THE ESSENTIALHOUSEBOOK

THE ESSENTIAL

TERENCE CONRAN

General Editor: Elizabeth Wilhide

Contributors: Elizabeth Wilhide, Dinah Hall, Deborah Morant and Gareth Parry

BCA

LONDON   NEW YORK   SYDNEY   TORONTO

ation to exterior

Fridge

e flooring

Line of rooflight above

N

ets 30 mm thick white Sicilian marble
top with undermounted circular S/S bowl set in.

d wiring for
nter

ase and atrium treatment,
wings 018, 019 and 020.

New
D17

New flush doors in
flush detailed frames

Plastered stud fin walls
to receive appliances.

150mm high plate glass upstand set into counter

1.1
LIVING ROOM

Oak T&G floorboards
(Detail to be approved b

100mm high solid oak skirting

1 5
WC

New
D18

HOUSEBOOK

Project Editor: Simon Willis
Art Editor: Helen Lewis
Production Manager: Sonya Sibbons

Copy Editor: Charyn Jones
Editorial Assistant: Charlotte Coleman-Smith
Proof-reader: Gareth Jones
Indexer: Karin Woodruff

Designers: Karen Bowen, Alistair Plumb,
 Robin Whitecross
Visualizer: Jean Morley
Illustrators: Paul Bryant, Angus Shepherd,
 Brian Ma Siy
Production Controller: Jill Macey

Picture Editor: Nadine Bazar
Picture Researcher: Emily Hedges
Picture Research Assistant: Ann Hallwood

Contributors
 Part 1: Sir Terence Conran
 Part 2: Elizabeth Wilhide
 Part 3: Dinah Hall
 Part 4: Deborah Morant
 Part 5: Gareth Parry

Consultants
 Parts 2 and 5: John McGowan
 Part 2: Robin Hillier

This edition published 1994
by BCA by arrangement with
Conran Octopus Limited
37 Shelton Street,
London, WC2H 9HN

Copyright © 1994
Conran Octopus Limited

A catalogue record for this book is available
from the British Library

CN 2097

Printed in Singapore by Star Standard

Publisher's Acknowledgments
*The publisher would like to thank the following for
their invaluable assistance with this book:*
Craig Allen, Bridget Bodoano, Chris Vercoe and
the staff at The Conran Shop, London;
Anderson-Schwartz Architects; Amanda Baker;
Antoine Bootz; Alison Cathie; Peter Cook;
Disabled Living Foundation; Dr Jonathan Fisk;
Kate Fontana and Tony Niblock; Louise Hillier;
Kiss + Zwigard Architects; Richard Lavenstein;
Sabine Léon-Dufour; Nadia Mackenzie; Rick
Mather Architects; Brain Mindel; Jasper
Morrison; Munkenbeck + Marshall Architects;
Ted Muehling; John Newman; Paxton-Locher
Architects; Michael and Jo Peters; Yanni
Petsopoulos; Nico Rensch; Ben Richardson;
Amanda Robinson; Robin Rout; Paul Ryan;
Christian Sarramon; Ron Smith; Jessica
Walton; Deborah Weintraub; Jonathan Woolf.

End papers based on a design by Sir Terence
Conran in association with James Lambert
Architects

CONTENTS

The Essential House Book was originally going to be called *Back to Basics*, until certain politicians adopted the phrase and managed to turn it into a joke! Never the less, both versions of the title indicate that the book is intended to be much more than a simple guide to interior decoration. Rather, it is a serious attempt to explain how your house works in a fundamental way, much as a doctor might explain to you how your body functions and how its various systems interrelate.

Style isn't irrelevant – far from it – and our lives would be much less fun without it. But no style works well unless you pay some attention to what's underneath – the bare bones of structure, design, fixtures and fittings. For this reason, this book concentrates largely on design and architecture rather than decorating. While the visual appearance of the space you occupy is also of vital importance, you are unlikely to enjoy the decorative aspects if your home does not function efficiently, or provide you with the right framework to enjoy life to the full.

The mission of this book is to help you to understand the myriad options that are open to you in the design and fitting out of the space in which you live. It will, I hope, pose questions that will enable you to analyse what you really want and need from your surroundings, and offers a wide range of alternative solutions for you to consider and put into practice.

Working on this book has given me great pleasure. I would like to thank the homeowners from all over the world who have allowed us and our photographers to investigate the workings of their homes. Without them, the book would not have been possible.

Terence Conran.

A SENSE OF PLACE

Home is the heart of life. Unlike an office, a workshop or a school, typically defined by a limited range of functions, the place you live in has to accommodate a broad range of activities, from sleeping to cooking, washing to relaxing. For the daily routine to be comfortable and enjoyable, your home must function well in each of these spheres. As well as an arena of activity, the home is where all kinds of different equipment, provisions and personal possessions are kept – a storehouse of belongings all under one roof competing for space and accessibility. There will be private places for individuals to retreat to and public areas where family and friends can gather. As the years pass and needs alter, there will be changes of use and emphasis. To meet these far-reaching requirements demands careful planning, efficient servicing and sensible, flexible organization.

But a home is greater than the sum of its parts and getting the practicalities right is only half of the story. For most people, the special significance of 'home' lies at a deeper level. Home is where we feel at ease, where we belong, where we can create surroundings which reflect our tastes and pleasures. Creating a home has a lot to do with discovering those elements that convey a sense of place.

Investigating these basic ideas relegates 'style' to something of a side issue. Fashions in decorating fluctuate like hemlines, whereas notions of comfort and intimacy date back hundreds of years. This is not to say that style isn't fun or even useful. But it is ultimately more important to find out what you really like, the unique combination of space, light, colour and materials which will continue to refresh your spirits long after the latest 'look' has had its day.

Past and present

1 The presence of the past is close at hand in this serene room, with stone flagged floor, scrubbed refectory table and mellow plastered walls. At the same time, the simplicity of decoration and sculptural objects mark this as a contemporary space.

1

2

3

4

2 The easy sweep of a cantilevered stone staircase leads the eye upwards in the entrance hall of an old farmhouse. The raftered ceiling, brick paved floor and terracotta urns provide a reassuring sense of continuity in both tone and texture.

3 Simple American country furniture in a Long Island house lends character to a space arranged for modern convenience. Soft, neutral shades make a soothing background for a successful blend of old and new.
4 Bright blue paintwork frames a view through the living areas of a French house on the Isle de Ré. The freshness of the simple colour scheme enhances architectural detail without stooping to period pastiche.

There are no objective standards in design and decoration. What is airy and uplifting to one person is spartan and brutal to another; one person's cosy clutter may be someone else's visual indigestion. What we do share, despite all our differences, is a vocabulary of proportion, arrangement and decorative practice. These familiar traditions, developed over the centuries, shape the way we look at our surroundings and affect our expectations, however unconsciously; they aren't easy to ignore. Although it may be tempting to write off popular revivals of 'period' styles as exercises in nostalgia, beneath it all there lurks a desire to remain in touch with the architectural and decorative conventions and ideals that have stood the test of time.

Social historians trace the beginning of the domestic interior, as we understand it today, to the bourgeois households of seventeenth-century Holland. It is almost unimaginable, despite the best efforts of Hollywood, to conceive of life in a Norman castle, or to relate the way we live today to a ceremonial progression through the grand suites of a Baroque stately home. But the quiet interiors and intimate scenes painted by Vermeer, de Witte or de Hooch are instantly and recognizably home-like, human in scale and disposition.

In his book *Home*, the writer and architect Witold Rybczynski argues that the Dutch were the first to think of the house as a separate, special place and, owing to the pre-eminence of the Netherlands in trade and finance, this was an ideal that spread throughout the rest of northern Europe and eventually to the colonies of North America. Rybczynski lists many qualities of the Dutch interior which still seem familiar. An awareness of space and a delight in the play of light and shade, a taste for simple, practical furnishings, the serviceable beauty of black-and-white marble floors, polished brass, pewter, china and white linen are all features which recur in Dutch genre paintings of the period. Dutch houses were impeccably clean and ship-shape; the kitchen was an important room and the garden a lovingly tended private domain.

Each age has made a contribution to our concept of the interior. From late seventeenth-century France comes the idea of decorative unity, using furnishings, particularly fabric, to make an harmonious composition. Window drapery, fabric-hung walls and upholstery were coordinated for the first time. The salons at the court of Louis XV saw the first attempts to make furniture truly comfortable for relaxation and leisure in the way we understand it today.

The classically inspired architects and designers of Georgian England transformed the ordinary town house into a model of order, symmetry and elegance. The proportions, scale and detailing of eighteenth-century rooms – derived from the classical orders of the ancient world – still look comfortable and appropriate to the modern eye. For these designers 'beauty' and 'usefulness' were inseparable notions.

By the beginning of the nineteenth century different rooms were becoming associated with distinct functions. The 'dining-room' became a fixed feature in the late eighteenth century; by the nineteenth, bedrooms were always private, drawing-rooms the most prestigiously decorated. More importantly, with working life taking place in factories and offices, the house became the bastion of the family, a sanctuary expressing personal tastes and aspirations.

From the Aesthetic Movement of the late nineteenth century came the idea that decoration, particularly colour, could express ambience, a notion that promoters of modern paint ranges take for granted. The same period saw William Morris and his followers in the Arts and Crafts Movement challenge the mediocrity of mass production, championing traditional forms and reviving handcraft skills, the genesis of what we now call 'country style'. By promoting an 'honest' use of materials and rejecting derivative ornament, Morris anticipated many principles of modern design.

In the last 100 years, the advances in domestic technology – electric light and power for labour-saving appliances, central heating and modern plumbing – have made entirely new uses and arrangements of interior space possible. The radical designers of the Modern Movement expressed these changes by rationalizing the home, applying principles of industrial production to make 'machines for living in'. The fact that Modernism in its purest form remains a minority enthusiasm has not lessened its impact on our ideas of how a home should actually function.

The extent to which technology has transformed daily life can partly be measured by how much we take it for granted. In the mid-1930s making fires accounted for an estimated ten hours' housework a week, time freed by the arrival of central heating. The advent of electricity meant houses became cleaner, fresher, brighter and easier to run.

1

2

■ Intense and vibrant primary colours articulate bold planes in this modern room, achieving depth and sophistication despite the relative simplicity of both the detailing and finishes.

2 A room in the Hancock Shaker Village, Pittsfield, Massachusetts is a powerful demonstration of the beauty of ordinary things. The high pegboard, use of plain textiles and meticulous woodwork are characteristic of the work of this nineteenth-century sect.
3 Matchboarded walls and floorboards painted chalky white create a luminous, light-filled interior. Displays of twigs and leaves in weathered metal containers add a natural vitality.
4 There is nothing hesitant about this creative clutter of colour and pattern. Calligraphic squiggles and bold shapes create both a dynamic sense of movement and an irrepressible warmth and cheerfulness.

When we select soft, light colours for a bedroom, we are echoing a style that began with Madame de Pompadour. When we place a dado one third of the way up the wall, we are preserving a basic eighteenth-century proportion. But when we organize the kitchen to make an efficient workspace, we are inescapably modern. The expectation that the home should be comfortable and convenient on a more profound level than ever before is the single most important contribution of this century. Few devotees of period decoration would be keen to revive eighteenth-century sanitary arrangements or nineteenth-century heating systems, though they may go to some lengths to conceal radiators, telephones and televisions in otherwise historically accurate rooms.

On the other hand, a recent American survey discovered that over 90 per cent of those questioned wanted a fireplace in their home, even those who lived in areas which were warm all year round. The reasons can hardly be practical. The fireplace, as our ancestors knew too well, is an inefficient source of heat; it creates dirt and waste, and in many areas of the world the types of fuel which may be burned are now subject to strict environmental controls. But the association of hearth and home is ancient and has proved to be a tie which even technology cannot break.

You do not have to be a social historian to have absorbed a host of preconceptions about how rooms should look and how they should work. Today, design books, lifestyle manuals, glossy magazines, film and television provide a deluge of images, presenting every conceivable variation on the theme of the interior, from beach houses to inner-city lofts, suburban villas to rustic retreats. Thanks to a burgeoning industry in home-improvement products, today's consumers are offered a wide variety of affordable colours, patterns, materials and furnishings, enabling them to turn their ideas into reality.

From a house to a home

The sheer range of decorating and furnishing options available can confuse as much as inspire; understandably many people still approach the process of creating a home in piecemeal fashion, acquiring a sofa here, a lampshade there, without any coherent idea of how it's all going to fit together. The aim of this book is to simplify and direct your decision-making by analysing spatial, organizational and structural issues relating to the whole house; by looking at the common activities that take place under the same roof and different ways of accommodating them; and by supplying a comprehensive and up-to-date directory to make selection easier.

There is one thing no book can do, and that is tell you how you want to live. Before you start to consider floor plans, storage requirements, tables and chairs, it is vital to discover your own tastes and preferences. Once you have an idea about where you are going, it's relatively straightforward to get there.

Making a home is a form of creativity open to everyone. Fear of ridicule, lack of confidence, or simply a sense of being overwhelmed by too many alternatives can still be inhibiting. We expect to be able to 'read' rooms and assess a person's character – and much else – from the way they choose to live; this level of exposure can force the self-conscious into conventional, predictable solutions that won't worry the neighbours but do little to enhance their own lives.

The idea that a home can be a vehicle for self-expression is relatively new, the means to make it so, newer still. When you consider how much time you spend at home and how much money you invest on improvements, it's only natural to fashion your home in a way that means something to you. Successful interiors have a definite flavour, an unmistakable vitality that allows personality to come through. 'Anonymous' rooms are depressing precisely because they lack individuality, or any sense of being inhabited by real people.

1

2

1 Inspired recycling contrives a 'pop' montage from urban debris in a New York loft. Packing crates and old timber create a partition between kitchen and living space, a witty low-tech framework to house modern apparatus.
2 The uncompromising natural look of this kitchen combines the bleached-out tones of driftwood and stone with basic furniture simply constructed from weathered planks and boards.

3

3 Direct and unpretentious, decoration that responds to climate creates a powerful sense of place. The cool ceramic tiled floor, whitewashed ceiling and uncluttered furnishings in this Corsican house are the visual equivalent of a breath of fresh air.

Many people only fully appreciate their surroundings once a year on holiday, when, relaxed and away from a familiar environment, they pay closer attention to colours, textures, form and light. Other impressions can be equally valuable. Holiday houses reacquaint us with the virtues of the simple life, a time when we find it surprisingly easy to make do with the minimum of equipment and technology, where furnishings are robust and economical and the emphasis is on enjoyment and basic everyday pleasures. Beyond acquiring the odd souvenir and preserving memories on film, however, few think to apply these inspirations in the context of their own home. Yet here is an ideal opportunity to assess what you can and cannot live without. If, by the end of the holiday, the whole family is climbing the walls for want of the television, so be it; but if you hardly missed it, you might consider moving the set somewhere less prominent when you get home.

A good starting place for discovering what you really like is to make a list of some of the houses, rooms, shops or even restaurants that have appealed to you in the past, no matter how vague or amorphous the reason. Dredge up your memories, indulge in a little creative day-dreaming and try to recall not just how such places looked, but how they sounded, smelled and felt. A house from your childhood, a place by the sea or in the country where you once stayed, a wonderful hotel, a room in a friend's home that you admire. Although its relevance may not appear immediately obvious, by analysing precisely why such places are evocative and meaningful, you can begin to distill the elements that might be put to work to enrich your own home.

I can personally relate the experience of being in a warm greenhouse, with its earthy musty smells, to my enjoyment of spaces which act as a transition between interiors and the world outside,

where nature can be brought closer and appreciated in relative comfort. Seaside houses have a similar elemental quality, a 'look' which can be suggested in bright colours and natural textures even if traffic noise and police sirens are the unwelcome urban equivalents to the restful sound of waves lapping or crashing against the seashore.

4

4 The simple pleasure of strong, bright colours in vibrant sunlight is universal.
5 Getting away from it all was never more appealing. This slatted summerhouse on stilts makes an irresistible retreat, lookout and hideaway.

5

■

I enjoy the luxury of space – my ideal would be a great open room which could be subdivided whenever I wanted, in the flexible manner of Japanese houses with their sliding partition screens. In the same spirit, I like interiors which merge with their settings, where there are no hard boundaries between inside and outside, where there are views and vistas that emphasize the sense of expansiveness. I like objects to be solid and well-made, not flimsy, and made of materials that mature well, ageing gracefully and acquiring their own beauty with use and time. It doesn't worry me when the edges of a stair carpet show signs of wear and tear, when curtains bleach in the light or ceilings darken and mellow. At the same time, cheerfulness and optimism are important to me, the freshness of a room after a really good spring clean, the vitality of flowers, the way a room can change its dynamics through subtle rearrangement to reflect the seasons. Finally, I enjoy comforting, hospitable houses which are well-stocked with provisions.

When it comes to creating your own home, you can derive personal inspiration from a wide variety of sources. As well as houses you have visited or seen, theatre sets, films, books, exhibitions and magazines can all generate ideas for

■ As elemental as its setting, Tigre del Mar by Mexican designer Gian Franco Brignone and architect Jean-Claude Galibert blurs the distinction between outdoors and indoors. Natural pigments rubbed into the exterior dissolve the walls into the horizon.

2 Warm ochre walls and wood strip flooring create an atmosphere of tranquillity that makes the most of natural light. The simple lines of the furniture complement the angles and planes of walls and ceiling.

doors and walls, bathrooms in view of the front door, visible plumbing and poor maintenance are bad. Remedies for awkward or oppressive features include mirrors to increase light and openness, growing plants indoors, wind chimes and blinds. It may be difficult to accept the interpretations – evil spirits rushing around a house are thwarted by a well-placed mirror – but *feng shui* encapsulates a universal response to fresh air, light and harmony in the interior.

What I've called 'a sense of place' is a barely definable, abstract quality, a combination of many factors that generates a specific atmosphere. The remainder of this chapter is an exploration of some of these elements. In practice, they aren't experienced in isolation and although it is useful to consider each individually, keeping the whole picture in mind will help bring them together in an harmonious whole.

3 A small London studio apartment overcomes the restriction of size with minimal furnishings and a fastidious attention to architectural detail. The base of the walls are finished with inset metal beading which provides a clean, graphic edge.

3

the use of colours, patterns, textures and materials to be adapted in your surroundings: some of the most original and satisfying interior schemes have arisen from cross-fertilizing ideas from different disciplines. Keep a scrapbook of tear sheets from magazines, postcards, scraps of fabric – anything which serves to jog your memory and foster your creativity. It's all part of the same process of discovering what you like.

It is instinctive to identify with the place in which you live. In dream analysis the house is usually interpreted as a symbol for the human body. Artists and writers have made extensive use of this psychological insight to portray and describe interiors that evoke states of mind or aspects of character. The artist Leonora Carrington believes there is a 'psychic shape' to a house, its form moulded like a container to its occupants over a period of time.

Less profoundly, it can be entertaining to extend the metaphor. Like the body, the house has its own physical systems of ventilation, energy and plumbing! Equally, it can be dressed up and decorated, cosmetically improved and fashionably turned out. The way that furnishing styles mimic changes in dress has been remarked upon by many

historians of the interior – high-waisted Empire dresses echoed in filmy window drapery, Victorian layers of upholstery and trimming corresponding to the intricately detailed layers of fashionable nineteenth-century clothing.

The ancient Chinese discipline *feng shui* – 'the science of wind and water' – also relates the house to the body, the house possessing its own metabolism which channels *ch'i* (the life force) to determine the health, prosperity and luck of its occupants. Even the most sceptical cannot disagree that human beings function better in favourable locations, or fail to appreciate the enlightened common sense of many *feng shui* rules, based on centuries of close observation of the way people react to their surroundings. Some *feng shui* practices have to do with preserving the vitality of a house by paying attention to light, the movement of air, orientation, shape and scale – elements which play upon the senses, not just sight.

In Chinese society, *feng shui* experts are consulted on everything from the placing of a chair to the siting of a new restaurant. Generous, light entrances, graceful curving stairs, windows that open wide and uncluttered living-rooms are good *feng shui*; low beams, slanting

Space and light

Space is the greatest luxury of the twentieth century. With most of us crowded into towns and cities, battling through traffic jams or jostling for elbow room in packed commuter trains, there is an acute need for our personal surroundings to allow us room to relax in comfort and relative privacy.

Space – as in square metres – is expensive. For many people there comes a point when moving house to gain another bedroom or a bigger kitchen becomes financially impossible. The answer is to find other ways of increasing the sense of space. 'Room for Change' (pages 30–113) addresses the structural, technical and organizational ways in which space can be maximized – physical changes that can enable you to make better use of the space you have at your disposal or to extend your house relatively economically.

But there is another side to the issue which is to do with the *quality* of the space at your disposal and how this affects your perception of it. There are many small flats or cottages which give an appearance of being wonderfully spacious simply by virtue of being well-organized and appropriately used, or because sympathetic and sensitive decorative choices work to dispel any feeling of the rooms being cramped or enclosed. On the other hand, there are plenty of large houses in which generous space is wasted by poor planning and arrangement. Big rooms can be just so much 'dead' space if they are badly designed and shoddily detailed.

One important element is unity. Rooms look awkward when there is a mishmash of conflicting styles and tastes clamouring for attention. Using the same sorts of colours and textures in connecting areas such as hallways and stairs, employing the same family of basic materials for surfaces and finishes and avoiding abrupt aesthetic leaps from style to style bring a sense of coherence to a sequence of rooms and help to define the essence of a home.

Another vital issue to address is the question of proportion. A common response to the problem of small rooms is to knock down partition walls and open up the spaces into one large area. In many cases the result is an immediate improvement, particularly if the new room serves two complementary functions such as cooking and eating. But imposing an open-plan layout on a conventionally arranged house isn't always successful. Proportions which look right when the rooms are separate can look distinctly odd when you take away the walls. Doors, windows, fireplaces and other architectural details may suddenly seem out of scale. One solution is to retain a hint of separation by making distinct areas for different activities within the new space; another is to scale up furniture and fittings to provide definition and visual weight.

If you decide to accept the spatial limitations of a small room and work with them, you can bring out the special benefits of an enclosed space – cosiness and intimacy, the comfortable feeling of having everything within reach – without suffering the drawbacks. Study other small spaces, such as ships' cabins and caravans, places that are appealing because they are so intensely workable and well-considered. A small space with little in it will always remind you of its limited size, but one that is elegantly fitted out and thoughtfully furnished to an appropriate scale has its own atmosphere and character.

Quality of space has relatively little to do with room size. Thinking about the house as a whole, how each room relates to the other and to the world outside and, crucially, considering the needs of everyone who lives there, is the basic message of this book. Space is dynamic rather than static. It is appreciated through movement, use, sound and light – all fundamental aspects which cannot simply be reduced to the empirical facts of the habitable floor area within four walls.

There will always be the need for a balance between privacy and openness in any home – large communal areas for people to gather in and small private rooms to retreat to. It may seem an obvious point, but in houses where every space runs into the other life can become tiring: sound is amplified, intimate conversations are virtually impossible and different activities set up competing areas of attention. Whereas if your rooms are uniformly small, there is nowhere to celebrate and entertain without feeling claustrophobic.

As well as variations in room size and scale, there should also be places which delight and surprise. Alcoves, window seats or generous hallways with reading corners may appear superfluous in a strictly functional sense but these are all features which people enjoy precisely because they add a different and often unexpected dimension to the way in which the space is used.

1 A tiny studio flat converted from a mews garage presents a particular challenge: how to accommodate different areas of activity within the same proscribed space without sacrificing light and openness. A compact kitchen wall is screened from the sleeping area with a large hardwood panel.
2 A room with a view is inherently spacious. The tongue-and-groove panelled walls, low bed and sympathetic furnishings do not detract from the expansive outlook beyond the window.

3
4

3 Internal windows
bring light into the
heart of the house. A
large window provides
an appetizing view of
the kitchen in this
Italian house and
maintains a valuable
connection with the
outdoors. The pattern
of panes unifies the
different-sized open-
ings and makes the
effect look considered.

4 A pleasing play on
light and space is
achieved by the careful
positioning and detail
of internal walls. The
gentle curve of the
wall that divides the
living from dining
areas is accentuated by
the suspended ceiling,
leading the eye along
the main axis of the
house. Openings in the
flanking walls provide
views through, as well
as frames for display.

2 Like a liner at its moorings, the nautical design of this gleaming extension to a Brittany farmhouse makes a dramatic architectural point about its location. Port-hole windows, metal clad walls and a top deck play out the visual metaphor.
3 Inside the same extension, bulkhead lights, compact fittings and pristine surfaces recall the efficiency of a ship's interior. Natural light spilling into the space is a positive, dynamic element.

1 Dappled light filtered through leaves has a magical vitality. Houses which preserve the link with the outdoors are instinctively appealing.

2

Another key consideration has to do with the relationship between the interior and the outside. What you see beyond, through windows, doorways and adjoining areas is just as important as what the room itself contains. In *A Pattern Language* by Christopher Alexander and others there is a short passage on what the authors call a 'Zen' view, those tantalizing glimpses of the outside world offered by 'places of transition' – at entrances, on stairs, along hallways. These views remain fascinating because they are only experienced briefly as you move from place to place.

I have often referred to the work of Sir John Soane in this context and make no apologies for doing so again! His interiors, particularly at the London museum he created to house his collection of antiquities, show a mastery of interior space. At Lincoln's Inn Fields the relatively modest proportions of a Regency town house are transformed by a series of ingenious visual devices. The eye is not so much deceived as delighted by hidden vistas, sudden changes of scale and intriguing reflections. Soane fitted window reveals with thin mirror panels to reflect light and views; there are lowered ceilings and small entrances giving way to large open rooms and everywhere there is a wonderful sense of contrast. 'Hazard and surprise', the guiding principle of Soane's approach to design, is a recipe for vitality that does not depend on grand surroundings.

3

4

4 A glazed link between kitchen and living-room makes a core of light at the centre of a waterside house. Eating under a glass roof with open views to either side provides the best of both worlds. The wooden structure and shingled walls are naturally complementary in the woodland setting.

A lot of what makes a particular space enjoyable has to do with light: the two issues of space and light are really inseparable. Natural light enhances the spatial character of a room, throwing detail into relief, drawing the eye to warm sunny spots, shrouding corners in cool shadows, making dappled patterns where it is diffused and filtered. Uniformly bright artificial lighting, on the other hand, gives any room the subtlety of a hospital corridor. Many people view artificial lighting as a practical means of illumination without giving thought to its aesthetic impact; the results are surroundings which resist any attempt to bring them to life.

Natural light is always changing; at different times of the day and in different seasons there are variations of tone, intensity, colour. Part of the pleasure everyone experiences sitting outdoors on a summer's day comes from these infinitesimal changes. Artificial light is no substitute for daylight, but with modern lighting systems, sources and fittings it is still possible to filter, direct and modulate light to provide essential contrast and variety.

A positive enjoyment of natural light, views and spatial diversity are all part of the same picture. It isn't merely a case of trying to get closer to nature, but a question of making the home a more natural place, in tune with the instinctive ways in which people feel comfortable, healthy and happy.

5

5 Lighting is one of the most effective means of creating a sense of architectural drama and surprise. Two flights of narrow, enclosed steps are picked out with small lights inset in the treads and top lit by a skylight to make an exciting transition between levels.

Colour

Before you confront a colour card or sample book of fabric swatches, think in general terms about the kinds of room you enjoy. Do you like places that are bright and airy, cosy and cluttered, rich with colour and pattern, soothing and neutral?

Build up a picture in your mind of the kind of materials that might work together to create the effect you want. A wooden floor has pattern in its grain, texture in its finish and colour; a granite worktop is cool, hard, smooth and flecked. In practice, we don't dissociate these qualities, they all work together. In the past, there was a natural association of material with colour: woodwork was often painted and grained brown to enhance its 'woodiness'. It's worth going back to these basic associations to investigate why we respond to certain colours, patterns and textures and not to others. You could translate an affection for seaside places, for example, into a palette of grey-blue, aquamarine, buff and white, and chalky, sandy textures; into enlivening accents of sharp colour against misty neutral backgrounds; into nautical stripes, or into materials like bleached or painted wood, sisal and coir.

Colour is one of the most subjective areas in decoration and no amount of analysis is going to predict how two people will respond to the same shade. At the same time, almost any generalization you can make about a particular colour can be overturned in practice. Nevertheless, you have to start somewhere. Even if you don't have a 'favourite' colour, there will inevitably be a family of colours to which you are instinctively drawn, colours which keep cropping up in your choice of clothes, in treasured pictures or possessions; and there will be other colours you absolutely abhor.

Use these clues to guide your choice when it comes to decorating and don't be put off by the stock decrees that blue must be chilly, yellow is sunny and so on. Quite subtle differences in tone can make all the difference. If you love red, you don't have to paint your living-

Colour, pattern and texture are the decorative elements which express a sense of place, cosmetic in one sense, but more than skin deep in another. How you decorate your house, what you apply over the bare bones of the structure, can be as easy and economical to change as paint, or as integral as a floor-covering. The initial approach should be holistic, related to material use and mix, rather than a series of isolated decisions where the whole effect is never considered.

Decorating should be fun, a chance to give your creativity free rein. But a lot of people get bogged down in the fraught process of selection and end up retreating to predictable choices on the false assumption that these will prove practical or easy to live with. In fact, it's far easier to live with something you enjoy, rather than merely tolerate.

room walls crimson, you can derive just as much pleasure from details such as sofa upholstery or a tartan throw. And, of course, colours take on quite a different dynamic in combination, in electric partnerships of opposites or complementaries, in soft modulated tonal families, paired with crisp, refreshing white or graphically contrasted with black.

It takes time to gain a sense of how colour behaves; like everything else, it's a question of widening your visual horizons. If you decide to play safe, start with a neutral background, such as

1 Nature offers many examples of colourful harmony: a bougainvillaea in bloom provides a sharp accent against the distressed paint of an old shed door and the rustic charm of the wall and fence.
2 Simple, utilitarian objects can marry function with decoration. Powdered paints in ordinary glass jars gain much of their effect from their ad hoc arrangement.

5

3 Flowers are a simple means of ringing decorative changes. This bowl of yellow daisies forms a vibrant focal point against the turquoise paintwork.
4 A large window floods this room with light, giving breathing space to the colourful collection of objects.

8

6

7

white walls, plain floors, and experiment with colour in objects and furnishings which can be easily changed. How you decorate large surface areas will have a determining effect on the room, so give yourself time to live in the space and get used to its particular characteristics. Ask yourself how you intend to use the room, what it looks like in the morning, or at night, which features are worth emphasizing and which you want to play down. It's easy enough to paint the walls at a later date, or add rugs, curtains or blinds as your decorative sense develops.

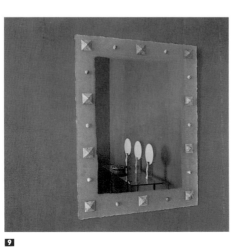

9

5 Bold planes of colour arrest the attention, delineating the space of a building.
6 As simple a device as picking out the dado rail in a contrasting colour can enliven the pace of a room.
7 Duck-egg green is elegant and simple.
8 Time and nature are the inspiration behind this still-life.
9 A mirror increases the dramatic intensity of the orange walls.

Pattern and texture

Neutral backgrounds leave you free to concentrate on another important dimension to the interior of a room – texture. The pleasing combinations of textures which arise from matching different materials and finishes gives any room depth and interest, which is why uniformly bland, artificial materials can seem so lifeless. Chalky matt paintwork, stripped, scrubbed and waxed floorboards, robust calico and nubbly linen may all be tonally very similar but they are inherently lively in combination simply by virtue of their textural differences.

What is evocative and stimulating about this approach is the way textures reinforce a link with nature, which has been a source of decorative inspiration through many centuries. There is no better way of going back to basics than revelling in the simplicity of wood, stone and natural fibres such as unbleached cotton – materials with a raw elemental beauty and an effortless way of working well together. Natural materials do not date and they tran-

scend conventional distinctions between styles; more importantly, they age well, wearing attractively with use and time. Synthetic finishes singularly lack this ability; any change to their original condition is inevitably a change for the worse. This is not to dismiss the undoubted practicality and benefits of using artificial materials in many situations, merely a reminder that natural materials repay your initial investment by improving with the years, mellowing and acquiring the patina of use, which, more than any other factor, contributes to a sense of place.

Pattern is inherent in decoration. As subtle as the self-coloured design of a damask cloth or as bold as a sofa layered in Oriental textiles, pattern transforms our appreciation of colour and texture, adding rhythm and movement, intrinsically suggestive of order and repose. A well-balanced print is a good way of living with the intensity of strong colour and an excellent mediating influence between strong shapes and plain surfaces. Pattern breaks up the

1

2

3

1 The pale tints of the plain rendered walls and stairs provide a subtle differentiation of tone and emphasize the chalky finish.
2 Pattern arises naturally in the way objects are arranged. A display of brightly coloured glass set off against a graphic abstract picture brings together different elements in a lively, companionable way.
3 Textural variety gives depth and physical presence to understated neutral backgrounds. In the absence of strong colour, metal, stone, carpet and paintwork provide essential contrast in the ways they reflect light.

4 One of the easiest ways of using pattern is as a decorative focal point. A patterned rug is the centrepiece of arrangement in the living area of a Greek island house, its soft muted colours accentuated by the vivid blue of the woodwork.
5 Blue-and-white striped bed linen emphasizes the crisp, fresh look of a clean-lined space.
6 The linear quality of venetian blinds, slatted chair backs and stripey table runner add a discreet sense of pattern to a modern interior and act as an effective counter-balance to the plain surfaces of the room.

expanse of large areas, giving depth and character: the success of broken-colour paint techniques demonstrates the effectiveness of tone-on-tone prints, which reveal the marks of brush, sponge or rag, at leading the eye beyond the flatness of a two-dimensional surface.

Pattern and texture do not, of course, arise solely in the context of textiles, carpets and wall finishes. A collection of glassware, a shelf full of books, a group of family photographs – all of these create a dynamic of their own and add to the texture of the room. Although, to an extent, they can be seen as finishing touches, you shouldn't underestimate the effect such displays will have. If you have a special item of furniture, a painting or a piece of sculpture that you know you want to keep in a particular room, this can provide a useful starting-point in establishing a decorative scheme.

During the nineteenth century there was an exceptional tolerance for rich, busy patterns, a level of visual distraction most people find uncongenial today. As with any other decorative element, the way in which pattern is used matters almost as much as what it looks like in isolation.

Pattern can be used to define – as in a border of chequered tile work – or to provide an accent and focus – as in a wonderfully rich kilim in a modern space, an effective contrast of mood and style. Although we are not attuned to the enveloping quality of nineteenth-century decoration – where surfaces were layered in intricately detailed fabrics, printed papers and floor coverings – mixing patterns that share some basic affinity can give a room a warm, embracing quality which feels both very comfortable and easy on the eye.

Arrangement and detail

1 Exactly judged, a symmetrical arrange-ment of decorative pots and glass candle-holders makes a wall of display in an eating area. The balance between detail and simplicity is carefully weighed; candlelight flickering at eye level prevents the effect from appearing static or austere.

People seem to fall into two distinct camps – either they like clutter, or they don't. In some mismatched households, you can sense a kind of open warfare between the person who is always tidy-ing away and the accumulator who leaves a trail of possessions in their wake.

I must admit to preferring less rather than more, the sparse and simple rather than rooms where the basic qualities of light and space are overwhelmed by objects and furnishings. Even so, I'm not a minimalist and there are some who adopt a much more rigorous approach, comfortable only in nearly empty spaces where very few of the accessories of daily life remain on view.

Whichever side of the divide you find yourself on, what counts is the courage of your convictions. Many people end up sharing their lives with unwanted and useless things because they can't work out what to do with them, or haven't the nerve to give them away – clutter by default. Over a hundred years ago William Morris formulated his 'golden rule': 'Have nothing in your houses which you do not know to be useful or believe to be beautiful', a mes-sage which retains its relevance today.

Teach yourself to evaluate what you see. Ask yourself what you really think about everything you own: do you posit-ively like it? If you do, why? What does it contribute – practicality, visual pleasure, a memory of a happy event or a special place? Plenty of people have experienced the shock of returning home after an absence and suddenly seeing familiar surroundings in a new, critical light. Make use of this feeling to change things for the better.

Exercise the same critical faculty when it comes to new possessions. It is better to wait until you find what works in a positive sense rather than to put up with second-best. If this means postpon-ing a purchase until you have saved up enough money, or spending more effort to source the right materials, it is well worth it. A sense of place grows with time, as different elements are juggled and refined until everything feels right.

Few really successful or interesting rooms are created overnight. Yet homes are never really 'finished': new stages in your life make their own demands, forc-ing you to adapt and reappraise the way you live. Your tastes may alter, perhaps radically. Instead of being frustrated or dismayed by this, you should welcome and even initiate change, since this is precisely what keeps houses alive.

2 A luminous Chinese porcelain dish balanced on a narrow ledge sings out against white walls in a near-empty room. This composition has the tension and precision of a technical drawing. **3** Everyday things in the corner of the small kitchen make a practical and pleasing display. The comfort and reassurance of familiar objects is part of what makes a home.

Room size and shape often dictate an optimum arrangement of fittings, services and at least the larger pieces of furniture. But there is usually a way to vary the positioning of some elements, even if it is only rearranging a display of objects, or putting some pieces away for the time being and bringing others out. Maintaining a room in the way it was first furnished and decorated, leaving furniture rooted to the same places from year to year, dusting objects and putting them back in exactly the same position means there will come a time when you hardly see them any more.

Even small changes can be refreshing. Use a good spring-clean or the coming of a new season to play about with emphasis and arrangement. A century ago, the advent of summer in many households meant rugs were taken up, loose covers slipped over heavy upholstery, thick curtains replaced with lightweight cotton versions – a general lightening of rooms to suit the warmer weather. There are many good reasons for reviving this practice, but perhaps the most persuasive is the fact that it fosters a new awareness of your surroundings.

Arrangement naturally has much to do with detail – such apparently small things as fresh flowers, or the witty, quirky or personal touches that make a disproportionately large impact on the way you view a room. At the same time, the importance of detail often lies in what you don't see. It means adopting a thoroughgoing approach right from the start so there aren't trailing wires and overloaded power points, clumsy junctions between finishes and flooring, unattractive skirting-boards or cheap handles that strike a jarring note. Detail is the narrow focus, the necessary complement to the wider picture.

Creating a home is a complex process, but it isn't mysterious. Getting it right isn't a question of adhering to a rule-book or toeing a fashionable line – it means finding out what you want and how you want to live.

ROOM FOR CHANGE

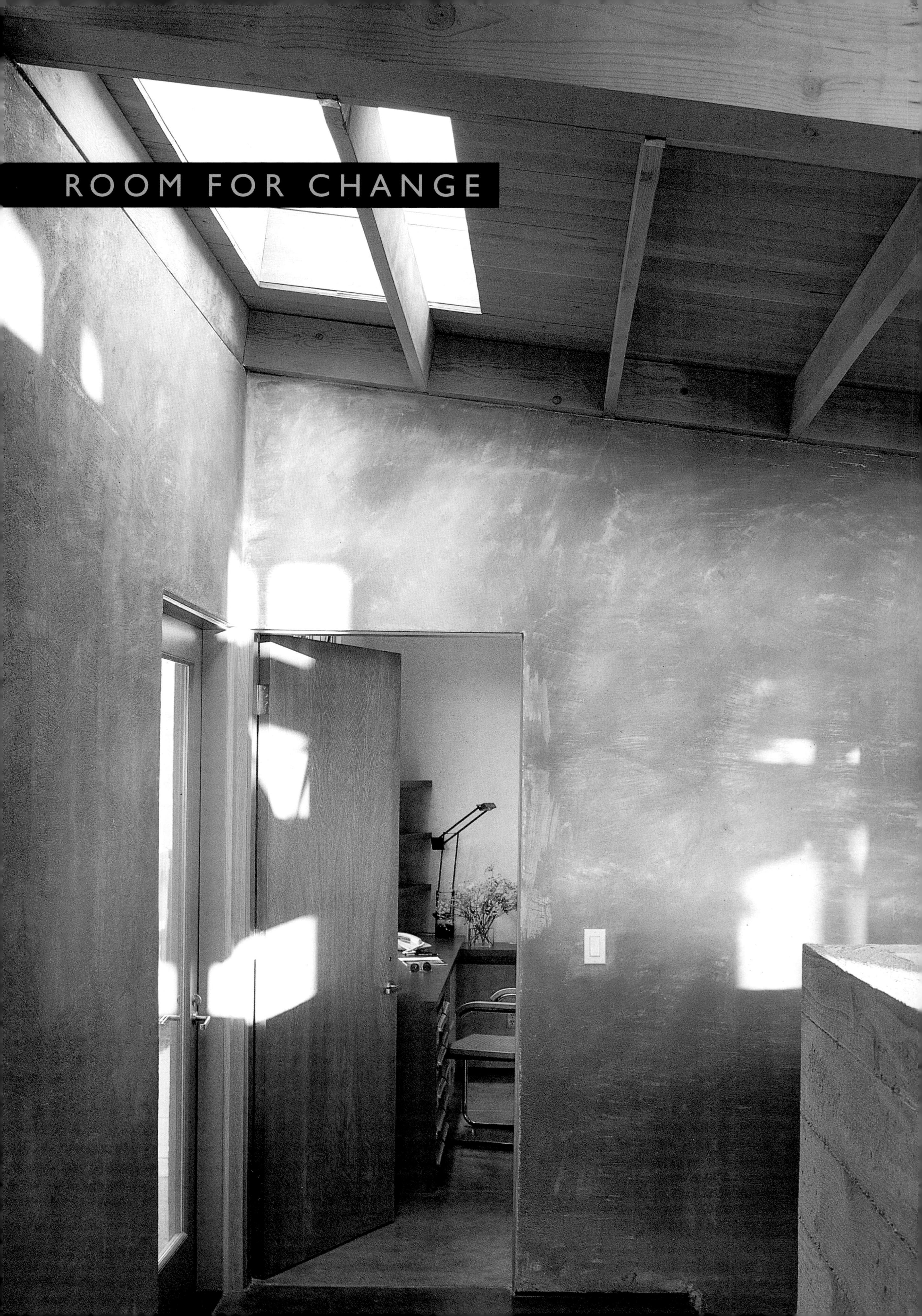

The main living areas of this house are at the back, down from the entrance level. A self-contained home office adjacent to the front door provides a means of separating work from social life. Roughwashed walls and painted trim give a warm feel to this modern building.

Our lives don't stand still. Work patterns, family circumstances, how we occupy our spare time may alter considerably from year to year. A new baby is guaranteed to turn most households upside down; the arrival of children instigates a sequence of changes as one stage of development quickly succeeds the next. With or without children, possessions accumulate, tastes are redefined. The surroundings which once suited our needs no longer fulfil our most basic requirements.

At certain critical points, the best solution may be to move to a new place. But it is neither possible nor practical to move each time your home fails to match up to a change in circumstances. In any case, it is more than likely that even a new home will meet only some of your needs, and that adjustments will be required to provide a perfect fit.

This section should enable you to envisage the scope and potential of spatial change. In this context, it is important to view your home as a complete entity, rather than a collection of disparate parts. Simple alterations to the fabric of your home can have a knock-on effect, bringing benefits which go beyond the obvious.

Major spatial changes always involve professional help. If you are thoroughly briefed on the range of possibilities, aware of potential hazards and familiar with common procedures, working with professionals becomes more of a partnership and less of a leap in the dark.

Even if you haven't reached an obvious turning point, there may be ways of improving your surroundings which will add to the pleasure and effectiveness of daily life. The following pages will show you how to take a fresh look at your home, challenge your preconceptions and discover room for change within your own four walls.

LOOKING FOR POTENTIAL

One of the most abused terms in the estate agent's lexicon, or the most useful, depending on your point of view, 'potential' generally denotes a property not so much alive with possibilities as neglected beyond belief. But neither 'room for change' nor 'looking for potential' necessarily mean you are confronting the dire prospect of total renovation and renewal. Each and every home has potential – if you know where to look for it. If you are among the fortunate few who are fairly satisfied with things as they are, there may still be ways of making improvements that you have overlooked. Or you may have the vague sense that you aren't making the best use of the space at your disposal, but find yourself unable to put a finger on exactly how it is you could improve the existing layout of your home.

People tend to be buzzing with plans and schemes when they move to a new home, but often find it difficult to establish which course of action would give the greatest long-term benefit or represent the best investment of time and money. Then, having settled in and spent a while in the same place, it's all too easy to become accustomed to the status quo and learn to tolerate imperfections and minor inconvenience. Even after the first flush of enthusiasm has died down there may be some problems, of course, that are too glaring to ignore. The solutions, however, may not be so obvious. Spatial, structural and organizational changes can be complex, disruptive and expensive, so it is understandable that many people only tinker round the edges without ever getting to grips with the underlying problems.

This section aims to provide you with the means to undertake a thorough analysis of your home: from identifying what you like and what you want to change, through to explanations of the various options available to you; from simple redecoration to more ambitious schemes that involve structural alteration. If you can look at your home in a fresh light, analysing its use in terms of how you live your life and the way in which different rooms do or do not respond to the demands you make, all manner of possibilities may suggest themselves to you. Provided you budget sensibly and schedule the work carefully, you can effect changes that will improve the quality of your life and, quite possibly, increase the resale value of your home.

1 The views through a house – from room to room, level to level, inside to out – make an important contribution to spatial quality. Colour underscores the sense of transition.
2 Contrast of materials defines different areas in a minimally furnished interior. In near-empty rooms, the focus falls on such telling details as switches, skirting-boards and the junction between finishes and floor coverings.

3 Entrances set the scene. An open stairwell creates a soaring sense of space and provides views in every direction. Hardwood flooring throughout the ground level emphasizes the expansive effect.

4

4 Dividing up the space need not entail loss of light. A kitchen is neatly contained within an area formed by two half-height partitions, providing a demarcation of activities within a large open room.

5

5 Open-plan living, where there are few divisions between rooms or even levels, dramatically alters the perception of interior space. It is important to incorporate private areas to maintain balance and flexibility.

Assessing your home

concerning services, technicalities or the basic structure. Are there deficiencies in the way the physical systems work? Which intrinsic spatial qualities would you take pains to point out, elements that perhaps aren't immediately obvious but ones you have come to appreciate through living there?

The next step is to identify precisely what needs changing. Think carefully about how you live, about the everyday experience of using your home. Ask everyone in the household to contribute their views, so that you have a rounded picture that takes everyone's perspective fully into account:

- What delights you most about your house or flat?
- What annoys you most?
- Are there bottlenecks where people always seem to be treading on each other's toes?
- How do you move around the house? Are there redundant doors or entrances that you never use?
- Do you have to travel too far between key areas, or are any of the main routes tortuous and awkward?
- Where does clutter accumulate despite all your best efforts at organization?
- What is each room used for? Are there conflicts of interest and activities?
- Which room do you feel most comfortable in, and why?
- In which rooms do family and friends naturally congregate?
- Can you entertain guests comfortably?
- Is there a room that is under-used, or one that people tend to avoid?
- Which areas are too small to accommodate your present needs?
- Is there enough natural light? Does the existing arrangement of artificial lighting serve your needs?
- Do you ever feel overwhelmed by the noise of your family or from the street?
- Is your home physically comfortable – is it warm enough in winter, temperate during the summer?
- Do you have enough power points?
- Do you suffer from regular break-ins?

1 The kitchen is the hardest-working area in the home. Integrating all of the elements to provide an efficient use of space requires thorough planning; the necessary improvements may amount to a substantial proportion of your budget, but the positive effects are far reaching.

Making a list of the positive and negative qualities of your home takes a degree of objectivity, a critical eye not dulled by overfamiliarity. To put yourself in the right frame of mind, imagine showing your home to a prospective buyer, or if that scenario is too ghastly to contemplate, imagine you're showing round a friend who has never been to your house, someone with an open mind, but who doesn't automatically share your affection for the place or isn't used to turning a blind eye to the state of the skirting-boards or the worn stair carpet.

Start at the front door and work your way through each area. How would you present what you see? There may be rooms that you would scuttle through, mumbling excuses; there may be outstanding features, fine details, good views you would emphasize. Think about all the questions a buyer might ask

- Do any of the main services, such as heating or plumbing, require constant and costly repair? Do you find your home expensive to run?
- Is your home safe for children, the elderly or for a family member with special needs?
- Are surfaces and finishes practical where they need to be – in the kitchen, the bathroom or children's areas?

If you intend to stay in your home for any length of time, try to imagine what your answers would be like in two, five or ten years' time. Which changes to your lifestyle can you anticipate?

This general exercise in consultation and analysis is an essential prelude to undertaking any major change on the home front. It is important to keep an open mind and identify any potential areas for change. Don't worry too much at this stage how such changes are to be

2 A bedroom
adjoining a living area
in a French house is
furnished with the
simplest elements. The
bare metal frame of
the bed creates the
sense of a room within
a room.
3 The central hearth
is open on two sides,
providing a visual
connection between
the bedroom and living
area, and a dramatic
double view of the fire.
4 Bedrooms which
are dominated by
clothes storage
generally fail to function
well as peaceful
retreats. In this small
bedroom, the dressing
area is just beyond the
glass doors – a logical
and practical use of
limited space.

implemented. And do not rule out alterations because you imagine they will be
too expensive or difficult to accomplish –
they may not be after all. Simply set
yourself the task of visualizing the best
possible surroundings for you and your
family and enumerate every obstacle
that currently stands in the way of you
achieving this goal.

It is important that you listen to the
views of others in your household. You
may be pleasantly surprised to discover
that everybody shares your reservations
about the condition of the bathroom or
chagrined to find that someone else has
designs on the spare room which don't
match your own. Compromise can come
later; now is the time to look at your
home as dispassionately as possible – as
an entity, with both strengths that
should be maximized and weaknesses
that you need to overcome.

5 Services – heat,
light, power, water –
constitute the
infrastructure of your
home. Making spatial
changes often involves
alterations behind the
scenes to ensure the
new layout functions
as it should.

A profile for change

1 An internal window offers a view into the kitchen area and counteracts any feeling of enclosure. Colour articulates the architectural elements.
2 In a Paris apartment, great attention has been paid to the materials used: white stucco walls and large oak floorboards open up the space. Steel beams enclose an open raised hearth that runs the full length of a wall, transforming the fireplace into a piece of modern sculpture.

Once you have made an initial assessment of your home, you can begin to analyse what you have discovered and determine the type and level of change required. Your preliminary list may include both specific observations – 'new bathroom flooring needed', 'overloaded power points in living room', 'grubby paintwork in hallway' – as well as the less tangible – 'kitchen feels closed in', 'breathtaking view from living-room window', 'nowhere to tackle paperwork quietly'. The following stages will help you to translate these impressions into a blueprint for action.

First take a look at your answers and try to determine whether there is a particular pattern to the responses. If many of your concerns have to do with storage, accessibility and the ease with which various functions can be carried out, the solutions may involve replanning or reorganization. If you are basically just short of space, conversion or extension may be the answer. If spatial quality is lacking, you can consider the possibility of architectural alteration. If there is a fundamental lack of efficiency in the way your home is serviced, you may need new technical systems. Or, as is often the case, if there is a scatter of problems across the board, you will need to think hard about where your real priorities lie.

The types of changes that are open to you fall into distinct categories, broadly determined by the extent of their impact on your home and on your budget. In practice, many improvements involve changes at different levels – if a wall needs replastering, it will also need redecorating, and so on – but it is important to be aware of what each type of change can offer.

REDECORATION

Technically the most superficial level of change, redecoration isn't necessarily the least important. You won't make your home structurally sound by giving it a new coat of paint, but you can make it more cheerful and allow its positive

3

qualities to shine through. Decorating is about enhancing what you have, bringing good features into focus, making the most of natural light and views, creating a sense of harmony and comfort. It also means choosing finishes and materials which are appropriate for the job they have to do and which will withstand the wear and tear they will receive.

If there are no outstanding problems with the basic structure or disposition of rooms, but you remain dissatisfied with your home, the solution probably lies in its presentation. In this sense, the term presentation encompasses all the main surface treatments for walls, ceilings and floors, as well as the way your home is furnished and lit. Good, sensitive lighting is a vital element in creating sympathetic, safe and workable surroundings and should never be underestimated.

Many of the options that fall within this category are relatively inexpensive and painless to carry out, involving far less disruption than building work or major repair. Particularly if you live in rented accommodation, are severely restricted financially, or expect to stay in

your home for only a short period, redecoration may be the sensible course of action; the furnishings you acquire can easily be transplanted to a new location. But if the real problems lie deeper and it is within your power to rectify them, redecoration is largely irrelevant until they are sorted out, and it may even be a waste of time and money.

REPAIRWORK

The physical condition of your home is of prime importance. If you own your property, its structural health will be inextricably tied to your financial fortunes. Repairwork isn't a creative option, but it will prevent unwelcome and expensive changes being forced upon you and halt deterioration before it becomes disastrous.

Major structural faults will require immediate action and you may need to consult a number of experts to determine the precise nature of the problem and to help you to put it right. Buildings are attacked by a range of adverse factors, from land settlement to dry rot and pest infestation. The symptoms may not

always be obvious, but unexplained cracking, patches of damp, persistent musty smells, sudden leaks, wobbly floors and bulging plasterwork are signs that something is going wrong somewhere. While every home-owner dreads the discovery of a major defect, delay will usually only make matters worse. Large-scale repair is generally disruptive and expensive, but you can make the best of a bad situation by taking the opportunity to extend the work and incorporate changes which actually improve your home, rather than merely restore it to a sound condition.

You should also allow money in your budget and time in your schedule for minor repairs and upkeep. Poor surfaces aren't necessarily symptomatic of underlying decay. However, they effectively counteract any improvements you make elsewhere; painting battered plasterwork will give it a superficial freshness but won't disguise the basic problem. And, as far as maintenance is concerned, keeping on top of little problems as they crop up dramatically lessens the risk of a major calamity at a later date.

3 Partition walls that fall just short of the ceiling create a box room that separates the kitchen from the living area in this architect-designed house in San Francisco. The open fire, with its warmth and vitality, makes a natural focal point, an established tradition that retains a powerful appeal in period and contemporary interiors alike.

REORGANIZATION

Some of the most immediate and far-reaching changes you can effect on your home have to do with its organization. Reorganization can conjure space from thin air and transform those irritating daily routines into models of clock-like efficiency. Many of the solutions are, in fact, startlingly simple.

Many people are surprisingly conventional when it comes to assigning uses to rooms. Yet in many houses and flats there is scope for choice, and breaking away from an unthinking acceptance of traditional arrangements can liberate much useful space. There's no reason, for example, why the biggest upstairs room should be the parents' bedroom when it is the children who would really benefit from the extra floor area. Provided relocation doesn't involve moving services around, this is one of the simplest changes you can make. Only marginally more complex are the types of alterations which reorganize 'circulation', or the way you travel from room to room. Blocking up doorways or creating new entrances (see page 91) can simplify room use dramatically and greatly add to the convenience of daily life.

Home organization naturally has a great deal to do with how and where things are kept. As your possessions accumulate, storage facilities often lag behind until there comes a time when confusion threatens to take over. Well-planned, accessible storage is vital for a smooth-running household and represents a great space-saver in itself.

CHANGING SERVICES

The physical systems that serve your home – its heating, electricity, drainage and ventilation – are elementary for health, comfort and general well-being. Deficient or faulty services are at best both inconvenient and uneconomical; at worst, they may pose a real physical danger to yourself or to the fabric of your home. Replanning services to suit new spatial layouts varies in complexity and expense, but it is fair to say that the majority of this type of work requires professional assistance and is best if it is carried out as early as possible in your programme of alterations.

The environmentally aware hold a wider definition of health and efficiency, which encompasses the long-term effects on the community and the planet. This has particular implications for energy consumption and waste disposal in the home and, as altruism is increasingly reinforced by public legislation, this dimension of home design and planning assumes greater importance.

ALTERING SPACE

For a real improvement in spatial quality, a fundamental change in light, volume and scale, you will need to alter the basic framework of your home: move walls, erect partitions, create openings, change levels or convert redundant space. The prospect of major restructuring fills most people with real dread, understandably given the horror stories that survivors of this type of home improvement like to tell. But if the risks are greater, so are the benefits, and if you prepare yourself properly and are thoroughly acquainted with the pitfalls, you are less likely to tumble into them.

A good deal of the complexity, and hence expense, of such work hinges on whether the alterations are structural or not. Knocking a hole in an internal wall may not be; whereas knocking a hole in an external wall almost certainly will be. You may need an architect, engineer or surveyor to tell you which is which. Some alterations require legal consent; for most you will need the services of a qualified builder at the very least.

CREATING SPACE

In order to provide a real increase in available floor space, the only option short of moving is to extend your home by adding on a new room or rooms, adding a new level, or by making existing rooms bigger. The direct benefits of

1 Roughly white-washed plywood partitions divide up a New York loft. A low platform covered in coir defines the sleeping area; a roll of thick industrial sheet-plastic serves as a blind to screen the space. Cork tiling inset in painted floorboards defines the sitting area.
2 In an Italian warehouse converted into a fashion designer's studio, large pieces of free-standing furniture provide practical storage and a means of visually anchoring and demarcating the space.

3 Stairs that double as drawers and cubby-holes make ingenious use of the space and provide storage for household necessities. **4** A thorough-going architectural approach to storage is evident in this imposing full-height library wall bisected by a mezzanine.

3

4

gaining more space are easy to imagine, but the implications go much wider than a simple increase in floor area. Any extension will affect your neighbours (and there are laws governing what you can and cannot do); it may affect the structure and stability of your home (which is why you need professional guidance from the outset); it will affect the external appearance of your home and possibly decrease the usable area of your garden; and it will affect the value of your property.

The decision to add on to your home must ultimately rest on whether you would be better staying put and carrying out the work, or moving somewhere new. But if you're prepared to evaluate all the options clearly and objectively, and employ professional help to carry out the job, the results will more than repay your time and trouble.

Building from scratch

The ultimate challenge on the domestic front is to build your own home. The advantages are obvious, considerable and very real. No other option allows you to express your preferences to the full. You can, if you wish, specify every element of the design, materials and finishes, from the shape of the windows to the type of doorknobs, and take advantage of the latest technical know-how in terms of construction and materials. In areas where land is readily available and relatively cheap, building your own home can be very cost effective, provided you don't get too carried away.

In many parts of the world, building a new house rather than moving into an old one, is far from unusual. In Scandinavia, for example, it has been common practice for people to build their own homes for many years and standards are high, thanks to considerable official encouragement. In Britain, regrettably, the opportunities for what is generally termed 'self-build' are more limited, but they do exist.

'Self-build' conjures up an image of pioneer cabins rough-hewn from tree trunks and field stones. In fact, the term covers all one-off houses, from bespoke cottages to gleaming Modernist masterpieces to detailed, ready-made plans you can buy from specialist companies. In most instances, the usual services of an architect, surveyor and builder are required. Designing a private house is a commission beloved of architects. If you and your architect are well matched in terms of aims and aesthetics, both sides will benefit from the creative freedom.

In Britain, a combination of rigorous planning laws and high land prices makes the process of finding a site somewhat tortuous. Desirable sites on the fringes of villages or county towns are hard to acquire and agricultural land is rarely awarded change of use. It is sometimes possible to buy a derelict property, demolish it and replace it with your dream home. But you may find that you have to rebuild within the 'footprint' of

1

the original structure, which effectively rules out replacing a tiny cottage with a rambling family home. In the city, you may be required to match the façade of your new house with existing properties in the street, which will not only affect its external appearance but may also determine its internal layout.

Unless you want to run the risk of buying land you are then unable to build on, the safest route is to approach a land agent and buy a plot which has already received outline planning permission for domestic use. Local authority planners will then have plenty to say about the materials you can and cannot use in construction, as well as the appearance, size and style of your new house.

If you can surmount these obstacles, the opportunities open to you are limited only by your imagination and your budget. Building your own home – or commissioning someone to build it for you – allows you to create an environment which suits you in every respect.

2 Creating a new building in an urban setting entails sensitivity to architectural context. The A-line structure of this modern design in Paris reflects the proximity of a church, the shape echoing the view of the spire from the glazed end wall. A mezzanine level with a glass floor retains the sense of openness internally.

2

1 With all the appeal of an outsize tree-house, this Australian home makes brilliantly imaginative use of simple materials. The sail-like corrugated-iron roof follows the lines of the landscape and the path of the sun. The basic timber construction and expansive panels of glass form a three-storey tower of single rooms – a powerful design which makes the most of the wilderness setting.

3 Perched on the rim of California's Napa Valley, a small family house commands great views of the countryside. The attic space forms a large bedroom, with big dormers that punctuate the roof and open up vistas through the surrounding trees.
4 Nestling among a wood of oak and pine trees, the south face of the house is almost a complete wall of windows on the ground floor, with a thin band of windows above, sheltered by the broad pyramidal roof.

3

4

Smith House, New York

Situated in the Catskill Mountains, New York, this new house is a small structure with a large voice. Its rigorous simplicity consists of three basic elements that converge to form the house: an L-shaped concrete wall, poured in place and forming a wall to the garden and the house; a two-storey, wood-framed barrelled vault which incorporates all the service functions (entrance hall, utility room, stairs, bathrooms and kitchen); and a perforated, wood-framed L-shaped wall sheathed in corrugated metal.

Perched on top of a small mountain, the house is approached up an inclined drive, the top of which becomes a circular parking court which sets up a formal and geometric relationship between house and garden. This is the public face of the building. On the northern side, the long concrete wall is punctuated first by a 'picture' window framing a view of the back of the house and thereafter by the sparse rhythm of tall, thin windows to the interior. The barrel-vaulted 'barn' intersects this wall at a slight angle.

The rear, which faces south, enjoys spectacular views of the mountains, a ski slope and a small village in the valley below. This private façade opens up to the light, and is mostly windows.

The interior design is predetermined largely by the formal clarity of the architecture. Although the house is small, its open-plan layout treats the interior as a complementary extension of the exterior, using a simple palette of materials. The kitchen cabinetry, for example, is built flush along one wall of the barrelled

1

1 An impression of the perspectives afforded by the house and its site: from the back, windows open out on to the valley and surrounding mountains; the end of the concrete wall affords a view through the 'picture' window; the public façade at the front of the building.
2 The corrugated metal wall at the rear of the house is punctuated by tall windows, some of which, in fact, are doors. The living area is simply furnished and decorated so as not to distract from the simplicity of the structure.

2

3

vault using the same marine mahogany plywood as the exterior. This creates one continuous surface, inside and out, the kitchen disappearing into the wall when not in use. In the ground-floor bedroom, large sliding doors play up to the scale set by the expanse of wood, concrete and glass. When closed, the doors offer privacy; when open, they slide across to become a part of the wall, enclosing the entrance to the bathroom. Throughout, lighting is integrated to highlight the architecture and finishes. Colour is used as a mediator of the architecture, rather than as decorative punctuation, blending interior with exterior, house with environment.

4

5

3 An exploded view of the house shows the location of the main rooms and services.
4 The large window in the poured-concrete wall affords spectacular views through to the open countryside.
5 The three basic elements of the house create a juxtaposition of form and materials that is at once both bold and harmonious.

6 This proposed site plan was produced by a later firm of architects after completion of the main house, and takes the geometries of the structure as the starting-point for the surrounding design. Approached by a circular drive that incorporates a clear-roofed car porch, a gravel path leads either to the house or across to the formal garden; this is the view that greets visitors and neighbours. Much of this design has yet to be completed.

Cliff edge

House

Gravel path

Car porch

Hedge

Formal garden

Drive

North

6

1 Brazilian walnut flooring runs through the main living area, which enjoys abundant natural light. The wood-burning stove supplements the forced-air heating and natural solar heat gain.

2 At the top of the staircase, a glass landing bridges the master bedroom and bathroom. The wooden stair treads, metal rail and glass floor unite three materials used in the main construction.

1

2

3

3 From the groundfloor bedroom, doors open on to the white marble entrance foyer, which in turn leads to the main living area. The view also looks up behind the staircase to the glass landing above.

4 Apart from the island-unit sink, all the major kitchen utilities are housed in the barrelled vault. When not in use, they are seamlessly integrated with the wall behind marine mahogany doors.

4

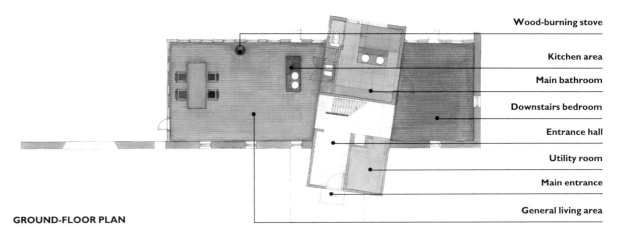

Wood-burning stove

Kitchen area

Main bathroom

Downstairs bedroom

Entrance hall

Utility room

Main entrance

General living area

GROUND-FLOOR PLAN

Upstairs bedroom

Glass landing

Clothes storage

Shower room

Lavatory

FIRST-FLOOR PLAN

5

5 The shower in the main bathroom is in a step-down area behind the basins. The wall of sandblasted glass blocks floods the room with natural light at the same time as retaining a sense of privacy.

6 Vermont slate tiles on the floor and walls complement the two cast-bronze basins. The mirrored wall enhances the sense of space and light in the room. The sliding Japanese-screen doors lead to the lavatory.

6

7 The upstairs bedroom makes a feature of the barrelled roof. As downstairs, the cupboard doors slide along the full width of the room and have a dual function. As shown here they form doors to the clothes cupboard; when pushed aside they cover the entrances to the lavatory and shower room beyond.

Architects: Deborah Weintraub, A.I.A. and Scott Lane; additional interior detailing by Richard Lavenstein; subsequent site plan and proposed landscaping by Kiss + Zwigard.

See 'Useful Addresses' (pages 258-65) for full details.

KNOW YOUR HOME

A precondition for change is knowing what you've got to start with. You may think you know your home, and if you've lived there for a while, you'll certainly be familiar with it, but do you really understand how it works, how each room relates to the others in terms of scale, shape and orientation? Do you know the dimensions of the rooms, the ceiling heights and sizes of the windows? Do you know the date when your house was built, or the materials from which it is constructed? If you're sensitive to the age, layout and environment of your home, you'll be far more likely to arrive at a scheme for change that fulfils as many of your criteria as possible than if you embark on an ill-thought-through plan to knock down as many internal walls as possible, just because you're fed up with the pokey dimensions of the existing kitchen. Similarly, if your budget will only allow you to undertake essential work at the moment, it's still worth drawing up a list of long-term objectives rather than embarking on alterations in a piecemeal fashion as funds become available.

Part of the process of assessment is providing yourself with a concrete framework to test your ideas. You may already have determined where improvements could be made, but before you rush out to commission the work, it is important to establish how your ideas tally with and complement existing conditions. This may take the form of measuring up, making floor plans and scale models, taking advice or engaging in local research. This preliminary work should also enable you to make a realistic assessment of the extent to which you can carry out some or all of the work yourself. Many people are unduly suspicious of architects, designers and builders — qualified professionals who should be there to make life easier for you. If you undertake an overambitious task yourself you are on a certain road to ruin. Undoing the damage will be costly and involve even further disruption; it is far better to ask around for personal recommendations of people in the building trade, to inspect examples of their work, and to let someone better qualified take on the task of realizing your plans. If you have a good understanding of the cost, scale and potential pitfalls of the job, you won't be taken for a ride.

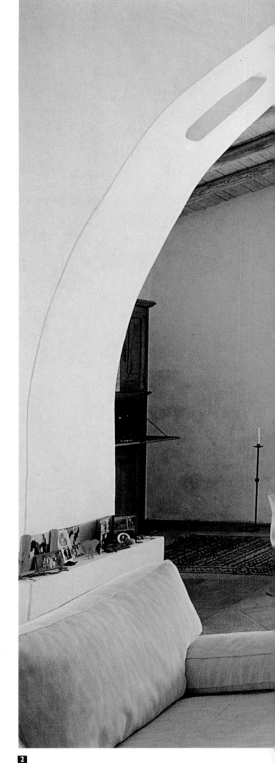

1 Part of the process of assessment is to identify those details and features of your home which are intrinsically appealing. This shallow flight of curved steps calls for no improvement.
2 A pristine conversion of an old farm building in Portugal allows the form of the original structure to shine through without compromising comfort or intimacy.

3 An American town house has undergone a bold conversion in which the back is opened up to form a wall of glass. In the living area, a modern fireplace dramatically inset in the glass wall takes centre stage.

4 Thoughtful allocation of space is essential for the smooth functioning of a multi-purpose layout. A dining area forms the buffer between living space and the kitchen fitted along the end wall.

5 The sheer delight of this flight of stairs, fanned like a deck of cards, makes a strong architectural state- ment. Assessing your home is as much to do with identifying what you like as it is what you want to change.

4

5

Making a floor plan

■ A conventional kitchen layout – the L-shape – is turned inside out in an unusual plan that takes advantage of the view of an internal courtyard in this Parisian home.

Making a floor plan is time-consuming but otherwise presents few problems. Begin by making a rough plan of the room in question, then measure and fill in all the dimensions; from this you can draw up a scale plan on graph paper. Elevations – wall plans – are produced in exactly the same way: first make a rough sketch on to which you should transfer dimensions; then make a scale plan on graph paper.

Anyone can make a plan of their home. Getting it all down on paper will give you a much clearer picture of your home's space and proportions. It is very easy to misjudge the size and shape of rooms when you're relying exclusively on visual evidence and comparisons; there's no arguing with accurate measurements.

Making floor plans is an exercise in objectivity, enabling you to regard your home dispassionately. Plans are also an invaluable means of communicating your wishes to others, and can prevent a lot of misunderstanding when you come to instruct builders, architects or suppliers. They are essential for testing the feasibility of your schemes and proposals.

Begin by sketching a rough diagram of each floor or room, showing the approximate shape and size, together with any connecting hallways, and the position of doors, windows and fixed features such as alcoves, fireplaces, radiators and built-in storage. If you aren't used to thinking diagrammatically, you may find this difficult initially, but persevere until you have a fairly clear representation of the existing layout.

Now you should measure up. Work as accurately as you can, using a tape measure or extendible wooden rule. Don't rely on pacing – the figures need to be as precise as possible. Adopt the system of measurement (imperial or metric) you

feel comfortable with and stick to it. Measure the length and breadth of each room, including the dimensions of features such as chimney breasts and alcoves. Measure the thickness of walls or partitions, the width of doorways and windows and the dimensions of built-in fixtures such as kitchen units. Transfer each measurement to the appropriate position on your sketch plan.

The dimensions you have taken may already indicate some inaccuracies in your sketch plan. You will now need to use your measurements to convert the sketch plan into a proper scale drawing. This task is easier than it sounds, as long as you're prepared to work methodically. Equip yourself with a good ruler, a set square, graph paper and a calculator.

A scale drawing is made using a fixed ratio that translates actual dimensions into ones of manageable proportions. In other words, you decide on a scale of conversion – say 2cm to 1m or ¼in to 1ft – and use this as the basis for converting all the dimensions you took into the dimensions of your drawing. Architects work at different scales, depending on the level of detail required on the plan. You may wish to double the scale given above for representing intensely planned areas such as a kitchen or a bathroom, but do not combine different scales on the same drawing. Remember, if you took the dimensions in metric, work to a metric scale on centimetre-square graph paper; whereas if you measured in feet and inches, work to an imperial scale on ¼in-square graph paper.

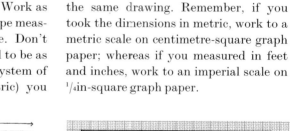

ROUGH FLOOR PLAN

SCALE FLOOR PLAN

ROUGH WALL PLAN

SCALE WALL PLAN

With a sharp, hard pencil, draw in the walls, using a set square to form right angles at the corners (provided they exist). Mark on all the features in their correct positions. There are a number of conventional symbols you may wish to adopt to show details such as the direction in which doors open, or the position of switches, radiators and power points. Include all relevant detail, remaining accurate at all times. You might also include a note of ceiling heights, the principal orientation of each room and the times of day it receives direct sunlight.

Once you are satisfied with your plans, make several photocopies of each so you can begin to try out your ideas. You may wish to draw in a furniture layout on one set – remember to work to the same scale, and measure each item accurately.

2

2 This kitchen alcove has been rigorously planned to make the most of the available space. Shelves suspended from the ceiling provide storage overhead; a high counter serves as a breakfast bar and space divider. Accurate measuring is essential to integrate fitted units with appliances.

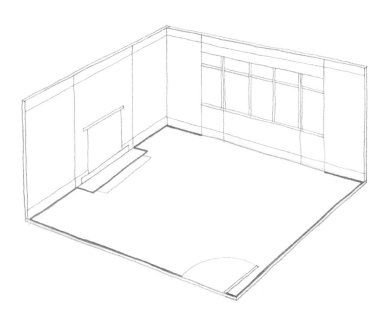

Using the scale floor plan and scale wall plans you can make a model of any room you are planning to change.

Alternatively, you can cut out furniture shapes and move the pieces around on the plan, trying out new arrangements. Again, work to the same scale, label each piece and colour them in if it helps. You can envisage different spatial layouts by placing tracing paper over your original drawing and sketching out alternatives. Reserve one set to mark with the details of defects and essential repairs.

OTHER VISUAL AIDS

You can apply the same basic technique that is involved in drawing up a floor plan to construct a three-dimensional impression of any rooms in your home that you are planning to change. For this, you need to consider the vertical elements of the structure, as opposed to the horizontal features shown on a plan. What an architect terms the 'elevation' is basically a plan of each wall seen face on, represented diagrammatically and exactly to scale.

Use the method already described to make sketches and then scale drawings of each wall in the area you are considering, showing the positions of windows, doors and other openings, as well as built-in features such as fireplaces or kitchen appliances. Stick the drawings, together with the appropriate floor plan, on sheets of card or polyboard and carefully cut each piece out. By attaching the pieces together with tape you can then assemble a scale model of a particular room or sequence of spaces.

Models are much easier for a lot of people to read than drawings because they give a clearer impression of volume and proportion. However, if you still find it difficult to visualize the effect that different alterations or arrangements may have, you can try working life-size. For this, you will need to buy a few rolls of lining-paper and draw out the features you wish to add or change, such as a new door, window or opening between rooms and tape the paper up on the wall in the appropriate position. As with scale plans, the more accurate you can be about dimensions the more useful the exercise. Conversely, you could use the lining-paper to mask out any openings you plan to block up. You can then rearrange furniture in the room to take account of the proposed changes and live with the new layout for a while to assess its impact on your home.

You could also make life-size cut-outs of existing furniture or of various pieces of furniture you plan to buy and then move these around on the floor. This will obviously save you a great deal of physical effort, while it will also help you to discover whether entrances are big enough to accommodate moving large items such as sofas, beds and dining tables in and out of various rooms.

Understanding structure

Until faced with the prospect of making major alterations, few people give much thought to the way their home is constructed. Most of us have some sketchy notions about how buildings manage to stand up, and even vaguer ideas about the implications of moving walls around or of changing windows and doors. Understanding a little more about the main structural elements will help you to assess the cost and feasibility of a whole range of spatial solutions.

Homes come in all shapes and sizes, but they all hold together in roughly the same way. You don't need a degree in physics or structural engineering to appreciate the principles of construction – if you've ever built a house of cards or a sandcastle on the beach, you'll realize instinctively that the main issue is how the weight of the building is supported. If you overload the structure or weaken it past a certain limit, the cards topple over and the castle caves in.

All houses have foundations, external and internal walls pierced by a number of openings, one or more floors and a roof covering it all. Starting at the top, the weight of the roof – slates, tiles, timber, perhaps glass – is largely carried by the outside walls of the house. These walls also support the floors that span across them, with some of the inside walls helping to carry the load. All of this great weight rests on the foundations. The roof and the upper floors are not merely passive loads to be supported, but also act to brace the entire structure and to give it rigidity and stability.

There are a number of variations in how the support systems of different buildings work. In large buildings, where the outside walls are widely spaced apart and the roof spans a great distance, there may be internal columns that provide additional support for the roof or there may be substantial tie beams or trusses between the walls to hold it all together. On a domestic scale, the main variables have to do with which internal walls play a supporting role and which do not.

Many of the walls inside your home are partitions – they divide up space but play no part in holding anything up. Others are structurally integral because they help to carry the weight of the floors above. Some walls may be semi-structural if they are positioned directly beneath walls on an upper level and therefore act as a support for this weight. If your house has timber floors, you can estimate which internal walls are structural by looking at the direction of the floorboards. The 'joists' or beams which support the floor run at right angles to the floorboards on the level above, which are generally laid across the width of the house. Any wall which carries the joists will be structural: these are likely to be the walls which also run side to side across the house.

If there is an element of doubt about the status of internal walls, there's no uncertainty about the external walls. It is likely that any substantial change to an outside wall will affect the entire structural system of the house. The same goes for major changes to the upper floors, roof and, of course, foundations.

1 A strong earthy red delineates the partition wall enclosing a bathroom. The wall is taken high enough to provide privacy but stops short of the ceiling, allowing light to spill down from the roof windows.

2 Part of the appeal of loft and warehouse conversions is the visibility of the main structural components. In domestic buildings, identifying which elements support the house and which do not may not be quite so straightforward.

If you took away one of the outside walls, your house would fall down. In the same way, if you remove a portion of the wall, to make a doorway for example, you adversely affect the ability of the wall to perform its essential supporting job. The way such alterations are accommodated is by compensating for the weakness by putting in a strengthening element, such as a beam or RSJ (rolled-steel joist) above the new opening. You need to ensure, at the same time, that the remaining wall and foundations can support this additional load.

From this account, it is also possible to see how certain defects can pose such a threat. Dry rot, which attacks timber beams and joists, and subsidence, which undermines foundations, are among the factors that can cause severe weakening of structural elements (see page 248).

3 Supported by steel beams, a new mezzanine level housing a bedroom and play space for two small children is slotted within a double-height space converted from a redundant warehouse. The toughened plate-glass window looks down on to the living space and kitchen area.

3

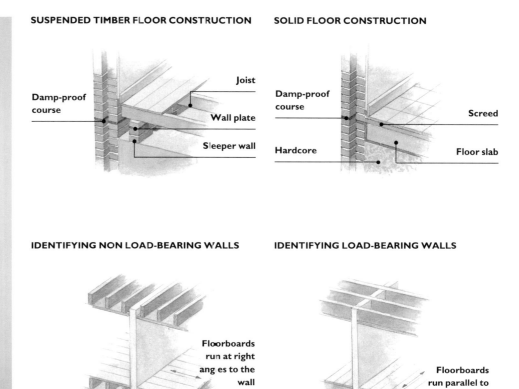

SUSPENDED TIMBER FLOOR CONSTRUCTION

Damp-proof course

Joist

Wall plate

Sleeper wall

SOLID FLOOR CONSTRUCTION

Damp-proof course

Hardcore

Screed

Floor slab

IDENTIFYING NON LOAD-BEARING WALLS

Floorboards run at right angles to the wall

Joists run parallel to the wall

IDENTIFYING LOAD-BEARING WALLS

Floorboards run parallel to the wall

Joists run at right angles to the wall

1

1 An internal box-bedroom formed within a New York loft is crisply defined with colour. Enclosing space with partition walls does not affect the structure of a building. **2** The kitchen, a step down from the living area, gains definition from the change in floor level. The same flooring throughout unifies the space.

This general picture should help you to assess some of the implications of spatial changes. All structural work should be properly appraised by an architect, surveyor or engineer to establish the precise change in loads and to advise you on effective substitutes and safeguards.

As a summary, work may have structural implications if it involves:

- Making a new opening in an outside wall, such as a window, door or French windows. This also applies if the opening forms a link with a new extension, such as a conservatory.
- Enlarging an existing opening in an outside wall, especially if the opening is widened, for example, by turning a single doorway into French windows. (Making an opening bigger by extending it downwards – for example, if you removed a lower section of wall under an existing window to turn the window into a doorway – may not have great structural implications.)
- Removing all or part of internal load-bearing walls, for example, by knocking two rooms together or creating an open-plan layout.
- Removing a chimney breast.
- Removing a portion of a floor to create a double-height space.
- Altering the position of a staircase.
- Excavating a basement below the existing foundations.
- Converting an attic into a habitable room, particularly if the ceiling joists have to be strengthened.
- Cutting away part of a roof to form a dormer window.
- Adding a new storey at roof level or on top of an existing extension.
- Renewing a roof, thereby increasing the weight of roofing material, such as replacing slates with concrete tiles.

STRUCTURAL SURVEYS

If you are buying a new property or about to embark on a major programme of alteration, it is a good idea to commission a full structural survey to determine the basic condition of your house. If there are any underlying problems of a serious nature, these must be put right before you go on to spend money on improvements. Even if your house has a clean bill of health, a survey can indicate precisely which elements are structural and help you to refine your plans. A surveyor should also be able to advise you on the condition of the various service systems – heating, plumbing and wiring.

Because surveyors, in Britain at least, are now legally accountable for the quality of their service, many are inclined to be cautious and even pessimistic about potential risk factors; this is to avoid any comeback in the form of a legal suit if they fail to spot a serious problem. Don't despair if a report seems excessively gloomy or unnecessarily vague and non-committal: obtain a second opinion to ensure you have been given a realistic picture of the situation. If there do turn out to be serious structural defects, a surveyor may suggest you go on to seek the advice of a structural engineer who will be able to tell you exactly what's involved in putting it right.

DATING YOUR HOUSE

The more you know about your house the better, and if your house is more than a few generations old, it makes sense to delve into its history. Most of us are insatiably curious about previous occupants and their way of life, and older houses have many other fascinating stories to tell about evolving styles and uses. The whole issue becomes one of more than passing interest if you intend to renovate a period house or you plan to restore special features and characteristics lost through unsympathetic conversion.

Documentary evidence in the form of maps, deeds and census rolls may provide information on houses built within the last 200 years, particularly in urban areas that have been systematically developed. The local records office or archivist may be able to supply you with an exact date, details of ownership and possibly even original plans of the house.

Information on property that was once tied to an estate may exist on early deeds or estate records, which may also be in the keeping of a local records office. In the same way, property once owned by the church may be fully documented. Wills, inventories and tax returns are other sources of written information and from these it may be possible to build up a surprisingly detailed picture of furnishings, size and use of rooms.

Where documentary evidence is sketchy, contradictory or missing altogether, you will have to look for clues in the architectural style of the house and any others like it that may be in the vicinity. Dating houses that have a long history can be problematic, since many will have been substantially altered and rebuilt over the years. It's by no means rare for old cottages or farmhouses to

have acquired false fronts added at a much later date than the original building or for the core of the structure to be almost completely obliterated beneath layers of subsequent additions. In some cases, the true date of such houses only becomes apparent when repair or alteration brings evidence of much earlier construction to light.

Constructional methods and architectural styles are not an infallible guide, however, since in remote districts away from the fast-moving fashions of the town, innovations were slower to be adopted and older methods of building lingered on. The most important thing is to keep renovation and redecoration sympathetic to the period, scale and character of the property. If the building is listed, there will be restrictions on what you can and cannot do.

2

3

4

3 The mellow quality of worn quarry-tiled floor and battered wall finishes are pleasing indications of age and use. Natural materials wear attractively, acquiring character with the years.
4 Good architectural bones require little in the way of cosmetic dressing. Plain white walls and linen leave well enough alone.

Planning for change

The best-laid plans may often go awry, but setting out to change your home without any preparation is just asking for trouble. Planning is a state of mind that comes naturally to some people; others find it frustrating to curb their impetuosity. If you are one of the latter, console yourself with the thought that by cooling your heels temporarily and imposing a little order and method on your approach, you will save yourself from almost certain disaster later on. Astronomical bills, months of dust, mess and inconvenience and a botched job at the end of it is the sure fate of those who jump straight in the deep end without working their way carefully through all the variables, making contingencies for unexpected problems, and scheduling the work to cause as little disruption and frustration as possible.

Planning is the art of the possible. It involves reconciling ideals with reality and working out the best route to an end result. You shouldn't expect to sit down and hatch a detailed plan of action straight away; the process should be gradual, as needs are refined, information gathered and options weighed up until there comes a point when you know you are ready to begin, and what it is precisely that you want to achieve.

At the beginning of this process, the type of changes you wish to make may amount to a coherent programme or no more than a list of seemingly unrelated items, some of which conflict. But whatever shape your ideas are in, they are your starting place and represent one half of the planning equation. The other half comprises a number of vital issues which will determine how you proceed. Sooner or later you'll come up against a fixed point – it may be the amount of money you can spend, the time at your disposal, what is legally or technically feasible. These parameters give a plan shape and direction and suggest the best way of going forward. Without limits, plans remain vague and unfocused – as long as a piece of string.

WORKING OUT A BUDGET

Money is probably the biggest determining factor in any home-improvement scheme. No one likes nasty financial surprises and since many types of alteration carry the risk of unforeseen expense, your financial planning should be detailed, cautious and conservative.

The advice given here assumes that you are a home owner; if you rent, different considerations come into play. As a tenant, you may be able to claim money for repairs and essential improvements from your landlord, depending on the terms of the lease. Anything else that you intend to do must be strictly affordable within your present budget, and achievable well within the timescale of the period you propose to stay in your home. You will need to consult your landlord for approval. Unless you have the security of a long lease, it is better to put your money into economical forms of decorating and furnishings you can take with you when you leave.

3

The first step is to work out what you can afford. Most people accept the need to budget for large-scale projects, such as a conversion or extension, but resist forward planning for on-going schemes of decoration and furnishing. However, even if your plans merely consist of a rolling programme of relatively small-scale improvements, unless you set aside specific sums for the expenses you will incur, you may find yourself living in the middle of a building site, badly out of pocket, in no time at all.

Consult your accountant, bank manager, or any other financial adviser to whom you have access, to work out the safest and most sensible way of funding your proposals. Advisers will help you to compare the costs of different options and can advise whether or not you will be eligible for assistance such as tax relief.

Options for financing include:
- Utilizing a lump sum, such as all or part of your savings, an inheritance, or the balance on the sale of a property.

You may discover that borrowing part of the money, even if you have ready cash, may be cheaper in the long run; you may have other uses for your capital which have to be weighed against the benefits of paying for the entire scheme up front.
- Credit, such as short-term loans, overdrafts, credit-card borrowing. This is often an expensive solution and is best restricted to the funding of small-scale decorating and furnishing projects.
- Home-improvement loans. You will need to work out how much you can afford to repay each month and whether your income will support this additional expenditure for the duration of the loan period.
- Remortgaging. If your mortgage is currently much lower than the resale value of your home, the remainder – the 'equity' – can provide a basis for extra borrowing. The risk associated with this approach is that property values can, and do, fluctuate and being

mortgaged up to the hilt is an uncomfortable position in a declining market. You need to be sure that the improvements you are planning will add real value to your home, so you stand some chance of recouping your investment when you come to sell.
- Grants. Houses in conservation areas or those of 'listed' historic interest are often eligible for government grants. Grants come with strings attached, however, and there are often stringent requirements about the standard and type of work that can be carried out.
- Making economies. To raise small amounts of money you may be able to cut back in other areas, forgo the annual holiday or the new car, for example, or earn a little more by taking in a lodger or working overtime.

Once you have arrived at a realistic figure which represents both what you can afford and what you are prepared to spend, the next step is to cost out your proposals and see how it all adds up. This is where many people go astray, preferring vague optimism to cold, hard fact. Some unscrupulous builders and suppliers are all too happy to encourage the folly of this approach, knowing that once work is under way you will be most vulnerable to extra demands for cash and least likely to resist digging deeper into your pocket.

To arrive at a likely total expenditure, first do your homework. Research the market. If you are buying materials or furnishings yourself, compare different suppliers with a ruthless eye for variations in quality. If you are planning any kind of building work, find out what the work should cost. Ask neighbours or friends who have had similar schemes carried out what they paid for it. Get at least two or three detailed estimates in writing from recommended builders or professionals. Make sure that estimates cover the cost of labour *and* materials, up to and including all those little extras, such as handles, catches, fittings and fixtures. Remember to add in the cost of

■

■ **Dividing up space offers the opportunity for imaginative constructions, such as this plywood-faced structure containing a mezzanine level used as a sleeping area.**

finishing off. The true cost of rewiring, for example, includes replastering and redecoration as well as the electrician's fee and the cost of new fittings.

These are the direct costs of your proposals. But there will also be hidden costs. These may include:

- The cost of financing, such as interest on loans or fixed repayments. You should also consider how your improvements will affect the investment potential of your home – will you be adding to its value in real terms? Some idiosyncratic alterations may make your home harder to sell.
- Fees for advice, from accountants, architects, surveyors or any other professionals whom you consult before commissioning the work.
- The cost of your time, if you plan to carry out some or all of the work yourself. Even if you delegate the entire job to a builder, you should allow time for supervision or administration.
- An allowance for potential disruption or inconvenience. You can't put a price on sheer aggravation, but you can

allow for the cost of eating out while a kitchen is out of commission, or for the price of having carpets and furnishings cleaned professionally if dust and debris prove excessive.

- Additional running costs. Will your home cost more to heat, light or insure once the work is complete? Will your property tax be higher?

Life is nothing if not full of surprises and some forms of building work seem guaranteed to come up with the unexpected. If there is the chance that you may uncover more than you bargained for, you should also set aside a percentage of the total cost as a hedge against disaster. This 'contingency allowance', as it is generally known, is roughly ten per cent for large jobs, but each case should be considered individually, depending on the scope of the job. Decorating, furnishing, applying new surfaces and finishes are largely predictable procedures if well planned, but the more invasive operations, including any form of remodelling, major repair or new building work, may expose hidden

difficulties along with the underlying structure. When the builder brings you the bad news about the patch of damp that has just been uncovered, knowing your budget can take the strain will help soften the blow. Overestimating how much you need to spend also allows you some flexibility as work progresses, if a chosen material proves to be impossible to get and the alternative is more expensive, for example. Don't give yourself too much leeway, however, or you may be tempted to respecify and upgrade the work as you go along – there are few more certain short cuts to financial ruin!

ECONOMIES: TRUE AND FALSE

By now you should have some idea of how much you want to spend and how much your plan is going to cost. Unless you have relatively modest ambitions, the two figures are bound not to tally and you will have to look at ways of bringing the cost down in line with your budget. The simplest and perhaps most sensible course is to tackle the really essential work first and postpone the rest

2 Sleek minimal interiors demand superb detailing and rigorous planning. Only the shelves of cookery books betray the presence of a kitchen area, installed behind a waist-high counter in an open-plan space.
3 Thorough planning is essential to achieve the best possible organization of fittings in a bathroom. In a small space, a matter of a few centimetres in either direction may make the difference between a layout that works and one that does not.

Another temptation is to reduce the costs of labour by doing it yourself. Only you can realistically assess your level of skill, but beware the new-found over-confidence that follows a high builder's estimate. If you originally planned to hire a builder or other professionals to do a particular stage of the job, you should trust this original assessment of your abilities and look for other possible ways of economizing. Don't forget that your time has value, too, and DIY is not doing-it-for-free. Basic materials will cost more, since you will not be eligible for the builder's 'trade discount'. You may also need to hire or acquire special tools for certain stages of the job. If you are inexperienced, you run the risk of ruining expensive materials, causing damage to your home or even yourself, not to mention taking twice the time to complete the work. Is it really worth it?

of your proposals until you are better able to afford them. This enables you to complete a stage at a time to the required standard of finish, which is ultimately more satisfactory than making do with second best. It's important to see each stage right through to completion; half-finished projects have a tendency to stay that way indefinitely.

Excessive cost may indicate that your plans could bear simplification. Run through your ideas with an architect, designer or builder to look at other ways of providing the same result for less money. Standard components and building techniques are always cheaper than idiosyncratic features: a simple, straight partition wall costs less to build than a curved wall, for example. If the design is based on the dimensions of standard units – such as stair flights, kitchen units, windows and doors – it will be much simpler and hence more economical to realize. This type of economy can be creative and you may even end up with a solution that is neater and more elegant than your original plan .

False economies are the type which turn out to have an expensive sting in the tail. Cheapening up by downgrading materials, doing without specialist help and taking on more of the work than you are qualified to do can lead to untold heartache and ultimately extra cost.

The price of materials usually forms a substantial part of the cost of any altera-tion, and there is a temptation to cut corners in this department. If you've specified a luxury finish, there may be an affordable option which will do the job just as well for a fraction of the outlay, or a cheaper lateral solution of the same quality. But there is a line below which you should not go. Substandard prod-ucts perform badly right from the start and you may have to redo the entire job. Cheap paint, for example, has such poor coverage that more coats will be needed to achieve a decent finish and it wears badly as well, so repainting will be more frequent. If you cost out the greater quantity of paint needed and extra time spent, what little you appeared to save at the beginning will have evaporated.

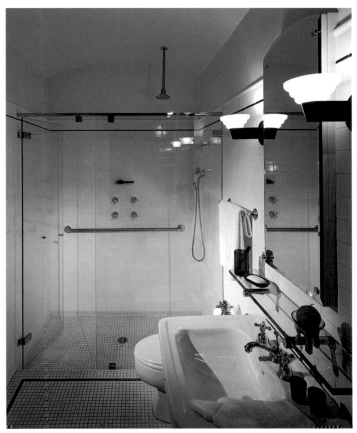

A two-storey house has been opened up to bring daylight from the roof windows down into the ground-floor rooms such as the kitchen and significantly increases the perception of volume. Running above the kitchen, a high-level walkway made of perforated steel makes a dramatic connection between different areas of the home, bridging rooms on the first floor and offering dynamic views through the space that offer multiple readings of the house and make it feel considerably larger than it is. The extractor unit above the hob sits in an industrial air-conditioning duct made from galvanized sheet steel and hangs from the ceiling way above, again emphasizing the height and maximizing the potential of the opened-up space.

Yet another common form of false economy is to do without professional advice. Obviously, there are plenty of home improvements that do not require outside assistance, but for large, complex projects that affect services and basic structure, some form of informed guidance is essential. Only politicians and lawyers are viewed with less esteem than building professionals. A lot of people fear exorbitant fees, or being bulldozed into solutions that they don't want, or being confused by terminology and unable to convey their wishes. These can be persuasive arguments for doing without advice when a little financial belt-tightening is in order.

Such objections largely spring from a misconception of what it is that design professionals actually do. The right architect, surveyor or designer should save you time, trouble and money by rationalizing your plans, anticipating possible areas of difficulty and negotiating legal consents.

A properly accredited professional with experience in the type of work you require is worth every penny of the fee (which may not be that high, especially for simple consultation). If you are unhappy with the work, you will have some comeback in the form of an appeal to the institution or body that regulates the profession. By the same token, anyone you employ to work on your home should come from a reputable firm.

ASSESSING PRIORITIES

A glance at the price tag may be enough to enable you to decide which changes are essential changes and which you could happily live without. If money is tight, repair work should take precedence over cosmetic improvements.

It is more difficult to assess priorities in cases where there are competing demands for the same space. If you're both clamouring for a study at a time when the children need separate bedrooms, you will probably have to accept that someone is going to lose out. Here it is best to opt for the changes which will benefit the whole household over the longest period, giving greatest value all round. A study may not be essential for the person who already has an outside office, whereas it may dramatically increase the efficiency of someone who exclusively works from home; separate bedrooms for growing children can cut down on sibling squabbles and give everyone a more peaceful life. As tricky as such negotiations can be, coming up against irreconcilable desires can force you to re-examine how you make use of your entire home; in the process you may find a better way of organizing space.

TIMING

Time is money; and in building terms, time also equals disruption. The cost of changing your home may be nothing compared to the emotional price of living on a building site for weeks on end. Before you put your plans into action, you should be aware how long it will take to complete the work and decide whether this is acceptable to you and the other members of your household.

Just as your budget should include contingency allowances, you should be generous in your allocation of the time needed to realize any project. Building work initiates a complex sequence of events which has the potential to break down at any point. Thorough planning can minimize hold-ups, but there are always factors you can't predict.

Ensuring that work proceeds in the correct order is vital for avoiding costly and frustrating delays. This is the most difficult aspect to organize and varies widely depending on the complexity of the work. There are some procedures which can be grouped; others which can't. There may be work which needs to be officially inspected and passed before the next stage can take place.

You should also plan to undertake the work at a time which fits in with your other commitments. Don't turn your home upside down and inside out when you're already overstretched at work, or you'll be battling on two fronts. The same applies if you've just had a new baby, if you've just changed jobs, if someone in the household is studying for exams or getting over an illness. There may not be a perfect time, but some are definitely more sensible than others.

Scheduling should also take account of the seasons. If you are building extensions or making structural alterations that involve external works, choose a period of the year when the weather is on your side; winter is no time to replace a roof or cut a hole in the back wall. But if you live in an area where the weather is unpredictable, where winters can be unseasonably mild or summers stormy and rainy, there may be no certain advantage in postponing work until the spring. Builders are usually less busy off-season and may therefore price the job more competitively and finish it faster than during the peak building period.

FEASIBILITY

The remaining constraints concern the practicalities of achieving what you hope to do and whether or not your plans are legal. It shouldn't be too difficult to discover if what you envisage is physically possible or not. Take advice early on and be prepared to modify your proposals accordingly. You may find that the work is more complex and more expensive than you'd imagined because of unforeseen structural implications, or that it is virtually ruled out for technical reasons to do with servicing. More often, if you seek professional advice along the way, you'll discover that what you want is broadly feasible but that there may be a few complications you hadn't considered.

Large-scale alterations and new building work generally have to comply with a number of legal requirements designed to ensure that what you do is safe, sound and acceptable to the community. Planning laws may determine the size and scale of an addition, the materials out of which it can be constructed and its

1

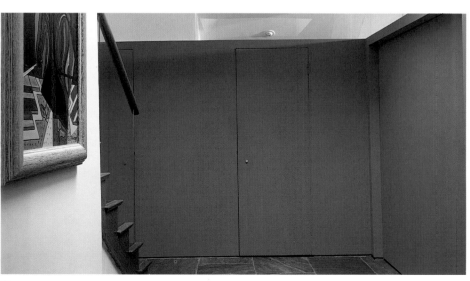

2

2 Three-quarter height partitioning encloses the entrance hall to this house without blocking out natural light.

relationship with adjoining properties. If you live in a house of designated historic interest, the rules about what you can and can't do have been framed with the intention of preserving the architectural integrity of the original building and they are usually both strict and specific.

While more detailed, specific requirements are given in appropriate sections of the book, the main areas affected by legal restrictions include:

- External appearance. There are regulations about the size, scale and extent of what you can build on to your home and how the general appearance of the proposed alterations affects the overall character of the street and the surrounding properties. An alteration which is prohibited to the front of your house may be allowed at the back, away from public view.

- Positioning. Building on to walls shared with neighbours (party walls) is always subject to agreement. You also have to ensure that your plans won't block natural light from other houses in your area. However, there is no legal right to a 'view'.

- Density. If you increase the amount of accommodation your home provides, the new density level (i.e., the number of habitable rooms per hectare) must conform to agreed limits.

- Structure. All structural alterations must be approved to ensure that your home will still stand up after you've made changes.

- Health. New rooms or a new layout of space must meet certain standards in terms of size, height, ventilation, heat loss, soundproofing and natural light.

- Fire risk. Both protection from fire and means of escape in case of fire are strictly controlled.

- Heritage. Changes to the fabric, appearance and design of historic houses are closely scrutinized.

- Specific approvals may need to be obtained from your gas, electricity or water boards, or from drainage or building inspectors.

Running a job

1

1 Basement areas are notoriously dark and enclosed. This glazed extension, half a level down from the garden, introduces light to a basement bedroom and provides a welcome sense of connection with the world outside.

There's an obvious difference between planning to paint the back bedroom on the next rainy afternoon and planning to extend the kitchen by constructing a new conservatory or creating an extra bedroom in your roof. In the first case, you can afford to act on impulse, put down your brush when you've had enough and pick it up again when the mood strikes; whereas the second type of plan demands careful forethought and discipline if you're not going to make a complete hash of things.

Matters are complicated infinitely when a job requires outside assistance. Even before a single tool has been lifted, you will need to have devoted considerable time and effort to making sure that everything has been properly organized. Hiring people to carry out work for you is the only safe and sensible course of action for tasks that demand specialist knowledge, skills and equipment, but finding the right professional help is more than a matter of dialling a number found in the Yellow Pages. Researching the market, thorough briefing and consultation and efficient scheduling won't guarantee a successful result, but should tip the balance in your favour.

WHO DOES WHAT

Before you can employ anyone, you have to know what services you require. The more complicated the job, the more advice and assistance you'll need. Most jobs can be broken down into three stages: planning and design; supervision and administration; and the actual building work. You may need help in all or some of these spheres to see your plans through to completion.

PLANNING AND DESIGN

Architects, designers and surveyors can help make a job run smoothly; more importantly, they can play a critical role in formulating what needs to be done. The architectural profession regularly attracts controversy, the mystique of the design process accounting for at least some of the bad press that it receives. However, for every high-profile designer of some contentious landmark building, there are hundreds of others who work happily on the domestic scale, carrying out sensitive and appropriate alterations to ordinary homes. On this level, if you choose the right person, you needn't worry about sky-high fees, avant-garde solutions (unless that's what you want) or professional arrogance. What an architect should offer is a new way of solving a spatial problem; a special knowledge of building materials and techniques; legal requirements; and structural constraints. The work may range from an hour's consultation to a more ongoing involvement producing a detailed specification for a builder to work to, or a set of drawings to submit for planning permission. An architect may also be able to put you in touch with the right building firm for the job. Fees are scaled appropriately, according to the level of involvement.

You may also need the services of a surveyor or structural engineer at this initial stage if you require a detailed assessment of structural defects to your house or flat or a report on the condition of existing services.

SUPERVISION

A full architectural service includes inspection of the job 'on site'. As such, the architect acts as your representative and ensures that all the contractors work to plan, schedule, budget and agreed standard. If the work involves legal consents or official inspections, the architect will handle these administrative matters as well. When the builder announces that the job is complete, the architect will inspect the work to ensure it is truly satisfactory, an invaluable service if your eye isn't trained to spot oversights and imperfections. In Britain, this stage is picturesquely termed 'snagging'. It is difficult to overestimate the importance of this function.

On a large job, organizing and scheduling the work is a major headache and it may be well worth the extra money to have someone else run it for you, whether this is the architect or the main contractor. For an uncomplicated alteration, there's no real reason why you can't manage this role yourself, provided you understand what's involved, and it may well be difficult to find an architect who's prepared to oversee a small job in any case. A comprehensive architectural service is usually billed as a percentage of the overall cost of the work.

BUILDING WORK

There is a vast range of trades associated with building work. Some firms are expert in only one or two related fields; others are multi-discipline; most employ a core of staff which is supplemented by subcontractors for the more specialist work. You need to be sure that the range of skills implicated in the proposed work is adequately covered by the firm you eventually engage to carry it out.

The alternative, especially for alterations such as rewiring, changes to your plumbing arrangements, new plasterwork, and so on, is to employ tradespeople on a direct basis, without using a builder as an intermediary. If the job demands only one or two disciplines, it may be more effective to hire a different person for each stage – say, an electrician to do the rewiring and a decorator to make good surfaces afterwards. This is only feasible if there aren't too many separate stages to go through, unless you really want the bother of finding a whole number of different tradespeople, briefing each one and obtaining a series of estimates for each job. It is also essential to identify the correct sequence of procedures; and remember, if you decide to go it alone, you may also have to take responsibility for organizing deliveries of materials and fixtures.

On the other hand, you may discover that it's hard to track down a general contractor prepared to tackle a really small job. Small jobs simply aren't cost-effective, even for many small firms; and, together with the aggravation factor, this may mean you either get an unreasonably large estimate for the work or an open-ended commitment to fit the job in when larger, more profitable projects permit. Either you can pay up, sit out the wait (which may be considerable), or revise your plans so that you group a number of related jobs together to make a more attractive package for pricing and scheduling.

The advantages of using a main or general contractor, especially for a large, complex job, are obvious. You will pay more for the service, but there are hidden savings to be made. When work is extensive, there are inevitably areas of overlap and the role of the contractor is to co-ordinate everyone's efforts so that each job proceeds in the most efficient way. Without anyone on site acting in this supervisory role, it is all too easy to waste time, money and effort. If, for example, an electrician lifts some floorboards to lay a new length of cable, replacing the boards afterwards, and then a plumber comes along the next day and needs to take up the same section of floor to install pipework, you can see how, by failing to anticipate the implications of each procedure, you might end

up effectively paying for work twice, not to mention suffering the consequent delays and bad tempers all round. Subcontractors – such as electricians, plumbers and heating engineers – like to target their efforts and hate being kept waiting. They expect the building to be ready for them when they arrive so they can get on with the job and proceed to the next as fast as possible.

Some builders also offer a 'design and build' package, which can be an attractive alternative to using an architect if your proposed plans are straightforward. In this case, the builder will commission drawings of the changes, which can form the basis of a planning submission if one is required. But if you're after an original solution or an approach that departs from standard building practice, it's far better to employ a professional designer.

FINDING HELP
Hiring the right person or firm for the job is half the battle. It's up to you to match skills and experience to the type and scale of the work; after that, it's up to them to execute it properly. Whoever you hire should be accredited professionals in their own field, trained and equipped to carry out the work to an acceptable standard, and experienced in jobs of a similar size and nature. It's easy to imagine the kind of difficulties you could get yourself into if you employ someone who is unqualified, unscrupulous and unreliable; easy to imagine, but apparently not so easy to avoid, since it happens all too frequently.

Whether it's an architect, a builder, a plasterer or a plumber you're looking for, the best route is usually personal recommendation. Ask around your circle of friends and acquaintances to find out who they would recommend for the type of work you're planning; you're much more likely to gain an honest assessment this way and you can always ask to view the finished work to double check that your friend's definition of a good job matches your own.

2

A personal testimonial isn't enough, however; you should go on to establish whether there are proper qualifications or affiliations to back it up. Most of the professions are controlled by national bodies who seek to maintain standards of training and workmanship in a particular field. If you can't find anyone through word of mouth, you could make a start by ringing one of the organizations listed at the back of this book and ask for a list of reputable firms to approach. None the less, professional status is increasingly a grey area; beware vague, professional-sounding titles such as 'architectural designer' which are no guarantee of full training. First of all, you need to be sure the people you intend to employ can accomplish what you want; secondly, and more cynically, you need to know you have some legal redress if anything goes wrong.

Once you've drawn up a short list of possible contenders, ask for references from previous clients or details of jobs completed. Don't hesitate to follow these up; a good professional has nothing to hide and won't balk at providing you with the sort of information you need to make up your mind.

2 A single-line kitchen makes good, hard-working use of a narrow area. The same basic ergonomic principles apply to kitchen design, however much – or little – space you have at your disposal.

Commissioning the work

If you intend to commission the building work directly, without architectural help, you need to be able to compare costs. This entails coming up with a specific brief for the work and getting a number (not less than two, and preferably three) written estimates from those on your short list. Don't cut corners here; prices can vary widely and by doing your homework and a little extra research, you may make a substantial saving. Bear in mind, however, that the lowest estimate may not always be the best bet. A really low tender for a job should arouse your suspicions as much as an inflated one. What you're looking for is a reasonable, realistic price for the work and a good overall level of performance.

An estimate is only as accurate as the brief – so be specific. If you're in doubt about what you want, take advice and firm up your decisions before any of the building work begins. Put everything in writing, preferably with annotated plans attached and keep copies of all of your correspondence on every point, however minor, especially if you change your mind. Don't take anything as read; if you don't specify the standard you want or the finish you require, you are more likely to be horribly dismayed than pleasantly surprised by the result. In addition to a firm idea of the eventual cost, an estimate should also provide you with a starting date and a schedule for completion. You must make clear that any subcontracts which arise and which have not been agreed at the outset will have to be approved by you before payment can be made.

Briefing anyone who's going to carry out work on your behalf is about good lines of communication. You don't have to learn a new language to make your wishes plain, although it clearly helps if you're informed and have some passing acquaintance with common terms. When you don't understand a technicality, don't be afraid to ask for an explanation. If you find it easy to be swayed by fast talk, delegate the briefing role to a partner or friend who will stand their ground. Finally, remember that you aren't asking for a favour, you're asking – and paying – for a service and you're entitled (within reason) to get what you want. At the same time, you may find that some of your ideas simply aren't feasible, practical or legal: in this case, listen to the advice you're given and adjust your sights accordingly.

Once you have made your decision and approved an estimate, it's a sensible idea to formalize the arrangement with the people you're employing in a written contract. An architect, for example, might be commissioned on the basis of a letter of agreement, setting out clearly the services you expect, the time-scale and the fee you will pay. For builders, any written agreement should stipulate the time in which a job may be finished, often including a penalty clause for late completion. It is also usual to set aside a percentage of the overall fee (about 5 per cent), which is retained for a period of up to six months in case of defects. The contract should also set out the terms of payment: after completion for a small job; at agreed interim stages for more complicated work. By staggering your payments, you have the option of withholding the next installment if you are dissatisfied with the work to date.

THE SEQUENCE OF WORK

Coordinating the work so that everything happens in the right order is a fine art. Get it wrong, and you will have holdups, work unnecessarily duplicated and extra wear and tear on your home, wallet and peace of mind. Good tradespeople tend to have full diaries and if a booking is missed because the work has not progressed to the appropriate stage for them to do their job, you may lose their services altogether. It's no less heartbreaking to see newly plastered and painted walls ruined because the electrician wasn't called in early enough, or to have to dig up a freshly laid floor so the drains can be passed by local inspectors.

As a general guide, the rough sequence of events, whether you're building an extension or carrying out internal works, is as follows:
- Obtaining planning permission and other preliminary consents.
- Clearance and demolition. Depending on the work, this may range from moving the furniture out of the way to knocking down existing structures and stripping out your old servicing. Unsupported structural elements will need to be propped, skips organized to remove rubbish.
- Preventative or curative treatments, such as damp-proofing, spraying against rot or pest infestation.
- Earthworks, such as digging foundations or drainage trenches.
- Laying new drains, with inspection by the local authority if required.
- Installation of major external connections to services, such as electricity and gas mains and telephone cables.
- New walls built and solid floors laid.
- Roof structure built and covered as quickly as possible.
- 'First fix' of services, such as the installation of boilers and pipework or electrical conduits.
- 'First fix' of carpentry work, framing up doors and windows, studwork, floor joists, etc.
- Plastering.
- 'Second fix' of services, such as installing baths and basins, fitting socket plates, radiators, fuse boxes. Alternatively, some elements of this work may not take place until after decoration is finished.
- 'Second fix of carpentry work, such as hanging doors, fixing door linings, skirting boards and mouldings.
- Some floor finishes, depending on what other work remains.
- Built-in fixtures and fittings, such as kitchen units and appliances, bedroom wardrobes and fixed shelving.
- Decoration.
- Carpeting.
- Furnishing and arrangement.

Because each job is different, this summary can only indicate the approximate order of various procedures. If you're using a main contractor or an architect to supervise and administer the work, these guidelines should help you understand what's going on. But if you're intending to run a job yourself, you'll have to go into greater detail. Consult suppliers and subcontractors to determine precisely how long they expect to take at each stage and the conditions they will require to do their job properly. This also means getting firm delivery dates for materials and fittings. You need to ensure that not only will the plumber turn up on the right day, but so will the wash-basin that's going to be installed. If necessary, you may have to organize a meeting of all concerned to work out a definitive schedule.

ON SITE

The big day has finally arrived and your house echoes to the sound of hammering and the clump of big boots. You may think you can sit back, fingers crossed and wait for your home to emerge, like a butterfly from a chrysalis, in its stunning new incarnation. Unfortunately, your role does not end with your signature at the bottom of the builder's contract. There's still a job to be done ensuring that work on site proceeds smoothly.

Close encounters with the building trade can fray the steadiest nerves. What began as an amicable relationship can rapidly deteriorate to all-out war if you and your builder don't establish some ground rules from the start. Before the builders put a foot on site, remove valuables to safe keeping and store breakable objects. This includes lamps, pictures, light fittings – anything easily toppled or shattered. Clear the space where the work is to take place and wrap or cover as much as possible in the vicinity to keep off dust – dust can travel an amazing distance, especially if the work involves hacking off old plasterwork. Electronic equipment is particularly vulnerable.

You don't have to run a full catering service, but it is reasonable for you to provide access to the kitchen for heating up meals or making hot drinks, as well as access to the lavatory. In return, you should make it clear that you don't expect your freezer or drinks cupboard to be raided or to find a heap of your best dishes dirty in the sink.

Mess is unavoidable and some jobs are dirtier than others. Within reason, you can ask your builder to tidy up at the end of each day and allocate a place where tools and materials can be stored overnight. Obviously, thorough cleaning is a waste of time until the really messy work is complete, but you are entitled to expect a certain standard of care.

When it comes to supervision, it is important to strike the right balance. Don't hover in the background, offering what you imagine to be helpful advice – no one appreciates being told how to do their job and you'll only be in the way. On the other hand, don't disappear from the scene if there is work to inspect: you may find that by the time you come back it's too late to change anything you don't like. At the beginning of each day, ask what's likely to happen and if there are any stages that you need to approve. In the normal course of events, the end of the day is the right time to view the work and make sure everything is going to plan. With a little luck – and you'll need that, too – it will be.

1 Inspiration can come from the most unlikely quarters. *St Jerome in his Study* by Antonella da Mesina (1456-79) was the point of departure for the design of a home office.
2 The contemporary reworking of St Jerome's study translates the idea of a raised, self-contained room within a room into a high-tech construction of steel and glass.

CHANGING SERVICES

Like the human body, the home has its own physical systems – heating and cooling to regulate temperature, electricity to power light and domestic appliances, plumbing and drainage to bring in fresh water and remove waste – and lines of communication. Equally, there are services that are supplied through largely hidden networks of cable, pipework and wiring buried within the structure. We depend on these systems for our personal comfort and convenience as well as health and safety, but we often don't know much about them – until, that is, they suddenly break down or need replacement, when technical specifications and professional prognosis generally prove no more intelligible than medical jargon.

Technology has brought enormous changes to our standard of living in an incredibly short space of time. The physical conditions we now enjoy in the home would have astonished most people 100 years ago, and the pace of change is accelerating. Keeping up with what's available isn't always easy, especially if you start with only a sketchy notion of how the servicing of your home operates. You can't expect to acquire the expertise of a heating engineer or a qualified electrician overnight, but learning a little about the infrastructure of your home and the utilities that service it will enable you to make sensible decisions and better use of professional advice.

Changes to services don't always arise through breakdown; they are also implicated in many of the spatial alterations you carry out to improve your home, such as building an extension, converting an attic or basement, installing a new kitchen or bathroom. If you are planning substantial changes to the layout and organization of your home, this will generally entail disruption of existing systems, and a rerouteing of supplies or even new installation. In many cases, changing the services accounts for the greater part of the work and the expense, so it's worth taking some time to understand the options available and the processes involved. There are only a limited number of procedures that you can expect to carry out yourself. Sound professional help is advisable both to plan and execute the work. Additionally, approval may be required to ensure that any changes to services meet minimum standards of health and safety.

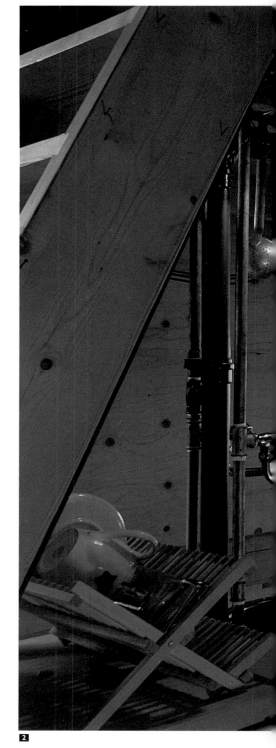

1 High-quality materials, fixtures and fittings repay the investment in practical performance, durability and good looks.
2 Exposed ducting and pipework and a spaghetti of cables let it all hang out in the servicing arrangements of this mountain-side kitchen.

2

3 Heating your home can be a complex business, not least because of the increasing range of options. The polished steel flue of this modern wood-burning stove is an architectural element in its own right.

3

4 A wall-mounted Anglepoise lamp provides versatile and unobtrusive bedside lighting. You need to plan the position of power points and built-in light fittings from the outset to gain the maximum benefit.

5 The conventional view is that radiators should be as discreet as possible, concealed behind grilles or paint-ed in with the walls. Painted black, this classic radiator has a retro appeal in a New York apartment.

Heating

Central heating has quietly revolutionized the way we live, even the way our homes look. Dependably warm interiors don't need layers of heavy drapery and aren't proscribed in scale by the heat-emitting power of a single source.

Central-heating systems essentially convert fuel to heat in a boiler or furnace and then distribute it to different parts of the house. In wet systems, the heat is conducted via hot water in radiators; in dry systems, warmed air circulates in ducts, escaping via grilles (the system can be adapted for air conditioning). The alternative, for areas of the world where there are no prolonged cold spells, is to warm rooms as required with individually controlled space heaters.

Choosing a system involves taking into account a wide variety of factors, such as the cost of installation and fuel consumption, maintenance, comfort and control, flexibility and the visual appearance of heat sources. The age of your house and the degree of insulation, your pattern of room use, the area in which you live and the availability of different fuels will also influence your decision.

In general, it is better to spend more initially on a system in order to use fuel more efficiently. Similarly, staggering on from one year to the next with an old boiler will cost much more in the long run than fitting a new appliance with all of the advantages of an energy-efficient, updated design. The benefits from all heating systems are maximized by good insulation; great strides have been made in this area of home technology to reduce energy consumption and minimize environmental damage.

A critical factor in any heating system is thermostatic control. A central thermostat must be sited carefully to avoid overheating the upper levels of a house and thus wasting fuel; the hallway is generally recommended as a sensible location; a better and more flexible solution is to fit individual thermostats on each radiator or else to use room thermostats which allow you to read the temperature of each area. Modern central thermostats offer digital control, allowing you to pre-set the time and temperature of both the hot water and heating, either separately or together.

ELECTRICITY

The most popular forms of electrical heating are by storage heaters or cables set into floors or ceilings. Hot water is provided by an immersion heater, which is thermostatically controlled. Storage heaters generally operate off-peak, using cheap electricity to generate heat which is then stored within the heater.

■ The cliché of fake burning logs or coals is wittily subverted by this strikingly original customized design for a gas fire. The heavy iron chain glows red as it heats up.

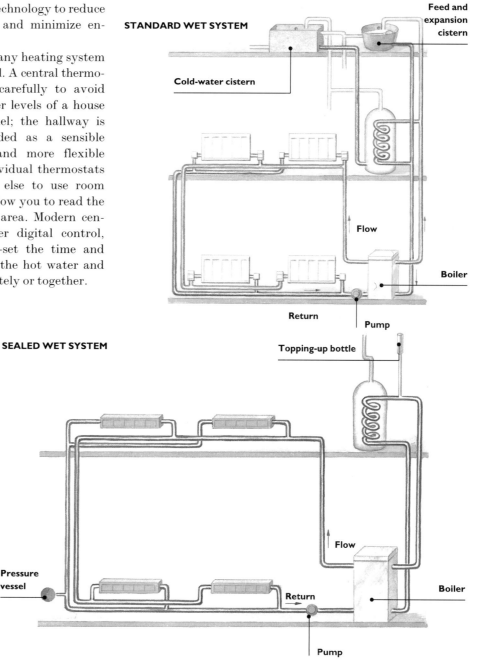

STANDARD WET SYSTEM

Feed and expansion cistern

Cold-water cistern

Flow

Boiler

Return

Pump

Topping-up bottle

DRY SYSTEM (WARM AIR)

Outlet grille

Warm-air ducts

Return air ducts

Heater

SEALED WET SYSTEM

Pressure vessel

Flow

Return

Boiler

Pump

The advantages of electricity include the facts that all homes already have a power supply, although this may need upgrading, while the cost of installation is low; and heaters can be individually controlled. In new homes and where insulation is good, electricity can be very efficient and easy to operate. In older houses with poor insulation, storage heaters may only be affordable as background heating. However, as insulation levels rise and the heating element of a home's energy bill becomes less significant, and as electricity costs fall relative to other 'fuels', individual low-power room heaters may regain popularity.

GAS

Gas is used to power boilers in wet or warm-air systems. A new development is wet underfloor heating systems, sunk in solid floors or running in metal trays in suspended floors. Because gas is burned in the appliance, there must be a flue to vent the waste gases, either via an existing chimney or fitted in an external wall. New boiler designs are far more efficient than previous generations and often more compact; condensing boilers allow heat to be recovered from the flue gases; anti-cycling controls minimize the heat loss that occurs each time the boiler switches off. Increasingly, standard combination boilers heat water directly from the mains, eliminating the need for either hot-water cylinders or cold-water cisterns. Powerful enough to run a whole system of radiators, they may pose a problem of immediate hot-water supply when simultaneous demands are made.

OIL

Oil-fired central heating is declining in many areas due to the scarcity of the natural resource and its associated high cost. A storage tank outside the house holds the supply for a boiler, which can be used with wet or warm-air systems. A check must be made on the level of oil in the tank and deliveries arranged to avoid interruption to heating.

1 The simple device of panelling the flanking walls with mirror accentuates a white-painted brick fireplace, multiplying views and increasing the sense of spaciousness.

2

SOLID FUEL AND WOOD

Central heating can be powered by burning coal to heat a back boiler serving a wet system. Closed coal fires allow an attractive view of the heat source and can be installed in existing chimneys that are fitted with an appropriate flue lining. However, they are messy and bothersome to light. Only certain types of coal are allowed to be burned, to lessen damage to the environment; some coal-burning appliances contain a 'smoke-consuming' element to minimize the emission of waste gases still further. You need adequate storage facilities for fuel deliveries and regular cleaning and maintenance of the flue is vital if the system is to operate efficiently.

Wood-burning stoves generate a great deal of heat and somewhat less pollution than coal ones. Because the heat source is generally within living areas, there are stringent safety precautions for flue maintenance and installation. Wood must be properly seasoned beforehand, and some species deliver better heat than others. Your supply of firewood should always be from either natural wastage or a sustainable, managed source.

2 A wood-burning stove supplies additional heat and a handsome focal point. Neat and unobtrusive, low-level warm-air convectors fitted at the base of the curved exterior wall maintain a stable background temperature.
3 The radiator as space divider: the traditional chunky design of this fixture forms a low barrier at the head of the stairs.

3

DESIGNING A SYSTEM

It is essential that you always work with accredited professionals to design or adapt a heating system to deliver your specific requirements. If you extend your system appreciably, into a new area, for example, you may need to upgrade the boiler to deal with the extra demand. Use a floor plan to work out where radiators or other heat emitters are best positioned, so that they provide you with maximum flexibility when positioning furniture, and so that you will minimize heat loss and simplify any new pipe runs that are required. Take advice and seek several opinions.

Radiators, as the name suggests, work by radiating heat and ideally should not be shielded by heavy drapery or large pieces of furniture. Proximity to a heat source can damage fine finishes and ruin musical instruments, such as pianos. There are many styles available, including standard single or double panels, which can be decorated to match wall finishes, low-level skirting radiators, finned radiators to maximize heat surface and warm air convectors that run off wet systems. Reclaimed radiators have a retro appeal. Don't compromise efficiency for looks: the graphic quality of many radiant heaters can be a positive asset, not an eyesore to be concealed behind fancy covers and grilles.

INSTALLATION

Gas, electricity and water come from the mains supply. The appropriate utility board is responsible for bringing a communication pipe to your property boundary; from there to your home, the supply is at your expense. Increasingly, there are attempts to coordinate services so that they can be routed in together, minimizing disruption to the road. Installing any mains supply is the job of the utility concerned.

The position of meters – the route, type and dimension of pipe or wiring – is strictly controlled. Gas pipes can't be run in cavity walls and the supply must be in vented pipes; electric meters are not allowed in bedrooms, bathrooms, over kitchen sinks or in coal cellars. Siting and ventilation of boilers and siting of flues is also subject to approval. Utility companies prefer meters to be external – siting can present a visual challenge!

Insulation and plumbing

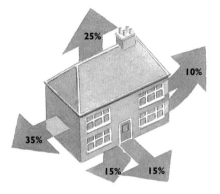

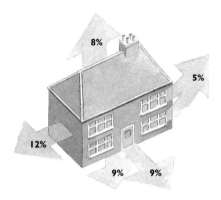

■ These two houses represent the percentage of heat lost before (top) and after (below) insulation. The figures vary according to the type of building you live in – a bungalow loses an even greater proportion of heat through the roof, whilst in a ground-floor flat there is less heat lost through the ceiling than there is through the roof of a house – but wherever you make you home it is worth ensuring it is properly insulated (see page 250).

INSULATION AND VENTILATION

Insulation keeps heat from escaping through the walls, floors, roof, windows and doors, and means you use less fuel and spend less money. It works both ways too, keeping homes cool during the summer months. Once considered merely a desirable or even optional extra, it is now increasingly viewed as one of the principal ways of maintaining even temperature levels in the home. Low-energy specialists are devising new methods of insulated construction that cut fuel needs practically to zero, although the capital costs of installation are high. However, it makes absolutely no sense to turn up the heating to cope with the results of poor insulation – you are literally throwing money out the window.

The areas of a building to insulate include the walls, under the ground floor and in lofts between ceiling joists (leaving the roof space well ventilated). Draught-proofing windows and doors, laying carpet and hanging lined curtains at windows are simple ways of keeping the heat in. In addition, hot water pipes, cylinders and storage cisterns should be lagged. Choose insulants that are HFC- (hydro-fluorocarbon) and CFC- (chloro-fluorocarbon) free.

Some forms of insulation, including double glazing, work by almost sealing the house hermetically, which means that no air, warm or cool, can escape. The result is often unacceptable levels of interior condensation, building up on windows and at 'cold bridges' or gaps between insulation. Condensation is uncomfortable and rots materials and finishes. The technological answer is to provide mechanical ventilation, such as extractor fans, to supplement other external openings; specific mechanical ventilation requirements are stipulated by law for kitchens and bathrooms. Environmentalists have pointed out that the insulation-condensation-ventilation sequence still results in warm air being needlessly expelled from the home, and they offer alternative solutions.

PLUMBING AND DRAINAGE

Alterations to kitchens and bathrooms can affect the supply and route of water around your home. Simple jobs, like plumbing in a new washing machine or dishwasher, involve very little effort or expense; but any work which entails alteration to drains is going to be both costly and disruptive.

Installing a connection from your home to a mains supply is the job of the utility; laying drains must be done professionally and meet building regulations. There are strict rules about the height and position of soil stacks, the accessibility of drains for inspection, traps in outside drains and gullies to prevent foul air entering your own house or your neighbours' and the diameter and construction of pipework.

In the most traditional arrangement for water supply in British houses, a rising main brings cold water from the mains to a storage cistern, generally in the attic space. The rising main also directly supplies drinking water for the kitchen tap. From the cistern there are connections to all other cold taps, the lavatory and the hot-water cylinder.

Drains take waste water from sinks and bath-tubs and sewage from lavatories away for connection to main sewer drains or to a septic tank, which is periodically pumped. Waste water reaches the drains via a trapped gully which has a water seal to prevent smells coming back into the house. The waste pipe from downstairs lavatories is connected directly to the drain; at upper levels, waste pipes feed into a vertical soil stack (which provides ventilation and prevents air blockages) and from there to the main sewer drains.

In general, the simpler the layout of your plumbing the fewer the problems. Pipes which weave all over the place, with frequent changes of direction, much branching and many different gradients greatly increase the potential for blockage and breakdown. There should be easy access at a number of points for clearing

2

2 Clad in ribbed terracotta tile, this bathroom designed by architect François Roche features sculptural stainless steel sinks and a low sunken tub.
3 A kitchen sink with a difference, by San Fancisco architects John Randolph and Bruce Tomb, wittily evokes the form of an ironing board. The waste pipe is plumbed through an opaque glass panel to connect with the bathroom services. The sink is portable and can be moved further into the room when in use.

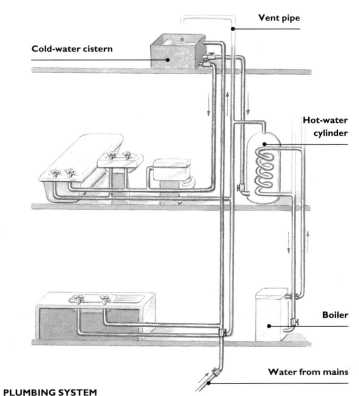

Vent pipe

Cold-water cistern

Hot-water cylinder

Boiler

Water from mains

PLUMBING SYSTEM

blockages if these should occur. There should be a stopcock for cutting off mains supply within the house as well as a water authority stopcock between the water main and the rising main.

Drainage services generally stack above each other in a vertical format for storied houses, or can be arranged in a central core. This means that adding a new bathroom on a level directly above an existing one is considerably easier than installing a bathroom on the other side of the house. Depending on the structure and layout of your home, you may find out it is impossible to achieve an adequate fall for waste pipes in a new location. In this context, it is also worth noting that, for reasons of health and hygiene, it is preferable for a lavatory not to be directly accessible from a food-preparation area. If the kitchen and lavatory are adjacent, it makes sense to include provision for a wash-basin.

If you plan to install a new shower in your bathroom, it may be necessary to fit a pump to supply water of sufficient pressure and/or an additional heater to handle the increased demand for hot water. In a windowless room, ventilation may also need upgrading.

3

4

4 A striking ladder-like arrangement of jointed hot-water pipes forms a heated towel rail in a bathroom.

Electricity

With electricity, flicking a switch is the instinctive command that summons light, power and, in many homes, heat. Its effectiveness is entirely dependent on convenience, which means ensuring there are enough power outlets to serve your needs and enough flexibility to accommodate change.

You need professional help to ensure that the existing electrical systems are safe, up to date and able to support the demands you place on them. You will also need help to change, extend or install new systems while, of course, hooking up to the mains supply is the job of the utility. Regulations vary from

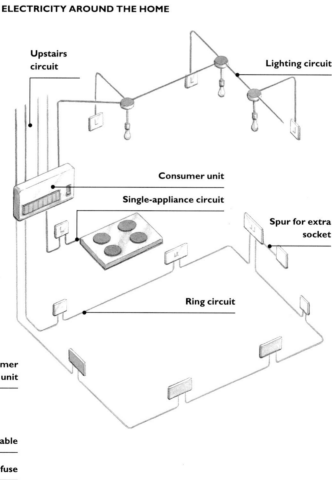

2

country to country about how much – if any – electrical work can be tackled on an amateur basis. Electricity is potentially extremely dangerous so you must be sure you know what you are doing before embarking on even what may seem the simplest task.

Wiring systems vary. In Britain, the main arrangement consists of ring circuits; elsewhere there may be spurs, or linear arrangements – sometimes both exist together. From the mains supply, cables feed power to a fuse box and meter and thence to a sealed distribution box or consumer unit. A number of circuits, each fused, then carries electricity to different parts of the house. Different circuits accommodate power points, lighting and major appliances such as cookers, hobs, ovens or storage heaters. Installing new appliances which make heavy demands on electricity may warrant extra circuitry.

To plan your needs, consider:
- The age of the wiring. Any system over 15 years old will probably need replacing. You should have your wiring checked every five years by a qualified electrician.
- Special appliances make new demands on the circuit, especially where these increase loads.
- Alterations to lighting.

1

ELECTRICITY AROUND THE HOME

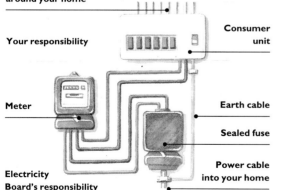

Upstairs circuit

Lighting circuit

Consumer unit

Single-appliance circuit

Spur for extra socket

Ring circuit

DOMESTIC FUSEBOX

Cables to circuits around your home

Your responsibility

Consumer unit

Meter

Earth cable

Sealed fuse

Power cable into your home

Electricity Board's responsibility

- The number and position of power sockets. Ideally, except in bathrooms, there should be a double power point on each wall to allow flexibility. Converting a single socket to a double one is not difficult.

The great boon of electricity is its invisibility. But this discretion is won at the cost of routing cable and wire through walls, ceilings and under floors. Naturally, this involves forethought, and subsequent alteration, if a major overhaul is needed, can be disruptive. If you need to rewire your entire home, you may consider tacking on a few other alterations while you're at it.

SAFETY

- Socket provision should be more than adequate to prevent trailing wires, which can cause accidents, and overloaded power points.
- Water and electricity are dangerous companions. In the bathroom, there are various regulations, which vary from country to country, concerning the types of sockets and switches that are allowed and the wiring of lighting, heaters and installation of appliances such as washing-machines.
- Layout of kitchen appliances must be planned in conjunction with their power supply.

- Outdoor power supplies should ideally be routed underground in special cables. Wiring in out-buildings is best encased in steel or plastic conduits.
- Sockets for outdoor appliances should be protected by individual circuit breakers and have some covering to shield them from the elements.

LINES OF COMMUNICATION

Lines supplying television, telephones and other communication systems are often approached as an afterthought, resulting in a spaghetti of wiring that disfigures the façade of your house. There is no reason why such wiring should not be neat and properly planned; separate ducting can improve the overall appearance and maintain accessibility.

THE CUTTING EDGE

People have widely different attitudes to technology in the home. For some, each new development is irresistible and within a short space of time, indispensable; others are fundamentally uneasy. Most of us have a love-hate relationship, enjoying the convenience and comfort, but unsure about the long-term effects. On the most basic level, everyone is familiar with the tempting gadget that promises much, but frequently delivers extra maintenance, takes up too much

1 Electrical servicing in the kitchen demands careful thought to ensure that there are adequate sockets for appliances where they are needed, as well as flexible provision for lighting. Major appliances require their own circuits.
2 A music system is inconspicuously integrated within an alcove separating two areas of the living-room.
3 Power points on landings and in hallways provide the opportunity to colonize the space for work or study.

storage space and then breaks down when you most need it. Environmental awareness has also revealed the dark side of technological change.

Predicting how the home of the future will work is guaranteed to cause amusement ten years on. But based on what currently exists in other fields and applications, it's possible to show the impact technology could have – if we want it to.

With new communications networks replacing conventional wiring, domestic services, appliances and media equipment should soon be fully integrated, programmable and interactive.

Microchip technology also means that it is conceivable that appliances could be self-diagnostic and even self-servicing. Infrared sensors have been developed that can activate showers, pre-set for intensity, duration and temperature, as soon as you step within a designated area. Multi-media hook-ups bring sound, pictures and text together in a single package for interactive reference and educational use. Remote controls or voice-activated electronics could replace manual switches and many other routine functions. Virtual reality could revolutionize home planning, just as computer programmes now enable sophisticated calculations of energy use.

Whether the average home boasts such features in ten years' time will depend on attitude. Changes that are backed up by low running costs and real gains in energy use may ultimately prove preferable to those that simply promise convenience. Technology smoothes your path, but it also distances. The sacrifice is physical presence, the sheer hands-on quality of daily life, which is often missed most after it has gone. Remote-controlled door locking may be a security boon and time-saver; but doors that swing open on a voice command may be too alienating for comfort. Cocooned in a pre-set, fully adjustable environment, will we long for the good old days when we could grasp a door handle, throw open a window or run our own bath?

Lighting

The huge seductive range of modern light fittings and fixtures now available encourages selection on a purely decorative basis. For many, lighting is often an afterthought, with choices and decisions made too far down the line. You can afford to wait until the basic framework is right before tracking down the perfect sofa, but you must consider lighting right from the outset.

Artificial lighting is a supplement and substitute for natural light. It enables you to function practically, safely and comfortably when it's dark or dull outside; it enhances architectural detail, and decorative features; it accentuates colour and reveals texture. Literally, it generates 'atmosphere'. The most exciting space on earth will still look like a launderette if it is lit by an overhead fluorescent tube, while the most sensitively chosen designer lamp is no use if you can't see to read the newspaper. Successfully balancing the functional and the aesthetic qualities requires thinking about lighting and incorporating it into your earliest plans.

Choice of fitting and light source are integral decisions. Although you may delay the final selection, you should know the type of lighting you require in each area of the home before you begin to furnish and decorate. Planning lighting involves a degree of flexibility, allowing for anticipated different layouts and spatial uses. (For a full discussion of the range of fittings and light sources, see pages 228-30.)

The best lighting schemes offer you flexibility, variety of light level, direction, intensity and fitness for purpose; a new consideration is low energy. The sheer variety and moods of natural light and its partner, shadow, are the secret of its profound appeal. Until really quite recently, artificial lighting did not even begin to mimic this diversity of effect, but technology now allows much more subtle and stimulating interior lighting conditions. Getting this right lies at the heart of a comfortable room.

1 Tube lights and halogen spots are suspended from steel wire running across a double-height space in an innovative and practical arrangement.
2 Modern light sources complement natural light. The clear white light of halogen spots accentuates a dining-table.
3 A variety of small light sources provides flexible illumination for a cooking and eating area. Spotlights over the preparation area give bright, shadowless light for detailed work; ceiling spots offer a good level of background light; pendant fittings add sparkle to the table.

1

2

3

4 Uplights bounce light off the ceiling for a soft, diffused glow. Track lights can be adjusted to highlight display shelves.
5 Lights fitted inside these kitchen cupboards are automatically switched on when the doors are slid back, providing discreet accent and information lighting. Halogen spots above the island unit offer directional task lighting.
6 Hallways and circulation areas must be well lit. Wall-mounted fittings illuminate the space with an even wash of light; avoid spotlights in such areas, as they create pools of brightness and shadow.

4

5

6

GENERAL LIGHTING

TASK LIGHTING

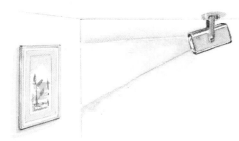

ACCENT LIGHTING

2 The quality of artificial light depends on the type and power of bulb, and also on the fixture. Left to right: a recessed ceiling tungsten spot; a pendant light with low-energy tungsten bulb; a halogen uplight; a tungsten multiple spotlight; a wall-mounted tungsten uplight; an eyeball tungsten downlight; a free-standing halogen uplight; a tungsten wall lamp.

PLANNING LIGHTING

Lighting has a dramatic effect on both our perception of space and the way we operate within it, yet it is one of the most economical and versatile elements in the spatial equation. Because it is powered by electricity, lighting should be planned in conjunction with changes to the wiring. In the case of built-in or recessed fittings, such as downlights, it is obviously less disruptive to fit these features before you decorate, ideally while the surfaces are being overhauled.

Use a basic floor plan to plot out the type of lighting you need in each area. Each room will need a combination of three basic types: general or background illumination; specific task light; and accent or decorative lighting. You can achieve these functions in a variety of stylistic ways; what is essential at this planning stage is to build in sufficient infrastructure to accommodate a variety of light sources.

Background light has been traditionally supplied by a ceiling fixture. In many cases, this solution is ugly and dull, resulting in flat, even and often over-bright conditions. The same level of illumination can be arranged by employing a variety of sources around the room which create overlapping pools of light and shade. Side lights, spots, uplights and downlights are all alternative means of achieving this effect.

1 Natural light is supplemented by a subtle variety of artificial light sources to create a tranquil mood in a bedroom in Provence. Plain plaster uplights, decorated in with the wall, give discreet background light; pivoting bedside lamps provide more focused illumination for reading.
3 A spotlight fixed to a beam lights a bathroom mirror for activities such as shaving or putting on make-up.

1

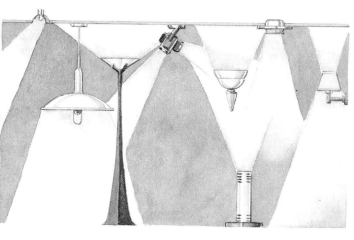

2

Task light is targeted lighting. Bright, concentrated and directed, it enables activities such as reading, keyboard work and food preparation to be carried out with ease and safety. Spotlights are the classic solution, although there are other fittings that offer the same result.

Accent lighting operates on a much lower level to enhance the architecture or decoration. Accent lighting which is too insistent or bright defeats the purpose of subtle differentiation and can throw a room off balance. Many kinds of fittings can work as accents if they are dimmed.

3

4 Single light sources, such as pendant fixtures, can cast hard shadows which quickly divest a room of atmosphere. A variety of small points of light in this hall and living area have just the opposite effect.

5 A low-level uplight, concealed to one side of the sofa, washes the wall with soft light. Task lighting at the desk is good for working by.

4

5

1 Living-rooms need varied sources of light for maximum flexibility. The wall uplight and table lamp provide general background illumination, and could be paired with a central pendant light. Spot-lighting in the alcove and a picture lamp above the fireplace give accent lighting, while the anglepoise can be adjusted to give task lighting when reading.

1

TASK LIGHTING IN A KITCHEN

2

2 Halls and stairways require a good level of general lighting. These recessed ceiling lights make locating a book a simple task, whatever the time of day. This corridor – with the desk looking out on to an open-plan layout and with a skylight above the area in the foreground of the picture – is not as gloomy as many in older homes.
3 Outdoor lighting can create dramatic night-time effects, such as these pools of light in a Japanese-style garden. Inside, high-density general lighting allows the open-plan space to revel in its clutter-less simplicity.

Specific lighting requirements include:
- Stairs, halls and passageways need to be well lit for safety. Avoid bright, directional lighting which causes glare and deep shadow. Stair treads can be lit individually.
- Exteriors, such as main entrances, front and rear, need to be lit for safety and security.
- Bathroom or dressing-room mirrors need even lighting from all sides for making up and shaving.
- Deep cupboards and the interiors of storerooms need lighting to reveal their contents and improve accessibility.
- Bookcases, paintings, display cabinets, and so on benefit from accent lighting.
- Outdoor lighting can be installed to highlight the garden at night, extending the time in which it can be used.

In Britain, there is usually a lighting circuit for each floor, designed to power up to ten 100-watt lamps. If you increase the load, you may need extra circuitry. Lighting circuits run around the ceiling, down to wall switches or fixtures, or across to central ceiling points. To fit overhead lights, it may be possible to minimize disruption by working from the floor above. Otherwise, wiring may have to be routed through a cavity wall or set into the plasterwork of a solid wall. Lighting track can be connected at one single point to a power source, accommodating a full range of lights without having to install each one separately.

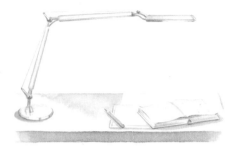

TASK LIGHTING FOR A DESK

READING LAMPS ABOVE A BED

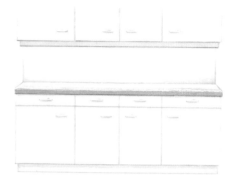

STRIP LIGHTING FOR A KITCHEN WORKTOP

POINTS TO REMEMBER

When planning the infrastructure for lighting consider:

- Socket provision – ensure that you have plenty of power points for your current and anticipated needs. This increases flexibility and avoids the hazard of trailing wires.
- The position of wall switches – these should be easily accessible from all main room entrances.
- Individual lamps and lights within the same room can be wired to a single switch for central control.
- Dimmers multiply the effects you can achieve with the same lighting and allow fine adjustment to take account of natural lighting conditions.
- Time switches are useful for security, or for arranging safety lighting in circulation areas.
- Some types of light source require adaptors or transformers.

LIGHTING FOR A BATHROOM MIRROR

3

4 An adjustable pendant lamp, preferably fitted to a dimmer, allows you to focus attention on the table at mealtimes, creating a mood of intimacy in an open-plan layout. A reading lamp clipped to the skirting board becomes an innovative uplight, while strip bulbs give accent to the display shelves and spots above the kitchen worktop ensure adequate task lighting. More general light could be achieved by adding ceiling spots or fitting a wall light.

4

Green living

Increasingly, making the most of our homes means making the most of the planet. Environmental issues are complex and often controversial. Solving the Earth's woes can appear too Herculean a task for anyone to believe their individual efforts would make any difference. But the cumulative effect of debates on the state of the ozone layer, the future of the rain forests, the impact of pollution and the depletion of energy resources has been a sure but steady increase in our ecological awareness.

There are different ways of living green. On the most basic level, you can change the products you consume. It's a logical step to go on to adapt your living habits so that you cut energy use and wastage. More effective is to incorporate ecological principles into the way your home is constructed and designed. Even small changes can make a difference.

Environmental concern is not merely a question of altruism. What's good for the planet is generally healthy for the individual and easy on the wallet. Green living design uncannily echoes many traditional building methods, age-old and appealing ways of planning layout and responding to the needs of climate and site. Green living is also in tune with our aesthetic preference for natural materials and finishes – back to the fundamental ways in which humans feel at ease with their surroundings.

ENVIRONMENTAL DESIGN

Environmental design is not merely a question of substituting an environmentally friendly product for one that isn't. It involves an intricate analysis of interrelated factors: pollution, threat to health, renewability and energy costs.

When you turn down the thermostat on the boiler, you reduce the energy you use in direct terms. Environmentalists look further, at the hidden energy costs involved in production and construction. The energy cost of producing brick, for example, is four times higher than that of timber; standard mineral wool insula-

tion costs 30 times as much energy to produce as the insulation provided by recycled newspaper. In addition to these calculations are the energy costs of construction and transportation. There is also the question of how materials are used. 'Low energy' timber construction entails less energy consumed in construction as well as less energy consumed in running the house during its lifetime.

Green designers advocate using building materials such as timber and stone which are found naturally and therefore produce less carbon dioxide. Softwood timber is a renewable resource and home-grown, mixed-species forestry not only encourages local employment but also reduces transportation costs.

Modern water- and oil-based paints and other petrochemical products are especially wasteful. Some paints produce as much as 90 per cent waste as a by-product of their manufacture, waste which is unrecyclable. Organic paints, by contrast, produce only 10 per cent waste, all of which is compostible; components include pine resin, linseed oil, chalk, beeswax and citrus fruits. Safe to apply, organic paint comes in a range of subtle plant colours, close to those traditional paint recipes much favoured by heritage specialists. All organic finishes – paints, stains and waxes – allow the underlying material to breathe, so that moisture is not trapped inside, which means, in turn, that materials wear well.

For those fortunate enough to build their home from scratch, incorporating ecological principles into house design means avoiding plastics, rigid foam insulants and synthetic finishes, using timber and stone wherever possible as well as achieving low-energy use through high levels of insulation and natural forms of design. It starts with the site, tailoring the shape and orientation of the home to protect it from wind and encourage passive sunlight. Large overhangs shelter the house in winter, cool it in summer; rooftop openings allow winter sun to penetrate into the heart of the building,

1

1 This Scottish house, by GAIA Architects, was designed to have minimum impact on the environment. The panoramic view of the Perthshire countryside is the attractive by-product of positioning the house to make the best use of passive solar heat. The windows are double glazed, and the house is built from renewable European softwood, treated with non-toxic borax salts. All interior finishes are environmentally friendly.
2 Nestling in its wooded site, the house blends well with its surroundings. The highly insulated roof is finished with reclaimed Welsh slate.

2

3

enabling air to circulate freely. The traditional transition areas – conservatories, lobbies and verandahs – act as a buffer between inside and outside, a natural form of temperature control. Living roofs of meadow grass and wild flowers restore the ground dug for foundations and provide miniature wildlife habitats; they protect the roof membrane from deterioration through ultraviolet light and temperature changes – and, what's more, they look attractive!

Insulation can be provided by recycled pelleted paper treated against rot and fire with borax, a natural non-toxic material. Some designers are experimenting with a form of construction that allows walls to breathe and avoids the problems of condensation associated with modern vapour-barrier construction. Timber finished with wax instead of toxic polyurethane, organic finishes and recycled-paper insulation add up to an efficient, healthy building which can retain a great deal of heat and which also regulates its own levels of humidity.

In conjunction with modern heating systems, the energy efficiency of such houses can be very high indeed. Equally persuasive is a dramatic reduction in annual heating bills. In these circumstances, low-power individual room heaters provide a heat source that is both effective and surprisingly economical.

There are various high-tech devices which can help a conventional heating system run more effectively and reduce energy use and cost. Computerized thermostatic controls read air temperature and adjust timing accordingly, working out how long a boiler needs to cycle to reach a given temperature and calculating when the heating should come on to reach this level at a specified time. These 'boiler managers' actually learn your living patterns, ironically reusing microchip technology developed for guided missiles in the Gulf War of 1991.

Heat recovery units are available in the form of individual fans or central systems which constantly suck stale air from each room and eject it from the house, after transferring the heat to incoming fresh air, which is then filtered and ducted into each room. Although not hugely expensive, these systems can only supplement a main heating system, not replace it, and the cost of running the unit has to be considered as part of the overall energy cost. Advocates claim that these devices improve the quality of the air and can provide relief to hayfever sufferers. There are also units that reclaim the heat from boiler or stove flues, as well as heat pumps which can boost the efficiency of heat-recovery units (though the cost of these is high).

SOLAR ENERGY

In northern areas, active solar energy is normally used to supplement water heating, but provides little energy when it is most needed in the winter months, as this is the time when light levels are low.

New forms of solar-energy collection, employing photovoltaic cells on the roof instead of the conventional tubes, may become more popular and could be used to generate a contribution to electric space heating. Surplus energy could be directed back into the national grid.

Passive solar energy can be achieved within the overall design by using south-facing windows and conservatories to gather the sun's heat and store it within the fabric of the building. Timber-framed houses heat up more quickly and vertical windows are better than roof glazing to trap the low rays of winter sun. Overheating can occur in summer, however.

3 This award-winning scheme by Architype Design Co-operative consists of nine self-build houses in a wooded Sussex valley. 'Living' roofs of scabious, tufted vetch, ox-eye daisy and birds'-foot trefoil recreate wildflower meadowland, replacing the area lost to construction. Limited soil depth means that the roofs do not require mowing. As well as providing a habitat for wildlife, the roofs help to cleanse the air by absorbing carbon dioxide. Most modern buildings are made out of a variety of synthetic materials such as foam insulation, vinyl floors and petro-chemically based paints and stains, all of which contain toxic chemicals which 'outgas' into the building. Natural materials and non-toxic finishes such as organic paints, stains and waxes work with, rather than against, nature.

AN ECOLOGICAL HOUSE

Summer sun

Maximum window area to the south to utilize warmth from the sun

'Living' green roof

South

Minimum wall and window area to the north

North

Winter sun

Large overhang shelters house in winter, keeps it cool in summer

Shelter from prevailing winds

Natural finishes on floor, walls and ceiling, such as organic paints, stains and wax

Timber and plasterboard framework

'Breathing wall' insulated with recycled newspaper – the whole outer shell of house is porous, allowing ventilation

RECYCLING

Conventional 'open' system dumps waste products after use

Shop

Using

Dumping

New 'closed' system recycles household waste in various ways

Shop

Using

Recycling centre

Garden

Compost

Recycling

1

2

3

1 Set on a hillside in Queensland, Australia, this steel-frame canvas-clad tent house – the home of architect Gabriel Poole and artist Elizabeth Frith – is an appropriate response to the tropical climate. Louvres over the balcony drive air through the house, cooling it without recourse to air-conditioning. The outside walls can be rolled up to merge indoors with out.
2 The tent house, designed by Poole, is cyclone-proof and sits gently on the land, ideal for environmentally sensitive sites where major construction would be too disruptive.
4 An annex, a short distance from the main house, serves as guest accommodation. Mosquito netting provides essential protection from insect life in a house open to the elements.

4

3 This Swedish holiday house is part of a prize-winning scheme by Norwegian architect Sverre Fehn. Modules for sleeping, living and dining are grouped around an inner patio. The open kitchen is installed in a long corridor running the length of the house.
5 The barrel-vaulted living/dining area contains a fireplace that screens the view of the kitchen corridor.

5

6 The bedroom opens on to the outside patio at the heart of the structure.
7 Blending with its site, the house is a timber construction faced in exterior blocks made of dried fine-ground straw mixed with clay, an environmentally friendly material which is also an effective heat and sound insulator. The wooden roof is protected with bituminous tiles.

DRAINAGE

An eco-alternative to a septic tank, where connection to a main sewer is not possible, is a reed bed. This consists of passing waste from a house through a series of living ponds, which clean the water using natural biological processes. Obviously, specialist design is required, not to mention enough land to site the installation. Soil waste demands a much larger system than 'grey' water from sinks, baths and basins.

Less radical and more affordable solutions include storing rainwater in butts to use in the garden, or even in lavatory cisterns. 'Grey' water can also be recycled for garden irrigation.

RADIATION

Electrical and electromagnetic radiation from domestic cables are considered by some people to be sources of stress and ill health, particularly where live cables run in close proximity to sleeping areas – where, after all, we spend nearly one third of our lives. In certain countries, it is common practice to make use of shielded cable as a protection from radiation. An alternative solution, available in Britain, is to fit an automatic switch which disconnects the electrical supply when there is no demand (such as at night-time), but which automatically reconnects the supply as soon as a demand is made (for example, when a light is switched on).

THE GREEN HOUSEHOLD

There are a vast number of ways in which the daily routine of your family can be modified or adapted to reduce pollution, waste and cut energy use. Green housekeeping is often a question of going back to the old-fashioned virtues of thrift and elbow grease.

We've grown accustomed to miracle products which promise all kinds of instant benefits, but the nasty side effects of many common household chemicals pose a long-term hazard. Making a few simple substitutions can improve your health, along with the state of the planet. Read labels and avoid cleaning products that contain toxic chemicals such as chlorine, formaldehyde, halogenated hydrocarbons or pollutants such as CFCs, as well as those in aerosol sprays.

- Choose organic paint and natural finishes – wax and organic wood stains, and natural preservatives.
- Choose natural cleansers – borax, ammonia, vinegar or soda.
- Buy furniture made from sustainable woods and natural-fibre upholstery.
- Opt for natural materials – linoleum rather than vinyl, cotton rather than synthetic blends.
- Recycling is the modern version of 'waste not, want not'. Packaging is a great offender – choose loose rather than packaged fruit and vegetables.
- Recycle glass jars and bottles, paper and aluminium cans.
- Reuse plastic food containers.
- Buy rechargeable batteries.
- Buy recycled paper products.
- Recycle old clothes, towels and sheets as cleaning rags.
- Compost organic waste.
- Reuse shopping bags.
- Choose products with less packaging.

In addition to shopping more considerately, you can 'go green' by reducing your energy consumption:

- Insulate your home with non-CFC insulants.
- Fit thermostatic controls to boilers and radiators or, better still, use a 'boiler manager'.
- Fit large single-panel radiators instead of air convectors. (Radiant heat provides more apparent comfort at lower temperatures than convected heat, which creates draughts.)
- Choose low-energy compact fluorescent light bulbs.
- Air-dry your wet clothing.
- Maintain appliances in good order for a longer life.
- Run only full loads in the washing-machine and dishwasher.

ALTERING SPACE

Decoration puts a smart new face on things, good organization brings order and efficiency to your every-day routine, but spatial changes get to the very heart of the matter. Altering space entails thinking about volume and scale, privacy and openness, natural light, views and vistas. In essence, it means thinking architecturally, which is consider-ably more demanding than it seems. The biggest hurdle, however, is not lack of professional training, but lack of imagination. It's easy to tinker around with the existing configuration of rooms; but it may be more fruitful to consider the volume of your home in a more abstract way – as a space that must fulfil the various demands and activities you expect of it on a day-to-day basis.

Living in unsatisfactory surroundings doesn't necessarily promote a desire for change; it can just as easily blunt the awareness of how improve-ments could be made. In such cases, natural caution can be reinforced by the perceived complexity of structural work and the aggravation it can cause. Furthermore, substantial sums of money can be involved, and there is always the residual fear that change may be for the worse – rooms stripped of their architectural character or 'conservatories' that are little more than lean-to sheds tacked to the back of a house have, in the past, given conver-sions something of a bad name.

Overcoming these obstacles and fears isn't a leap in the dark when you take the time to explore all the options and seek professional help to put ideas into practice. Improving the spatial quality of your home may be as relatively straightforward as removing a partition wall to open up internal views and reconfigure your living space, or it may involve more significant alterations, from converting roof space into an extra bedroom or home office, adding a mezzanine level or building an extension.

Ultimately, radical alteration to the structure of your home may be the only means to improve the way you live – to give you more space, more light and a better use of indoor and outdoor areas. You need to weigh the cost of change against the benefits it will bring, both to the way you live and, poss-ibly, to the value of your home. In the long term, the alternative – doing nothing – may work out to be the most expensive course of action of all.

1 The intersecting planes of walls and curved ceiling create architectural interest in this modern hallway.
2 Architect Rick Mather's conversion of a nineteenth-century artist's studio stripped away years of badly considered alteration to create a light-filled gallery for living in. A spiral plaster-shell staircase connects with a U-shaped upper level.

3 A bathroom tucked under the eaves derives the greatest practical benefit from otherwise wasted floor space. Adding a roof light makes the room feel less enclosed and provides a contempla-tive view when soaking in the bath. Sliding doors neatly enclose clothes-hanging space.

4 A large pivoting solid wood panel separates a dining area from a kitchen, making a dynamic connection between the two rooms. The thick, roughwashed terra-cotta walls contrast with and soften the gleaming stainless-steel kitchen units and appliances beyond.

5 The elemental qualities of light and space are orchestrated to maximum effect in this Majorcan house designed by Claudio Silvestrin.

4

5

Envisaging change

1

1 In a London flat, juxtapositions in scale create witty illusions in a small space. A low-level bed sheltering under the plane of the roof makes an intimate sleeping space in this imaginative attic conversion. Open and closed storage space is fitted under the eaves. **2** Staircases and hallways in older houses can be exceptionally wasteful of space. This modern open stairway has a graphic simplicity.

2

An architect may be able to imagine your ideal home better than you can. There are many low-key spatial changes which don't require much in the way of professional guidance or only a degree of technical expertise on how the work is to be carried out. But if you're planning to make major changes, it's a good idea to consult an architect as early as possible to help you to formulate your ideas.

The conventional view is that the architect is the person who brings the client down to earth, setting limits on fanciful schemes and replacing dreams with sober reality. In practice, many architects find that it is their clients who have the mental brakes on, imagining obstacles to change which don't really exist. The architect's most important role is to envisage what would be the best possible solution to a spatial issue. This isn't a question of talking you into more work than you want done; instead, it is a synthetic approach to problem solving

which enables you to gain the maximum benefits from any change. If your home needs a thorough overhaul of services, an architect can suggest ways of incorporating structural alterations into your plans which won't add much to your budget but may add a great deal to the spatial quality of your home.

BASIC SPATIAL PRINCIPLES

Architects are trained to think three dimensionally, to analyse and plan buildings systematically in terms of layout, elevation and section. You can't achieve such expertise without such experience but an appreciation of some of the fundamental issues will help you to approach the subject more creatively and communicate your ideas better.

Balance between privacy and openness is a major consideration. In general, older houses tend to comprise a series of self-contained rooms, originally designed to accommodate separate activities, all clustered around a staircase. Repetitive and conventional in their planning, these houses can frustrate a desire for more flexibility and communality. Open-plan living, on the other hand, is a more recent phenomenon, largely the result of improvements in heating. In the first flush of enthusiasm for what promised to be a new spatial freedom, many older houses were also opened up from top to bottom to create large, multi-purpose areas – a dramatic swing from one extreme to another.

It has taken time to appreciate what we've probably known all along, that there should be a balance between openness and privacy. If you take down all the internal divisions between areas, remove doors, knock down walls, integrate stairways and corridors, you may achieve a dramatic new space only to find you don't really like living in it. If all your living spaces run into each other, you run the risk of losing your bearings; there's simply nowhere to escape to when you need to sit quietly with a book or have a private conversation. Large spaces are exhilarating, but they can also be tiring, noisy and muddled, the more so when there are no small enclaves to vary the pace and scale. You may also find that you have lost much usable wall space for storage, for radiators or simply as an anchor for furniture arrangement.

The same type of approach applies whether you're considering knocking two rooms together or converting one large open space, such as a warehouse or loft floor, into living quarters. You may require privacy for sleeping, bathing and work, but would equally enjoy a layout which allows you to combine living and eating areas, cooking and eating areas, or even all three. Providing a contrast between open and enclosed areas modulates and gives rhythm to spaces, an important dimension that is lacking when every room is either a poky cell or a vast featureless concourse.

A related issue is thinking about space as volume. With a little practice, it's easy enough to envisage changes to internal planning and layout; what is harder to imagine are alterations that involve changes to levels. Opening up by removing portions of floor, or dividing up by adding galleries and mezzanines are changes that alter the volume of a space along with the floor area. Such schemes offer dramatic scope for spilling natural light down the centre of a building, providing a sweeping, soaring sense of space, creating internal views and vistas that link different areas together in visually exciting ways.

Even if you are only moving around partitions, you should never view your home in isolation from its setting. Changes to the inside often imply alterations to the way the interior relates to the exterior, by providing better access to a garden, for example, or by making better visual connections or responding more sympathetically to the site and orientation. You should know which direction the main rooms in your house face, where the light comes from at different times of the day, which rooms are warm

3

and sunny, which are dark and cool. In extreme climates, no home would be comfortable or practical if the design failed to take account of these basic factors. They are no less important in areas of the world where conditions are more temperate. People are profoundly affected by natural light and by the ability to move freely from inside to outside; if you live in an area where there are not many sunny days in a year, it's even more important to be able to make the most of them when they occur.

Alterations to space can be graded in complexity, with demolishing or erecting partitions fairly low down the scale and adding an extension to an existing building fairly high up. In practice, however, there may be an interrelated series of changes, some of which are simple and straightforward, others less so. It's more instructive to think about the end result that you are trying to achieve, and to plan backwards from there.

3 A free-standing white panel doubles as a bedhead and partition that screens the raised bathroom area from view without blocking light from the rear wall of windows.
4 Converted lofts and warehouses are the ultimate urban spaces – one-room living at its most expansive. Setting up home in a building which was not originally designed for domestic use provides great creative freedom.

4

Views and vistas

■

■ **The rippled contours of these kitchen doors make a playful contrast with the clean, neat lines of the fitted cupboards beyond.**

Perception of space is as important to the layout of a room as the floor area at your disposal. The simple truth is that the desire to increase the 'feeling' of spaciousness probably lies at the back of many decisions to knock down walls or integrate different areas. Of course, it makes sense to link rooms with related functions. Living and eating rooms, and eating and cooking rooms are prime candidates for merger, with connecting or ante-areas, such as hallways, running a close second. Although practicalities may tip the balance, the sheer expansiveness of a large room constitutes a powerful argument in itself. In a typical terraced house, with rooms running front to back, knocking through dividing walls provides a dual aspect, with light and views coming from two directions.

People don't need views, but they crave them. Windowless rooms are the stuff of nightmares and, in law, only 'non-habitable' rooms such as utility rooms, bathrooms, lavatories, and, curiously, kitchens can be fully internal. They must be well ventilated but need have no direct visual connection with the outside world. Where the opportunity exists, creating rooms so that light falls from two sides is infinitely preferable to spaces lit by only one window. Better still is to arrange the layout of rooms so that there are internal views and vistas across a space, giving glimpses of outdoor life in different directions. These can be oblique aspects, such as the view from a stairway or from a gallery level – vantage points that offer a choice of stimulating perspectives.

Putting in internal 'windows', either glazed or open, can help to spread light around and offer the type of intriguing views that liven up the experience of moving about from room to room. A porthole between an internal bathroom and a hall or a glazed panel over the sink in an internal galley kitchen can help to counteract feelings of claustrophobia while maintaining the separation of private activities from public spaces.

Older houses often turn their backs on the garden spaces that surround them, and ill-judged additions and extensions may have made access outside even more proscribed. Reorganizing the layout can often improve the ease with which you reach the outdoors, as well as offering the opportunity to bring it closer visually.

New openings, internal and external, have a positive effect on the air flow, ventilating rooms naturally and stirring up the atmosphere in a pleasant and stimulating way. Arranging the position of windows so that breezes blow through them from one end of the house to the other can cool rooms dramatically on a hot day and avoid the need for artificial air-conditioning.

The overriding caveat is that you must pay attention to proportion, scale and detail when creating any new opening, either internally or externally. Taking out a floor to create a double-height space may mean that existing windows appear too small. It's relatively straightforward to extend a window by lowering the sill – big rooms do need more light and openings of a larger scale. In old houses, taking down the wall between a living-room and a dining-room, for example, can result in a new room that has two fireplaces and two chimney breasts along the length of one wall; this may prove unsettling, an uncomfortable visual reminder that the space was once divided. It's worth remembering that you can gain many of the most positive benefits of integrating two rooms by retaining a portion of the wall on either side of the new opening, retaining a hint of separation. If you want to maintain an element of flexibility, you can fit the opening with double doors, glazed or unglazed, or shutters that fold back within the reveal. In this case, it's often easier and more economical to find the doors first and then scale the opening to fit them; joinery that has to be custom-made to fit the new opening would add extra expense to what is in other respects a relatively straightforward project.

2 Large pivoting windows allow access to a balcony with an enviable view.

3 A washing area fitted in a corridor expresses the curve of an exterior wall in a modern Australian house. Panels of mirror reflect the view.

4 Where the climate is hospitable and the view spectacular, large openings bring in light and air and allow free movement between outdoors and in.

1

1 A window wall in this Corsican house provides an eagle's eye view of the lush valley. **2** A cylindrical drum containing a deep curved bath is lit by a large port-hole window. The circular mirror suspended at right angles above the basin appears to float in the recessed space.

2

3 Massive double doors offer a tantalizing slice of view that takes the eye along the axis of the space into the landscape beyond.

3

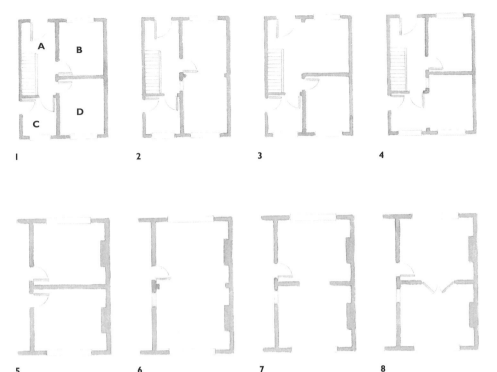

The general layout of a sequence of rooms can be altered by removing an internal wall: (1) a conventional layout might have an entrance hall ('A'), living-room ('B'), kitchen ('C') and dining-room('D'); removing the wall between the living- and dining-room (2) or the hallway and living-room (3) gives more general living space; removing the wall between the kitchen and dining-room creates a large open-plan eating room (4). Two separate rooms (5) can be integrated into a single room (6), perhaps retaining part of the dividing wall (7); double doors between such an opening maxi-mize flexibility (8).

In the case of external openings, too big can be as unsatisfactory as too small. Picture windows – unbroken expanses of plate glass – may seem like a good way of revelling in a view, but they often have a curiously deadening effect. Windows articulated with panes, or French doors that open on to a terrace often have a greater degree of vitality. Ensure that the view you reveal is worth looking at: a new window which leads the eye down the garden to a shed won't improve the quality of view from the living-room. Work out the best aspects for external openings, and design the landscape and interior to complement each other.

The difficulty of such work hinges on whether structural walls and other elements are involved or not. There may be added complications if the alterations involve changes to services – the loss of a radiator, changes in drainage, wiring or lighting, for example. If a load-bearing wall is affected, the opening must be reinforced by adding in a beam, concrete lintel or steel joist. Except in simple cases of extending windows downwards, all changes to external walls will entail some form of reinforcement. Inside, it depends on the wall. With structural implications, you will need approval from building regulators, although plan-ning permission is not required. In a building where interiors are listed, you are unlikely to be allowed to make any changes at all.

Options for change include:
• Removing a wall between two rooms.
• Making a large connection between rooms, leaving wall area to either side.
• Making an oversized doorway between rooms and fitting doors or a screen.
• Taking out the wall between a stair or hallway and a room.
• Making internal windows.
• Putting in French doors.
• Widening existing windows.
• Deepening existing windows.
• Removing a portion of floor or all of a floor to open up to the roof.
• Adding windows in a roof.

4 The supporting framework of columns and beams provides a hint of separation in a large airy room. Banishing all internal divisions from a house can create 'problem' spaces with no points of reference.

New space for old

Achieving a feeling of spaciousness in your surroundings won't necessarily win you more usable space. If you have a pressing need to house more people, more activities or more storage under the same roof, it may be a matter of redesigning the layout, partitioning a large room to make two separate ones, or of changing levels to insert an extra floor. No-go areas like basements and attics are often ripe for extensions.

Partitioning is simple and normally you don't have to worry about structural problems. Dividing up a large nursery to give the children separate bedrooms, for example, involves a few commonsense decisions about where to place the wall and how to arrange access. The critical issue for 'habitable' rooms is making sure each new area has at least one window, and you may lose some floor area in forming separate entrances or lobbies to each new room. You must also consider the proportions of the new spaces; a high-ceilinged room divided in two may look odd unless you also adjust the levels by dropping the ceiling or raising the floor. If there isn't an extreme disparity, you can accommodate the eye to such changes by running a plain cornice or coving around each new room and repeating details such as decorative mouldings and skirting-boards.

Partitions don't have to be full height or full width and they don't necessarily have to follow straight lines. A curved wall that encloses part of a space can be an elegant way of gaining privacy or segregating activities; a half-height wall often makes a useful buffer between an integrated kitchen and eating room.

In an older multi-storied house, where ceiling heights are generous, you can sometimes squeeze in extra rooms by juggling the levels and adding a mezzanine. If you've got to rework services anyway, this can provide you with the opportunity to turn the house topsy-turvy, rethinking layout from the ground up. In Victorian terraced houses, the kitchen generally occupies the least

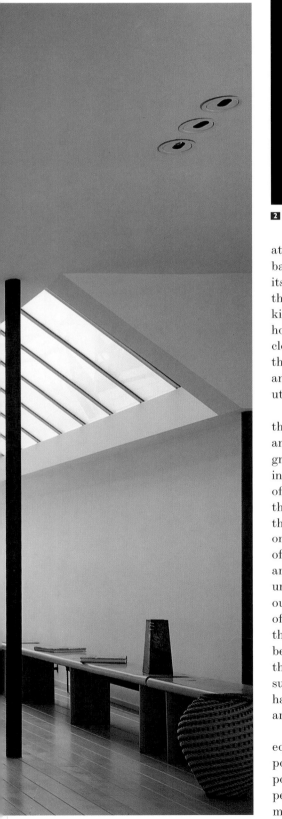

2

attractive, lowest position, usually in the basement or semi-basement, reflecting its former status as a utilitarian room, the servants' domain. Moving the kitchen further up into the heart of the house allows you to integrate it more closely with other living areas, releasing the lowest level for more flexible use as an extra bedroom, home office or study, utility room, or even self-contained flat.

Planning changes to levels entails thinking about 'section', and this is truly an architectural skill. The section, or diagrammatic vertical cut through a building, enables you to work out the best way of using volume, as opposed to planning the horizontal layout of each storey. In this context, it is essential to get a grip on the fact that the ceiling is not the floor of the room above. Ceilings, because they are cosmetic finishes applied to the underside of a floor, can be lowered without difficulty to improve the proportions of a room. Lowering or raising a floor, on the other hand, is structural work, because you are moving the position of the floor itself. Adding in a new level – such as a mezzanine in a loft space – also has structural consequences, since you are increasing the load on the main walls.

Basement conversions are not the equal of loft conversions in terms of potential. They are understandably less popular, at least partly because most people find it less pleasant to spend very much of their time underground. Head

height and daylight are the two critical factors. A semi-basement on a sloping site, which is deep enough for you to move around in comfortably and which has some form of external opening, offers the greatest potential. You can excavate the ground outside to improve access to a garden or extend windows to increase natural light. Digging down to create a new basement or extend a shallow underfloor space involves a lot of disruption and expense – underpinning existing foundations, rerouteing drainage, waterproofing, substantial building work and all the associated permissions are usually enough to put most people off the idea very quickly. If there is some basement area, but it is not sufficient to make fullscale conversion feasible, you could still look at dropping the ground-floor level as far as possible to create more volume in the ground-floor rooms.

Changes to levels generally imply changes to stairways, too. You can sometimes gain extra space by relocating and rebuilding an existing staircase. Old houses tend to waste a considerable amount of space in this department. New stairs to galleries or mezzanines can be exciting and dynamic additions; the thrill of open cantilevered steps or the bold sculptural beauty of a spiral staircase brings an agreeable theatricality to everyday life, especially when combined with other dramatic features such as roof windows or skylights.

An Edwardian terraced house in west London has been radically remodelled by architects Munkenbeck and Marshall. From the outside, the house is indistinguishable from its neighbours, but inside the space has been gutted to convert the layout of small, self-contained rooms (which themselves had split to form a pair of flats) into a loft-style open-plan layout (see plans overleaf).
1 Daylight floods into the ground-floor room through a new glass ceiling, the French doors, and a glass landing above the kitchen worktop that looks up through the whole height of the house to a skylight in the roof. Activity areas are zoned by the use of furniture and fittings: a dining table and chairs; the kitchen island; and (in the front bay window, not shown) two sofas at right angles to the fireplace.
2 From the back garden, a spectacular view of the interior: the maple floor, island unit and graphic staircase add a touch of warmth to the understated minimalism.

1 This unique kitchen, designed by David Pocknell, is fitted into the wall of MDF cabinets, with an inset stainless-steel worktop. Additional work space is provided by the island unit. Above the gas hob, the extractor fan is housed in an MDF cabinet. On top of this sits a clock which can be seen when crossing the glass landing above.

2 At the top of the stairs on the first floor, a glass landing leads to the study, the only conventional room (in the sense of four walls and a door) in the house. The landing is a focal point in the reconfigured space, a point from which the opening up process reaches its fullest potential, looking down to the living area, and up to a metal walkway and skylight beyond.

1

2

3 The bathroom on the first floor is the second-largest space in the house. The free-standing bathtub occupies a prominent place, with double basins built into the unit beyond it. Hinged mirrors play with the geometry of the room, reflecting back the sleek walls of built-in wardrobes made from varnished MDF; beneath the staircase, one of the 'wardrobe' doors opens to reveal a small dressing-room.

3

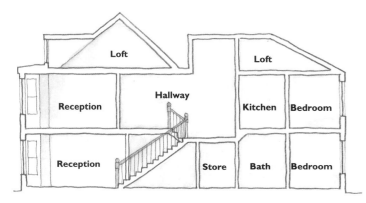

PREVIOUS CROSS-SECTION

Loft

Loft

Reception   Hallway

Kitchen   Bedroom

Reception

Store   Bath   Bedroom

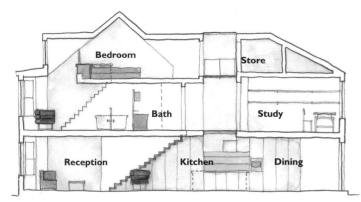

NEW CROSS-SECTION

Bedroom

Store

Bath

Study

Reception   Kitchen   Dining

4 The bedroom is located in the roof of the house, immediately above the bathroom. Low-level shelves form an extended bedhead, a place for the owners' collection of tin toys and automata.

5 The formal paved garden at the back of the house is dominated by the russet concrete slab, from which spouts a mini waterfall spilling into a trough. The slab, in fact, is a small shed that conceals a barbecue behind it.

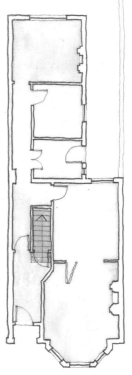

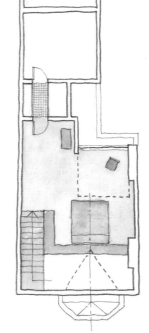

PREVIOUS GROUND-FLOOR   **NEW GROUND-FLOOR**   **NEW FIRST-FLOOR**   **NEW SECOND-FLOOR**   **5**

Into the roof

1

Going up into the roof offers a wide choice of spatial solutions. An attic can often be converted into a habitable room by adding a skylight, lining with new finishes and fitting snug storage space under the eaves where the head height diminishes. The popularity of this type of alteration is evident in the number of companies specializing in purpose-made 'conversion kits' which supply you with the relevant components. If you live in the city, and garden area is precious, roof space may be the most feasible way of providing extra room. At the same time, opening up to the roof, by removing all or part of the ceiling, can transform the upper level of your home into a soaring, light-filled space. Attic spaces – with angles formed by the planes of the roof, the potential for top lighting and panoramic views – have their own special appeal. The only drawback is that some people find loft conversions noisy – in practice, the sound of rain drumming on the roof can prove to be more annoying than romantic. And, unfortunately, this type of conversion is largely ruled out in new houses with preformed roof trusses.

Access is a major issue. If you're going to use the new room on a regular basis, you'll need to install a proper staircase, rather than a folding loft ladder. Changes to an existing staircase or to the layout of upper rooms may be necessary to fit the new stairway in. You may have to extend the ceiling opening if you plan to move in large pieces of furniture.

The type of window you install should be easy to clean. Windows that pivot on special hinges make cleaning easier; there are also various tools designed for the purpose. Cleaning is not a side issue for a roof window; the pleasure of gazing up at a clear blue sky will be lost if you're forced to look through grimy glass. Any window that can be fitted from the inside will mean you don't have to erect scaffolding to install it. Windows facing the sun will need blinds, awnings or cover to filter strong light and keep the temperature within reasonable limits.

2

Structurally speaking, the work varies. Ceiling joists in an attic are unlikely to be strong enough to support you and the furniture: you will probably have to double them up by adding extra beams alongside. A roof light – a window in the flat plane of the roof – is the minimum needed for 'habitable' status and it is advisable to double up roof rafters on either side of it for support. A dormer may be necessary to increase the floor area with adequate head height, and this may require planning permission. Some rafters or beams may have to be removed to gain enough clear space, which will necessitate alternative means of support.

3

1 Converting an attic to a home office can liberate your pattern of work without encroaching on the space of people you live with.
2 In large buildings, the area beneath the roof can be significant. Excellent sources of natural light and the potential for unusual storage arrangements showcase the bonuses of 'loft living'.
3 Attic bedrooms remove the sleeping area from the general domain, enhancing the sense of privacy.

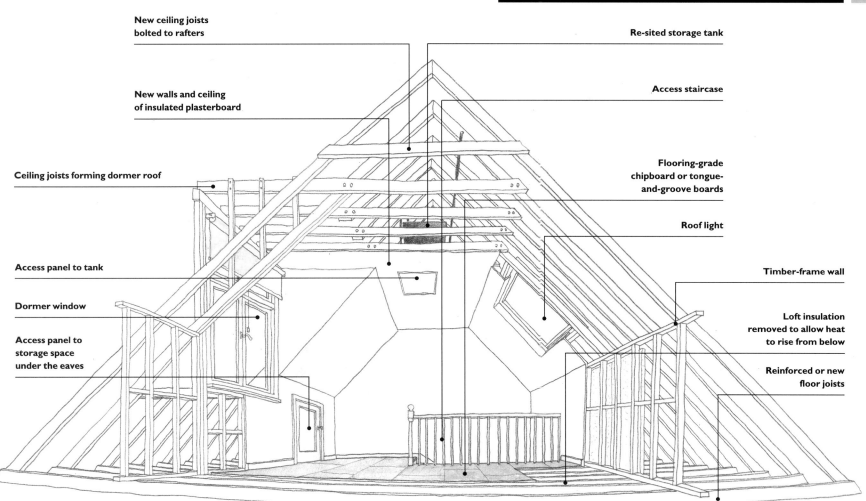

New ceiling joists bolted to rafters

Re-sited storage tank

New walls and ceiling of insulated plasterboard

Access staircase

Ceiling joists forming dormer roof

Flooring-grade chipboard or tongue-and-groove boards

Roof light

Access panel to tank

Timber-frame wall

Dormer window

Loft insulation removed to allow heat to rise from below

Access panel to storage space under the eaves

Reinforced or new floor joists

POINTS TO REMEMBER

- Planning permission is required if you split your house into two separate dwellings. If you wish to retain a connection between the two units, you will need to install a fire door.
- You will need building regulations approval for any structural alterations to your home, including underpinning.
- Soil stacks have to be extended away from new windows.
- Reroofing or adding a roof light does not require planning permission if you are not changing the shape of the roof – except in conservation areas.
- Planning permission is normally required for dormers that overlook a 'highway', which doesn't just mean the front of the house, but may include side roads as well, and, in some areas, parks and public gardens.
- There are planning restrictions on how extensive dormers can be.
- Changes to layout and loft conversions have to comply with fire regulations. These may specify fire-resistant doors to seal off new areas, type of flooring or size, operation and position of windows. Three- and four-storey houses have more stringent requirements than two-storey ones.
- Ladders may be acceptable as a means of escape from a loft.

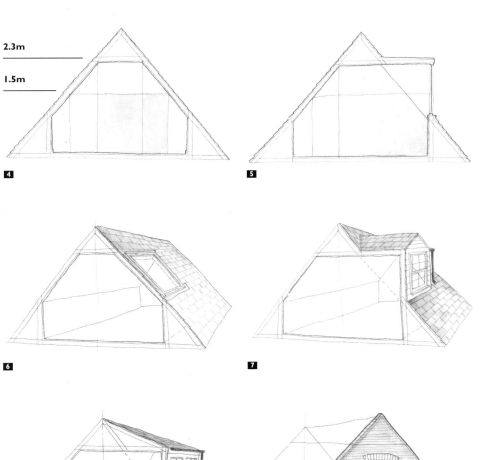

2.3m

1.5m

4

5

6

7

8

9

4 Floor area in a loft is calculated to be the space at which the roof is 1.5m (5ft) above the floor level. Most building requirements stipulate a minimum finished ceiling height of 2.3m (7ft) over at least half the floor area.
5 The addition of a dormer window can significantly increase habitable floor area.
6 Standard roof light.
7 Gabled dormer window.
8 Dormer window.
9 Casement or sash window set in gable end.

Adding on

Home extensions range from building on a wing which doubles your living space to that perennial favourite, the conservatory. Well-executed and properly planned, adding on to your home can increase its value as well as its floor area. On the other hand, a mean back extension, shoddily made, is never a desirable feature and might even make the rooms you do have less pleasant to live in. Clever siting, sensitive design and careful integration with existing layout is essential to reap the most of the investment.

First decide on the purpose of the extra area. Do you want to extend existing rooms to make a bigger kitchen or living area? Do you need another bedroom or a place to work from home? If you feel the need for more space, first establish which function the new area could fulfil that would ease congestion in the rest of the house. Extending your home can have a knock-on effect, forcing you to rethink layout and organization. An example might involve converting an integral garage into a study or playroom with a new entrance through to the main house, then building a separate garage on the other side of the plot. In this case, the new structure has made better use of the original building, although it has not directly provided more living area.

Siting is another key issue, and should take account of the direction of natural light, views and the relationship with outside areas. There's little point in adding a conservatory to the side of the house which gets little direct sun, nor to extending your living-room towards a neighbour's brick wall. Ground-level extensions entail the loss of part of your garden – ensure this is a sacrifice worth making. Clearing away old out-buildings or tacked-on extensions can give you more ground area to play with. If you live in a city and space is scarce, a roof-level extension may be better – at the top of your house, on top of an existing extension or over an adjoining garage. Balconies or roof terraces can achieve the same sense of connection with outdoors.

Properly conceived, an extension should rationalize routes indoors and out and increase the sense of spaciousness and light, rather than rob internal rooms of their best aspects. For these reasons, half- or fully-glazed garden rooms are popular additions and their transitional nature, mediating between house and garden, helps to reduce the impact of the construction. If your house is sitting on a large plot of land, an alternative is to build or convert an out-building at some distance from the main house and form a connecting link between the two. Courtyards or planted garden 'rooms' make the whole effect look considered.

As far as style is concerned, you can opt for a sensitive addition that repeats the details and materials of the original construction or go for a blatant contrast. In this context, a near miss is as good as a mile: it will either look like you haven't tried hard enough, or that you lack the courage of your convictions.

As far as building work is concerned, there are three main aspects to consider. First, you will have to form a connection with the existing house, which normally means work to the original external walls. Secondly, a new ground-level structure will need its own foundations; a rooftop extension may require existing foundations to be strengthened to cope with the new loads. Thirdly, there is the question of extending heating, electricity and drainage to the new area.

POINTS TO WATCH OUT FOR

- You don't need permission to build a small single-storey extension, if it is under a certain height, within a certain distance of the existing property boundary and the 'cubic content' of the original house is not extended by more than about 10 per cent. This exempts most small conservatories, for example. However, if your home was extended any time after 1948, you may have already used up this entitlement and you will thus need planning permission for the new work.

1

2

1 Adding on extra rooms often has implications for the existing internal arrangement. This extension to a studio flat provided a conservatory-diner, new kitchen and – up the stairs – a small, self-contained bedroom.
2 Usable ground-floor space can be found to the rear or side of a building if the garden is not made unacceptably small. This new bathroom is part of a rear addition.

3 A double-height side extension covered by a glazed pitched roof makes a dramatic eating area with a powerful connection to the garden.

3

4 In cities, many older houses are inward-looking. This conservatory kitchen at the back of a London town house takes the heart of the home to the heart of the garden.

4

- For larger extensions, planning permission may hinge on whether the proposed addition will deprive your neighbours of natural light and how the extension affects the character of the surrounding area.
- In some areas, you may need planning permission to build on to party walls shared with neighbours.
- All internal rooms must be adequately ventilated, at least mechanically for kitchens and bathrooms, by a window for any other room.
- It may not be permitted to build over an existing sewer manhole.

- For large-scale extensions, current insulation standards must be met, even if these do not exist in the original building.
- New foundations may have to be tied into existing ones; this can add to both the schedule and cost of the work.
- Detached buildings not used for living purposes – such as garages, poolhouses or summer houses – do not require planning permission if they are under a certain height and within a specified distance from the house and its main boundary with a highway. Check local regulations carefully.

Conversions

Most buildings outlive their original occupants and, barring natural accidents, planning blight and redevelopment, many even go on to outlive their original function. There's nothing particularly new about setting up home in a structure that began life with another purpose, but in recent times the attractions of living in a converted building have become ever-more appreciated.

The reasons are pretty clear. Large parts of our cities, towns and suburbs are given over to street upon street of remarkably similar houses. Modern builders are no less original than their Victorian and Edwardian counterparts. If you are familiar with a few house types, old and new, you may have a passing acquaintance with the layout of about half the homes in your area. The sheer predictability of knowing that the bathroom will be 'first on the right at the top of the stair' makes many people long for a change. Conversions can offer a whole new freedom of layout, and room for the quirky and unexpected.

Ever since smart young things first discovered that a handy pied-à-terre could be fashioned from a humble mews, the potential for development of otherwise-redundant buildings has been increasingly explored. For aficionados of modern design, converted factories or warehouses offer a rugged utility and spare functional beauty; for conservationists, there is the opportunity to renovate, preserve and cherish unique architectural forms, such as old barns, chapels and tiny village schools. Loft-living was a simple expedient for New York artists who, in the late 1970s, started to colonize the old light-industrial buildings of lower Manhattan and found the acres of cheap studio space they were looking for. From these pioneering efforts has come a whole 'loft' style of living, with associated trends in design, such as hi-tech. In the process, a wide range of inner-city buildings has escaped being razed to the ground, recyling useful space and rejuvenating neglected districts from whence local industries have long since departed.

Conversions usually offer more space than the average domestic house. At the same time, they generally encourage flexibility in the layout and arrangement of the space and throw in unusual architectural detail for good measure. You may secure many of these advantages by buying or renting a space which has already been converted, and there are now many highly sophisticated makeovers on the market. True enthusiasts prefer to start with the bare bones. The downside is that, while many of the spatial considerations that apply to an ordinary house are the same, there are extra demands, both structurally and organizationally, and the sheer scale of such projects can be daunting.

First of all, however, you have to find your building. Church commissioners may be able to tell you if any church or chapel properties are being offered for sale; local authorities may have the same information on small schools designated

1 Translucent sliding screens section off a sleeping area in a loft conversion. The metal framework of the screens complements the industrial aesthetic of the building.
2 Rough-and-ready plywood partitions subdivide space in a New York loft – a surprisingly sleek use of a basic material.

for closure. Light-industrial or warehouse buildings are handled by commercial agents; there is the chance that you might stumble on a suitable property by scouting out areas in which you would like to live. There are often workshops, old meeting halls and small factories tucked away behind and between residential streets, but the larger premises are likely to be in parts of town which aren't well served by standard amenities.

Depending on the size of the building, the next stage may be to find a number of like-minded people to share the space, and who are willing to join you in setting up a cooperative or limited company to fund the sale or take on the leasehold. You will need sound advice from the appropriate professionals on financing and contractual matters from the start.

Even more essentially, you need to secure planning permission for both change of use and the concomitant necessary alterations. 'Change of use' is the tricky part. Buildings are classified according to the functions they fulfil, with 'residential' being only one of many categories. A planner's response to your proposal to set up home in a former piano factory or infant's school will often depend on political issues, such as whether or not the powers that be are trying to encourage new business in the area. If your scheme includes working premises, such as a photographer's studio or a pottery, you may stand a better chance of success. The only really safe course of action is to make the sale or tenancy conditional on securing permission; otherwise you may find yourself the proud owner of a large building that you aren't allowed to live in. At the same time, you should submit an outline scheme indicating the alterations you propose to make. Take advice from an architect, and commission a thorough survey. The requirements for adequate fire protection are likely to be stringent. You may have to deal with conservation agencies if your building is listed – many old barns and agricultural buildings are.

3 Old beams and roof trusses reveal the past in an elegant conversion of an old barn. Redundant agricultural buildings provide original and characterful space for those seeking to move away from conventional domestic surroundings. **4** Gridded partitions infilled with glass separate private areas from open living space in a warehouse conversion.

3

Naturally, it is easier to bypass such hurdles and look for a floor or loft space in a building that is already managed by someone else. Whichever route you take, adapting the space to meet your personal requirements involves exactly the same kind of approach detailed elsewhere in this section, only on a much larger scale. However, the potential rewards are great. Services for the kitchen and bathroom areas are best grouped in a 'core', which can form the basis for a division of space into private and open areas. Some partitioning will be necessary, or you may soon find your new home has the intimacy of a football field. At the same time, it is essential to acknowledge the scale of the original building and to play up to it; you may be able to salvage some of the original fittings. Let the original character of the building show through: respect the existing architectural features and other structural elements.

4

Putting back the style

1 While the practical role of the fireplace may have diminished considerably, the aesthetic and symbolic contributions it makes to the interior are more valued than ever. This empty hearth frames a large ceramic urn, and provides a decorative focus for the room.
2 Panelled doors, architraves and a simple fire surround painted in with the walls lend detail, focus and character without compromising the essentially contemporary mood of this bedroom.

Putting back the style amounts to a moral crusade for some devotees, an enterprise which demands diligence, detective work and spare cash. In such instances it becomes a question of how far to go. It is perfectly possible to restore an interior to a semblance of its original condition, down to historically accurate door furniture and paint recipes. Generally, however, there comes a point when the convenience of modern services becomes too persuasive and period flavour rather than period reality appears more attractive. Others are aware that old houses are the product of many changes over the years and that the date of origin carries no special significance. For most people, the issue is how to reconcile the old with the new.

Period restoration is most feasible, practical and effective on the level of architectural detail. 'Detail', however, is a more powerful element than the word might imply. The aggregate effect of such subtle and seemingly redundant features is easy to judge when you see an old house without them. Detail civilizes proportions, makes sense of scale and adds quality to finishes. Mouldings and trim adjust the eye to the breaks between ceiling and wall, wall and floor. Cornices and skirting-boards edge the plane of the wall, and in the process elegantly conceal the type of superficial cracking which can occur at these major joints. Dado rails, generally positioned about one-third of the way up the wall, were intended to signal the break

An old house with a history reveals its character in a variety of ways – through materials and construction, design and layout, and, critically, what is generally referred to as 'architectural detail'. This is a loose term that encompasses all those intrinsic, evocative features, such as mouldings, cornices, dados, picture rails, fireplaces and architraves which define, embellish and articulate the plain surfaces of the interior.

Not so long ago, in the frenzied rush to modernize old properties with updated services and more flexible internal arrangements, many such 'details' found themselves in a builder's skip. Eventually, post-war conversions became notorious for historical vandalism and in a short space of time people began to realize what they were missing in their homes. Nowadays it is unthinkable that a period house might be adapted in such a way as to strip away all of its most distinctive features – features which, increasingly, add real value to a home. Coincidental with this renewed appreciation and spirit of conservation has come a flourishing trade in architectural salvage and the reproduction of period detail. None the less, restoration is a vexed issue.

2

3

3 The traditional detailing of this Mediterranean house is subtly emphasized by slate grey paintwork. In the past, doors, panelling shutters and wooden trim were common y made of softwood which was always painted.
4 Half-height pan-elling, fine architraves and the glossy polished floor pay homage to early American interiors without resorting to wholesale restoration.
5 An elaborate plas-terwork ceiling in a studio flat provides a superb foil to the contemporary design.

4

between different types of wall finish – the lower half (the dado) robust and hard-wearing, the upper part fine and decorative. The rail itself was originally intended to prevent chair backs from scraping away at the fabric of the wall.

A study of historical interiors can acquaint you with the various forms of these decorative features and their stand-ard positioning. There may be a house in your neighbourhood which has retained its details and you might wish to copy these. Alternatively, you might have semi-intact mouldings from which you can cast replacements for the missing portions. Synthetic versions are avail-able off the peg; lightweight, easy to install and virtually indistinguishable from the real thing once painted and installed, these can be a practical option.

Avoid period gloss and restore only those elements that make a positive con-tribution, either in a decorative or a practical way. If you want to run picture rails around your room, hang pictures from them; if you put back a dado rail, restore the dado, too. You don't have to opt for excessively decorative flights of fancy; a relatively plain moulding will do the same job as one with all the curlicues.

Larger period pieces, such as fire-places, often contribute an important focus to a room. You don't have to be slavishly accurate, but it is important to suit the fire surround to the scale of the room and match its style to the overall character of the space. A tiny cast-iron grate will be swamped in a high-ceilinged room; a baroque marble edifice won't do much for a bedroom unless the decoration is suitably extravagant to support it.

Adding on the style isn't likely to involve you in much building work, although installing a fireplace does entail opening up a blocked chimney breast. Since chimney breasts form part of the structure of the house, it may first be necessary to get help to establish how far you can excavate.

Removing unwanted features, in the form of modern additions, is another matter. Occasionally something totally unexpected turns up – a Tudor inglenook has been known to be found nestling under layers of Victorian brickwork in the heart of an old farmhouse – but not all discoveries are welcome. Thorough-going archaeology on the fabric of your home demands proper surveying, as well as architectural and historical advice.

5

GETTING ORGANIZED

Homes house things as much as they do people. Even the most dedicated minimalist needs belongings, equipment and basic necessities; most of us travel through life with rather more baggage, some of it clearly redundant. When possessions start to get the upper hand, it's time to rethink just how, where and why we hang on to things.

Good organization should be largely invisible; whereas chaos and muddle stare you in the face, slow you up at every turn and make aggravating chores out of simple everyday routines. Organizing your

home properly need not involve major upheavals, expense or structural change; it can be as straightforward as reassigning rooms new functions or setting up a designated storage area. If you organize your storage properly, you'll rediscover space you never knew you had and enjoy using it all the more.

Storage is a workaday word for what is, in fact, one of the key elements in the way your home looks and functions. How and where you accommodate your possessions has a radical effect on the way you use the remaining space, particularly on the ease and efficiency with which you perform almost any task, from getting dressed to cooking a meal, taking a bath to playing with the children. And your basic approach – whether you like to leave everything out on view or to banish all your belongings to cupboards and closets – will determine the basic character of your home more surely than any palette of paint colours or soft furnishing style. An entrance hall that is cluttered with bicycles, discarded coats and unopened junk mail speaks volumes about the value of good storage – and the mess has a habit of spreading insidiously throughout the rest of the house.

For all these reasons, it's not an issue which can be approached piecemeal or reactively. You need to look at all the items in your possession, at how often you use them and in what contexts, so that you can then store them somewhere sensible, know where to find them and access them as easily as possible. Good storage also means that your possessions are well cared for and don't get damaged or age prematurely. It's common knowledge that you need twice as much storage space as you think; reorganize your home and you'll probably find it within your own four walls.

1 Kitchens demand special organizational skills. Fresh food, basic provisions, equipment and utensils all need to be stored safely and readily to hand for efficient food preparation and cooking.
2 A well-proportioned storage wall combines closed base cupboards for clutter with open book shelves for display. Framing a doorway with shelving in this way has an appealing solidity and strength.

3 Hide it all from view in floor-to-ceiling cupboards fitted with shelves at different heights to provide flexible storage space.

4 Plywood door fronts stained in different colours liven up these bathroom units.

5 The beauty and fragility of glassware is accentuated by glass display shelves, seamlessly fitted into an alcove.

4

5

Less is more

Before you begin to reorganize, it makes sense to review what you actually own. Most of us share our lives with a great many unwanted things, possessions which once deserved house room but no longer serve a useful purpose, articles accumulated over the years that have established squatters' rights in the hall closet or spare room. Be ruthless with yourself and evaluate your belongings frankly and objectively, discarding what you no longer need, like or use. There are plenty of outlets for anything which still has some usable life left in it — junk shops, secondhand or charity shops, school fairs, jumble sales, garage or car boot sales are good forms of recycling anything from old clothes and furniture to toys and books. What no one in their right mind would want, throw out.

The idea behind this strategy is not to force you into Spartan self-denial or to pare your belongings down to a list of desert-island necessities, but to get the maximum pleasure and usefulness out of both space and possessions. Though good organization isn't incompatible with a relaxed attitude to tidiness, true clutter is profoundly uneconomical, a waste of precious space and a guarantee that essentials will be overlooked, lost and even uselessly duplicated.

Once you have discarded as much as you can, analyse what you have left into categories based on frequency of use. There will be many things in constant, everyday demand, which need to be readily accessible; others which are used fairly frequently, perhaps for specific activities; some items which are needed on a seasonal basis; and a few which you may require only once a year or less.

In most cases, the items that fall into the last category can go into deep storage in dead areas such as lofts, box-rooms, basements or sheds and you can more or less forget about them until the rare occasion arises when you need them again. Take the time to list what you have stored in out-of-the-way areas to make retrieval easier. It's often a good

1 Halls and stairways are often spacious enough to double as storage areas, liberating useful space in the main living areas.
2 In a compact kitchen, cabinets above and below the worktop store pots and pans from view. A wire rack hung on the wall organizes kitchen utensils in everyday use, a pleasing and practical display.

1

idea to rotate seasonally defined belongings in and out of deep storage as well, exchanging winter wear and sports equipment for their summer equivalents at the appropriate times: making this kind of effort twice a year isn't unreasonable. What remains when you have made these basic decisions is what you have to accommodate and organize in a more visible and accessible fashion.

A PLACE FOR EVERYTHING

In most cases, the things with which we surround ourselves are indivisible from the activities or functions for which we use them. No one would be foolish enough to keep kitchen utensils in the bedroom or put the lawnmower away in the attic each time the grass is cut. These are absurd examples, but in minor ways we often act no more logically, making difficulties and obstacles for ourselves by failing to take account of when and where things are actually needed. The

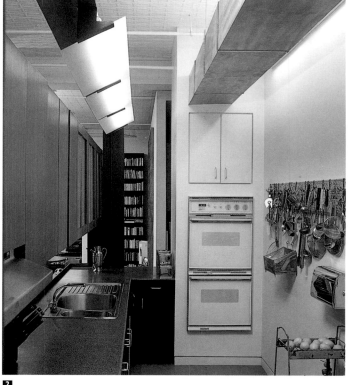

2

3

4

5

3 A kitchen area in an open-plan space receives rather more attention than one behind closed doors. An array of sleek fitted units allows the kitchen to blend into the background when it's not in use.

4 Storage that is fitted flush with the walls of a room is seamlessly integrated. Fitted out with sliding drawers and shelves, the cupboards provide generous levels of discreet storage in the sleeping area.

5 In a fashion designer's London apartment, solid wood display shelving, partly concealed behind a false wall, provides space for a few carefully chosen objects.

6 Living in a minimal interior demands rigorous behind-the-scenes organization to maintain the purity of space. Household necessities have to be kept somewhere; integrating storage within rooms devoid of conventional fittings and furnishings is a precise art.

result is that valuable, accessible space is wasted storing articles which are barely used, or that undertaking a simple, everyday procedure needlessly becomes a major exercise, turning the house upside down to find the articles we need to carry it out.

Few people are so instinctively tidy that they will return an item to its rightful place the instant they've stopped using it. But if things have a proper home, and it's in the neighbourhood of where they are most frequently used, they are more likely to end up being put away — and easily found again, in good condition, on the occasion when they're next required. The possessions that float from room to room, hang about in limbo on the stairs and eventually vanish into thin air often either have no home to go to or one which is basically too remote for anyone to bother with. For example, if children like to play in the kitchen and you like to have them there, it's better to provide them with a place close at hand where they can keep their things than to sweep up an armful of toys at the end of the day and return them to a bedroom several flights of stair away — or not, as the case may be. A cupboard given over to toy storage may not quite be what one expects to find in a kitchen, but in this situation it makes a lot more sense than using the same cupboard space to keep a pasta-maker that is simply languishing between its annual outings.

On this mundane level, there are many similar decisions to make, based on the way you actually live, rather than the way you think you ought to live. Inevitably, there will be the odd pocket of disorder, a drawer filled with the kind of bits and pieces normally found in the bottom of handbags. Unless you are obsessively organized by nature, it's inhuman to suggest that you should itemize every possession, filing everything away neatly; but if every drawer is threatening to turn into a bits-and-pieces drawer, it's time for a thorough sort-out and reorganization.

Finding space

Home organization tends to lag behind changes in lifestyle or circumstance and if you're feeling the pinch in a particular area, it may be because your expectations or activities have altered. If your culinary horizons have broadened over the years, you may require more storage space in the kitchen; if you now work at home instead of going out to an office, you'll need a place to keep the accessories of your professional life. And if you have children, you'll know how fast their needs change and how important it is to keep a step ahead organizationally.

Micro-planning can get you just so far. Usually what's needed is a more thorough investigation of how you use the space at your disposal. Finding space to put things involves understanding how you use or underuse different areas.

The first aspect to consider is room use. Simple reallocation of space can go a long way to solving many organizational problems. Consider the most common

1 As Le Corbusier pointed out, the practice of keeping clothes in the bedroom is neither practical nor conducive to relaxation. Dressing areas can be fashioned from vestibules, box-rooms and adjoining hallways.
2 A walk-in closet framed in unfinished plywood makes an idiosyncratic library fitted with floor-to-ceiling shelves.

arrangement, with parents in a large 'master' bedroom, the eldest child in a smaller bedroom and baby in a tiny nursery. However, if the children were to share the big room, the parents move to the medium-sized room and the nursery converted to a study-cum-guest room, the benefits for everyone could be wide-ranging. From three rooms dominated by a single use, there would be a new flexibility with positive implications for the entire household. Big bedrooms often make sense for small children, giving them a base where they can play and romp with their friends: if they have their own domain, they are much less likely to invade the rest of the house leaving a trail of Lego in their wake. Similarly, a small study for quiet reading, homework or hobbies, perhaps with facilities for putting up overnight guests, is a positive asset in many families, while a baby will quickly outgrow the confines of a tiny room and will soon be longing for the company of siblings.

Next, consider the 'between-spaces' – such as under the stairs, in landings and hallways – places which have no specifically defined function but which often, especially in older houses, account for a significant amount of floor area. Lining one wall of a hallway with shelves to house all of your books or converting the area under the stairs into a study area, play corner or fitted storage space can dramatically benefit the spatial quality of adjacent rooms burdened with too many activities. There's a world of difference between letting heaps of clutter clog up the hall because you haven't found anywhere else for it to go and a wholehearted, architecturally conceived solution that transforms redundant space into one with its own specific character and appeal. Provided you don't shrink main traffic routes unacceptably and make it awkward, uncomfortable or even dangerous to move from place to place, decanting storage into circulation areas can be very successful all round.

3

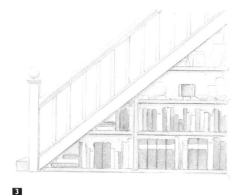

4

5

6

7

8

9

10

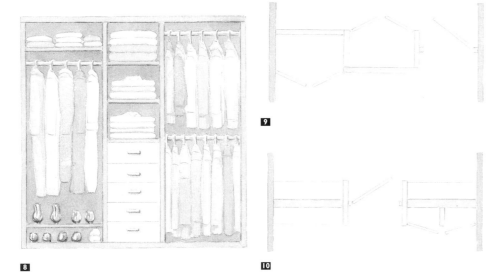

11

3 The space beneath conventional staircases is often overlooked, but offers great storage potential for shelves of books.

4 Used as book-shelves – rather than for aesthetic display – a wall of shelving makes particularly effective use of space in a hall or landing.

5 If you need a quiet corner for settling bills and occasional work from home, the below-stairs area could be turned into a small home office.

6 Even a small alcove fitted with a shelf at desk height can be put to use as a study area.

7 Fitting a wall of shelving around a door-way can be strikingly graphic.

8 Wardrobe storage can be much more effi-ciently organized if you think about the types of clothes you own: shelves at the bottom for shoes; full-length hanging space for longer clothes; open shelves for shirts and sweaters; drawers for small items and accessories; and half-height rails for jackets, skirts or other shorter-length items.

9 Stagger the dividing wall between two rooms to provide wardrobe space in the alcoves created.

10 Alcoves on either side of a doorway can be used for open-shelf storage or cupboards.

11 A hard-working corner doubles as a window seat and spare sleeping area, with generous storage space fitted underneath the mattress.

An extension of the same idea is to transform partitions between rooms into storage walls, with both inner and outer sides fitted with closets, cupboards or closed shelving. Here is an opportunity to tailor the fitted space to the precise dimensions of what you need to store, which always makes good sense. Storage walls act as buffers to sound and are effective heat insulators, too.

Another way to achieve more storage space is to reorganize the connections between rooms. If you plot how you actually travel around your home, you may be surprised how rarely you use cer-tain entrances to rooms where there's a choice of routes. In this case, blocking up the redundant doorway will win you that much more wall space which can be used for storage needs or could offer the opportunity, for example, to extend a run of kitchen units.

Finally, there is the option of devoting an entire room to storage. Linen rooms, larders, dressing-rooms and other areas principally given over to the housing and management of belongings immediately recall the type of planning associated with great country houses with their myriad household offices. Few of us live on such a grand scale but, even when space is tight, fitting out a specific area to house clothes, provisions or books can make good spatial sense. A separate dressing area can make the bedroom a much more relaxing place; you don't have to sacrifice an entire room for the purpose, a vestibule adjacent to the main bathroom would do. The larder, the indispensable store cupboard in our grandmothers' day, fell from favour with the advent of kitchen technology, but there is nothing old-fashioned about the benefits of natural refrigeration and orderly keeping of stocks and supplies. With the kitchen often functioning as a family room, separate storage areas are making a comeback. Storage rooms are instinctively appealing, liberating other parts of the house from the burden of catering for too many different needs.

Storage versus display

1 Lighting can be fixed behind a strip at the front of a shelf to illuminate the surface underneath.
2 Brackets are the quickest and simplest means of supporting a run of shelving.
3 Adding a lip to the front edge of a shelf gives the appearance of it having more substance and also helps to hide the supporting brackets at the back.
4 A half-round moulding fixed across the length of the shelf is an effective way of supporting display plates; alternatively, rout a groove along the length of the shelf and fix a retaining rail above (not shown).
5 Books furnish rooms in unexpected ways; in this instance, the tilting spines and triangular bookends provide a lively visual theme echoed in the design of the rug.

Attitudes to home organization range from the seamless concealment of the devoted minimalist, at one extreme, to the rampant clutter of those who prefer everything out on view. Neither stance could be described as typical, and most people look for a middle ground, storing some of their possessions behind closed doors and organizing other items in more visibly accessible ways.

The attractions of a happy medium are fairly obvious. Even minimalists have to brush their teeth and wash the dishes; near-empty interiors, with little to distract the eye from the pristine walls and gleaming floors, aren't really empty, it's just that you can't see where all the accessories of daily life are kept hidden. The strict discipline required to provide storage space for absolutely everything, in such a fashion that cupboards and closets scarcely draw any attention to themselves but are elegantly integrated within the structure, is as great as the discipline required to keep it that way. A relatively high degree of expenditure is the necessary corollary of such perfection. But on the other hand, sharing your

living space with all your possessions out in the open is confusing to say the least. Cereal packets and cleaning products just don't offer the same visual delight as an array of crockery or glassware. Achieving a good, sympathetic balance between open and closed systems of storage enables you to relish the beauty of pleasing everyday objects without either descending to the most trivial level or banishing all evidence of human existence from your surroundings.

There's room for storage as display in almost every area of the home. In the kitchen, utensils and ingredients in constant demand make a practical and appetizing arrangement on open shelves or hanging from racking systems. People often overlook the potential of everyday display, the sort of organization evident in a bathroom shelf of shampoos and soaps or in a row of books. In the bedroom of her Venetian palazzo, the American heiress Peggy Guggenheim arranged a display of her favourite earrings, hung on the wall like miniature trophies. Such marriages of practicality with pleasure double the benefits.

TYPES OF STORAGE

Storage facilities come in all shapes and sizes, from bespoke cupboards tailored to the precise dimensions of what will be stored to a stack of labelled cardboard boxes in a workroom; from antique armoires to metal shop-rails. Whatever system you adopt, you need to balance precision with flexibility.

Make sure that the basic dimensions of what you need to store are comfortably accommodated – an obvious point, but it's surprising how often attempts are made to shove round pegs into square holes. The dimensions of mass-produced modular systems and storage units often reflect the exigencies of a manufacturing process to a greater degree than the shapes and sizes of what they are intended to house, which is why advertised versatility can be sadly lacking in practice. If necessary, you can customize interiors of standard units with racks, baskets, hooks or drawers to suit more specific storage requirements.

Another vital consideration is ease of use. Top shelves or cupboards should be accessible without having to clamber on to a chair to reach them and reserved for storing infrequently used and fairly lightweight items. Deep shelves above eye-level are inefficient, because you won't be able to see contents at a glance or rearrange them easily to reveal what is lurking at the back. Heavy objects are best stored at waist-height to prevent back strain when lifting. Independent light fittings for closets, deep cupboards and hallway shelving allow you to see what's inside more readily. If you are cramped for space, don't compromise valuable floor area with hinged cupboard doors that swing out – fit sliding or retractable doors instead.

The style and appearance of your storage should reflect the character of the room so the overall effect is well-considered. This is particularly relevant to shelving, one of the most adaptable and useful of storage arrangements, but often the least well-handled. Shelving is

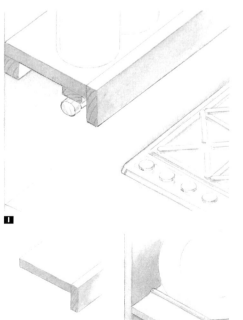

1

2   **3**   **4**

5

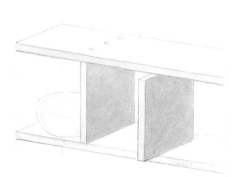

6

7

8

best treated almost architecturally, so that it appears to form part of the wall. One of the simplest ways is to paint it to match the wall colour and to attach a beading or lipping to the leading edges of the shelves to increase apparent solidity. In a room with period details, you can devise shelving to follow the horizontal wall breaks at dado and frieze height, with deeper shelves or closed cupboards forming a lower plinth and open shelves above – the classic proportions of a wide

range of traditional storage furniture, from dressers to china cupboards and secretaires. Lining an entire wall with shelves, including the areas surrounding doorways and windows, can also have great visual appeal, but you must take care to ensure there is adequate support. For built-in or bought storage units, try to match finishes, mouldings and accessories such as handles to those used elsewhere in the room to provide as much visual unity as possible.

9

10

6 Add interest to basic alcove shelving by adding dividers to form pigeon-holes.
7 Rather than filling a whole wall, you can nail together a simple box unit with shelves slotted in as required.
8 Economical and full of character, these cupboard fronts are robustly assembled from basic materials.
9 Wooden plate racks over a Belfast sink drain dishes dry.
10 The traditional dresser, with glass-fronted shelves, is a household standby.
11 Old commercial fittings such as these apothecary's drawers are irresistible to those with a hoarder's instinct.

11

Thinking laterally

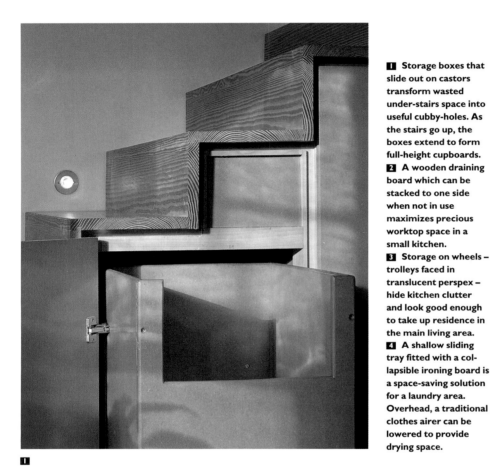

2

1 Storage boxes that slide out on castors transform wasted under-stairs space into useful cubby-holes. As the stairs go up, the boxes extend to form full-height cupboards.
2 A wooden draining board which can be stacked to one side when not in use maximizes precious worktop space in a small kitchen.
3 Storage on wheels – trolleys faced in translucent perspex – hide kitchen clutter and look good enough to take up residence in the main living area.
4 A shallow sliding tray fitted with a collapsible ironing board is a space-saving solution for a laundry area. Overhead, a traditional clothes airer can be lowered to provide drying space.

1

3

4

Adaptability is the secret of successful storage; make a sideways step and you can discover unconventional solutions which work brilliantly. Hi-tech style alerted many people to the potential of borrowing equipment and accessories designed for factories, offices and shops; if you aren't enamoured of the industrial aesthetic, you don't have to look that far for ideas, you should merely be prepared to consider different uses for fittings and fixtures from those for which they were originally intended. A plastic-coated wire mesh container may be on sale as a laundry bin, but if it turns out to be the ideal solution for storing rolled up drawings, then why not make use of it? You could import a vegetable trolley into the bathroom as a home for toiletries, or fill a log basket with a great many other things besides logs — from the children's toys to dirty laundry.

Lateral thinking also applies to finding new uses for traditional free-standing storage furniture. Chests, armoires, dressers, and cupboards are generally adaptable enough to house a wide range of items, not merely those which their makers first envisaged. Given a face-lift, there's no reason why an old bedroom chest of drawers shouldn't be put to use in the kitchen. Hat boxes can make a good home for needles, thread and other sewing equipment; neatly stacked shoeboxes can store a range of knick-knacks. Useful items to salvage or adapt include:
• Shop fittings, such as display cabinets, hanging rails, banks of drawers
• Wire mesh baskets, trolleys and bins
• Metal shelving originally designed for catering or industrial use
• School lockers and cupboards
• Filing cabinets, plan chests and other office storage systems.

5 In a kitchen, a compromise is often struck between squeezing in major appliances and allocating enough worktop and cabinet space. This ingenious solution takes the built-in oven and hob out of the equation by building them into a wooden framework that forms a piece of free-standing kitchen furniture. By incorporating work surfaces to either side, there is still somewhere to transfer pots and pans when the food is ready. The wall-hung spice rack and *batterie de cuisine* keep utensils and basic ingredients readily to hand.

5

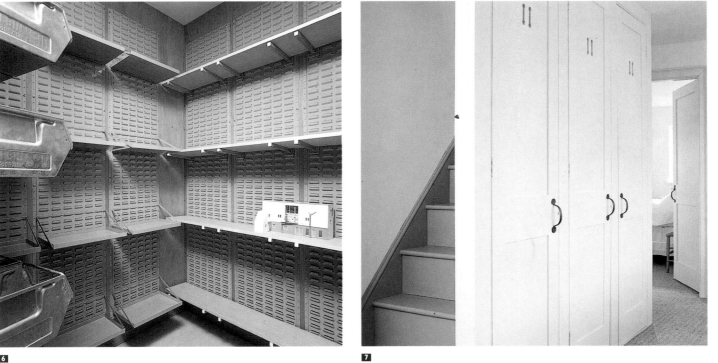

6

7

6 Ideal for fitting out a workshop or studio, this high-tech storage system with movable shelves and metal bins racked on to back plates – originally designed to store industrial components – can organize a vast amount of clutter.

7 What appears – from the landing – to be a wall of built-in wardrobes in fact hides the staircase up to an attic study. The 'wardrobe' doors do open, however, providing progressively greater storage space as the stairs behind rise. The far door conceals a full-height cupboard for hanging up coats and stowing away outdoor gear.

Walls shape our lives. Most of us live by house rules in rooms whose nature is dictated by their names. We sleep in the bedroom, we bathe in the bathroom, we cook in the kitchen. Yet, historically, the house has always been a fairly amorphous organism that changes in response to society. In the Middle Ages, domestic activity took place in one room, centred around the hearth (so much for open-plan being a modern concept). Two hundred years ago it was the done thing to receive company in your bedroom. One hundred years ago it would have been unthinkable not to have a dining-room. Times change; walls, metaphorically, dissolve.

The term 'living-room' disturbed the status quo when it first entered our vocabulary in the post-War era. Before the coining of this loose appellation, living-rooms were specifically defined in a way that clearly denoted their function and, at the same time, the status of their owner. At its crudest, the rich had drawing-rooms (literally a withdrawing-room) and the genteel poor had what was called a 'front room'. Both terms carried a certain hands-off, Sunday-best implication. 'Living-room' seemed better suited to a society that was becoming less class and gender bound. It had an egalitarian ring to it, though for many the lack of definition implied a freedom they could not cope with. Gradually, this strange concept of 'living' in, as opposed to merely inhabiting rooms, spread beyond the former drawing-room or front room to the kitchen. To have your decorating style described as the 'lived-in' look during the 1980s was the ultimate compliment: thus did a practical way of life become a stylistic conceit.

You and your home

1 Clearly a kitchen belonging to someone with nothing to hide. Shop-display cold-storage cabinets would not suit every lifestyle – but for anyone who does a minimum amount of cooking (or who chooses what they buy with great attention to the packaging) they make an interesting alternative to a conventional fridge.

2 An easy blend of comfort and style, with none of the artificial gloss associated with a stick-on lifestyle. The enormous cabinet copes with the clutter generated by multi-function rooms.

3 Uniformity is not always the right solution for a small bathroom. Here, using different materials has the effect of actually opening up the space, with the glass-firebrick wall and elegant curves of the roll-top bath providing a visual counterbalance to the solid MDF cabinetry.

1

2

4 Strong architecture makes its own decorative statement – interfere with it at your peril. In an interior where the beauty lies in the structure, keep fabric and fuss to a minimum: curtains at the window and drapes over the bed could have killed this bedroom.

5 The pure lines of a clean, modern space offer the perfect back-drop for different textures and styles: design classics and rustic antiques can be successfully mixed because both share the bond of simplicity.

3

4

5

Property booms, like those in the 1980s, have a detrimental effect on the quality of interiors; concepts of 'lifestyle' are culled from the pages of magazines with an eye to resale value. Instead of tailoring houses to personal preferences and a unique way of life, those with an eye for a quick profit respond by clipping on conservatories, building in kitchens and hanging swag curtains in every room. Nothing too individual is done while there is the spectre of 'other people's taste' foremost in the mind.

If anything good can be said to come from economic hardship, it has to be a rejection of these artificial values which accompany an inflated sense of wealth. People come down to earth, turning towards more natural materials – a

preference for rough textures over the slick gloss of boom consumerism. This 'new-age' attitude, combined with a return to the reality of a house being a home rather than an investment, should encourage us to look at our houses with a fresh eye and open mind, seeing rooms as areas of potential, sculpted around our individual lifestyles.

Comfort is a word we'll be hearing a lot more of in the future, and it doesn't necessarily mean plump armchairs and deep-pile carpets. It is what Witold Rybczynski calls 'domestic well-being' – something 'too important to be left to experts; it is... the business of the family and the individual'. As such, comfort goes way beyond the angle of a chair back or the wattage of a light-bulb.

At the beginning of the twentieth century books made much of the concept of 'homemaking'. Stripped of their servants, embarrassed by their naked ignorance as to quite how their houses functioned, the middle classes were forced to adapt to new lifestyles. And from the jaunty pioneering tones of some of the books, it was clearly an adventure they rather relished. Homemaking might have a deeply unfashionable ring about it today, but it may be that in mastering the art of shaping a home around our individual and family lifestyle, instead of trying to fit the glossy dictates of magazine and showroom within our own restricted walls, we will rediscover the power of domestic well-being.

First impressions

1

From a visual point of view, a home's exterior is felt by many of us to be low on the list of priorities. The money it takes to give the front of the house a lick of white paint could go quite a long way in the living-room. Given the choice between a new sofa or a smart façade, most of us would probably plump for the sofa. The longer you live with a shabby exterior, the less you realize it (until, that is, the day you notice it crumbling around you...).

For many reasons, then, the first impressions are often dealt with last. This is perfectly understandable, if short-sighted – you do, after all, spend more time inside, and from a purely selfish point of view it is passers-by and your neighbours who suffer from the visual assault if your house is the one in the street that looks like a rotten tooth in an otherwise gleaming smile. However, as soon as you begin to make improvements you see that it makes a disproportionate difference to the feel of your house: a freshly painted front door can give a tremendous lift to appearance, only you'll then notice just how shabby the door furniture looks.

Even something as simple as a row of geraniums up the front steps can have enormous impact on style. Other improvements may involve more thought and cost. You may, for example, need to claim the front garden back from the street by growing a hedge, or putting up a fence to give a sense of enclosure and privacy. Replacing flimsy wrought-iron gates with a solid, custom-built gate will add to the sense of this being personal space.

However, as with all changes to the façade. the whims of the individual must be balanced against the constraints of the public. Take into account both the architectural period of your house and its surroundings. A row of terraced houses can look pretty all painted in different colours if they share the same depth of tone – it's the bay window with bottle-glass panes that strikes the discordant note. In fact, there is probably no quicker way to devalue your house, both aesthetically and in terms of resale, than to mess around with original windows.

1 The British habit of giving their houses names instead of numbers – even if it is nothing more original than *Casa Nostra* – is considered to be a sign of affection for the concept of the home. A nicely detailed number, however, conveys the same sense of care with considerably more panache.
2 Not everybody feels the need to shrink anonymously into the urban fabric. Witness this house-cum-studio belonging to London artist, Andrew Logan: forged out of a former garage, it uses a terracotta render and vivid blue to give the building a strong identity that is neither domestic nor industrial.

2

3

3 The range of colours to these San Francisco houses gives them a greater harmony – the differences in detailing would be more obvious if they were all painted white.
4 In London, the same effect is achieved using similar intensities of different colours.

4

6

7

5

5 A long roof unites separate buildings that enclose that most magical of spaces, an internal courtyard. The real beauty of this building, apart from the spectacular location, is the appropriateness of the construction materials: built of timber, the house seems to grow naturally out of the environment.
6 A metal door suits the industrial aesthetic of this development.

8

10

7 Strong vernacular styles of building – such as the richly tiled façade of this house in Portugal – should be tampered with as little as possible.
9 The white stucco front of a London town house leaves only the front door as an area for experimentation.

9

8 An imaginative conversion of a mews garage has left the original garage doors in place.
10 When the seemingly commonplace doors are opened they reveal a stunning glass-fronted studio. Buildings which retain part of their past have charisma.

Halls and stairways

Entrance halls are important both from a symbolic and purely practical point of view. In a small house, getting rid of the hall to open up and enlarge the living space may seem like a good idea, but stepping straight from the street into the living-room is a psychologically uncomfortable experience. It may extend your floor space, but it deprives you of the ceremony of entry, that brief period of transition in which you shake off the outside before you can truly feel at ease in a house. It's almost as if coming straight in from the elements to the living-room is too much of a shock to the system, because you are denied that breathing-space in which to adapt

Because a hall is just such a breathing-space, it is best not to clog it up with clutter. If it is very narrow, even coat hooks, when fully loaded, can induce a feeling of claustrophobia. If it is wide enough for furniture but it is still very much a thoroughfare as opposed to a room, it is unlikely to feel comfortable as a space for sitting and relaxing but it may be a very good location for purely decorative pieces of furniture.

As an introduction to other rooms it is probably wise to stick with a simple decorative scheme. Fussy wallpapers and dark paintwork give a gloomy overbearing first impression. Light, neutral colours are best, particularly as the hallway is often chosen as a gallery space for a collection of pictures.

Floors need to be durable and washable: consider the period and character of your house before deciding on the material. Architectural salvage yards are a good source for authentic flooring, but beware of getting carried away. Mellow eighteenth-century Provençal tiles may be beautiful, but they will look totally out of place in a Victorian terraced house. Original encaustic tiles still exist in many Victorian hallways – if there are one or two missing from the pattern there are companies who have revived the method and can produce replacement tiles to order.

1 Barely-there balustrading gives a sense of space. Instead of using wood, many designers choose metal for stairway detailing – rigging wire from yachting chandlery specialists is particularly effective.
2 A sculptural stairway in wood and metal is graphic and strong.
3 If a hall is wide enough, a wall of cupboards is invaluable for storing coats and shoes. Solid doors would be too heavy – louvered panels, as here, work well.

1

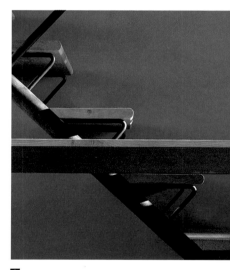

2

3

Bear in mind the material and colour of floor surfaces in the rooms which lead off the hall so that you can avoid any jarring contrasts. This is one obvious reason why the ever-popular black-and-white tiled floor never fails to look good, as long as you have got the size of tiles in proportion to the floor space.

In a house, the hall is usually dominated by the staircase, and this is often the first thing you and your visitors will see on entering. For most of us – living in standard spec-built Victorian or post-War houses – a staircase is simply a

4

5

6

place that leads up to one floor or down to another, and a lick of paint is about the most it ever receives in terms of decorative attention. But in modern, architect-designed homes the staircase often takes on a much more active part; accorded the status of something of an icon, its important role in linking different levels is given a sculptural form.

However, staircases that make a dramatic statement – which sweep into a room or suggest themselves as places to sit – are comparatively rare, and the potential to make something of the existing arrangement is limited unless you are having work done to other parts of your home. The average staircase is generally undistinguished rather than downright ugly, so beyond replacing missing banisters, it is probably simply a matter of deciding whether to strip, paint or French polish the wood.

As for stair treads, if they are in good condition and are of elegant proportion, it is a shame to hide them under fitted carpet. Bare treads, none the less, are noisy, so a good compromise is a runner. Matting is hard wearing and visually appealing, but avoid materials that are too tough and unyielding – they will be difficult to fit properly and are often scratchy under foot.

4 Conventional stairways use up a huge amount of floorspace: where this is restricted a spiral staircase is the obvious solution.
5 The hall is a linking space: vistas from it should be an integral part of the design.
6 Any horizontal surface becomes a natural dumping ground in the hall – a cunningly placed glass shelf prevents people hanging their coats on the art.

COOKING

'Woman's place is in the kitchen'. How absurd that sounds to us now, and how inflammatory such a remark would have been only twenty years ago. But it is only because 'woman's place' and the kitchen have been so closely associated during the twentieth century that the whole concept of the role of the kitchen and our feelings about it have so radically altered.

At the turn of the century the kitchen was not a place that one mentioned in polite society: it was considered very much as the bowels of the house, where – even in quite modest households – the servants presided. Most design books ignored it – provided a reliable stream of well-cooked meals emerged from it, no one really cared how it functioned as a room or what it looked like. But by the 1930s servants had disappeared from all but the richest households and the kitchen became the 'woman's place'. This did not mean, however, that overnight the kitchen suddenly became a haven of beauty and comfort; at this stage, the main priority was to turn it into a labour-saving room – the germ of the 'dream kitchen'. This was not just a matter of practicality, it was a question of dissociating the woman from the servant, the theory being that all sorts of clever machines would liberate women from housework. But whatever the theory, it didn't work in practice. 'The invention of the washing-machine has meant more washing, of the vacuum cleaner more cleaning, of new fuels and cooking equipment, more courses and more elaborately cooked food', wrote Hazel Kyrk perceptively, and prophetically, in 1933. What really emphasized the woman's position as surrogate servant was the kitchen's splendid isolation from the life of the rest of the house.

It is no coincidence that the shift of a woman's place in Western society, the gradual moving away from the house to an outside place of work, coincided with a complete change in attitude towards the kitchen. The pursuit of the dream kitchen has now been replaced by an almost emotional relationship with this room. When the kitchen stopped being a prison and became a place to which all members of the family gravitated – for meals, for company, for conversation – it made way for the equally pervasive, and equally clichéd, concept of the kitchen as 'the heart of the house'.

Cooking is a true celebration of the senses, a tactile, olfactory and visual feast before the finished dish hits the table and our tastebuds get to work. Getting the design and decoration of the cooking area right should allow the cook to enjoy the preparation as much as everyone else enjoys eating the food.

Living in the kitchen

1 The slick work-man-like lines of a compact fitted kitchen are softened by its relationship to the living-room.

1

2

Liberated from negative associations we are free to enjoy the kitchen as never before. Where once it was barely considered as a room, it is now felt by many to be quite the most important space in the whole house – a place where we are sustained both physically and emotionally. Although it is primarily functional, a place in which to cook, it is also, in practice, an informal living-room; in many ways it probably plays the role of the eighteenth- and nine-teenth-century morning-room where visitors were received in the daytime, so that its style and comfort are almost as important as its functional fit-out.

Our kitchens give out signals to other people, both about our character and our attitude to food. This may be only a stylistic front. Take, say, what can loosely be called the farmhouse kitchen, where a central table doubling as a work surface is the focus of a generally cosy-looking space – lined with cup-boards, shelves and perhaps a dresser – that conveys a welcoming air.

Undoubtedly, this look involves a certain amount of self-deception. There is something slightly ludicrous about the idea of a farmhouse kitchen in an urban environment, but this probably reflects a general escapism: the harder the outside world gets, the worse the economy, the bleaker the six o'clock news, the cosier the kitchen becomes.

If you take the farmhouse kitchen as your basic format or guiding inspira-tion, you should work with materials that are suited to your house. Fitted kitchens can disguise themselves as an ad hoc arrangement of cupboards which look back, stylistically, to a gentler age. A farmhouse kitchen does not have to be nostalgic. You can still follow the pattern that has proved to be the most practical and successful way of combin-ing general family life and cooking, but use ultra-modern furniture and fittings or a contrasting combination of old and new. The table does not have to be a scrubbed pine, antique refectory table; it could be glass, metal or laminate.

This ideal of a large, hospitable 'lived-in' kitchen depends on a generous allocation of space. If you try to cram farmhouse style into a poky modern room, the creature of your dreams who

3

4

5

6

2 A fresh colour scheme of blue and neutral injects vitality into this practical kitchen, where a butcher's block adds an extra work surface.

3 With its tiled walls and high ceilings, the old-fashioned air of this room is emphasized by the free-standing furniture. Roller blinds half way down the windows afford privacy without sacrificing light and ventilation.

4 A separate utility room means there is nothing to disrupt the tonal harmony of this studio kitchen, where colour and texture are aesthetically blended.

5 The message of the lived-in kitchen is that cooking is a pleasure. Attention is focused on display and presentation, with clever use of mirror in the elegant wall of shelving.

7

inhabits this space – the one who gets back from a hard day's work and starts calmly baking bread while four angelic children create brilliant collages on the kitchen table – is likely to end up screaming and burning the cakes.

If you have the space, then the most workable solution is what the French call *le living* – an open-plan area with cooking facilities and a table at one end, a chair or sofa, cupboard for the children's toys and the dog basket at the other.

But this is a look that needs to be done with conviction. Penny-pinching, badly planned kitchens which take up a corner of a square, carpeted living-room do not have the same atmosphere as *le living*. The classic architecture and planning textbook, *A Pattern Language*, sees in this half-hearted measure 'the hidden supposition that cooking is a chore and that eating is a pleasure. So long as this mentality rules... the conflict which existed in the isolated kitchen is still present.'

6 Last night's wine bottle and this morning's jams cohabiting on the table spell the ultimate Bohemian dream for some, nightmare squalor for others. Of course, it helps to have signs of faded grandeur: remove this scene to a small, one-room flat and it loses its charm somewhat.

7 Different ceiling heights and the use of units to break up space create areas with a defined sense of their own while retaining the open plan.

The self-contained kitchen

1 Where the kitchen
is small, it is best to
avoid fussy detailing.
Fitted appliances and
neatly stocked shelving
are enlivened by the
bold red door, which
hides most of the
kitchen from view
when it is not in use.

3

4

Naturally there will always be those who do not look upon cooking as a spectator sport and who prefer to practise their craft in solitary confinement. For these reclusive cooks and also for those who simply do not have the flexibility of space to allow for combined living and cooking areas, there may be no alternative to the small, but not necessarily isolated, kitchen.

Even if there is no room for anything other than functional essentials, the kitchen does not have to feel cut off from the lifeblood of the home. If it opens on to a corridor, a double door may make it seem less like a cell. Look at how the kitchen relates to the spaces around it – perhaps you can open up at least partially to the living-room.

Styles of cooking have some, but not a major, impact on design. Consider planning and efficiency before getting bogged down in matters of style. It is best to choose a fairly basic style of kitchen and then dress it accordingly. Be realistic, too, about your culinary expectations. Seductive as they may be, sophisticated pieces of equipment will not turn you into a brilliant chef. An unused kitchen has a dead feel to it, so if you see food as only a means to an end, you are likely to be far happier in a farmhouse-style kitchen than in a kitchen-as-laboratory which puts the spotlight on performance.

Of course good cooks do not need an ostentatious kitchen. Custom-made kitchens have become so sophisticated that we have tended to lose sight of the basics. Cooking only demands ingredients, heat, water, a sharp knife and a set of saucepans. But by the time you

2 Even the paintings
are free-standing in
this low-tech kitchen,
which gives a new slant
on twin ovens.
3 The hatch hits new
heights of sophistica-
tion in this 'machine
for cooking in', to mis-
quote Le Corbusier,
where the work
surface doubles as
breakfast bar.
4 A high counter
with shelves above
shields the kitchen
from the dining area.

5

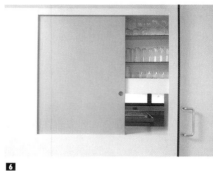

6

5 A high kitchen counter screens culinary clutter from general view.
6 A serving hatch can be closed off or open as convenience and sociability dictate, the perfect antidote to culinary claustrophobia.

7

8

9

7 Kitchens come alive as rooms when furniture, such as this grandfather clock, are used out of context.
8 The hard lines of a professional stainless-steel restaurant kitchen provide a good model for the compact domestic kitchen.
9 Where a galley kitchen extends off the main living-room a shared colour scheme works well.

have been through all the brochures, you can easily convince yourself that life simply isn't worth living without a wicker drawer for potatoes and a tin-lined one for organic waste.

If you are on a low budget, look for creative solutions rather than the cheapest thing on offer. You may find it works to buy a range of inexpensive self-assembly cupboards and replace the chipboard doors with ones made up by a local joiner. Painted tongue-and-groove, for example, can give you the custom-made look at a fraction of the price.

Kitchen planning

1

2

Good planning is the key to a successful kitchen, but don't be intimidated by its seemingly technical nature. Basically, planning is a question of assessing your requirements in terms of equipment and storage space, and balancing that against the architecture of the space you have available. There is no exact prescription because people's priorities are so different. One designer's clients living in the country were concerned that the fridge should be acoustically isolated so that its humming would not spoil their rural peace and quiet. Le Corbusier apparently thought it would be a good idea to put the kitchen at the top of the house to do away with the problem of cooking smells.

However, there are three fundamental factors in kitchen planning – where to site the sink, cooking facilities and fridge. Once you have established these it is relatively easy to design the kitchen in a logical fashion around them. Most kitchen designers base their plans on the 'work triangle', an imaginary line drawn between the three work centres of sink, hob and fridge. Ergonomically speaking no two centres should be more than a double arm span apart or so

close together as to cramp your movements. Individualists might balk at this prescription, but ergonomics is as much about common sense as it is about scientific precision. You may think it is no problem to walk from one end of the kitchen to the other to collect something from the fridge but repeating that sequence time and time again, day after day, year after year, will eventually wear down your resilience.

The siting of the sink is where you should start. Traditionally it is placed in front of a window. There is no law about this, and sometimes the layout of the room makes it impossible, but it does feel distinctly odd to stand in front of a sink without a view. And it makes sense to put the area of the kitchen where you are likely to spend most of your time nearest the source of natural light. If window space is unavailable, the next best thing is to have the sink facing outwards into the room – on an island, or peninsula layout. If none of these choices is feasible, at least try to avoid having cupboards above the sink; claustrophobic working conditions are certainly not going to increase the appeal of working there.

1 In this single-line kitchen, bulky cooking equipment is stored in the cupboards below the worktop, with ingredients neatly displayed above on glass shelves.
2 A combination of fitted and free-standing equipment allows for optimum flexibility in the layout of room, provided you have enough space. High-tech stainless steel appliances are moderated by the washed blue walls and the pink and yellow trim.

3
4

5

3 The classic L-shaped configuration, with a kitchen table providing an additional work surface.
4 Storage cabinets on castors are incredibly versatile. When not in use, this impressive kitchen is hidden away behind the wall of sliding doors.
5 In a large family kitchen, the island counter provides a breakfast bar, food-preparation surface and room divider all in one.

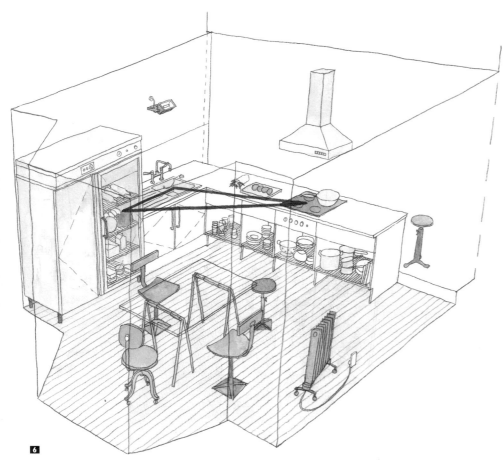

6

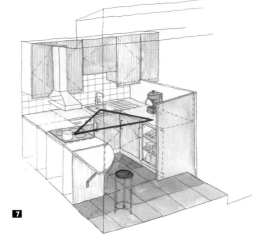

7

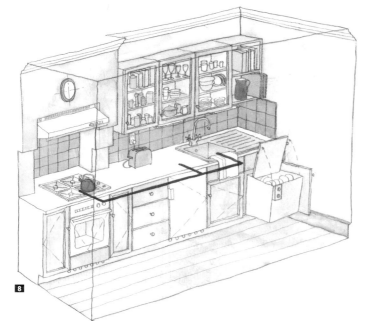

9 The galley kitchen is the most efficient use of space, with counters running along two par-allel walls. There should be a minimum 1200mm (48in) between facing units to allow easy access to under-counter cabinets.
10 The island kitchen requires plenty of floor space. Islands create a separate work area at the same time as open-ing up the kitchen. An island hob requires dedicated worktop ventilation or an extrac-tor hood.

8

For practical purposes dishwashers should be located near the sink. Siting of the oven is not so crucial; anyone with young children, and older people who want to avoid too much bending down, will probably choose an eye-level appli-ance. Don't choose a stranded position; you will need a surface close by for depositing hot dishes.

Disguising appliances as cupboards – the built-in look – is a hotly debated question of aesthetics. Many designers dislike the dishonesty of it, and put it on a par with hiding the television inside a fake antique cabinet. On the other hand a run of units, unbroken by knobs and dials, has a certain neatness. You can cel-ebrate technology by choosing appli-ances in stainless steel or gleaming enamel; or you can compromise – hide some, display others.

Portable appliances which are likely to stay permanently on the worktop must also be taken into consideration; toaster, microwave, food processor, espresso machine and kettle can soon eat up valu-able space. You also need to take the height of these into account when allow-ing for clearance between worktops and overhead cupboards.

6 The L-shaped kitchen allows ample space for a dining-table without interfering with the routes between the elements of the work triangle.
7 In a small U-shaped kitchen, a flap-down counter provides useful additional work space. Positioning the fridge at the end of a run allows easy general access to it.
8 The single-line kitchen works well in any room with a run of at least 3m (10ft). It should be carefully planned to provide as much worktop space as possible.

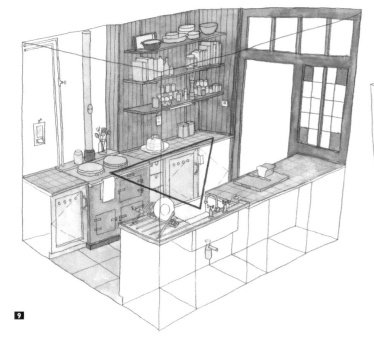

9

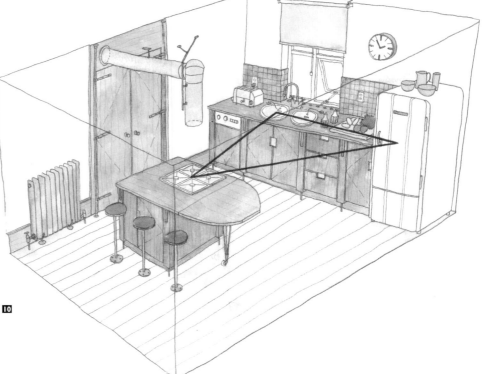

10

Storage space

1 A plate rack serves as vertical drainer and plate storage.
2 Open cupboards and wicker baskets are a cost-effective and stylish alternative to solid rows of doors in a large kitchen. Unsightly essentials are hidden behind a simple white curtain.

2

How much storage space do you need in a kitchen? The answer is probably much more than you think. There is no precise formula for calculating it, though there are those who measure their kitchen chattels and do complex mathematical calculations to determine the appropriate shelf area. Unfortunately, real life never fits happily into algebraic formulations. There is a standard height – 900mm (36in) – for kitchen units, but human beings rather inconveniently tend to come in non-standard heights. The American women at the beginning of the century who tried to extend principles of scientific management from the office to domestic use soon realized that. Although most houses could benefit from better planning and organization, it is neither possible – nor desirable – to iron out all domestic idiosyncrasy.

It is probably more helpful to group together all the different items you need to keep in the kitchen and plan their accommodation according to type and where they are needed. Are you going to keep saucepans in a cupboard beneath the hob, on a free-standing saucepan rack, or hanging from a suspended ceiling rack? What do you do with the lids? Cookery writer Anna del Conte keeps hers conveniently hanging from curtain wire on the backs of cupboard doors. Many French households rack the lids separately to save space.

Drawers will be needed for cutlery, tea towels and odds and ends. (At least one drawer will inevitably end up as the equivalent of a schoolboy's trouser pocket, where pieces of string and useful paraphernalia congregate.) Baking tins are best kept in capacious pull-out drawers, while trays and chopping boards need a handy vertical pocket of space somewhere. All these different requirements are catered for with great elegance by the smartest kitchen manufacturers. However, when it comes down to it, no one has ever improved on the basic storage options – cupboards, drawers, open shelves and racks. True,

1

the runners may not glide as smoothly, but a junk-shop chest of drawers will house cutlery, cake tins and children's toys just as effectively.

Open shelves require a high degree of visual discrimination: thick, Tuscan pottery bowls, yes; bags of flour, no. Similarly, glass-fronted cupboards have nostalgic appeal but require tidy owners who buy food with nice labels. There's a lot to be said for being able to close the door on a mess, not to mention hiding your taste in junk food.

Brooms, ironing-boards and other large, visually unappealing items need a tall cupboard, or, better still, an adjacent utility room where the boiler and washing-machine can be housed as well. Don't be tempted to sacrifice a utility room to the open-plan ideal: a washing-machine rumbling away in mid cycle adds nothing to the quality of life.

3

5

4

3 In this well-planned kitchen every possible corner is used as cupboard or shelf space.
4 High tech meets rustic: take inspiration from shop displays.
5 Custom-designed kitchens look efficient, but ad hoc solutions work equally well.

6 Accepted wisdom dictates that you should not build in front of windows, but if space is at a premium or the middle-distance view is not particularly life enhancing, try bending the rules. The strip of window across the bottom keeps claustrophobia at bay.

7 Windows and doors often preclude a straight run of cupboards. Here, an unglazed panel helps lighten, both literally and metaphorically, what might otherwise appear a rather heavy mass of cupboards.
8 Door furniture such as hinges and handles lend a distinguished look to even the simplest cabinets. Architectural ironmongers offer the greatest selection.

9 Alcoves either side of a chimney breast present an obvious location for cupboards: a skillful joiner has made this one a snug fit and matched the skirting board.
10 Shaker pegs, with their minimal styling, are at home in rustic and modern interiors.
11 Handy wine storage for those who prefer to drink now.
12 Tall sliding cupboards are convenient and space saving.
13 Mixing bowls are ideally kept close by the worktop.

EATING

The demise of the dining-room has been one of the most dramatic changes in the way we inhabit houses, and when we trace its death throes we see it goes hand in hand with the renaissance of the kitchen. The dining-room is not totally extinct; in grander houses, and more formal families, it would – even now – be unthinkable not to have a separate room for dining. But in most houses where there is space for one, the dining-room now doubles as a re-creation or work space.

Early in the twentieth century domestic wages and working conditions were generally so pitiful that even fairly modest households could afford at least one maid. For as long as there was no real alternative to domestic service, there was a ready supply of labour. But during and after the First World War, jobs for women in factories – with better salaries and shorter working hours – became available. Thereafter, those that remained in domestic service were in a stronger position to demand higher wages and regulated working conditions so that only the wealthiest people could afford to continue employing servants.

New books like *First Aid to the Servantless* and *The Servantless House* made housework seem like rather a jolly adventure and extolled the virtues of extraordinary cleaning machines like the 'Ukanusa Drudgee' and the 'Dreadnought' dishwasher. But when the first flush of enthusiasm had died down, people began to look much more seriously at the practicality of their houses. When servants had been taken for granted the kitchen was often positioned some distance from the dining-room. During the First World War many families – 'though respectability might hardly countenance it', wrote a shocked Randall Phillips in 1921 – were actually eating their meals in the kitchen. Having broached the subject Phillips goes on tentatively to suggest the idea of 'eliminating the sitting-room from the middle-class house and having instead one large living-room – large enough, indeed, to allow a dining-table to be set comfortably at one side of it, leaving plenty of space around for sitting, writing or reading.' The dining-room was not yet dead, but there were certainly signs of its mortal decline. Seventy-five years on the dining-room as a formal, monolithic space is probably only seen where old habits die hardest.

Eating is about more than just physical sustenance. Meals can be an intensely social occasion, a chance for family and friends to gather together. Whether the main eating room is the kitchen, living-room or a separate dining-room, we require the space to be relaxed, congenial and adaptable to various moods and occasions.

Formal dining

1 The most flexible dining-room is one that can be dressed up or down. Simple furniture and fresh sunny walls play down the sophistication of the chandelier by day.

1

2

3

Traditionalists may mourn the passing of the dining-room, but it was always something of a parvenu. In the eighteenth century the 'moveable feast' was a common practice; small tables were positioned in whichever room took one's fancy. In Europe, the dining-room was at its most firmly established in the second half of the nineteenth century, during which time it was ruled by a strict set of social customs and manners. Indeed, the unease which people feel at the loss of the dining-room is possibly more an expression of sadness at the demise of the etiquette that went with it.

The order imposed by eating in a formal dining-room still has adherents amongst those who believe there is a link between social breakdown and the TV dinner. Eating should be a social and life-enhancing activity, not just a refuelling process. In countries where the family unit is most secure, the notion of family meals eaten together around the table is almost sacred. The question is where should it take place?

Ideally, the setting for a meal should be as joyous as the sharing of it. One reason for the decline of the dining-room is probably that it rarely felt comfortable. Rooms which are not used much lose that sense of animation that comes from being lived in – they become dead space. In the case of the dining-room it was often also smelly space, the odours of the last meal clinging to the carpets and curtains. And its decoration reflected its unsure status – somewhere between a strictly functional room and a rather staid reception room.

For good reason the dining-room has never been very interesting to modern women; this, after all, was where, in less enlightened times, the strange practice took place of women retiring from the room after a meal to leave the gentlemen to their cigars. 'The whole appearance of the room ought to be that of masculine importance' wrote architect Robert Kerr with masculine importance in 1864. And even if the attitude changed over the next century the style that went with it did not. Hermann Muthesius noted that the dining-room was 'by long tradition . . . serious and dignified in character, its colour scheme dark rather than light, its furniture heavy and made of polished mahogany: it has a Turkish carpet on the floor and oil paintings, preferably family portraits, in heavy gilt frames on the walls'. The dismal room with dark green striped wallpaper and an intimidating, polished-mahogany table with a silver candelabra plonked in the middle is the enduring legacy of this look.

2 Formal dining no longer necessarily means a sit-down, knives-and-forks affair. When not in use for meals, this Japanese-inspired dining-room takes on a tranquil, meditative air.
3 Separate dining-rooms work well when the space relates to other rooms.
4 Your decoration will inevitably be influenced by your style of entertaining. Everything about this room – circular table, comfortable chairs and dog basket – invites expectations of cosy suppers rather than stiff dinner parties.

5 Bare wood has both aesthetic and practical advantages in an eating room: its warm tones provide a neutral setting for food, and it is easily kept clean.

4

5

6

6 The move away from soft furnishings in the dining-room has echoes of the 'purity and hygiene' movement at the beginning of this century. There are no curtains, carpets or upholstered chairs to retain lingering smells of food.

7 Few people any longer consider the sideboard to be an essential piece of furniture in the dining-room, as it was until the 1950s; but here a console table serves as a modern alternative. This dining-room benefits from a sense of animation and light coming in from the hallway beyond.

7

If you have the space, a dining-room can be a real luxury, though it should have some other function, doubling as a study or library, perhaps. Even if it is the place where children do their homework, it will benefit from the animation.

If you have a separate dining-room, you need to create some of the atmosphere that seeps quite naturally from the kitchen into the open-plan eating space – connotations of warmth and comfort that accompany the making of food. A dining-room with the table as a solitary focal point is a sterile kind of place; tables generally look depressing when bare, and debauched in the untidy aftermath of a meal. There is only a short period in between when they are at their optimum, so it is as well to have the focus of the room elsewhere. For this reason the dining-room doubles well as a library or print room.

The open plan

1

2

3

The open-plan kitchen is brilliant for rushed family breakfasts and relaxed suppers but it has one huge drawback – the formal entertaining side. It requires formidable powers of organization and tidiness to present an impressive three-course meal within the same space that you have produced it – particularly if the table doubles as a work surface.

In an ideal world, you would not have people around to dinner whom you felt it necessary to impress. But in real life it happens, and even the most relaxed among us feel the need to change tempo and have the kind of refined evening that demands something more exotic than pasta and candles in bottles. There is also the cynical but historically justi-fied view that perhaps the open plan is fashion-motivated, and that we shall all soon revert to more formal lifestyles.

Whatever the reasoning, it is sensible to make your eating spaces flexible. If you are restricted to eating in the kitchen this will largely be a matter of styling – replacing the muesli-splattered plastic cloth with white linen and dress-ing the table accordingly. Lighting is an essential factor in defining spaces and orchestrating mood. In *A Pattern Language*, Christopher Alexander advoc-ates a low-hung light, central to the

4

5

2 Varying the height of the ceiling and using different materials creates interesting pockets of space within an open-plan structure. A sunny enclosed verandah makes a perfect dining spot.
3 Use of a single colour brings unity to a small, open-plan area. It also helps to have dual-purpose seating: this table can be moved across to the built-in sofa at mealtimes.
4 An enclosed room works well within open-plan space only if it asserts itself boldly.
5 A worktop counter carves out space for the kitchen.

1 What a room gains in space from an open plan it can lose in intimacy. The natural inclination is to move table and chairs into an area with some sense of enclosure, such as under the sloping ceiling, as here.

6

table, with dark walls around so that the light acts as a focal, gathering point. In the farmhouse-style kitchen this has the added advantage of de-emphasizing the work surfaces and drawing the eye to the decorated table. The same effect can be created using modern, low-voltage downlights: position a narrow-beamed spot over the centre of the table with wide-beamed spots providing more general illumination. The ultimate, low-tech solution is soft, flattering candlelight.

In a room where there is only space for a large table with chairs drawn up to it, the transition from formal to informal is difficult to make. A room that is elegant by candlelight and perfectly suited for dinner can seem cold and uninviting at breakfast. Even when the kitchen is cramped, people instinctively gravitate there in the morning. In a large room it might be possible to create a more appropriate ambience by setting up a smaller table in an alcove or by a window that catches the morning light.

By using different flooring materials you can give some sense of demarcation to cooking and dining areas. It can work well, for example, to have the eating area fitted with wooden floorboards while the cooking and preparation space has some kind of tiled or stone floor.

7

8

6 A steel kitchen needs to be balanced with equally strong statements in the dining area. The false ceiling over the kitchen neatly conceals the workings of the lighting and ventilation, an essential consideration in open-plan layouts.
7 In an artist's studio the boundaries between work and relaxation are effortlessly blended.
8 Semi-open plan, where enough of the dividing wall remains to form a partition, may be more suitable in an older house. The exposed pipework adds to the charm.

Breaking down barriers

The serving hatch, which became popular in the 1930s, acted as both a physical and psychological breaking down of the barrier between kitchen and dining-room. It paved the way for the 'knocked-through' phenomenon of the 1960s, after which time the serving hatch was viewed as the ultimate in suburban naffness. It was too mediocre, too middle of the road – sneered at by those fashionable enough to have gone open-plan, and also by traditionalists who trudged the long way round from kitchen to dining-room on principle.

For most people today the kitchen-diner is the most practical use of space. Within the span of a few decades the idea of eating in the kitchen has gone from working-class necessity or bohemian eccentricity to the accepted norm. It suits our more informal but busy lifestyle: increasingly, people tend to issue carefully worded invitations to 'supper' rather than the more challenging and labour-intensive 'dinner party'. Even our food has undergone a change to accommodate the new eating habitat – somehow cordon bleu spectacles belong in the formal setting of a dining-room and the more relaxed style of peasant food is better suited to the kitchen.

Even at the height of the dining-room's popularity it was appreciated that different meals, or types of food, required different settings. The breakfast room has long existed as a corollary to the dining-room, although it is now becoming rarer as houses are smaller and people combine a breakfast room with the kitchen. There would seem to be no practical point in keeping a breakfast room as a separate room, though if it doubles in function as a study or as a playroom, some form of screening to allow a measure of privacy without obstructing the circulation flow might be useful. The obvious drawback with dual-function rooms is the constant interruption of activities and clearing of tables to make way for different uses of the room. Good organization and planning

enable different activities to coexist and this should be taken into consideration when choosing your furniture – the old-fashioned dresser, for example, is ideal for storing plates on the shelves while children's toys can be stuffed into the cupboard space beneath. A table with a large drawer is also useful.

Most of us do like to eat with a change of scene, at its most prosaic in front of the television. The question is, do we dignify the practice with some kind of permanent design solution? Possibly not, though would a couple of small tables by the sofa really be such an admission of guilt? Fortunately, there is no social stigma attached to eating outside. Even if the climate only makes this feasible for a few weeks each year, open-air eating is so pleasurable that it is worth the effort of staking out an area for that purpose. The chances are that you will be instinctively drawn to the right spot – somewhere that has some sense of enclosure, perhaps from a hedge, a trellis or an external wall. It is worth investing in solid, permanent outdoor furniture, particularly in a climate where good weather only comes in snatches and eating al fresco is likely to be spontaneous. If every time you consider having a coffee outside you have to go to the garden shed to retrieve a fold-up chair, you will very rarely go beyond the consideration stage.

1

2

3

1 The more loved – and lived-in – the kitchen the less obvious its primary function appears. Decorative objects with no culinary associations and pretty furniture which could happily house children's toys and baking tins create a room of irresistible charm.
2 A covered patio is the ideal spot for a summer barbecue.
3 If you can afford to sacrifice the under-counter space for a couple of stools, one side of an island unit can be commandeered as a breakfast bar.
4 All of the elegance of al fresco dining, with none of the risk.

4

5 Breakfast in bed is a languorous, self-indulgent luxury.
6 Eating outside is best in an enclosed spot, preferably somewhere close to the kitchen that receives the morning or evening sun. Foliage-green garden furniture looks unobtrusive, as does the tablecloth, which takes the lead from nature's colour scheme.
7 Where a kitchen is not big enough to take a full-scale dining-table, install a small table and a couple of chairs for cosy breakfasts or suppers *à deux*. The kitchen can be the perfect place for rationed television viewing, as it is not quite comfortable enough for all-out vegetation. Here the set has been cleverly incorporated into the overall design, not added as an untidy afterthought.
8 A convenient spot for casual meals, with the window acting as a serving hatch.
9 Cooking outdoors satisfies a primitive instinct in even the most sophisticated among us.

5

6

7

8

9

Furnishing

1 Mix-and-match
Arne Jacobsen chairs,
designed in the 1950s
but having found their
true niche in the '90s,
bring a splash of con-
temporary colour to
an open-plan kitchen
and eating area.

2 An eating alcove,
with a custom-built
bench and cantilevered
seating, makes effect-
ive use of a small space.
3 In our less formal
society, matching sets
of dining-chairs are no
longer *de rigeur*: in fact,
they can look positively
overbearing. Complete
sets of chairs, with
carvers, can cost a
fortune, whereas you
can buy odd pairs of
chairs quite cheaply.
From a psychological
point of view, dinner
guests may feel under
less pressure to con-
form when seated on
mismatched chairs.

The trend when furnishing eating rooms
tends to fall into two distinct categories
– humble in the kitchen and monumen-
tal in the dining-room. Even the most
unlikely people choose rich wood or its
simulation for dining-rooms. In the
kitchen, old chairs are chosen because
they are cheap and suitably rugged for
family use, if not the height of comfort.

This doesn't have to be the rule.
Going up the scale halfway in price and
comfort, the armless dining-chair with
tall back and upholstered seat is good
for its elegance in the dining-room or for
dressing down with simple slip-covers to
protect against accidents in the kitchen.
If space is tight then folding chairs are a
practical solution – instead of chairs left

getting in the way around the table,
they can be folded away in a cupboard;
or you could adopt the Shaker solution,
hanging ordinary chairs from a peg rail.

The shape and position of the dining-
table is another vexed issue. A round
table is considered more sociable and
democratic than a rectangular one:
there is no 'head' of the table and therefore no need for power-statement chairs
with arms. This arrangement fits with
the opinion of Archbishop Grantly in
Anthony Trollope's *Barchester Towers*
that 'there was something democratic
and parvenu in a round table'. But if
you are catering for six or more people,
the proportions of a large rectangular
table are easier to live with than those

1

2

4 Gravitating
towards the light of
the French windows,
the positioning of this
dining-table frees up
the rest of the room
for other purposes.
The directors' chair is
immensely versatile: it
can be used inside or
outside, and folded
away when not in use.
However, it is not a
long-term solution:
after a year or two
they tend to look the
worse for wear.
5 Curved chairs have
been cleverly designed
to fit a round table.

3

4

5

6 Simple slip covers can transform directors' chairs into something more ceremonial, and they have the advantage of being washable. **7** Bentwood chairs have been fashionable since Le Corbusier controversially used the traditional restaurant chair in a domestic setting.

6

7

of a large round table. Most tables now incorporate ingenious leaves to tailor their size to the number of diners and make them compact when not in use. If your dining-table doubles as a play surface for small children there is no point in letting them practise their artistic skills on a wonderful piece of designer craftsmanship. Make do with a practical laminate or junk-shop table – no one need know what lies beneath the white damask when it comes to entertaining.

There is an accepted convention that the centre of the room is the right place for the table – and for fairly compelling reasons. The wall space is freed for other uses and, in a kitchen, the centred table can serve as an island work surface. If, however, the room is so small as to impede circulation around the table, it is better to have the table close to a wall, which will also enable you to make use of bench seating on one side.

Contrasts of style work very well in a kitchen dining area. A bland backdrop of modern kitchen units can be lifted by an old, characterful table. And while good modern lighting is essential for work surfaces, an antique chandelier, by being taken out of context, adds surreal glamour to an earthy kitchen.

RELAXING

Even the best modern designers and architects have a problem with their living-rooms. Closely allied to the dictate that form should follow function they are happiest designing bathrooms and kitchens because both have a clear function. But what is living – relaxing with a book, sprawling in front of the television, thinking, dreaming, talking, loving, playing with the kids? It is difficult to express this with only four walls and a three-piece suite, particularly when you add the desire for some kind of individual style, an expression of personality. Moreover, this problem is partly restricted to modern society. In previous eras living-rooms were subdivided and given spurious functions. There was the morning-room where the lady of the house would spend her mornings, receiving company or perhaps writing letters. There might have been a parlour or sitting-room reserved for the afternoons. The drawing-room was for more formal occasions – for withdrawing into after supper or for entertaining company too grand for the morning-room. When living was such a circumscribed affair, the decoration of these rooms was probably an easier task.

Today most of us view home as a place to which we retreat, a sanctuary from the stresses of working life. In fact, as Adrian Forty has pointed out, individualism in decoration is strongly linked to the growth of industrial society. For those who are subjugated at work, a style statement at home becomes 'a sign of being capable of independent thought and emotion, of having a life apart from the mill-wheels of the economy.'

The living-room should be a place where we feel totally at ease – a temple of the soul. It will also be a place in which other people can feel relaxed, too. However, the desire to impress others, tempting though it may be, should never override personal style and comfort. Whether you express yourself in white walls and architect-designed chrome and leather, wall-to-wall carpet and flouncy chintz, or bare boards and distressed antiques, the true test of the success of such a room is whether or not you choose to spend time there. If you retreat to the bedroom or kitchen instead, then something has gone badly wrong. Perhaps it is a showroom or a dead area? It certainly is not, in the fullest sense of the word, a living-room.

Relaxing, whether alone or with family and friends, is an essential antidote to daily stress. From a quiet corner where we can curl up with a book to a place where we can entertain friends, our living spaces need to be flexible, personal and, above all else, comfortable.

Setting the style

1

2

Adhering to a preconceived, self-conscious style is the very antithesis of relaxing. If you take comfort as your base point, and let the style evolve naturally from what you feel comfortable with, you are more likely to end up with a look that inherently 'gels'. Whereas if you set out with the aim of reproducing a 1950's living-room or the American colonial look, it will always have a forced air to it.

As Edward Gregory wrote in 1925, 'a really interesting drawing-room is very rarely perfect in style.' Gregory castigated rooms decorated in the 'painfully proper' style of Louis XV: 'You cannot walk into them yourself without shyly glancing in the mirrors and feeling that you are an anachronism. . . Yet the room is in most delightful taste. You cannot find fault with it. You only feel just a little bored and rather overcome.'

Anyone who has sat in some fogeyish room that looks like a museum will know what Gregory means. A room that forces you to behave out of character, that inhibits your actions or your dress may be a dazzling example of period accuracy, but if style hijacks comfort it can never be considered a success. On the other hand, at least the fogey's room is usually done with some passion. Too often people choose what

1 A stylishly eclectic room pays due attention to the vaulted ceiling and unusual proportions without taking them as a stylistic lead for decoration and furnishing.
2 A restricted colour scheme gives this elegantly constructed room a restful air.
3 Rooms need not be all of a period: this one is unified by a love of art: from 1950s chairs to a collection of turn-of-the-century vases.

3

they consider to be the 'modern' look – usually dating from the 1930s – because they believe it delivers effect for very little effort. Paint the walls white, add a large photographer's light and a black, leather Eileen Gray armchair and finish with an abstract rug – a Modernist's room, totally devoid of feeling.

There is no reason why you shouldn't indulge a certain style of decorating. But if you can discern which elements of the style appeal to you, and adapt those to your own way of life, you are more likely to be successful than if you try to fit the style into an environment for which it was never intended.

A living-room is more than just an assemblage of objects – it needs some sort of foundation. This is not to be confused with giving a 'theme' to a room. Look at the space you have, commune with its architecture and work with it instead of trying to superimpose flimsy notions of decorative style. You need to work out what it is you want from the room – whether you want it to be warm and cosy or light and airy, a day-time or a night-time space. It is no use adopting someone else's style from a magazine because you probably have different needs and priorities. By all means take inspiration from books,

5 Cosy rooms do not have to be small, dark and cluttered. The symmetry and ordered neatness of this room does not impose a stiff formality on its occupants: window-ledge seats and cushions invite a casual, relaxed way of life.
6 Comfort is not an abiding priority for everyone: this room is an ode to '50s design, each piece existing in spectacular isolation, and yet drawn together by the obvious passion that lies behind them.
7 Cross-cultural influences are more effective than attempts to recreate a particular national style, as in this cool Western interpretation of Asian design.
8 In some cases, interiors are led by the outside environment. The cool white and blue of this beach house are an obvious response to the view, while slatted furniture is a perfect complement to the climate.

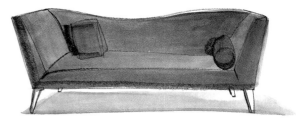

4 When work is an all-embracing obsession it can enhance – rather than intrude upon – the living-room. In this living-room cum studio, the work of an artist is complemented by the comfortable curves of the furniture.

4

5

6

7

8

magazines, fabrics, paintings, museums and other houses, but do not use these as the starting point. The foundation from which you must always begin is your own lifestyle, an honest appraisal of your needs. Taking style as your foundation will always result in a room that has a kind of emptiness to it.

Gregory was very good at defining what it is that makes rooms which are in 'perfect taste' so peculiarly unsatisfying to be in. 'The fact is,' he wrote 'that there is nothing in sight which suggests an idea; nothing which sets one's wits working, or stimulates an entertaining train of thought.'

A calm retreat

1

For social relaxation the drawing-room lives on in spirit if not in name. Today, perhaps, we make the mistake of equating relaxation with mess and clutter – wading through plastic toys and dolls in order to clear a place on the sofa. In fact it is incredibly stressful not to have somewhere calm and peaceful to retreat to. Houses need to be able to accommodate changes of mood and at least one room, particularly in a raucous, family household, should supply this need.

Having child-free zones tends to smack of Victorian values – Muthesius noted that 'children are on the whole not allowed into the drawing-room except as visitors in their best clothes.' It needn't be the children who are excluded, just the detritus that goes with them. Children are just as capable of appreciating the different moods of different rooms as are adults – and it's a good opportunity to instill in them an appreciation of finely made pieces. If they have adequate space to play elsewhere then the living-room can become the special place where they have a bedtime story or for quiet times – perhaps

2

3

4

1 In Victorian times it was common practice to change curtains and loose covers twice a year as the dark, heavy upholstery which contributed to a cosy warmth in winter could feel stifling in summer. A cheaper modern equivalent is to use dust sheets which, apart from the practical application of hiding ugly upholstery, give rooms an ethereal, floating quality.
2 Our concepts of comfort have changed radically over the last few decades. Many people feel more comfortable with sparse elegance than wall-to-wall carpet and overstuffed chairs.

5

6

3 Most people do not have unerring, one-dimensional taste that they apply throughout their homes. They like different things to suit their different moods, and so will feel most relaxed in rooms that reflect different facets of their taste. Bold and comfortable, this room has both cosiness and coolness, antiquity and modernity, meshed together in the general ambience of relaxation that comes from its owners' confidence in their own taste.

4 The drawing-room traditionally pays homage to the notion of social relaxation, and is laid out in the classical configuration of chairs and sofas drawn up to each other to facilitate easy conversation. Here, a chair and footstool turn their back on company to allow a bit of solitary communion with the view.

5 A tranquil room, unfettered by any needs other than somewhere comfortable to sit and something beautiful to look at. No colours are better suited to express the feeling of calm, unhurried living than white and cream.

6 Port-hole windows, white walls and a couple of sofas and an armchair contribute an understated calm.

7 In holiday houses and weekend cottages decoration is best left underdone: improvization, with cheap but striking fabrics, is both more effective and appropriate than full-scale, overblown decorative schemes.

7

for watching television. If, however, the living-room has to double as playroom and family room, then make sure there is a large basket or chest into which all the toys can be thrown when it's time for the room to make the transition to grown-up space.

Criticisms of the formal living-room voiced down the century are that its decoration reflects what goes on there, that somehow the triviality of conversation seeped through to the furnishings. 'It [the drawing-room] has the least style of all the rooms', was Muthesius's verdict at the beginning of the century. He felt it suffered 'from having too many odds and ends packed into it and the deliberate informality all too often degenerates into confusion.' Edward Gregory, however, felt obliged to defend it from 'reformers' who believed the drawing-room encouraged snobbish ostentation: 'They point out that a house is to live in, not to pose in, perhaps forgetting or ignoring the fact that it is just as easy for the superior person to tilt the nose while wearing homespun garments and occupying an arts-and-crafts "houseplace" as to condescend in conventional evening dress surrounded by the decorative accessories of a drawing-room.' Gregory's argument was that even if the drawing-room did lead to 'an artificial, self-conscious propriety', at least such a room 'prevents the household degenerating into slovenliness, which is even worse.'

Gregory's words may now ring rather severely, but they are worth thinking about. Today we are altogether more circumspect in our criticism of others' taste but it remains true that environment affects behaviour to a profound, usually subconscious, degree. Certain living-rooms – those that are a spontaneous expression of the owner's taste and personality – instantly put you at ease, while others – perhaps because the seating is wrong, perhaps because the room is living a lie – make you feel awkward and uncomfortable.

Comfort

1

3

2

Making comfort the priority for your living space is neither as obvious, nor as simple, as it might appear. Physical comfort – somewhere soft to put your bottom, somewhere supportive to lean your back – is a comparatively modern concern. It did not really figure in domestic life until the eighteenth century; until then, home was not much more than shelter for the poor, while for the rich it was a means of conveying status.

When we talk about comfort now, we don't just mean a physical sensation; it has a much wider definition which takes in a range of sensory satisfactions. Comfort, as Witold Rybczynski has pointed out, is multi-layered: it involves 'convenience, efficiency, leisure, ease, pleasure, domesticity, intimacy and privacy – all of which contribute to the experience.' Today, comfort, wholesomeness and honesty are packaged as a fashion commodity and labelled 'natural', hence the wool throw for the sofa, the seagrass matting for the floor, the beeswax candles for the mantelpiece.

1 When the interior architecture of a space is as spectacular as this, it is wrong to try to cover it over with the conventions of comfort like curtains. Heavy, dark furniture would have weighed the place down, whereas the white sofa and chair with the checked rug echoing the small square window panes keep the visual flow of the space perfectly balanced.
2 Another space in which the decoration is a response to the architecture. The sloping walls and beamed ceilings are complemented by the simple, unpretentious furniture and fittings.

4

5

5 Tall ceilings can
make a room seem
austere. Here, the
sociable seating
arrangement gives
intimacy, while the
indoor tree breaks up
the distance between
chairs and ceiling and
provides a point of
focus as an alternative
to the fireplace.

6

3 A room where,
apart from the chair,
comfort is probably
more visual than
physical. Nothing jars
the eye in this natural
colour scheme.
4 Comfort and order
are not mutually
exclusive as this snug
but stylish living-room
proves. Yellow makes
a perfect background
for the warm, earthy
tones and green
accents of the confident
colour scheme. The
ladder leads up to a
mezzanine level.

It is difficult to predict what is going
to make you feel comfortable – especially
since you may know what you like without knowing why. People recognize
comfort when they experience it.
Rybczynski says that 'this recognition
involves a combination of sensations –
many of them subconscious – and not
only physical, but also emotional as well
as intellectual...' Given that comfort is a
multi-layered thing, it is probably best
to start with the most tangible layer –
physical comfort. Establishing your
needs in this sphere gives you a good
foundation on which to build.

7

The essentials are warmth and light.
In planning where to site radiators, you
need to take into account architectural
and functional considerations, but you
must also have some idea of seating
arrangements. If you put radiators
against walls where you are likely to
want to place sofas, the heat will be
wasted. Under windows is ideal because
the warm air, hitting the cold coming
from the window, is well circulated.
However, from the point of view of
light, this is also a good place for a sofa.

Lighting is fundamental to comfort.
The need to alter it according to mood
and the time of day corresponds to
human physiology as well as to the biological clock. In a living-room you need
general, ambient light, topped up with
task and spot lighting. A low-voltage
lighting scheme requires professional
installation, but the flexibility it offers
is worth the expense. If you are stuck
with a central pendant light fixing, at
least fit a dimmer switch, which will
allow you some mood changes.

6 The human instinct
to gravitate towards a
fire is supplemented in
this room by the pro-
vision of seating ledges
which, semi-enclosed,
give a sense of security,
the perfect place to
curl up with a book.
7 A room at ease
with itself and the
environment, its palette
of natural colours and
materials blending
seamlessly with the
landscape outside.

Seating

Seating affects behaviour. You can see the truth of this in any waiting-room with its hard, straight-backed chairs set in rows against the wall which force you into an alert, expectant posture while discouraging socialization. Historically the design and placing of chairs has been determined by the mood of society. Sitting only became a recreational pursuit (as opposed to a statement of authority or a means to an end) in the more leisurely eighteenth century when many different types of upholstered furniture were designed.

The grouping of chairs to aid conversation was something of a social skill in the eighteenth century. Mark Girouard details the 'formal circle' arrangement in *Life in the English Country House*. Maria Edgeworth describes this as 'of all the figures in nature or art . . . universally the most obnoxious to conversation' in a contemporary novel. This circular grouping reigned supreme until about 1780 when a more informal grouping to accommodate different clusters of people found favour.

1 A huge, deep sofa is the epitome of luxury if you have the space to take it. Socially, however, it only works if the company is relaxed enough with each other to sprawl across it. Perching on the edge of a large sofa intensifies any feeling of unease and discomfort.
2 Versatility is a key consideration of seating arrangements: a cool grouping of designer classics is the perfect accompaniment to the bare architectural lines of this space, but a stone ledge for display can be commandeered for extra seating when entertaining large numbers of people.

Girouard quotes a wonderful description by Fanny Burney of being entertained in the 'new style' by an anxious hostess. 'When some other guests came in and instinctively started to form the traditional grouping of chairs, the hostess exclaimed: "My whole care is to prevent a circle," and, hastily rising, she pulled about the chairs, and planted the people in groups with as dextrous disorder as you would desire to see.'

Today we are rather less artful in our social manipulation but most people instinctively arrange furniture so as to facilitate conversation and make others feel at ease. Grouping sofas and chairs loosely around a focal point such as the fireplace works well – as long as you remember that in a social situation a sofa never pulls its full weight. Unless you are on intimate

3 The success of this banquette seat lies in its organic curves which make it both visually and physically comfortable.

4

4 With such striking upholstery, these sofas need to keep their distance, but are linked by matching side tables.
5 In a fairly confined space, two small sofas may work better than one sofa and a couple of chairs.

6 Modern sofas come in all shapes and sizes, not necessarily with arms and a back. Such sculptural seating works well in a contemporary interior.
7 Cushions and throws add exoticism to plain sofas.

5

6

terms, a two-seater sofa will only accommodate one person who can then spread; two people sitting side by side are forced into a formal pose. Similarly, even a large three-seater is awkward for any more than two. In conversation people like to turn their whole bodies towards each other and furniture should not inhibit body language. There can be something too confrontational about two sofas facing each other.

Furniture can also be used to 'zone' areas of the room for different types of activity. For example, if you have a television in the room, don't arrange the seating in such a way that everyone is forced to watch it. If the television is set up in a corner in front of a sofa or chairs it should be possible to make another grouping of seats that relate to each other to facilitate conversation or for solitary occupations such as reading.

A mixture of sofas and armchairs is good both visually and psychologically. The combination breaks up the space of a room in an interesting way and allows for differences in sitting style – upright and more sprawling – in addition to permitting different levels of intimacy. If you are entertaining an insurance assessor you would probably prefer not to have to chum up on the sofa. On the other hand, a room with only single chairs can seem rather unfriendly and distinctly formal.

The tyranny of the three-piece suite, however, is probably over. Its smug respectability hampers the flexibility of a room, and does not sit well with the new informality. A mixture of seating – the strict, clean lines of a modern sofa, perhaps, set against the voluptuous curves of an antique chair – can lend a stylistic signature to the whole room.

7

Recreation

When the television first became widely available, nobody tried to conceal the fact that they had one. The television took pride of place in the living-room, an icon of a new age, and less fortunate friends and neighbours – without a set of their own – were invited round specifically to watch it. The change from black-and-white to colour broadcasting simply reinforced its standing as a status symbol. If the set was housed in an elegant wooden cabinet, this was not so much to hide it as to honour it. In most Western households television became a kind of altar, a place of honour – until the advent of 24-hour broadcasting.

Today the question of where to put the set is not so simple, bound up as it is with increasingly ambivalent feelings: perhaps we watch it a lot, but wish that we didn't; maybe we watch it but don't want other people to know that we do; maybe we watch it so seldom that we don't want it dominating the room.

Where the television is sited affects your viewing habits so it is best to start from a considered position. Now that many homes have more than one television, and it is turned on rather as a radio used to be, the television is an appliance that needs to be integrated into the room so that viewing is comfortable but the set does not unduly dominate. For passive viewing while getting on with household chores, it might be better to fix the television to a bracket on the kitchen wall or to buy a miniature portable set.

Hiding the television need not be furtive or dishonest: it is quite a good means of restricting yourself only to programmes you genuinely want to watch. Free-standing television cabinets have a bad image; they are expensive and pretend to be something they are not. It is probably better to find a well-designed television set.

Fortunately music systems come without any cultural hang-ups and value judgements, and as most modern hi-fi systems are neat and compact, they rarely cause too much visual disturbance. For a state-of-the-art sound system – speakers in every room, for example – it is probably best to consult a specialist retailer.

You may survive happily without a stereo or television but a living-room without books or pictures is a barren place. A few purist souls consider books too untidy and hide them in cupboards or remove all the dust jackets so that the colours don't jar. But a lot more common is the 'displayed reading' style with books used as decorative objects – a forgivable conceit, really, when books are visually so luscious.

1 A less furtive alternative to hiding the television completely is to use sliding screens which, when closed, give the room a clean, uncluttered look.
3 Is the television, after all, such a visually contemptible object? As a plain, black square, it is no less offensive than a hole-in-the-wall fireplace, and it does not appear incongruous set between the pile of logs and display of ethnic baskets in this room.

2 The solution favoured by those of the 'honesty' school of design is to bare all. The living-room and bedroom televisions here are unashamedly displayed, while the downstairs set is even flanked by candlesticks as if it were a modern-day altar.

4 In ultra-modern interiors, too much new technology can look like a parody of itself, or overly osten-tatious: this is an artful blend of high and low tech, with its modest floor cushions and old-fashioned telephone.

4

5

5 With studio living there is no room to be discreet about tele-vision viewing: when your bed-making technique is on full view, why worry about hiding the speakers? In fact, this style perfectly suits the stripped-back archi-tecture of the room.
6 Recreational icons: why should only vases of flowers and works of art be viewed as suitable objects to display, when some people may feel just as passionate, if not more so, about their bicycle or electric guitar?

6

Storing and display

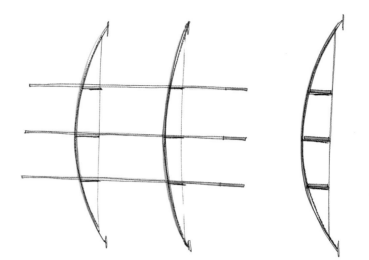

A room that is used primarily for relaxation may not be as strictly 'functional' as the kitchen or bathroom but it is not enough just to think of a living-room in terms of somewhere to sit. Relaxation generates clutter as surely as cooking or playing. Think of flopping down in a chair to read a newspaper – you need somewhere for your coffee cup, wine glass or papers. Surfaces for putting things on are often overlooked and a room can be uncomfortable without them, as anyone who has sat rigidly clutching a glass, not daring to put it on the floor, will know. Unfortunately, occasional tables conjure up visions of gentility – the once-ubiquitous 'nest of tables'. A blanket box can do just as well and double as storage.

Those with minimalist inclinations need more cupboard space for storing videos, compact discs, drinks, games, sewing things and all the odds and ends that tend to accumulate. The problem is that wall space is already punctuated by doors, windows, radiators and sofas. Often the obvious place to build cupboards is either side of a chimney breast but recesses need to be deep enough so that the cupboards don't jut out too far. You may find it works better to have base cupboards to about dado height and then build shelves above them. Have the best joinery you can afford in the living-room, though you can add wooden beading or scalloped leather library edging to customize ordinary

chipboard shelves. Upholstering less than perfect shelving in felt is quicker than making good with filler and paint. Metal industrial shelving looks effective if the rest of the room is in roughly the same idiom, though it can seem uncomfortably out of place with wall-to-wall carpet and homely loose covers. Glass shelves work best when displaying rough or rustic objects as a contrast. Anything too precious starts to look sterile. The danger with any collection is that the room can be made to feel like a self-conscious exhibition space.

Unbroken rows of books are good for absorbing sound but sometimes make a room feel oppressive and claustrophobic. Punctuating blocks of books with vases, small pictures and favourite objects can counteract this. When locating shelves, look at less obvious spots – above doors or between windows where the window dressing is not expansive, for example. Short sections of shelving, placed high and seemingly erratically around the walls, can be particularly effective – and childproof – for displaying special objects.

1 It is worth having a selection of glass vases in different shapes and sizes. They make less of a decorative statement than ceramic vases and are therefore easier to mix with a variety of styles.
2 Etched-glass room dividers separate the living area from a display of antiquarian objects, perhaps in the belief that overexposure dulls the senses, that tantalizing glimpses of beauty are more powerful.
3 Walls can hang a variety of objects, not just paintings. This asymmetrical arrangement around the fireplace is balanced by the giant cactus.

4

5

4 A wall of low-level cupboards provides a useful surface for decorative display. But beware the temptation to allow it to degenerate in to a general dumping ground.
5 The chest of drawers, a staple of every junk shop, is one of the most useful pieces of furniture you can buy.

7 Whenever television programme-makers want to suggest that the subject they are interviewing is intelligent, they film the person against a background of books. By that reckoning, the owner of this splendid wall of books must be immensely clever, but also something of an aesthete judging by the artful interjection of birds' nests and the display of old-fashioned washboards. Some people find the use of books as decorative space fillers morally reprehensible, but books have always been valued for their beauty. Buying fake book spines by the yard (though not necessarily any less honest than shelves full of unread books) is no alternative, because the visual pleasure of books is in the mixture of their sizes, colours and textures.

6

6 Shelves add drama and definition to a doorway, but should not be filled half-heartedly. Ideally, they should evolve naturally over the years, with things added as they accumulate. Die-hard minimalists can get away with bare shelves, or one or two seminal objects, but when you are desperately trying to fill space for the sake of it, it shows.
8 Well-seasoned shelves framing the view through a door are packed with books, magazines and curios.

7

8

Focal points

A room without a focal point is a strangely disconcerting one. There may be warmth, light and a comfortable place to sit, but without a feature to which all eyes instinctively turn in moments of repose it will never be a room in which people feel really at ease.

Traditionally the focal point is the fireplace, which has never really been ousted from its position as 'hearth' or heart of the home. Staring into the flames of a fire is a universal, primeval satisfaction; it elicits identical behaviour from young and old alike. It is as if the fire puts us in touch with our most primitive, instinctual nature.

An open fire is surely the ultimate comfort. Many people opt for the convenience of a 'real' gas fire which gives instant warmth and saves you having to clean out the ashes next morning, but it cannot compare with the multi-sensory pleasure of a coal or wood fire. A fire without companionable sound is a fire that warms the room but not the soul.

Muthesius recognized the significance of the fireplace to the English. 'All ideas of domestic comfort,' he wrote 'of family happiness, of inward-looking personal life, of spiritual well-being centre round the fireplace. The fire as the symbol of home is...the central idea both of the living-room and of the whole house; the fireplace is the domestic altar before which, daily and hourly, [the Englishman] sacrifices the household gods. . . To remove the fireplace from the home would be like removing the soul from the body.'

Perhaps this is why, even when the chimney has been boarded up and the fireplace has been made redundant, people like to keep it as an architectural feature, filled with a basket of dried flowers or a paper fan. While this has to be better than a hole plugged up with an electric fire, there is something rather sad and sterile about a fireplace devoid of function. One that burns, for however brief a season, gives life to a room. And an open fireplace also allows a natural circulation of air.

In summer there are more unusual alternatives to filling the black hole with dried flowers: a pile of brightly coloured witches' balls, perhaps, or a found sculpture of bleached driftwood. The naked fireplace used to be concealed behind a decorative fire-screen. You can still find these in antique shops, though this will not appeal to practitioners of the 'honesty' school of design. The architectural solution, advocated by Christopher Alexander, is that there should always be something else to attract the circle of chairs around the fireplace when the fire is not burning, like a window or a view. Only then, he says, 'will the circle of chairs which forms around the fire be stable and keep the place alive, both when the fire is burning and when it isn't.'

For some people the whole point of having a fireplace is the decorative focus of the mantelpiece above it. Not for them the limp formation of the central carriage clock and symmetrical candlesticks. The most striking displays are either rigorously minimalist – a single beautiful or esoteric object dramatically lit – or a rich assemblage of different textures and colours. These miniature exhibitions of taste need not be written in stone, although it is strange how the majority of mantelpiece displays hardly change from year to year.

Does this indicate that the mantelpiece is the true repository of a person's real taste, uninfluenced by fashion?

1 A table laden with flowers and candlesticks carries connotations of the altar, itself the focal point in a church. Here, the strength of the image is intensified by the use of old pillars and two large mirrors.

3

2 A stunning piece of visual imagery – log store and piece of art rolled into one. The question is, where do you take the logs from – top or bottom?

3 Exploit every corner for its decorative potential.

4

5

8

6

4 An assemblage of objects has more impact if there is some sort of visual link between them, however abstruse. Here, the shape of the compasses echoes the three sculpted lower torsos.

5 The cultural significance of the fireplace is played up here in this architectural homage to the hearth, which is almost like a theatrical set dropped in to an open-plan space.

7

Or is it simply visual laziness? The mantelpiece should change and evolve with us, like a chronicle of our lives, a three-dimensional scrapbook. The best mantelpiece displays are never the ones with the perfect collection of Chinese porcelain but are, by contrast, the ones which combine the exotic with the personal and the familiar, where a child's first attempt at pottery is seen to be as priceless as the adjacent Art Deco vase, where a photograph or postcard with fleeting appeal is given temporary lean-to residence, where a memory resides in a beautiful stone or shell.

6 Without the gnarled twig, this table would not draw attention. The appeal lies in the differences in scale and in the way the twig follows the twisted line of the base.

7 During seasonal redundancy, the fireplace can be rather dismal. In this room, the eye is drawn to the painting to the side.

8 Careful choreography gives the two areas of this room their distinct orientation.

Special places

1

2

3

4

5

Like the siting of sacred buildings in auspicious landscapes, there are corners of most houses where areas of seating have become firmly and permanently established. It may be a window-seat that gets the morning sun, a quiet alcove or a front porch – but there is something almost magical about these places which draws us to them. One of the worst things about modern estate houses is that they are so bland and featureless, that they are completely lacking in idiosyncratic space.

As with all magic, however, the appeal of these special places is founded in logic. These are places which have become fixed refuges because they are in a favourable position regarding light and sun. Or perhaps there is a wonderful view from them. Christopher Alexander believes that alcoves are fundamental to healthy living spaces from the point of view of relationships between the occupants of a house and their need for a degree of privacy. 'No homogeneous room, of homogeneous height, can serve a group of people well. To give a group a chance to be together, as a group, a room must also give them the chance to be alone, in ones and twos in the same space.'

Alexander suggests that what he calls 'window places' are not just the luxury that modern cost-cutting house building would suggest them to be, but are, in fact, a necessity. A room without a window place, he believes, keep its occupants in a 'state of perpetual unresolved conflict and tension - slight, perhaps, but definite.' This is not as crackpot a theory as it might at first appear for, as Alexander goes on to explain, we are naturally drawn towards windows for the light, but at the same time we have an equal need to sit somewhere comfortable and if all the comfortable places are situated away from the windows there is a conflict.

In a very old house, the chances are that these places will already have been established by history and human inclination. Otherwise you may need to seek them out and build on their potential. Windows, as Alexander points out, need to be 'taken seriously as a space, a volume, not merely treated as a hole in the wall.' A bay window, for example, is the perfect place for a window-seat; topped with a comfortable cushion along its length and fitted with cupboard space below, it doubles as useful storage space. If your joinery budget

does not run to cupboards, a simple bench or an extended window-sill with a curtained skirt concealing the clutter underneath has a cottage-like charm.

If no such place suggests itself to you, it is worth considering adding a conservatory. These always work best if they are seen as an extension to a room; too often they are indiscriminate additions, perhaps a dining-room, that relate badly to the rest of the house. You may find that adding a glazed alcove to an existing room gives you as much useful extra space as a whole new room.

The average town house often has a corridor of outdoor space running between it and the neighbouring house which seldom gets used because it is too narrow – no more than a thoroughfare to the garden. This is an ideal area to convert from redundant space to a living alcove with a glazed roof to let in as much light as possible. As the external wall is always structural anyway it makes sense to use this to partition space rather than trying to open out completely. In most houses the room that it annexes will be the kitchen and it will probably be just wide enough to make into a cosy sitting space or a good study area looking out on the garden.

1 Landings are often wasted space. A chair and small table have turned this into a quiet reading retreat.

2 A bedroom open to the countryside is the ultimate room with a view.

3 What patio umbrella could possibly compare with the romance of sitting in the shade of an ancient tree? It only takes a few floor cushions to turn dream to reality.

4 Alcoves are magical spaces for adults and children alike. It may seem indulgent to squander storage space, but measure that against quality of life. The owners have niftily incorporated storage potential above and below this alcove.

5 You may not share the idyllic setting, but conservatory furniture on a sun deck makes the most of summer just as much in Peckham as paradise.

6

6 Though the raised platform was probably added to improve the wall-to-floor proportions of the high-set window, it has also created a cosy nook.

7 Window seats provide a pleasure quite out of scale to the space they take up. If they are not incorporated in to the architecture of your home, it is worth investigating the possibility of building some in.

8 The tropical equivalent of the conservatory is a cool, shady verandah.

7

8

SLEEPING

Bedrooms are probably the most neglected area of any house. True, we spend a third of our lives there, but most people require only that the room contains a comfortable bed. After all, the reasoning goes, if the greatest proportion of that time is spent visually unconscious, who cares how the room looks?

In fact, through pressure on space, the bedroom is gradually becoming a room with multifarious purposes, often combining as a study and personal living-room. But even when it retains its single, primary function, it should not be undervalued. We don't, after all, drop into sleep from a vacuum. Those moments just before we go to sleep, taking stock of the day and winding down, and when we wake up recharged are, or should be, prime time for reflection and contemplation. How you wake up can affect the whole of your day. So your sleeping environment needs every bit as much, if not more, consideration as your living-room.

A bedroom is usually a fairly good indicator of the inhabitant's self-respect. People are generally happy to put all their energy into decorating a living-room because they believe by that they will be judged. In some cases living-rooms are decorated purely with other people's perceptions in mind. But a bedroom, usually out of bounds to others, is selfish space at its purest. It is a shrine to the personal and the private. It is where children can create their secret world; teenagers can make rebellious statements; adults can seek sanctuary. There is no more depressing sight than the institutional bedroom, devoid of personality. This is why any decent old people's home allows residents to have treasured pieces of furniture in their rooms.

Even in the houses of people we know well it feels like trespassing on intimacy to go uninvited into the bedroom, though in the seventeenth and early eighteenth centuries the bedroom was used as a reception room. It seems that the bed is the object of embarrassment – not necessarily because it is the most usual place for lovemaking but because it is witness to all our most private thoughts and dreams. This is why, when a bedroom doubles as living-room its owner usually goes to some effort to cast off slumbering associations and disguises the bed as a sofa. Night-time must be welcoming, but easy to banish by day – that is the real dilemma of the bedroom.

Sleep recharges the body's batteries. It is a universal need, one of the great levellers. Yet if the basic require-ments of shelter and a bed are fairly simple, we none the less personalize our sleep-ing spaces as much as we do any other area of the home.

Orientation and position

2

1

3

The history of the bedroom and the history of privacy are closely intertwined. Domestic privacy did not really exist until around the beginning of the seventeenth century: people ate, entertained and slept in the same rooms, with much use made of collapsible beds. As Philippe Aries points out in *Centuries of Childhood*, people rarely slept alone; there might be several beds in one room, but the fact that a room contained a bed (or beds) did not make it a bedroom – it was still a public place. When beds became less mobile in the seventeenth century they were fitted with curtains to afford a degree of privacy, but often servants slept alongside masters on truckle-beds. Hard as it is to imagine now, 400 years ago 'nobody was ever left alone . . . people who managed to shut themselves up in a room for some time were regarded as exceptional characters'.

It was in the eighteenth century, when the notion of family life and privacy took root, that rooms with specialized functions took over from semi-public arrangements of space in a house. Most notably, bedrooms moved upstairs and became citadels of privacy.

The bedroom is beginning to revert to a less isolated position but it is not likely ever to become as public as it once was. Many people feel uneasy in ground-floor bedrooms, possibly because they feel more vulnerable sleeping at ground level but also because the upper floors – particularly of houses in built-up areas – receive more morning light. Christopher Alexander believes that natural light is crucial to healthy architecture: taking it even further he – along with the new generation of eco-designers – prescribes sleeping in rooms orientated towards the sunrise so that people wake up naturally with the sun. The theory is that our

4

1 A bedroom with the contemplative serenity of an abstract painting... unless there are children around, in which case the inviting open window becomes a nightmare of dangerous possibilities.
2 Despite the itchingly prosaic reason behind its existence, the mosquito net exerts a powerfully romantic pull through its colonial and bridal associations.
3 Another escapist's idyll – with its connotations of innocence, of lost childhood play in the garden shed – this look relies on total authenticity, though something of the effect could be recreated with painted tongue-and-groove boards in an attic bedroom.

5

6

bodies are attuned to the sun's cycle, and if you are gently nudged awake by the sun immediately after a period of REM sleep you are more likely to emerge refreshed and energetic; whereas if you are woken artificially in mid-sleep cycle you will have to drag yourself out of bed with bleary eyes and a heavy head. Certainly the idea of sleeping to the east has prevailed through different periods and various cultures. Some early twentieth-century cots had built-in compasses, presumably so that the baby could be healthily positioned.

Modern houses built on the principle of lateral space seem less odd with bedrooms on the ground floor, perhaps because they have been designed with good natural light. Also, they are not circumscribed by age-old conventions; freed of the restrictions of an out-dated architecture, more of us might look at our bedrooms without sleep in our eyes.

4 In rural locations where no interior should compete with the view, simplicity is the rule. By minimizing furniture and pattern, the inside takes its cue from outside.
5 In a sparsely furnished bedroom, a row of shirts provide a decorative focus. The shirts may not be neatly pressed and could not be accused of wearing their relationship with the laundry on their sleeves, but this is more than simply an artful conceit.
6 A feminine bed, with lots of frills and flounces, can emasculate its male occupant. Here, a comfortable compromise has been struck between feminine 'prettiness' and masculine sobriety.

Using the space

In many ways, those bedrooms that operate purely as a room for sleeping in do not make sense in an age where space is at such a premium. The bed is the dominant feature of the room and the space around it often tends to be rather awkward and unfocused. For most of us, in average-size bedrooms with a double- or king-size bed, the space we negotiate is that around the bed; quite often the fact that there is no easy circulation flow turns out to be what makes a bedroom such an uninviting, dead space during the daytime.

What can you do about it? Futon mattresses can be rolled away into a cupboard and sofa beds have the benefit of versatility, but as a permanent arrangement these alternatives are both time-consuming and demanding. Also, denying the existence of the bed is ultimately counter-productive – you have to work with it. The solution might be as simple as moving the bed to a different position in the room, though you will probably find that your options are fairly limited. Pushing a double bed into a corner may give you a more manageable space, but it makes access for one person difficult, is awkward when you come to change the sheets, and limits space for a bedside table – though there are built-in alternatives such as a shelf or small alcove in the wall.

Psychologically, most people seem happier with their bed cater-corner to the door: half concealed behind it, rather than facing it. In the West this is a hazy, subconscious notion, but in China it is formularized in the ancient science of *feng shui* which guides building and interior design, and behind whose often mystic-sounding dictates usually resides much rational common sense. The bed, it is believed, should be positioned so that its occupant can see anyone entering the room; and the bedhead should rest against a wall, not float in space, since the bed's occupant will otherwise feel similarly unanchored in life.

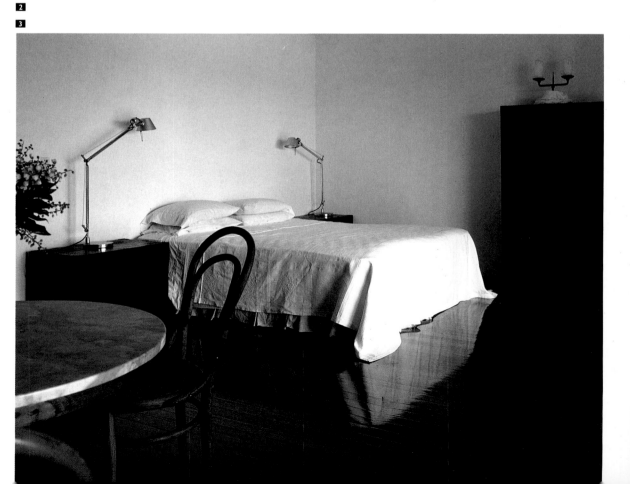

1 In a high-ceilinged room, a mezzanine level gives a sense of enclosure around the bed, at the same time as providing valuable storage space so that the floor area can remain uncluttered.
2 The bedroom in this converted warehouse has the luxury of plenty of floor space around the bed. This, together with the huge expanses of window flooding the room with natural light, make it a wonderful place to occupy during the day as well as the night.
3 If your bedroom is going to accommodate activities other than sleeping, it is best kept cool and uncluttered, with furniture that does not look too cosy.
4 A tranquil room focused on relaxation.
6 Bright colours need not be reserved for children's rooms: waking up to this wardrobe every morning should ensure the day at least starts on a cheerful note.

4

5 The bedroom is a good place for fantasy furniture: one avant-garde chair can have enormous impact, particularly where the bed is quite simple.
7 Vanitory basins have a slightly out-moded feel, but a more workmanlike sink opens up the room to new possibilities.
8 When there's no room for harbouring sentimental feelings for a bedroom, this is an efficient solution for a work-dominated environment: the bed folds away into a wall of cupboards.
9 High-tech hanging space: these wardrobes on casters form an impressive wall of clothes storage.

6

Perhaps the main problem with bedrooms is that we try to cram too many functions into them so that they fulfil none of them particularly well. These functions – dressing, toiletry, general storage and maybe even work space – carry with them bulky, often ugly pieces of furniture – wardrobes, dressing tables and the like – that clutter up the traditional bedroom. Where possible it is best to shift the emphasis of some of these functions to other rooms. Many of us, for example, dress in bedrooms simply from convention; it may make sense to fit hanging space elsewhere.

A combined study and bedroom is a practical combination. The space is used day and night, though some believe that it is unhealthy to keep a computer in the bedroom because of electromagnetic radiation. There is also no doubt that electrical office equipment attracts dust and pollutes the air, which certainly does not make for the healthiest sleeping atmosphere.

For some, the ideal sleeping space is a mezzanine platform, accommodating only a bed; this works well in a large open-plan space, but is not a solution for the average town-house.

5

7

8

9

Setting the style

The modern 'healthy' bedroom is as much about the visual as the physical conditions. Just as the late nineteenth-century obsession with hygiene hinged on the visible notion of cleanliness and resulted in furniture designed to have no hiding place for dust, one modern ideal of the bedroom rests somewhere between Scandinavian and Mediterranean style – bare boards, wafting muslin drapes and crisp white linen sheets.

Fundamentally, we associate sleep with purity – 'the sleep of the innocent' – which is why we are so concerned about sleeping in a benign atmosphere. At the same time, however, the bedroom has a sensual side, which some prefer to emphasize and which can be at odds with the pure, virginal look. Sex in a white and airy bedroom might be of the health and efficiency kind – an athletic tangling of showered and shiny, perfectly honed limbs – while the dark and exotic bedroom, with its curtained four-poster, advertises a more sultry, possibly more experimental, coupling. Perhaps this is why people don't often show off their bedrooms – it gives too much away. Small wonder that so many opt for the 'polite' bedroom which yields no clues – the floral, frilly affair deemed 'feminine', yet curiously sexless.

In the late nineteenth century the bedroom became the focus of an intensive campaign of dust- and germ-busting. Papers written at this time on the 'healthy house' were remarkably similar to 'green' design tracts of the 1980s. In the 1880s, bedroom floors were to be made of wood-block or good-quality boards: wall-to-wall carpeting was considered a dust-trap, so rugs were used and shaken out daily. Washable silk and cotton were recommended for curtains. Much the same advice is given by eco-designers 100 years on, though to the old enemies of dust and dirt they have also added the spectre of chemical pollution from synthetic materials.

1 Pristine and pure, the sharp lines of this bedroom are softened by the mosquito net.
2 Art as furniture: an extraordinary abstract assemblage in wood and metal forms a dramatic bedhead against which no patterned bed linen could compete.
3 The monastic cell has long been associated with cerebral personality, though this raw-textured bedroom perhaps owes as much to the aesthetic of the bounty hunter.

4

4 When a room is devoid of architectural features, be brave and go all out on colour.
5 Beamed ceilings have such a strong presence that most people opt for submissive white walls; but here, painted Shaker cupboards make a bold statement against the bare wooden beams.

5

6

8

7

6 Ship-shape and streamlined, this room hints at both nautical and log-cabin associations, but arrives at uncontrived simplicity.
7 Remember when we weren't so sophisticated that we couldn't just hang things from a nail in the wall?
8 A tall room is given more comfortable proportions with fabric hangings that make a private haven of the bed.
9 Bare brick and a rustic bedhead are balanced by the bold colour scheme.

Certain colours seem particularly well suited to the bedroom, depending on whether the room comes into its own for you in the morning or at night-time. White remains popular for its pure and romantic elegance while yellow – in spite of the late John Fowler's stipulation that it should not be used in a lady's bedroom because it made her complexion look sallow first thing in the morning – is a wonderful colour for making a room sunny, even if the skies are pewter. But those who make a point of never welcoming the morning light and who come alive at night choose dark, jewel-like colours to intensify a warm, enclosed atmosphere.

9

The bed

1 Allergic to dust or allergic to decoration, this is a room in which the purity of the space speaks for itself, a place for the committed minimalist.
2 This unusual antique box-bed gives wrap-around painted decoration and a sense of security.

When people say that a bed is the most important piece of furniture you will ever buy it is not strictly true: it is the mattress. Anyone who has spent a tortured night on a soft or lumpy mattress won't need to be told about the wisdom of buying the best you can afford. Sleeping night after night on an inferior mattress will result in back trouble in later life. A mattress should be firm enough to support your spine but not so hard that it throws the hips and shoulder out of their normal curvature. If it is too soft, rolling from side to side is difficult, impeding the natural movements you make during healthy sleep.

This does not mean that you are restricted to characterless bases. If you have a wonderful antique bed, you can have a mattress made to measure; if you want to commission an iron four-poster, you can have it made to fit the mattress of your choice. Alternatively you can customize basic beds simply by adding an unusual bedhead.

The importance of the bed does not merely lie in physical comfort. It has a symbolic significance we have sadly lost sight of. In the past the 'marriage bed' was a status symbol. In the Austrian Tyrol, for example, a carved and painted bed, often with the couple's initials worked into a highly decorative scene, formed part of a bride's dowry. The American architect and writer, Christopher Alexander, mourns the loss of the kind of bed 'which nourishes intimacy and love'. He envisages a true marriage bed, one with a headboard that can be carved and painted over the years as a kind of celebratory testimony to a couple's relationship. A little fanciful, maybe, but he has a point – we have lost the personal touch in our bedrooms. When it comes to buying a bed, back problems, house mites and dust allergies have all but obscured the romance.

However, the enduring appeal of the four-poster bed remains rooted in romantic notions. Although it lost favour in the hygiene purge of the late

3 A bed with powerful symbolism stands out from the bland places where most of us sleep. This is a monument to its owner's passion for tribal art.
4 A platform bed provides extra storage underneath.

5 Modern versions of the four-poster bed tend to trade the traditional heaviness and draught-excluding properties for a feeling of airiness and curtains that are more decorative than functional.

7

8

9

10

nineteenth century – it was considered unhealthy to sleep within the confines of a small, heavily curtained space – the four-poster is now considered a stately touch to bedrooms. This is fine where a stately touch is appropriate, but too often they look slightly ridiculous, dwarfing the proportions of a small room and aping grandeur in a way which diminishes natural style.

Modified versions of the four-poster often work better in modern rooms. There are some minimal black iron four-posters or pale wood frames over which a simple length of fabric can be hung to great effect. Alternatively do without the posts and hang a lightweight fabric canopy from ceiling-fixed rods.

From a stylistic point of view, one of the problems of 'historical' beds is that the duvet looks out of place. A lot of people conceal the practicality of the duvet under a bedspread or quilt, while others are returning to the comfort and nostalgia of crisp sheets turned over wool blankets. It is all very well to sneer at the duvet as the furnishing equivalent of fast food, but who is going to make the bed and iron the linen sheets?

6 Beds can be islands of individuality. This one uses a clash of materials and styles to stunning effect. The base, which incorporates a decorative brass grille, has echoes of a classical *bateau au lit*, while the skeletal metal top is uncompromisingly modern.
7 The celibate single bed always looks good because its proportions are often easier to work with than those of a double bed.
8 The rustic feel of this simple bedroom is reinforced by the old timber bedframe and the farm-gate style bedhead.
9 Upholstered bedheads may conjure up visions of pink buttonbacked nightmares, but they can be as cool and simple as this.
10 Iron and steel frames are increasingly ousting the more dated brass bed.

Children's bedrooms

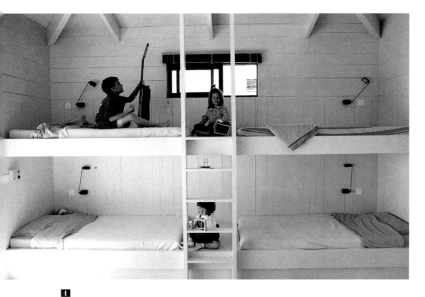

It is part of cultural mythology, perpetuated in films and books, that when a baby is expected the parents 'prepare the nursery'. Some blame it on hormones and claim it is a pregnancy-induced psychosis that results in a frenzy of furnishings and fluffy mobiles. Others believe that it is a way of distancing ourselves from our natural instincts – for the first few months of life all a baby wants is to be held and fed. Spending vast sums of money on nursery furniture is totally unnecessary, though it undoubtedly assuages guilt about spending less time with the baby than nature intended.

When the child has a sense of its own identity then a separate room becomes appropriate – or at least a room shared with siblings. Giving small children a room of their own is the adult's idea of a treat – to make them feel 'grown up'. And yet pre-teenage children generally prefer the comfort and security of others sleeping in close proximity. At the same time they do like to have some kind of base or private place where they can keep their special possessions or hide away. The old-fashioned box-beds are perfect for children who love the hidey-hole element; bunk-beds also give a good sense of territory.

1 In a holiday house, building platform beds across the entire width of a room economically accommodates four children. Wall-mounted reading lights are a necessity, and some might say a safety rail for the top bunk-beds is, as well. Although this sort of sleeping arrangement is an adventure on holiday – remember the excitement of bagging a bedroom – the lack of privacy might be a disadvantage on a more permanent basis.
2 An ingenious solution to accommodating the maximum number of children in the minimum amount of space, this attic conversion allows a couple to have all their grandchildren to stay for the weekend.
3 Mosquito nets add romance to the prosaic bunk-bed, enthusiasm for which has normally worn off by the age of ten. A room divider and muslin-swathed doorway gives the illusion of privacy for an older child.

Stringent safety regulations govern the dimensions of bunk-beds, particularly with regard to the safety rail on the top bunk, which should not have a space large enough for a child to slip through and then get its head stuck. If you look at the room through a child's eyes – as an exciting adventure playground – you may spot other potential hazards.

One can, however, become paranoid about safety. It is really not necessary to build special low children's beds in case they fall out at night: when children make the transition from cot to bed they inevitably tumble out a few times, but injury is rare. If you pre-empt your child's every move, you may well stifle the growth of self-confidence and self-motivation, and dull their own innate sense of danger.

In a house with limited bedrooms and more than a couple of children it makes sense to sacrifice the main bedroom to them. Often it is the room that receives the best light in the day, which will be wasted if it is only used for sleeping rather than for playing, too. A couple of bunk-beds leave plenty of floor space for toys which can be neatly stacked under the beds at night in boxes. Communal sleeping for children means that other bedrooms can then be put to other uses – at least until the teenage years when a 'room of one's own' becomes an issue.

Devoted parents are often tempted to indulge their children with decorative 'themes' – whether it's the latest cartoon-hero wallpaper or converting the room into an authentic wigwam. This should be resisted: the wallpaper will inevitably be deeply uncool next year and specific themes limit creative play. Far better to paint the walls a cheerful colour which will not have you gnashing your teeth every time they decide to personalize it with stickers and posters.

A bed, some good, ample storage and platforms or window-seats – a child needs very little else in a bedroom. It may not be so much fun for parents, but the best thing they can provide in a child's bedroom is potential.

4 More than two beds in a row may revive memories of school dormitories, but few can have been as stylish as this. The hand of an adult is evident, though: parents like their offspring's things to match; children prefer to express their individuality.

5

5 Most small children's clothes only need folding away in drawers; a row of Shaker pegs is perfectly adequate for the few which need hanging.
6 By the time children reach the age of 11 or 12 they need their own space, particularly somewhere to do their homework. A bed draped in a throw with cushions to match becomes a makeshift sofa, and may even encourage them to make their own bed.
7 A platform bed (with all-important safety rail) makes room for storage and play space beneath it.

6

8

7

9

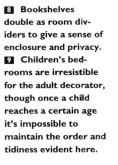

8 Bookshelves double as room dividers to give a sense of enclosure and privacy.
9 Children's bedrooms are irresistible for the adult decorator, though once a child reaches a certain age it's impossible to maintain the order and tidiness evident here.

WASHING AND BATHING

The history of bathing is not necessarily synonymous with the history of cleanliness. Though personal hygiene played a part in the rise of the bathroom, the bathing ritual is a more complex process, and the room in which it takes place is often referred to by such inflated titles as 'the temple of ablutions'.

The idea of cleanliness being next to Godliness is a fairly modern one: in the early Church bathing was frowned upon. St Francis of Assisi considered dirtiness to be one of the insignia of holiness and St Agnes is said never to have washed. Until the move towards more hygienic surfaces at the turn of the century, people tended to furnish their bathrooms much like other rooms in the house, with sanitary equipment treated like pieces of furniture, often cased in fine dark woods such as mahogany. With the drive against dirt the bathroom became rather less hospitable, with hard tiled surfaces and free-standing white cast-iron baths.

Interestingly, it was the 1920s when the middle classes started to spurn the clinical white look in favour of coloured suites and tiles. This coincided with subsidized housing which was fitted out with the same sanitary equipment as that which graced middle-class homes. When they could no longer distance themselves from the class below by being cleaner, the middle class distinguished themselves by the style of their bathrooms.

Using the bathroom as an arena of status and style has continued unabated – from gold-plated taps to the latest whirlpool technology, from avocado-green suites to the inconspicuous opulence of all-white rooms. Stripped of our outward vestments of status, reduced to the democracy of nakedness, perhaps the need to surround ourselves with the reassurance of material wealth has become all the more intense.

Recent thinking on the bathroom, however, is more concerned with its therapeutic value. Pope Gregory the Great thought baths were permissible only if they did not become a 'time-wasting luxury'. For today's generation this is perhaps the whole point of the exercise, with cleanliness merely being a by-product. In the history of contemplation, from the first 'eureka', the bath must rank at the top of inspirational locations. The bathroom is still a place for the quiet luxury of comfort and style.

Washing is about more than physical cleanliness. Soaking in a hot bath after a hard day's work, ruminating on the oddities of life, we are afforded some time on our own. It is little wonder, then, that the bathroom is decorated both to accommodate planning needs and to reflect personal comfort, a haven of peace and privacy.

Planning

The bathroom needs more planning than any other room in the house after the kitchen. Options are more limited, and mistakes irredeemable. Added to this, the room often tends to be what is left over after everything else is housed – a small, often windowless space. Once bathroom fittings have been plumbed in, they are permanent fixtures which you are unlikely to want to change.

Planning a small bathroom is like working out a puzzle. There is probably only one solution, given that you have to site the minimum of three items – bath or shower, lavatory and wash-basin – within a small space, taking into account the position of architectural features such as windows and doors, and not forgetting the plumbing and drainage pipework.

In some ways planning restrictions can work to your advantage. This gives you a starting point; the lavatory has to be sited close to the existing soil stack, unless you plan to go to the considerable expense of rerouting the pipes. The room usually has to be sited at the back or side of the house as local planning regulations often forbid pipework at the front. In a very small room, you may not have much choice as to where the bath is positioned; the dimensions of the average bath are 1700 × 700mm (67 ×

27in) and this may only fit along one of the walls. In a long, narrow room, the bath can be fitted across one end, with the ceiling lowered to make a cosy alcove.

The wash-basin must be sited with enough space in front of it so that you can comfortably bend over it to wash. For wet shavers and making-up, it is best by the window. You may have to do without a wall-mounted mirror, or attach a chrome extending mirror to the window surround. On the other hand the window-sill can be used as a shelf and you can always replace the glazed panes of the window with mirror glass, which will give you an illusion, at least, of space. Leave yourself plenty of elbow room either side – it is difficult to wash in comfort if the basin is jammed right up against a side wall.

The lavatory requires the same forethought. Make sure that there is enough room between the rim of the seat and the wall in front so that your knees are not up under your chin. The bidet needs space to the side and back for your legs.

In a very small bathroom, an inward-opening door can limit space even further. You can rehang the door to open outwards, or fit a sliding door or louvered-concertina door to free up a significant area of usable space. An outward-opening door works well in an *en*

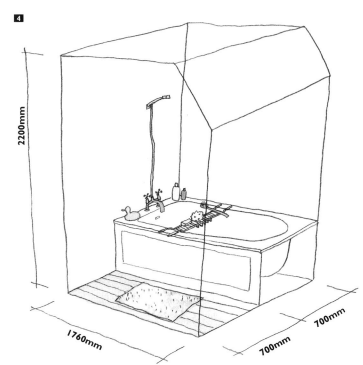

1 A bidet needs 600mm (24in) clear space in front of it, and a minimum ceiling height of 2m (6ft 6in).
2 A dado works to counteract the tall, narrow shape of this cloakroom.
3 Placing the basin near the light would have obscured part of the window; the alcove instead makes a blissful spot for a bath.
4 A bath needs its width again for comfortable manoeuvring.
5 The classic line-up for a narrow room.

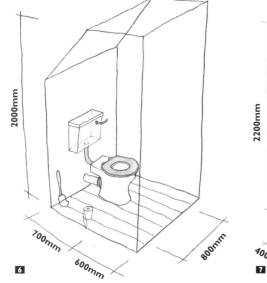

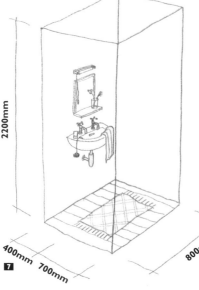

6

7

6 A lavatory needs 600mm (24in) clearance space in front.
7 A basin needs slightly greater clearance to either side.
8 The requirement of two basins has left a rather tight fit in this bathroom, but the glass tiles allay any claustrophobia.

8

10

suite bathroom but it is not practical if the door will then open out on to a narrow landing or corridor.

Even an average-size bathroom will need precision planning to fit everything in, particularly if you include a shower and bidet. Adopt the same approach as with kitchens (page 128), drawing up a room plan, cutting out sanitary equipment shapes to scale and fitting them into the space on paper.

In a large bathroom, space may not appear to be such a problem. However, large bathrooms often leave a vast expanse of empty floor in the middle, while the sanitary fittings hang around the edge. The answer may lie in placing a free-standing roll-top bath in the centre of the room, though not everybody feels comfortable with this. A raised platform can equally break up the floor space and provides space for a sunken bath which is still easy to clean.

It is essential to have enough storage space in your bathroom if you don't want bottles of bleach and packets of lavatory rolls on display. If you are concealing the cistern and pipework, this presents an ideal opportunity to create storage. The basin can be set in to a work surface with cupboards beneath, while the lavatory cistern can be hidden in a duct with shelves above or below it.

9 In a small attic bathroom a shower cabinet may fit where a bath would not, provided there is sufficient pressure to maintain a decent water supply. This can be a problem with top-floor bathrooms, but a special pump can be installed to remedy it.
10 Any less space than this would feel extremely cramped.
11 Separate showers need clearance space as shown if washing is not going to be a contorted affair.

11

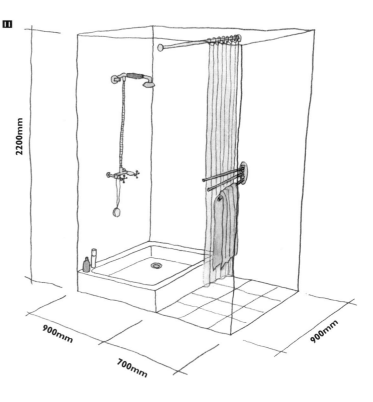

Fittings

Lavatory humour is proof of an almost universal embarrassment about bodily functions. So excruciatingly embarrassing did the turn-of-the-century British find the whole notion of 'lavatories' that, supposedly, there were strict rules governing the placement of the ground-floor facilities. A lavatory had to be always tucked away in an inconspicuous position and access must be through another room. But nor must it be too difficult to find, the prime requirement being that anyone should be able to slip in unobserved, with minimal fuss.

Today there are plenty of lavatories with plain unembarrassed lines in both classical and modern designs. The main choice to be made is between cistern types – the old fashioned wash-down flush or the syphonic which is quieter and more efficient, but costlier. It can look neater to hide the cistern behind ducting but you need to allow for easy access. Instead of going to the trouble and expense of tricky plumbing you may be better off choosing a nicely designed cistern which doesn't need to be hidden. Bidets are also designed to match the style of the lavatory although many people still tend to regard them as an optional extra.

Wash-basins come in pedestal and cantilevered style, which in theory, at least, conceals the plumbing; less dependent on the aesthetic skills of your plumber is the built-in basin housed in an all-concealing cupboard that will also provide room for cleaning fluids.

1 An unusual shallow, trough-like basin.
2 Raised sides and built-in splashbacks were a sensible feature of older basins, copied in good reproductions.
3 Old-fashioned taps and fittings are increasingly popular, rather more so with home-owners than with plumbers.
4 There is no need to match sanitaryware: most styles of basin go well with the traditional Victorian-style roll-top bath.
5 An interesting *ménage à trois* of handbasins built into a vanitory unit.

1

2

3

4

5

6

7

10
11

8

9

There are many designer toys for the bathroom, such as glass basins, though these should only be considered for obsessively clean individuals. If you opt for fancy equipment, the style may date quickly. Tasteful luxury is a standard bath shape, but big and deep; anything too adventurous – round, sunken, triangular – runs the risk of looking like something out of a James Bond movie. For the same reason, whirlpool baths have an image problem, though it is possible to have jets fitted discreetly to a standard bath. If you prefer the safety of nostalgia, there are modern versions of the Edwardian roll-top bath or you can have the genuine thing re-enamelled, though this may cost as much as a good-quality modern bath.

A shower offers manufacturers less scope for vulgarity, though some ready-made shower cabinets can look like alien space capsules in an otherwise well-designed bathroom. The most important aspect is sufficient pressure to deliver a shower worth having; for this you may have to install a pump.

6 Side-mounted taps work best on round-ended baths.
7 Cedarwood tubs, inspired by Japanese tradition, are undeniably elegant, but they are expensive and require maintenance, needing to be filled every day to prevent them springing leaks.
8 A school sink is set in to a wall of marble which also conceals the radiators.
9 Soap dishes come in a range of striking contemporary designs.
10 A towel rail gone crazy, windows on the slope and a basin set into a sculptural rock: who says there's no room for individuality in the bathroom?
11 Sanitaryware design is entering a new era, with the big companies taking the lead from individual designers.
12 A plain glass screen makes an economical shower cabinet.

12

Mood, atmosphere and privacy

1 If cleanliness is next to godliness, you're just that bit nearer on an urban rooftop. But al fresco bathing is sadly a rather pie-in-the-sky idea, brought down to earth by considerations of plumbing, drainage and load bearing.

1

2

Functionally the bathroom may have changed little over the past 100 years; the sanitary fittings are more sophisticated but they still perform exactly the same function. It is the spirit that has changed. Today we take hot and cold running water and the daily bath or shower for granted; relaxing in the bathroom has now become almost a metaphysical experience.

Unwinding from the stresses of the day with a good long soak in a deep hot bath is a simple luxury available to most people. Inevitably, then, some people will want to differentiate their bathroom, making it a personal haven of privacy and contemplation. In the last century you could be superior by having a bathroom instead of going to public baths. In the twentieth century you could distinguish yourself further by having an *en suite* bathroom, which emphasizes the privacy aspect.

Some feel that the *en suite* obsession has gone too far, that it is a further step in the process of giving our houses the luxurious but bland uniformity of the international hotel. Architect Christopher Alexander decries the trend: 'These separate, efficiency bathrooms never give the family the chance to share the intimacies and pleasures of bathing, of being naked and half-naked together.' He is one of the growing group of architects and designers who, perhaps inspired by trips to Japan where, at least in the traditional houses, bathing is not a private ritual, are exploring the bathhouse or communal bathing idea. But for most people, this runs counter to the cherished concept of the bathroom as a place for private contemplation in peace. Some of the Japanese techniques of bathing are gaining ground; the idea, for example, of showering the dirt off first and then

relaxing in a hot tub. Deep cedarwood baths can be used but, like wooden rowing boats, they have to be filled every day to keep them from springing a leak.

In some households the question of whether to house the lavatory in the bathroom is a contentious one. A bathroom without a lavatory does look deprived. The reason for putting it with the other sanitary fittings is largely one of convenience, so that all bodily functions can be dealt with in one room, without having to put clothes on, or take them off. Those who favour the separate lavatory think that it is more hygienic and causes less traffic jams in the morning. The problem with lonesome lavatories is that they tend to be housed in narrow claustrophobic rooms and are often overlooked when it comes to decorating. If the lavatory is situated next to an existing bathroom, it might make more sense to knock it through.

2 Modern plumbing need not restrict you to soulless acrylic basins: here a shallow stone trough, echoing the shape of the porthole and slotted into a window recess, turns hand-washing in to a spiritual experience... But note the vanitory basin in the background for more prosaic everyday use.
3 The lavatory as sculpture: one man's mission to put art in to the cistern.
4 What more invigorating way to start the day than in a deep tub in front of windows flung open to welcome the fresh air.

3

4

5

5 The cosy, lived-in bathroom, with its free-standing bath, comfortable chair, even, perhaps, the ultimate luxury of a real fire. A large, free-standing bathtub can look a bit like a beached whale, but here it is visually integrated by the simple means of colour.

6 Privacy is a cultural norm, not an absolute. This is a brazen alternative to the *en suite* bathroom, though it does require fittings that are good looking enough to bear their all.

7 The bathtub as icon in a minimalist bathroom, a shrine to purity and cleanliness.

6

7

Decoration

1

2

3

4

5

1 White tiles graphically grouted in black, and shiny exposed plumbing give this bathroom a crisp, masculine air.
2 Mosaic tiling, particularly in this watery blue, is the perfect material for bathrooms.
3 A bathroom in a Gothic house built by Lord Ellenborough for his mistress is given an ecclesiastical theme.
4 A brass curtain rail turns the bath into a shower and lends an air of Edwardian opulence, toned down by the simple Shaker pegs above the lavatory and basin.
5 Back-to-basics bathing: soaking up the atmosphere in an antique copper tub.

A bathroom can be the most satisfying of rooms to decorate: because it is usually fairly restricted in size it offers the chance to indulge in schemes and materials – a shell-encrusted grotto or a mosaic tiled hammam – that you might feel to be excessive in a larger space.

Just as the style of bathrooms in the early twentieth century was a reflection of society's emphasis on hygiene and cleanliness, today's interiors convey images of relaxation and escapism. Stretches of pristine white tiles or gleaming marble suggest a kind of cerebral hygiene, while the trend for Edwardian-style fittings and large bathrooms with armchairs to lounge in is the nostalgic face of escapism.

Certain practical considerations have to be taken into account, but none are particularly complicated. Obviously, surfaces need to be water resistant and easily cleaned, so wool carpets should be avoided as they rot easily if allowed to get wet; synthetic carpets with rubber backing can be used if you like the idea of padding on to a warm floor in the mornings, but on the whole a hard surface – marble, tile or vinyl – with the option of soft rugs is preferable.

Good lighting is essential for grooming tasks in the bathroom. The sparky white light of halogen downlighters recessed into the ceiling works particularly well here, but you may need to add extra 'task' lighting for shaving and make-up areas. If you prefer a more traditional lighting scheme, remember that for safety reasons light-bulbs have to be enclosed within shades that fit flush against the walls or ceilings: pendant light fittings are not suitable. Switches need to be operated by a pull cord or to be situated outside the room.

Wall treatments should be practical – but this need not cramp your style. While uncoated wallpaper and matt emulsion paint are ruled out, you can use ceramic tile, glass mosaic tile, eggshell paint, tongue-and-groove boarding, marble or granite. Bare plaster, sealed with a matt varnish, gives a kind of raw warmth to the room – you can embed jewels into the plaster for a touch of exoticism – while painted tongue-and-groove has an elegant simplicity that works particularly well in the bathroom. Using mirror as a wall

6

6 A huge panel of glass makes a simple splashback with strong visual impact. Old-style roll-top baths look particularly good when contrasted with contemporary accessories and fittings.
8 Saunas do not have to be all scrubbed knotty pine.

7

8

9

10

7 For the minimalist, space and clean lines are more of a luxury than the most opulent fittings. Shower cabinets are seen as ugly intrusions, and if you have a sloping floor with drainage at one end they are unnecessary anyway.
9 A marble-topped Edwardian washstand together with the colour scheme and mosaic detailing give a turn-of-the-century accent to this room.
10 Decorated with paintings and furniture, bathrooms can be just as homely as any of your other rooms.

surface gives the illusion of space and is often used to suggest luxury, but you may find that large expanses of mirror, as well as being a pain to clean, throw back too many unwanted reflections.

Accessories can follow any theme set by your choice of materials. If you have plaster walls a bit of glitter works well as a contrast, whether it is punched tin cabinets and ethnic mirrors or the clean lines of chrome-and-glass shelves and trolleys. With tongue-and-groove boarding, slightly rustic cupboards and mirrors with wide wooden frames look good, and the dado-level beading should be wide enough to provide an ideal opportunity for displaying pretty glass bottles or sea shells. As a general rule, the more clean-cut image of marble or granite is best left uncluttered, though luxurious thick white towels can be used for softening the look.

Showers and storage

Until quite recently a dressing-room was seen as something that only those with large houses or no children could aspire to. However, if a bathroom is large enough and there is another elsewhere in the house, it can double as a dressing room, though it will also double the time you spend in there at peak times. Take care to ensure that the room is well ventilated; a steamy room is far from ideally suited to clothes storage.

The ideal is a small, separate, well-lit room, reasonably close to the bathroom and bedroom. As well as clothes-hanging space and drawer space, you need 2m (6ft) square for dressing. If your funds don't run to custom-built joinery, you can create some very effective ad hoc solutions; use a dress rail for clothes and baskets on shelves for small garments and accessories. You can curtain off the area if it's part of another room.

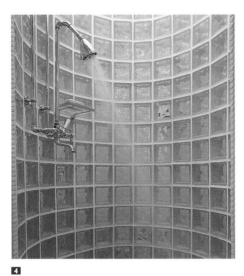

4

5

6

7

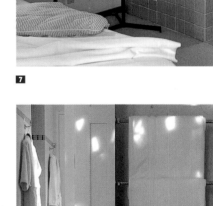

8

9

10

1 The general aesthetic standard of off-the-peg shower cabinets is fairly abysmal. Many designers prefer to make their own, despite the problems of sealing. Here, a sand-blasted sliding door has a clear square of glass for *Psycho*-phobes.
2 An integral sunken bath doubles as a shower tray.
3 A sylvan shower fitted in an old conservatory is a wonderful *folie de grandeur* that few of us would manage to take further than an idle fantasy. In fact, it's a lot more practical than it might appear, and the plants get watered at the same time.
4 A sweeping curve of glass fire bricks makes a stunning shower cubicle.

Some people would rather sacrifice the dressing room for a shower room if there is space. While the bath is for relaxing, a shower cleans and energizes; it is probably a more appropriate and efficient way to start the day, whereas a bath comes into its own in the evening. A proper self-contained shower unit is infinitely superior to any half-hearted measures. If you have two bathrooms it make sense to turn the smaller one into a shower room. Alternatively, a shower room could be situated on the ground floor, for use by someone coming in from outside exercise.

A downstairs cloakroom is perhaps a luxury in terms of space, but it can double as a boot hole and laundry room. A genuine cloakroom is not such a good idea; if possible allocate a 'dead' space under the stairs or in the hall to hang coats and hats.

7 A corner of the bedroom can be given over to a shower.
8 Baskets with tie-on labels are an effective means of storage.
9 Built-in cubby holes integrate more neatly than wall-mounted soap racks.
10 Generous towel rails make for easy airing and drying.

WORK AND PLAY

Whenever we consider ourselves radical in the way we live, there is invariably some long-distant precedent to remind us that nothing is ever new. Over the last twenty years, new technology has revolutionized the work field and meant that the option of working from home is available to administrative workers as well as creative artists. But, despite all the sophisticated equipment – the faxes and the desktop computers – that have allowed this to happen, we are merely coming round full circle to an older model of living whereby work and leisure were all based under one roof. A room of one's own is both a necessity and a luxury. Even in the most intimate household there is a need for individuals to be able to retreat to their own space. Christopher Alexander argues that all members of the household need their own private space, that it is necessary for psychological health, and that 'it helps develop one's own sense of identity; it strengthens one's relationship to the rest of the family; and it creates personal territory, thereby building ties with the house itself.' Virginia Woolf in her book whose title is perhaps better known than its contents argued that a room of one's own was a vital precondition of creativity.

When the idea of working from home began to take shape in the late 1970s, 'home offices' strived to be simultaneously 'hi-tech' and low cost – not a happy combination. It was almost as if the worker needed reassurance that this was really a place of work. In a commercial office the design and layout of furniture gives out subtle but unmistakable messages about the workers' status and authority. Many home workers may still feel unsure about their place without the security of an established hierarchy, and something of this insecurity manifests itself in the home office, giving out confusing signals. There is a need to separate working life from domestic routine, yet at the same time the office must be integrated into the house. As people become more relaxed about their working life, so this will be reflected in a confident handling of the design of their working environment. Certainly it seems ridiculous not to capitalize on the comforts of working from home – there is no point in abandoning a city office only to recreate exactly the same atmosphere at home.

Working from home frees us from the dull conformity of office life. Whether it's a dedicated room in daily use or a quiet corner for dealing with monthly bills, it need only look as formal as you want it to be. And if the children have their own playroom, why shouldn't you also devote a space to a favourite pastime?

Choosing the space

1

2

3

5

4

Choosing the best room in which to work from home involves several considerations. In a family house you need somewhere quiet, away from the main flow of household traffic – not the room through which the children trudge to the garden – but you also need good light and if possible a pleasant view. If you receive clients or colleagues at home, the space should be distanced from your domestic life. It is hard to keep up a professional front if you have to negotiate a path through drying underwear or past an unmade bed.

If your house is large enough, you may have the luxury of a whole room. As this is obviously the best option, it is worth trying to reorganize your living space to cater for an office – sacrifice the dining-room or turn the biggest bedroom into a communal sleeping space for the children so that you can use one of the smaller bedrooms as an office.

3 Even if you do no paid work from home it is good to devote a quiet corner to private study or domestic paper work.
4 The otherwise-wasted space under the stairs is a popular spot for a small personal office. The only drawback is that it might be short on natural light so you need to ensure good task lighting.
5 It may be important for professional credibility to give your office a commercial look distinct from the rest of your home.
6 Work space can be carved out of even the smallest room; but in a bedroom, as here, try to use bright furniture that does not have an office stamp to it.
7 An office environment does not have to be visually barren: objects that give you pleasure are as important here as anywhere else in the home.

8 A window alcove makes a perfect mini-office. At home you are free to explore unusual filing solutions.

6

7

8

The next best option is a room with dual functions. The bedroom tends to be redundant space in the daytime, but unless it is a very big room, the bed will dominate the space, though you could consider a sofa bed or a futon. It can be depressing to sleep in the same space that you have worked in all day, so it is important to separate – psychologically if not physically – the two functions. Try to create a fairly self-contained work area, by the window if possible, with your back to the bed. Under these circumstances, it is very important to take regular breaks from your work and have a change of environment.

The other room which is often only in part-time use and therefore makes a good working base is the dining-room. The dining-table can double up as a desk or work area although this is obviously not ideal if you have to keep clearing your work away.

Creating a work area in your living-room may not work well from a visual point of view, but you may be able to create a suitably self-contained working area. In any event you will need good storage and filing systems to keep unsightly paperwork or work samples under control. It may be worth having special cabinets made into which your equipment can disappear at night. Or, if your work is reasonably contained and not too dependent on high technology, an old-fashioned bureau or writing-desk may adequately cater for your needs.

If nowhere suggests itself inside your home, perhaps you should look to the outside. Sheds have always had a romantic allure – even an extremely prosaic larchlap self-assembly job can have its magic. This is a place to indulge your dreams, to revive the childish art of make-believe homes and to release your decorative *alter ego*!

Perhaps we need to rethink our whole attitude to the division of work and 'life'. For many people work is not a chore, but a part of their life from which they gain a great deal of enjoyment. In this case you may not feel like hiding your work away as if it were something to be ashamed of. Equally some people feel that their work actually benefits from being in the hub of domesticity. Where would we be, after all, without the kitchen-table novel?

Planning the layout

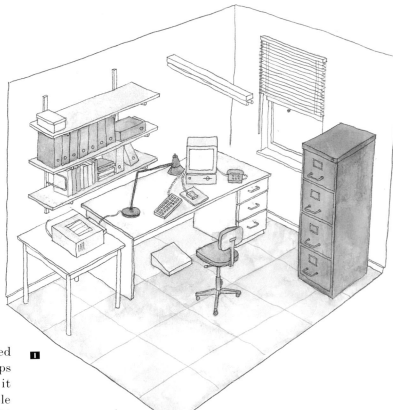

One of the joys of working from home is that you can plan your office to suit your particular way of working as well as your personal foibles and preferences. There is no office manager to dictate that your filing cabinet must be grey to match the carpet squares. In fact there is no reason why your work space should resemble an office at all, unless you need the status-support of an important-looking desk. Provided it is a comfortable height and stable – particularly important with computers – any work surface will do. But you cannot allow yourself quite so much freedom with the chair: a dining-chair is fine for the limited amount of time you are at the table, but when you are seated at a desk for hours every day you are placing considerable stress on your spine. So buy the best office chair you can afford: there are a few designs available which have a more 'domestic' feel than the bureaucratic grey swivel chairs.

If the work area can be partitioned off, even if only by suggestion – perhaps by the arrangement of furniture – it may restore equilibrium to the whole space. In converted warehouses and old factories with high ceilings, it does not make sense to divide the space with full-height walls. Often moveable partitions and storage systems work best, creating a wall on one side so that you still keep the flow of space, but with some sense of division. Different floor levels may help to orchestrate the space, and a sleeping platform is worth considering; psychologically it might be helpful to sleep at a distance from your work. If possible consult an architect or interior designer – a professional evaluation of the space and its potential will probably produce results you had not dreamed possible.

You don't have to endure utilitarian metal storage systems and filing cabinets either. You could use baskets to file papers in, while DIY shops make good

1 The minimum requirements for an efficient work space are a desk, easily accessible shelves, a filing cabinet, ergo-nomically designed chair and good light. Ideally, natural light should come from the side, particularly if you work with a VDU.
2 Good planning makes the best use of even the smallest corner. In a tight space like this, a raised side to the desk encloses the work space as well as providing extra work surface.

2

hunting grounds for drawers to house stationery accessories. If there is no alternative to living on top of your work then good organization is vital. Make storage for your work apparatus a priority, so that you are able to put things away neatly at the end of the day. If a table has to function as work surface and dining-table, make sure you have large cloths to transform it from work-horse to centrepiece.

Take advantage of the comforts that working at home can offer but also try to insulate yourself against the temptations and diversions. For instance, if you have to go into the kitchen to make yourself a cup of coffee you may find it difficult to ignore the unwashed break-fast dishes or the mountain of ironing. You could install a coffee maker or you could go even further and have a mini-kitchen fitted – a sink, small fridge, microwave and food store – preferably one that can be neatly closed away behind cupboard doors.

3 Industrial work space often has its own raw aesthetic which it is best not to tamper with: trying to tame the space with dom-estic imagery will be doomed to failure. Less than perfect walls give you the advantage of being able to knock in nails or extra shelves as the need arises.
4 Only a totally self-denying workaholic would turn their back on a view like this. The computer, however, is positioned away from the light source, and the shutters and venetian blinds are essential to cut down the glare and heat of a hot summer's day.

3

4

5

6

7

5 If working from home deprives you of a spare bedroom, it makes obvious sense to invest in a sofa bed. As a bed it will enable you to put up guests, while it can be used as a sofa for periods of relaxation during the day. If the idea seems too dangerously domestic, stick to plain-coloured upholstery while it is in office use – you can always add an exotic throw to brighten it up for guests.

It is impossible for any human being to work at a consistently high level of concentration without taking a break. Most people go through a natural 'low' in the early afternoon. If we obeyed our body clocks and took a 10-minute nap at this time, we would probably be more productive. Anyone who has nodded off, chin in hands, while pretending to read a report will know that it is simply not permissible in a commercial office. But in your home office a comfortable sofa or armchair can provide a haven for a rest or a change of pace – not all work needs to be done sitting at a desk.

There is no reason why your office should not be a joyful and pleasant place, where you enjoy spending time. Give shelf space to objects which you enjoy looking at, enliven the walls with favourite photographs and paintings. Capitalize on the visual quality of the things you work with: tools, brushes, fabrics can be both functional and a decorative display when not in use.

Lighting can be your most valuable ally in delineating work and leisure time, though one advantage of working from home is that you can juggle your hours to include night-time work. For work you need maximum voltage. But when you want to relax, it is important to switch to a gentler, mood lighting.

6 Even the most utilitarian furniture can be given executive status with a little imagination. Painting the trestles to match the filing cabinet transforms a cheap option in to an elegant solution. The printer is raised on a small colour-coordinated shelf while the paper tray is an ordinary box given glamour with a simple lick of paint.
7 For some people – notably writers and young fogeys who hanker after the days of Dickensian clerks – the appeal of high-tech is entirely resistible. An uncluttered table, good light and a sharp pencil may be all you need to write that masterpiece.

Playrooms

1 **Children need very little to fire their imaginations. Smart, expensive climbing frames may have far less play value than a pretty garden pavilion. A scrap yard to adult eyes is paradise to children, where an old iron bed doubles as den and trampoline.**

Play is essential to the development of children – without it the spirit of child-hood shrivels up and dies. Children need play space of their own with some sense of independence from their parents. For babies and toddlers play is a valuable prerequisite to more formal learning. But where there is potential space for one, the separate playroom has quite probably been squeezed out by the home office, and the take-over by tele-vision now means that in too many households passive entertainment has replaced active play.

While children are at the baby and toddler stage, their playroom may be a portable basket of toys which means they can play under the watchful eye of a parent. But once they get past the stage of swallowing marbles whenever the opportunity presents itself, they benefit from some independence. If you do not have the space for a separate playroom, the bedroom usually doubles up as one. Children seem to have no problem in dissociating the space from sleep: as soon as the first rays of day-light hit the room it readily takes on its daytime role – with a vengeance. But children also like to be near, so a room three floors up probably won't suit until they are at least seven or eight.

Generally, children's playthings fall into three categories which need to be considered when it comes to storage. There are boxed games which are prob-ably best stacked in vertical piles on shelves with the names on display. There are all the bits which go together to make a whole – Lego, bricks, plastic people etc. Keep these in brightly coloured plastic storage boxes – ice-cream boxes are also useful for keeping the smallest bits together. Hardback books obviously need shelves but you may find that a large basket on the floor is more useful for the paperback picture books of early childhood so that the children can flick through by them-selves to see the covers that might be overlooked in bookshelves.

2

3

2 Teenagers living at home need somewhere to call their own – and somewhere free from the decorative influence of their parents. If you have the space to indulge them, a bed-sitting room is ideal – with sofas and chairs to accommodate their friends – because however groovy you may feel yourselves to be as parents, they really do not want to sit around the kitchen table with you. With their constant craving for clothes, it does not make sense to waste space on a wardrobe which will soon be crammed to overflowing – a hanging rail will be able to take the load better.

3 Easily cleaned floors with soft rugs are best in a playroom.

4

5

4 A mezzanine level in a child's bedroom conveniently separates sleep from play and makes going to bed more of an adventure than an affliction – at least until the novelty wears off.

5 Many children feel liberated rather than repressed by a certain amount of order and discipline in an area set aside for quiet, creative activity. A healthy play environment, however, should also include a less structured area for dressing up and pretend play.

Generally speaking when it comes to children's toys, storage and display should be one and the same. Toys should be accessible and safe – don't keep them in heavy-lidded boxes which can trap fingers. And make sure shelves are firmly fixed to the wall: children will inevitably climb up them when trying to reach something on the shelf above.

If you are lucky enough to live in a house with non-standard features – deep window-sills, small alcoves and pockets of 'awkward space' – children will make a beeline for them. This is where they can spend the most valuable currency of childhood – their imagination. Be wary of buying things where the adult designer has done the imagining for them – the darling little lipstick-pink Chesterfield sofa, for example. For the same money you could buy them a real garden shed to use as a playhouse.

As children get older they need more space – whether for watching television, making model aeroplanes or homework. Where there is not much floor space a raised bed which houses a desk, drawers and wardrobe underneath is useful for this age group. The disadvantage is that they are difficult to move around for cleaning and may be considered deeply uncool by the teenager.

Accepted wisdom about teenagers seems to be to keep them as far away as possible from their parents. A caravan in the garden, as some advocate, may be a little excessive, but they do need somewhere private to go and listen to loud music. The mutual revulsion between teenagers and parents is much exaggerated; like all of us teenagers need to be given a degree of freedom. If you have the space and funds, a loft extension or basement flat is probably the ideal solution.

Individualizing personal space can counter an increasingly standardized world. This section provides a visual source book that shows the range of materials and finishes available to enable you to customize your surroundings. Since most of us are allergic to design that looks good but doesn't wear well, the text notes how different options combine form with function, design with economy. Character and a sense of budget are not mutually exclusive terms when it comes to remodelling or redecorating. While our homes are the perfect vehicle for expressing individuality, they must also be within our means. So in addition to the relative merits and maintenance of design options, the text also considers the practicality and relative costs to enable you to make the right choices for your home.

In the section on walls and ceilings, the emphasis is on decorative treatments that support style and substance. Without lifting a hammer, you can use materials such as paint and paper on walls and ceilings to make rooms wider and taller, in appearance, if not in fact. Textural surfaces, ranging from commercial sandpaper to concrete to natural fibres, grow more tactile at close range.

Flooring is a room's home base; always underfoot, acoustics and sense of touch enter into consideration. Choose a gently massaging surface – carpet for instance – and you cross a room as silently as if on tiptoe; a wooden floor that feels cool and smooth will have you marching. Materials that complement the use of the room and the other elements in the space is another factor of a good choice. If you increasingly find that the generic simply won't do, read on and open you sights to the range of options now open to you.

WALLS AND CEILINGS

Walls are boundaries that enclose a room and ceilings are the lofty extreme. Exploiting the decorative potential of these basic elements can dramatically affect the apparent proportions of a room and radically determine its overall character and mood. Backgrounds are not insignificant; the sheer area involved lends impact to any choice of finish.

Plain white walls and ceilings have become the trademark of contemporary interiors. If you're unsure how to proceed and need time to evolve your decorative instincts, there's nothing wrong with this tried-and-tested formula. But even the most hesitant decorator should eventually be liberated by the huge range of of techniques, materials and finishes. From silky smooth gloss paint to broken-colour effects, bold patterned papers to matchboarding, it is easier and more economical than ever to put decorative ideas into practice.

Colour, pattern and texture are the fundamental variables. Colour generates an almost emotional response, from the quiet contemplative quality of chalky whites, serene blue-greys and gentle greens through to the electric jolt of sunshine yellow, scarlet or marine blue. If a room seems bland and characterless, these basic associations can help to lift it out of the ordinary. Dark rich colours and dense pattern draw in the boundaries of a space, making it warm and enclosed. Light fresh colour allows walls to recede and promotes an airy, expansive quality. Pattern offers similar potential, but requires sophisticated handling. The scale of the repeat and type of design must be tailored to the proportions and size of the room: large-scale prints with a high degree of contrast will overwhelm a small, enclosed space; tiny, subdued motifs will fade to insignificance in a big high-ceilinged room. Texture is a vital component of any finish, bringing a tactile quality and a material expression which adds depth and character.

When you begin to draw attention to the walls, it's worth remembering that any applied treatment will only ever look as good as that which underlies it. In spatial terms, decoration can disguise and distract, but it can be cruelly revealing of substandard surfaces. Preparation may be dull and time-consuming, but it constitutes the essential means to your required ends, enabling you to gain maximum benefit from your decorative efforts.

1 Decorating doesn't have to be terribly costly or time consuming: even the simplest walls look better for a couple of fresh coats of white paint. Neutral colours focus attention on simple touches such as a vase of flowers in dappled sunlight.
2 Primarily used in the construction industry, simple builders' planks have been used to form a partition wall.

3 A dramatic plane of strong colour – as on this ceiling – can make a room seem larger by drawing the eye away from the enclosing walls.

4 Concrete breeze blocks follow the subtle curve of this window, and are juxtaposed against the smooth surface of the traditional plaster wall above. Concrete walls and floors are most feasible in new constructions or when adding an extension.

5 A wall of glass brick filters light from upstairs, refreshing the rooms below.

Making a choice

1

2

The walls and ceilings of your home have to withstand considerable wear and tear. They should be able to weather the dirt of day-to-day living and to sustain the occasional knock; they need to withstand condensation and, within reason, to be straight – though no house is made up entirely of right angles.

Before you even begin to consider a new decorative scheme, you need to check for (and, if necessary, eliminate) any structural problems: no finish can cover up a damp wall or a ceiling in poor condition. Injecting insulating foam into the wall or ceiling cavity reduces heat loss and mitigates condensation problems.

If heat loss remains a concern, consider warm, thick finishes such as plaster, timber and padded fabric panels. If noise pollution is an issue, walls of stone and fabric are better than plaster or wallpaper at hiding sound and providing privacy. Paint and wallpaper are versatile, generally cheaper, more easily changed and much less permanent than tile, stone and wood panelling, making them good interim choices.

ON THE SURFACE

One of the first things to consider is a general colour scheme, either for a particular room or for the whole of your house or flat. Do you want the walls to be a muted background to furniture and furnishings or do you want them to be bold in their own right? Do you prefer solid colour or pattern, a silky smooth gloss finish or a rougher texture? It is a good idea to concentrate on playing up good features and minimizing those that are less attractive. Different rooms have different moods: think in terms of the overall feeling you want to achieve, the function of the room and its contents.

When a room has disparate or dominant features – walls at odd angles, sloping ceilings, a staircase, more than two entries – a single decorative treatment or pattern often helps to unify the space. Alternatively, you can highlight irregularities by distinguishing between one plane and another with different shades of the same colour, by using the same colour but varying finishes and textures, or with

complementary colours. A block of bright colour on one wall articulates the space by making that particular wall the focus of attention. Using colour to pick out architectural details brings definition to the whole room, and can be a useful means of drawing the eye away from less than perfect finishes elsewhere. Pale wall finishes extend the boundaries of small and plain rooms by reflecting light; similarly, pastels and soft colours will make you less aware of a room's narrow confines.

Picture rails and chair rails provide an obvious boundary for different wall treatments. If they've been removed you can reinstate them with new mouldings or simply by painting a stencilled border, dado or stripe. Trim gives structure to a room: picture rails in tall rooms make the walls a more manageable proportion; omit skirting-boards and walls appear to float.

Glass walls and ceilings filter and diffuse natural light. Glass is not an expensive material to work with and can be used as a layer over plaster or MDF (medium-density fibreboard).

Setting up a dialogue between the walls and the upholstery works best when you stick to simple applications and clear colour as a foundation. Using colour that appears nowhere else but on walls or the ceiling can be clean and modern, but you need to have a good eye to know that the colours you've chosen will work together in a bold way rather than result in a migraine-inducing clash. A close harmony between the colours and textures of a room is the more obvious route for most of us.

Decorative paint effects – such as sponging, stippling or dragging – add depth to flat walls and can help to disguise uneven surfaces and poor plasterwork. You need to practise first on a patch of wall to ensure you have the necessary skills to apply the technique to good effect.

Bear in mind that whatever decorative treatment you choose should easily accommodate doors, windows and other built-in features such as shelves or a fireplace. The proportions of a room can be made to look very different according to the way in which walls are decorated.

1 Contrasting colours of paint on the walls and ceiling of this kitchen add wit and depth to a small space.
2 Old and new – in this case sheets of aluminium, ceramic floor tiles and a slatted wooden floor – can make an aesthetically pleasing combination.

3

4

CEILINGS

A ceiling is like the lid of a beautiful box. There are times when a white ceiling is appropriate, especially when the room's contents are what warrants notice. Ornamented ceilings, even those given a coat of high-gloss paint, are uplifting. Generally, the higher the ceiling the more reason to give it some texture, depth and reflectiveness. Silver and aluminium leaf, Adam-style plaster mouldings, thin beading and rough-hewn timber are some of the effective choices open to you. Picking out cornices in contrasting colours is one way of adding interest at ceiling height, especially if the walls and ceiling are painted the same colour.

To unify a room with several ceiling heights, you can establish a horizontal line around the space – perhaps at picture-rail height, or slightly higher – and use a different finish above and below the line. In upstairs rooms, skylights and dormer windows open up not only the ceiling but the whole room. In converted roof space, the pitch of the ceiling is a positive feature to exploit.

PROPORTION

If the ceiling of a room is nearer to eye-level than the floor, the room may feel particularly claustrophobic. Windows can reinforce this telescoped effect by drawing attention to the room's mid-section. By fiddling with the information walls and ceilings display about their size, you can control how the eye takes stock of space and fool it into reading rooms differently. Shifting the design focus to neglected wall areas or the ceiling through decorative treatment can make rooms perceptually more desirable.

Pattern and texture expand the horizons of walls and ceilings visually, creating a variety of moods and, if needs be, an illusion of spaciousness. Stripes can act as a frame, defining the boundaries of what they enclose. Vertical stripes, in either wallpaper or paint, direct the gaze up and down, which seems to raise a low ceiling. Horizontal stripes painted on walls effectively anchor a ceiling that floats too high. The thickness and spacing of stripes should broadly reflect the size of the room. If you

are painting quite broad stripes, it's best to plan quite carefully in advance so that features such as doors and windows are taken into account and the stripes aren't broken up in a complicated and visually distracting manner. Unless you want the illusion of living in a tent, stripes are best avoided on ceilings and crooked, imperfect walls whose faults will only be emphasized.

Horizontal patterns lead the eye around, visually broadening a small room. Painting in a dado rail below waist height, devising one from moulding, or using a wallpaper border as a dado helps widen a room by drawing attention downwards and making walls seem farther apart. Long, narrow rectangular panels entice the eye upwards; squat rectangles below a chair rail anchor the scheme to the floor.

Continuing the ceiling colour or material down to picture-rail height or painting it a darker shade than the walls are ways of lowering the apparent height of a ceiling. Tenting a ceiling with fabric or applying a rich colour makes a room seem wider.

3 Home improvements are as much about knowing when to leave well alone as what to change: these renovated oak floorboards and window shutters are complemented by the bare brick wall.
4 Dividing up part of a room with painted chipboard partitions and damask curtains also lends a warm touch to the stained concrete walls.

Paint

Paint is incredibly versatile, relatively cheap and offers an unbeatable immediacy. With a little practice, you can achieve exactly the colour and texture you want.

Though on the surface paint doesn't appear greatly to change things, appearances are deceiving. With a few tricks of scale and the sorcery of colour, a room can be made to appear larger or smaller, wider or taller. Horizontal patterns broaden and vertical designs seem to lengthen walls. You can lower the

1 Emulsion painted walls with contrasting trim on window-frame and above picture rail.
2 Paint effect on ceiling.
3 Broad emulsion painted stripes.
4 Contrasting glazed walls above and below dado rail.
5 Paint effect carried over from wall to door.
6 Rough textured plaster walls.
7 White emulsion walls against contrasting wall of rough plaster coloured yellow.

ceiling of a room by painting it a colour other than white or off-white. When the ceiling and cornice are painted the same colour, the eye lingers where colour changes between the walls and the cornicing, not at the true ceiling line. This also serves to lower the ceiling and instill architectural definition.

CHOOSING PAINT

Emulsion and oil-based paints come in five finishes from dull to shiny: flat; eggshell; satin; semi-gloss; and high-gloss. The shinier the paint, the easier it is to wash, but the better the finish has to be. Modern additives speed drying, prevent mildew and improve surface appearance. Eggshell and gloss finishes are oil-based; their durable finish can be washed down more successfully than emulsion. Gloss and eggshell are traditionally used on wood and metal and are recommended for fingerprint-prone doors and scuffable trim. Emulsion is water based and the least durable, but is suitable for walls and ceilings since it both covers easily (though

several coats may be needed) and dries very quickly. Solid emulsion paint comes in a tray and is non-drip, making it particularly suitable as a finish for ceilings

Eggshell and flat finishes are the most effective at hiding blemishes; high-gloss paint, by contrast, makes the most of flawless walls by refracting light and energizing the room. Lacquer is so reflective it can make quite undistinguished rooms seem brighter and larger.

Soft distemper and milk-based paints made from natural pigments bring warmth, earthy colourations and a chalky quality to wood, plaster or wallboard. These paints come in pre-mixed and powdered form. Rubbed down with steel wool, walls finished with distemper or milk-based paint have an instant patina. If a very fine sandpaper is used, the finish looks polished; by using a soft cloth, they appear burnished.

The best paint is costly, made from high-quality ingredients such as long-lasting pigments, pure oils and solvents. Look for titanium dioxide on the label; paints with it may need distilling, but those without it can clump, adhere poorly to surfaces and tend to yellow in sunlight.

You can also use paint to make up glazes and washes. A glaze is a mixture of turpentine and oil-based varnish, usually in the proportion of 2:1, to which oil-based paint is then added. Glazes are slow to dry, but give walls a rich luminous sheen. A wash consists of diluted water-based (usually emulsion) paint and can be applied instead of or over an existing paint finish. The translucent wash of colour brilliantly reflects the light.

COLOUR

Thinking of a wall, ceiling and trim as architectural elements can provide guidance for choosing one or more colours. Painting the walls a deep matt and the trim in a contrasting high shine, for example, would bring out the depth of the walls.

For older houses there were conventions of the day for painting interior and exterior architectural elements that can be easily researched. Visual sources, such as paintings of period interiors, provide wonderful clues.

Another way of choosing a colour is to approach paint the way an artist approaches a canvas. Adding coloured pigment to an eggshell suspension with varnish is a technique painters use to give a burnished depth to the canvas. When this sort of glaze is applied to an eggshell undercoat it gives a wall extraordinary depth of colour. Instead of coordinating walls with your furnishings, you could paint them in a colour that complements those of the furnishings. Literally mixing complementary colours, such as pink and blue, produces a rich 'bruised' shade. When in doubt, however, show restraint – remember that you will have to live with the results!

White walls are a tried-and-tested convention. Ethereal white, tinted with a hint of vanilla or cream, is more inspired and has a greater richness than plain white. Painting different rooms in a house with five or six tones of softly contrasting shades of white and grey provides a neutral backdrop for belongings, and the walls will reflect light in interesting ways.

If you are moving house or flat, the best initial response – if it is feasible – is to paint the interiors white and allow your design ideas to develop over time. However, in a gloomy basement or in a small room, white isn't always going to give you light or make the area less insipid. It is sometimes better to exploit the situation and use dark, rich colour. It's not always necessary to use the palest colours in order to create a feeling of space and light. Soft blue and creamy yellows, for example, work well in dark rooms.

Choosing a paint colour from a paint chart or sample pot is never an adequate gauge as to how the paint will look on a wall. It is worth the expense of purchasing several small samples first. Colour changes during the course of the day, according to the source of light. A sunny exposure makes any colour appear more yellow; cold winter light is whiter and less distorting, while rooms with eastern or western exposures fluctuate through the day according to the position of the sun. Tungsten

light is yellower than sunlight; halogen is white and tends to sap warmth away from paint hues; fluorescent lighting casts a greenish pallor over a room.

To test paint samples, buy a can of each chosen colour and brush a patch of pure white primer on a window wall, which is typically the darkest, on the wall where sunlight lands, at floor level and under your lighting, then apply a coat of your chosen colour on top. Look at these swatches under artificial light in the evening and at various times during daylight. Is the colour giving the effect you want it to? Try to picture the painted wall when furniture, window treatments, a rug and people are in the room.

Custom mixing enables you to achieve any colour you've seen and loved. You need to take care to mix up enough paint to cover the surface: if you run out of paint half way through the job it may be very difficult to match a new mix exactly. Many paint manufacturers now offer a colour-mixing service themselves.

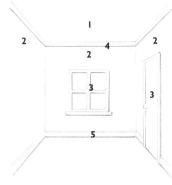

5

6

DECORATIVE PAINTING

Using paint instead of moulding to create wall details has a venerable history seen in eighteenth-century Scandinavian cottages, Mexican haciendas and medieval paintwork on half-timbered houses. The look is fresh and painted details are easy to amend. Painting a dado below waist height, for example, draws the eye downwards and makes walls seem further apart. This is a useful trick for hallways and other narrow areas.

Since their heyday in the early 1980s, some decorative techniques now look a little tired: sponging and ragging are both over-exposed, while marbling requires a deft hand if it's going to have the desired effect. Distressed surfaces call for a subtle approach and plenty of practice beforehand. More versatile and easily mastered methods such as graining, however, still have life left in them and make inexpensive ways to conceal flaws and gain texture. Today, decorative painting remains a fun form of camouflage.

With any decorative paint effect, it is important that you restrict your palette. Methods such as ragging and graining that involve broken colour generally work best when the base colour is close in tone to that used for the effect. If the tones are not carefully matched, the effect will look clumsy. Pattern and texture will partly be determined by the print left by whatever tool or material you use to apply the paint finish. You should always practise first on a piece of lining-paper so that you familiarize yourself with the technique and also so that you gain some idea of how the finished room will look. (For this reason, it's not a good idea to try out the technique on a scrap of paper, as you'll not get a very good idea of scale.)

Almost any paint effect can be used on woodwork as well as walls, but you should resist the temptation to go crazy with a new-found technique. A grained dado or carefully placed stencil will have much greater effect than a room in which every surface has been subject to one special effect or another.

7

If you are painting in or adding wall details, keep your design in proportion to the scale of the room. If you are unsure about the results a scheme may have on the room, transfer your idea to a piece of tracing paper, then sketch possible schemes on the paper with coloured pencils and tape these to the wall to see how it looks. Bear in mind that any design should take doors, windows and other built-in features into account. Use a metal rule and spirit-level to ensure that the lines on the wall are accurately marked out. Before you start painting, lightly tape along the proposed line and view it from a distance. If a wall slopes badly or is subsiding, a level line may actually accentuate the problem and unbalance the room. 'Straighten' the line until it looks right.

Start from a point in the room that will not be the centre of attention, and use a good-quality paint brush. Chinese bristle sash brushes are recommended for enamel paints and nylon bristle brushes for emulsion.

PLASTER

A lot of new construction and renovation in the interior is made from MDF (medium-density fibreboard) or chipboard. When you paint either of these materials, the finish is lacklustre, offering little in the way of depth and richness. If your budget allows, you can remedy this by applying a skim coat of plaster on new walls so the paint will have greater resonance. Plaster is a durable and relatively inexpensive finish spread on walls. It has the material quality of chalk and, unlike flat latex, it doesn't scuff.

Plaster is traditionally made of layers of lime and rough sand trowelled on to wire mesh. Its surface can be striped (by running a plasterer's comb over wet plaster), sparkled (by working in marble or metallic dust) or textured (by rubbing straw or sawdust into the surface). The most understated white plaster is produced by burnishing a plain plaster skim to white iridescence with kaolin from Germany, the substance that makes porcelain whiter than fine bone china. Bare plaster is such a lovely buff-pink colour that it can be worth leaving uncovered in some rooms.

PREPARATION

Proper preparation can add years to your paintwork. Make sure the walls are washed clean and have been lightly sanded, and that uneven surfaces have been patched before they are primed and sanded prior to a main coat. Gloss paints require undercoat; emulsions generally don't. Professionals recommend sanding between coats for a smoother finish.

ORDER OF PAINTING A ROOM

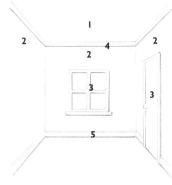

If you are painting the whole room, begin with the ceiling, working away from the main source of natural light. Next paint the walls in the order shown (right); then paint the door and window-frames. Finish by painting mouldings, architraves and skirting-boards.

ORDER OF PAINTING A CEILING

ORDER OF PAINTING A WALL

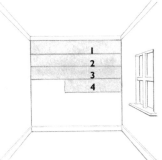

USING A PLATFORM

Wallcoverings

WALLPAPER
Potentially less anonymous than plain paint or plaster, wallpaper is a popular choice for decorating walls, offering plenty of character and style. The texture of some wallpapers can help to disguise a wall's flaws, while a wallpaper mural can deceive the eye about the proportions of a room. People have a tendency to forget how well wallpaper works on the ceiling. An architectural paper and border, perhaps illustrating *trompe-l'oeil* plasterwork, for instance, give a ceiling wonderful depth.

WALLPAPERING A ROOM

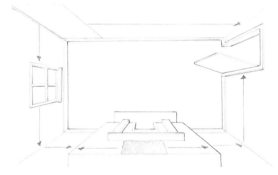

If you are hanging wallpaper with a large pattern, you should begin by centring a piece above the fireplace or other significant feature of the room. For all other wallpaper, hang the first sheet in the corner of the wall adjacent to the window wall and work away from the source of natural light.

Wallpapers also work well in combination with one another or with paint. Using one paper under a dado with a different design above, or using contrasting patterns in a room gives you a real feeling of dimension. These days, patterned wallpaper is not just huge floral bouquets and flocked Victoriana; contemporary patterns, stars, stripes and elegant repeat motifs lend vitality and boldness to a material that has not always been held in esteem.

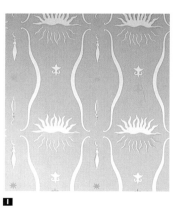

The perceived wisdom is that you should hang a large-scale wallpaper in a large-scale room, and a small-scale paper in a small-scale room. However, small rooms can be given style with a large-scale paper. Choice is governed more by personal taste than proportion and by how much you want the walls to be a backdrop to the rest of the room.

Before buying a wallpaper, invest in a large sample. Pin it to the wall and view it night and day, in natural and artificial light. Florals are easier to pattern match than plaid papers and natural fibres. Delicate and difficult to clean papers, such as grasscloth, woven raffia and foil papers, are only really suitable for walls that are not going to be subject to rough wear and tear. Vinyl wallpapers are the best choice for busy, trafficked areas such as the hallway and kitchen.

PREPARING WALLS
Before wallpapering, strip the existing decoration down to the base wall, and then apply a coat of size (a gelatinous substance usually used to stiffen textiles) to seal the walls. Hanging paper directly on to impervious painted or plastered walls requires high-contact adhesives. If the walls are in poor condition or contain lime, it's advisable to line them first with an inexpensive lining paper to provide a base of uniform porosity and colour. Lined walls give a smooth and less patchy finished result, and the wallpaper will adhere for longer than if it were applied to an unlined wall.

Generally, heavy wallpapers last longer and are easier to hang than lightweight papers. Always use the paste recommended by the manufacturer. Wallpaper shouldn't be hung immediately after it has been pasted; most wallpapers expand after pasting, a process which takes at least five minutes. If the paper is still expanding while it is hung, it will dry unevenly and shrink. Most professional paper-hangers also apply paste to the wall as well as the paper for better bonding. Follow the directional arrows (printed on the back) when hanging wallpaper to ensure that patterns are not hung upside down.

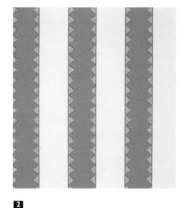

TYPES OF WALLPAPER
There are two basic categories of wallpaper – block printed and machine printed. The labour-intensiveness and quality of the finish is reflected in the cost of the paper. Hand-blocked wallpaper is the costliest variety. Designs are cut into wood blocks, and these are then dipped into chalky distemper paint and applied by hand to heavy paper. The paper is then hung up on rollers to dry between each colour print.

Hand-blocked paper is more difficult to hang. The longer pulp fibres of the strong paper (used to prevent tears during the printing process) make it prone to stretching and curling when it is wet with paste. Bought from source, hand-blocked paper can be printed in colours of your specification, and can last up to 30 years without the colours becoming dull or the paper tatty.

Machine-printed papers are either spongeable, washable or vinyl. Spongeable papers wipe down gently with soap and water. Washable papers are covered in a thin plastic film that allows you to use water (but not detergent) to clean them. Vinyls have a tough and thick plastic coating that makes them scrubbable. Most roller-printed wallpapers today incorporate vinyl, making them much less vulnerable to wear than the paper stock that is used for hand-blocked varieties.

What can be classified as wallpaper often goes beyond the inventory of design retailers. Brown kraft papers (the sort that are used in the manufacture of brown paper bags and commercial sandpaper) are brilliantly inexpensive alternatives to traditional wallpaper, and they don't look cheap or makeshift. Brown paper is simple and sophisticated; sandpaper reflects light beautifully and is a tactile surface. The biscuity-ochre colour of both becomes a neutral and warm backdrop. They work particularly well when counterbalanced with white-painted trim and stripped wooden floors.

NATURAL FIBRES
Natural fibres have a powerful, understated beauty. Their simplicity appeals to the eye. Wood veneers, woven raffia, dried grasses and hessian are backed with paper to make them easier to hang. The effect is as varied as the materials, from the luxury of silk to the rough appeal of hessian. Paper covered with a thin veneer of cork can be used on the walls in a child's room for posters, though most of these materials are delicate and will not withstand much wear. Natural materials cannot be matched: joins are noticeable, but can be concealed using borders or incorporated in the design.

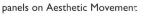

5

later. When putting up wall tile, don't attempt to align borders or dadoes with the grout seams of fixed tiles. It is historically incorrect and may lead to practical problems and superfluous cutting. Grout joints can pick up dirt, though new stain-resistant grout compounds and grout coloured to match tiles makes maintenance easier. Cutting tiles to fit around electric outlets, pipework and alike requires some skill.

Tile designs range from vibrant panels on Aesthetic Movement

8

6

7

FABRIC WALLS

If walls are pitted, the plaster is flaking, or you need to muffle sound, covering walls with fabric involves less headache than calling in builders. Fabric can be pasted like wallpaper, paper backed, sewn together, or put up in a panel system. The traditional style of fabric walling is to lay wadding or interlining on bumpers which are attached to battens nailed to the walls. Pattern-matched fabric is then sewn into panels and stapled

to the top and bottom of the walls. Glued strips of double piping or a braid hide the staples. There are quick DIY fabric panel systems using plastic tracks which enable you to remove and launder the fabric, but the joins can be seen. Fabric can be lightly gathered into casement curtains and hung from stretch wires at ceiling and skirting board.

Felt, cotton, linen, wool and any other light- or heavyweight fabric can go up on the walls. Generally, the

more body and stretch a fabric has the more it requires professional fitters to conceal joins and match the pattern. Thin silk dupion, which tears and gives, and plaids, which tend not to match particularly well, are less suitable than other materials

TILE

Tiled walls can be beautiful and resilient. There are rich possibilities in size, colour and finish, from iridescent to crackled, matt to metallic. Varieties include glazed and unglazed porcelain, vitreous glass, terracotta and clay. Hand-made, customized tile is available from artisans, while antique tile salvaged from old houses is obtainable from second-hand shops and architectural traders. If you hanker after the luxury and intense colour of hand-glazed tiles but are put off by the price, think of incorporating them to maximum effect, as a border or to form a focal point.

Tile comes in batches and can be subject to wide colour variations; buy extra to use as replacements

fireplaces to 1920s tiles comprising a field of plain tiles – a reminder that plain white tiles can be laid to great effect, perhaps at an angle, or in staggered rows. Among the authentic touches that you can revive is Victorian wafer-thin grouting, though a return to the traditional method of polishing unglazed tiles is ill-advised since modern polishers do the job much better. Tiled surfaces in older homes were frequently obliterated with paint or wallpaper as taste of the period dictated. Since they are hardwearing and durable, many tile walls will have survived relatively undamaged, waiting to be rediscovered and restored.

All unglazed tile must be sealed to protect it. Wax is a more time-consuming process, but is more colour-rich, wears better and produces a deeper patina than emulsion polish or acrylic varnish. Wall tiles should be applied with a faster-drying adhesive than floor and worktop tiles. Handmade tile is uneven and looks best if grout joints are not too tight - about 3mm ($\frac{1}{8}$in).

1 Hand-blocked wallpaper with large repeat motif.
2 Machine-printed striped wallpaper.
3 Machine-printed paper with small design.
4 Machine-printed wallpaper with repeat motif above a dado.
5 Small ceramic mosaic tile.
6 Natural fibre.
7 Ceramic tile.
8 Glass brick.

Wood and metal

WOOD

Wood panelling guards against heat loss and insulates noise, conceals uneven or crumbling walls and can be crafted anew or recycled. As the cost of hardwood rises and forests continue to be depleted, there is an increasing need to use timber that is not endangered. Period wood panelling can be found at architectural salvage yards and given new homes for less than the cost of new panelling. Hardwood doors and pieces of armoires and tables can be recrafted into wood panelling. Timber from ecologically farmed plantations provides an excellent substitute for mahogany and ebony, and is no more expensive.

Wooden wall panelling, traditionally known as wainscoting, has been used as a lovely and practical wall lining for principal rooms since the fifteenth century. As with most wooden wall finishes, it is mounted on battens fixed to the wall. Modern tongue-and-groove matchboarding is simpler to construct and usually features beaded moulding. Though it was

originally used in country homes, batten board and wood veneers avoids period clichés. Tongue-and-groove boards can be nailed to wall battens vertically, horizontally or diagonally. Depending on the quality of the wood used and the pattern of its grain, the surface may be stained, varnished or painted.

Tongue-and-groove panelling is popularly used in bathrooms, where it can be painted in seaside colours or to complement bathroom fittings. Wood panelling also makes good, practical sense in a hallway, since it is well able to sustain knocks and blows. Plywood makes inexpensive panelling and, when stained, the wood grain comes through beautifully – this can be an excellent treatment for a study or home office, where the effect is akin to clubs and old libraries. Battens are used to cover the seams between pieces and to create the panelled effect. Plywood is also a good surface for paint, particularly light colours such as khaki, olive green, wheat and white. Lime-rubbed woods and wire-brushed textures enhance doors.

Seal timber wall finishes as insurance against damp and stains and insulate them with metal sheets or fireproof material if they abut the cooker or hob in the kitchen or the fireplace in the living-room.

DADOES

Dadoes are decorative wall treatments that stop at chair-rail height, traditionally one third of the way up the wall; the dado and the moulding above it protected the walls from being damaged by chair

backs and general traffic. Today, dadoes can be just as useful in protecting surfaces and in visually breaking up walls in a way that follows classical principles. The Victorians built dadoes of frame-and-panel and tongue-and-groove boarding or they applied robust, textured paper; however, they can be painted or wallpapered.

METAL

Sheet metal is chic but expensive. Copper, zinc and aluminium are costly wall coverings but work well as panels under chair-rails. Stainless steel is even more of a luxury. Metals dull easily, needing frequent polishing. They come in sheet or tile form and should be adhered directly to smooth plaster or wood panels to deafen noise. Pressed tin ceilings, left bare or painted a pale colour, are an inexpensive way to add texture overhead. Steel diamond plate, used on fire engines and for commercial floors, adds modernity to a room. Painted white and glazed with verithane (used on boat decks), the wall or ceiling neatly diffuses light.

1 Sheet-metal cladding screwed to wall.
2 Tongue-and-groove boards used to create a dado.
3 Wood panelling.
4 White-painted tongue-and-groove walls.

Doors and openings

Doors introduce rooms or close off space, and they vary in importance. Doors to cupboards are very different in material, trim and hardware from doors leading to private rooms, which in turn differ from those opening on to public spaces. The way a door looks hints at the pretensions, scale and service of the room behind it.

All doors should be appropriate in style and proportion to the architecture of the house and the

corresponding room. If your budget allows, designing doors as a focus for the room is a wonderful opportunity. If doors are very large, they will have a much greater sweep, forcing a certain amount of the floor space to be left unoccupied, doubly emphasizing the room's grandeur. Exaggeratedly big doors shepherd you into a room, while small and narrow doors are more intimate.

INTERIOR DOORS

In most instances newly constructed, plain, flat, hollow-core doors need rescuing from banality. People tend to hope they will just fade into the background, but simply by adding an interesting door knob, a new trim around the door, or raised panels you can enhance their appearance for minimal time and money.

Flexibility is a good idea. When doors recess into the wall, the space is opened out. Unfortunately they are not always easy to operate. Doors that reach to the ceiling, such as pivot doors, interact with the room in a much more dynamic and conscious way, and occupy more

space than those of standard height with a frame. Pivot doors have one edge which rotates around a pin to swing the door open or shut. Ceiling-height doors add presence to a room, drawing attention to its height and playing with its proportions.

Since a door interrupts the view from one room to another, it is by its nature a focal point. With a little forethought, doors can add interest to boring and plain walls; depending on their style and treatment they can generate warmth or a cool demeanour, make a room appear large or cosy. Painting the door and door-frame contrasting colours exploits the tension between these two architectural components. Painting the door a dark colour in contrast to white or pale walls and using stencilling or *trompe-l'oeil* decorative painting gives a door impact and a colloquial drama. Veneering doors with wood, or covering them with thin sheets of stainless steel or *découpage* are among the many decorative options open to you.

It is a good idea to play down the doors with matching paint when they are not in alignment or if there are too many. It is also a sensible strategy for undistinguished doors and those in rooms with dadoes or other architectural features that might otherwise be overwhelmed. Glass doors offer acoustic privacy without closing out light or views and provide a continuity from space to space. In narrow houses and terraces, glass doors prove far less claustrophobic than timber doors.

1 Flush interior door.
2 Sliding partition door.
3 Glass rear door.
4 Traditional front door.

The patterning and size of the glazing creates decorative effects as well as welcoming light into the room. Glass doors which swing in both directions form a wall designed to open up your living spaces (though they are not ideal if you have young children).

Folding doors solve space problems. A folding door can create a room within a room, closing off a kitchen, for example, when the cook is hard at work, but folded aside to open it up to the general living area at other times. Doors originally designed for industrial or commercial use, such as for diners, catering kitchens or boats, can be just the quirky jolt a room needs. Space is made totally flexible by the pleated plastic screen doors that are designed to divide up offices.

For some homes nothing is as commendable as an old door. Dutch and French doors, garden and screen doors can be found second-hand, probably covered with layer upon layer of paint. Depending on the decoration of your home, you can strip the doors completely (it is easiest to have this done professionally) and then stain or repaint, or you can rub back the paint layers using wire wool to create a 'distressed' finish. Recycled pine, oak and walnut doors of varying degrees of age and pedigree can be found in salvage yards and recycled.

PAINTING A PANEL DOOR

Wedge the door open before starting to paint it. Tackle the job in the following order: (1) mouldings; (2) panels; (3) uprights between panels; (4) horizontals; (5) outer uprights; (6) door edge; (7) frame.

EXTERIOR DOORS

The front door gives a home focus. Traditionally, the grander the house, the greater the emphasis on the entrance. A front door with side lights creates a different feeling to a panelled door with columns and a pedestal. Painting the front door in a contrasting colour to the façade gives it impact. Coating a front door with firehouse red enamel – as scandalous Elsie de Wolfe did to Manhattan houses in the early 1900s and

designer Brian Murphy does on white stucco Los Angeles bungalows – is an immediate way to articulate an entry. Conversely, painting a front door the same colour as the exterior reduces its impact.

Garage doors, large and domineering, are best painted to blend with the façade. Glazed back doors and the frames of French doors are usually painted to match the window-frames.

Most manufactured exterior doors are ornamented. Unless it is appropriate for the period of your home, avoid bevelled glass, columns and pressed wood grain on sheet metal – they all look inauthentic. The simplest door with good hardware is far better than a door that pretends to have been crafted 100 years ago. For exterior doors, choose wood that can withstand weathering, such as oak, elm and teak. Unless the front door is protected by a deep porch or awning, stain or paint doors rather than varnish them. Door-frames can be painted to match window-frames, with the door a contrasting colour.

FLOORING

Floors form a large part of the surface area of any room, so the way in which they are treated will determine – or at least affect – other decorating and furnishing schemes. Different materials offer different results in terms of colour and texture as well as having properties that make some of them more suited to certain applications than others. In addition to finding a flooring material that complements the room and that falls within your budget, you need to consider your choice in terms of the functions it will need to fulfil. A soft wool carpet, for example, feels luxurious pet, for example, feels luxurious underfoot but will quickly wear in high-traffic areas such as entrance halls, and will prove a devil to keep clean in the kitchen; ceramic tile, by contrast, is cold to the touch (unless paired with underfloor heating) but wipes clean more easily. Still other materials – notably marble and various stone floors – need a solid sub-floor or heavily reinforced floor to take their weight.

Whether you are reconditioning existing floorboards or entirely reflooring a room, the financial outlay will be considerable. Whatever choice you ultimately make will be with you for many years to come. If in doubt, opt for a fairly neutral shade and material which won't interfere with other elements in the room and which, broadly speaking, increases the impression of space – you can always add colour and interest using rugs and other furnishings. Fairly neutral flooring will also keep your decorative options open, accommodating future changes of stylistic direction.

Another important consideration is the junction between different types of flooring. Make sure the transition between rooms is not too jarring and that joins are neatly finished. You can mix and match different flooring materials in the same room, perhaps to define different areas of activity – say, terracotta tiles in the kitchen area and wooden floorboards in the eating area of an open-plan family room. As long as there is some sort of tonal or textural harmony, such combinations can be both visually stimulating and highly practical. The range of options may seem vast and overwhelming, but a careful analysis of your own requirements and the relative merits of the materials available should result in you making a choice that is a pleasure to live with for many years to come.

1 Ceramic tiles – both water- and stain-resistant – make a practical floor.
2 Juxtaposing different flooring materials can add texture and interest to views and vistas. The rich glow of oak floorboards segue into muted flagstones in the adjacent hallway. Rugs delineate the living area and harmonize tonally with the wall finish and the upholstery.

3 Slate floors – whether tiles or slabs – come in a range of hues including purple, red, grey, blue, brown and green.

4 Genoa marble tiles have an understated elegance that works equally well in traditional and modern interiors.

5 Square ceramic tiles shouldn't necessarily limit you to rectilinear floor patterns. Contrasting colours follow the curve of the bathroom wall, forming a witty sea of water around the tub.

4

5

Making a choice

■ Painted concrete walls and hand-made terracotta floor tiles possess both sophistication and an inviting ambience. Scattered kelims and loose chair covers add comfort and warmth at relatively little cost.

■

When renovating, plan to start at the bottom and work up. This means you need to look at the floor first. Address any signs of rot, infestation or damp, then install a damp-proof course, heat and sound insulation and adequate ventilation. Concrete screed or sub-floors need rigid insulation above or below the floor so that feet won't freeze. Make sure water pipes are encased in sleeves or ducts; never run them in solid concrete floors or you risk leaks when pipes expand and contract – and subsequent major disruption. After these prosaic considerations, there is a vast range of surfaces and finishes to choose from including dozens of beautiful hardwoods and softwoods, brilliant modern materials and ageless stones and tile.

CONNECTIONS

After deciding on the material, consider floor colour and design. The floor is usually the background music to the symphony of grander collectibles and architecture in the room. Be wary of fashion's transitory images which may quickly appear dated. In large rooms, in particular, it's important to think carefully before you buy: whatever material you choose will be expensive if you have to cover a large area, so you'll want it to be able to live through changes of use and lifestyle.

Take into consideration the room's relationship to its surrounding areas. If there is a view into other spaces with different floor coverings, do you want to separate or unite the rooms? Brick and stone integrate the indoors and out, especially when an organic relationship to the patio or garden is important. Simple and monochromatic flooring runs seamlessly from room to room conveys space, unity and pedigree, but you have to take into consideration the different functions of different rooms: the main routes through the house and rooms – particularly the kitchen – that see a high level of activity need to have flooring that either shrugs off the dirt or is easily cleaned. Carpet, in particular, is best restricted to rooms where self-indulgence is the order of the day.

The ground rule when deciding on a floor is to select the right material. Base your decision on price, wear and tear, maintenance, comfort, how the room will be lived in and the type of atmosphere you want in the room. Ensure floors are sufficiently robust and adaptable for the contrariness of daily use. Is your floor going to see children and pets bringing in dirt day in and day out, toddlers experimenting with food or crawling about? Terracotta, slate and wood are durable, natural materials that will stand up under these sorts of demands. The manner in which they wear with age is all part of their attraction. If it's an exterior floor, will it be subjected to freezing and thawing or exposure to rain? Some floors – such as stone or concrete – will withstand brutal weather; others – like some types of tile – will crack or lose their glaze when exposed to the elements.

Quarry tile and stone combine function with patina, but are less sound insulating than carpeting and linoleum, which are easier to install and cheaper. Concrete, aluminium

and rubber are also durable, though the acoustics caused by an aluminium or stainless steel floor mean they should be used with discretion.

On the other hand, if 'natural' is your byword for a good material, floors ingrained with nature – such as timber and stone, seagrass and terracotta – come with positive, ecologically friendly virtue. Their earthy palette is versatile enough for both city and country life. Raw materials and textures, such as coir and sisal, add depth.

Lesser-known materials can be cheaper and more acceptable. For example, cultivating birch (considered a weed by millers) and olive ash for flooring is a way to increase the economic value of small, specially planted woodlands where these timbers grow native and in plentiful, cheap supply. Dirt is hidden in the irregular pattern of the khaki-brown streaks of olive ash. Species of pale woods veined with blue fungal stains are also good value for money. They are uncommonly beautiful but considered imperfect and often sold below market value. These timbers

are alive with colour only; fungi are harmless, dying when the moisture content of the wood falls below 22 per cent, which will occur after cutting anyway. For similar reasons of looks and economy, consider flecked granite and other stones available from companies that carve tombstones. They are less expensive and come in larger sizes than stock from a stone mason and are a neutral foil to a room's decoration.

Since a floor is a large plane, its treatment influences the overall look of the room. You want it to have impact – but without trying too hard and dominating the other elements. Strong, large patterns and dark, vivid colours take your mind off the boxiness of a room and can also be used to make it look smaller. Conversely, tight patterns, light colours, and plain surfaces tend to look more expansive, increasing the sense of space and tranquillity.

It's also worth taking into account accessibility to under-floor services, your home's architecture, existing decor and furniture and how much disruption you're likely to encounter.

3 A poured concrete floor coated with grey exterior paint shimmers when it rains; the climate of this California beach house encourages an open-door policy. By placing the mattress on the floor, an illusion of height is given in this low-ceilinged bedroom.

2

3

2 Sand-blasted glass doors, a semi-circular wall and rough plastered ceiling give the room a clean, modern look. Thin wooden floorboards temper the dramatic architecture. Windows of opaque glass screen less-than-neighbourly views while still letting in natural light.

4 Slate is used indoors and out, creating an organic relationship between house and garden. Interior built-in sofas mimic outdoor bench seating to blur the extension between the two further.

4

Hard flooring

BRICK

Bricks are basic building blocks, non-slip and waterproof. Bricks of soft orange-red, buffs and browns lean to the cosy and rustic; those in blues, purples and yellows are cooler, and those of green flint and lime are rare. Old bricks sold by the tonne in salvage yards look best, since they have already acquired the patina of age. Like sponge, brick is absorbent. Spills and messes seep into all but engineering brick, which is fired to a higher temperature until vitrified and not absorbent.

Laying Bricks can be laid in a variety of patterns on a damp-proof base, bedded into mortar. Bricks can only be laid on floors that have a high load-bearing capacity. Elsewhere in the home, you could consider using thin brick tiles.

Treatment Sealing plasticizes the character of brick considerably and can be tricky to apply.

TILE

Tile resists heat and is hard wearing, easy to clean and immune to water and most household chemicals. Installation can cost as much as, or more than, the tiles themselves. By surface area, tiled floors are more expensive than linoleum or vinyl, but similar in price to hardwood flooring.

Tiles are not for the clumsy; any china dropped on the floor will probably break. They are noisy, hard on the feet, and cold – though a tile floor can be paired with underfloor radiant heating for warmth. Floor tiles must be non-slip, though water on any hard surface is always slippery – no material is skid proof. Unglazed quarry, terracotta and cement tiles

are naturally non-slip, won't blister, burn, or discolour, though they can be slightly absorbent. Hand-made, unglazed tiles, glazed tiles with an undulating, uneven surface and machine-made glazed tiles with an abrasive grit added are also suitable. Glass tiles are too slippery (even when sandblasted) and fragile for a floor, as are high-glazed tiles with smooth surfaces which mark.

Burnished terracotta is the warmest floor tile. Hand-made terracotta tiles are of natural clay, fired in a kiln. Terracotta never quite loses its propensity to retain heat, which makes it kind on bare feet. In about a year, terracotta develops a rich patina which glows with a quiet fire, though walked-in grit – such as pebbles and stones – acts like sandpaper on the surface.

Ceramic tiles are crisp and smooth underfoot. Encaustic (inlaid) tiles can be remarkably beautiful, but some don't react well to pets and babies: urine is acidic and apt to stain if the encaustics are unsealed. With machine-made embossed tiles, the

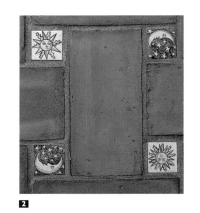

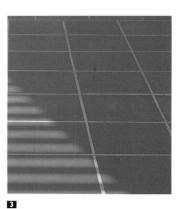

first ones out of a particular mould are clear and crisp, while the last – many hundreds of castings later – are fuzzier and less distinct.

Quarry tiles are a dense, durable, extruded tile that are widely used. Made from unrefined high-silica clay, they have a basic appearance that suits country cottages. They are available in a similar range of colours to brick, and are slightly less durable than ceramic tiles.

Laying Tiles can be laid in a variety of patterns and with decorative borders though, especially over large areas, simple treatments usually look best. Tile needs a level, rigid base. If you have concrete screed, you can tile directly on top. If you have a wooden floor, the movement of floorboards will eventually crack the bond between the adhesive, causing tiles to rear up. Cover timber floors with hardboard first or use a malleable glue that when mixed into the adhesive and brushed on a bendable floor allows movement without breaking the adhesive. If you have lovely old tile or stone floors with bad grout, you can take up the floor and reset tiles and slabs in fresh grout. Old quarry and encaustic floor tiles can be prised up from their soft mortar base, cleaned and relaid in sanded, cement-based mortar.

Grout is used to fill the gaps between the tiles. It is a mixture of Portland cement and sand and comes as a powder to be mixed with water to a quick-drying paste. New acrylic latex additives have improved grout, preventing cracking, loosening and staining. Grout on floors is bound to stain, so opt for colours that will camouflage wear. (Bear in mind that

dark grout will set up a noticeable grid pattern.) If you are using coloured grouts, choose non-porous tiles so the colourants won't be absorbed. For aesthetic reasons, tight grout lines are recommended.

Tiling requires honest toil. Tiles are difficult to cut and space. Badly laid tiles may lift up and lead to water seepage.

Treatment Sealants are normally used to protect tile floors, but may darken the tile colour. Resin sealants are available in a liquid form that solidifies over the floor like a heavy-duty polish, and particularly suits stone and terracotta. Silicone sealants, similar to those used to waterproof shoes, also deepen colour, usually evenly.

Unglazed tiles are traditionally sealed with linseed oil and wax, a method which deepens their colour several shades, protects from food stains but requires periodic re-waxing. Since tile floors are costly, sample potential sealants on spare tiles to gauge the effect before covering the entire floor.

Quarry tile is never glazed; it remains the colour of the base clay. Although the floor can be left unsealed, it is best to coat quarry tile with a penetrating oil before it is laid to build up immunity to stains.

Soap and water mops up most messes on tiled floors. For grease and oil stains, try a neutral pH detergent. Berry juices come clean with mild bleach. Tougher grime can be removed with a mild mix of phosphoric acid, but take care as harsh abrasives can damage the glaze.

6

STONE

There is a wide acceptance of stone's imperfect beauty. It is available in hues from winter's pallor to spring's lush green, in custom-cut tile and slabs. Stone floors work best when the colour, texture and weight of the stone is in scale with the architecture, decor and volume of the room. As a rule, the bigger the slab, the better the floor looks. Other varieties include granite, York stone, bluestone and fieldstone.

Stone is as hardwearing as tile, but bears the irregularities of nature. Sold as slabs, stone is costlier, colder, heavier and noisier than ceramic and quarry tiles. Stone chippings cast with cement into slabs or tiles are a cheaper alternative. Costs vary according to type. For example, sandstone is cheaper and tougher than limestone, and needs no sealant which makes it easier to lay.
Laying Stone is very thick and most fragile during installation, making it a Herculean task for one person. Stone must be laid in a cement bed on a concrete sub-floor with a damp course. For some types of stone, you might have to allow up to 100mm (4in) in depth for the new floor; slabs under 80mm (3in) thick are scarce. Calculate the weight of stone slabs, then check the load-bearing capacity of your sub-floor with a surveyor.
Treatment Some stone is porous and can be sealed, while other less porous varieties cannot. Check with your supplier as to whether sealing is recommended. A coating may alter the stone's coveted (and costly) character by changing its colour or causing chipping. Once laid, it needs a sweep, wash and polish.

7

MARBLE

Marble is opulent. The veining flatters floors and its rich colour strikes the eye. But marble is as rich in price as appearance; it is also formal and slippery. You can maximize its use by honing the surface, choosing darker colours (green, red and brown hide stains better) and using a mineral sealant.

Marble comes in slabs or tiles and a stunning selection of more affordable choices, such as inlaid tiles.
Laying As tile, marble must be laid on a level, solid floor, such as a concrete sub-floor, with cement or sand screed, or any smooth sub-floor with a latex screed. Thin veneer marble tiles place less strain on suspended timber sub-floors.
Treatment Polishing can prove a problem and needs frequent repeats. Scrub marble with non-acid cleaners.

SLATE

Slate is cold, hard, durable, waterproof and cuts easily. It can be honed or left rugged, evocative of the mountain regions where it is

hewn. Darker colours, such as purple and black, show dirt, dust and scratches, leaving footprints and spills more visible than on grey, green, red, sienna and mottled slate. An economic, non-porous alternative to marble and granite, slate is reasonably stain resistant, and some suppliers advise against sealants.

Slate tiles come in smooth or rippled finishes, but slabs can be custom-cut without much of a difference in price. Random cuts laid in abstract patterns highlight the textural variations in the stone.
Laying Install slate on a concrete slab, screed or plywood sub-floor. To ensure you have the minimum deflection in the floor and to reduce the likelihood of it bending or of joints cracking, lay slate on a base of 20mm (¾in) plywood with a 12mm (½in) thick underlay board screwed on top of it.
Treatment Slate holds up well untreated or it can be polished with wax, vegetable oil or olive oil (all of which change its appearance slightly). Slates from India, Africa and China

8

tend to have a higher absorption rate, and for these it's probably worth experimenting with a protective coat. Wipe clean with a damp cloth. Surface scratches and stains erase with sandpaper.

TERRAZZO

This aggregate of concrete and granular marble chippings has a beauty that lasts, requiring little upkeep. Terrazzo is tough and streamlined, fairly non-slip and available in hundreds of colours. A paganized version of marble, splodged or mottled rather than veined, it is nevertheless no cheaper.
Laying Terrazzo can be trowelled or rolled on by professionals, laid down in the form of slabs or in even more durable hydraulically pressed tiles. Terrazzo floors must be laid on a screeded sub-floor, and – unless trowelled – are best in panels of about 8m (26ft), with brass or zinc dividing strips. Because of its strength, it can be as thin as 9mm (⅜in).
Treatment Seal as for tile. Wash clean with hot, soapy water.

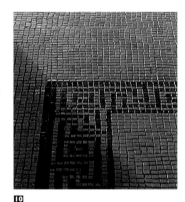

10

MOSAIC

As a focal point or on its own, mosaic can imbue a room in floaty, ethereal romance or give it the humble charm of a cobbled street. The labour required to piece mosaics of glass silica, clay or marble into a floor is dearer than the cost of materials. More reasonably priced ceramic floor tiles create mosaics at half the price. Mosaic floors are as durable and noisy as tile; they should be cared for and installed like tile, and come in a huge range of colours.

9

1 Untreated brick.
2 Glazed brick laid around small encaustic tile.
3 Machine-made terracotta tile.
4 Black-and-white ceramic tile.
5 Quarry tile.
6 Old flagstones.
7 Marble tile with border.
8 Terrazzo.
9 Slate.
10 Hand-made mosaic tile laid in 'Greek key' pattern.

Synthetic flooring

CONCRETE

One of the basic building materials emerges as the simplest, most affordable flooring solution. A mixture of cement powder, sand and water, concrete is sensitive to site and climate, and it is able to take on any shape or thickness. Concrete has an austere quality in slab form, much less so as tiles, or when waxed or stained. It can be packed like clay, veined, textured with shards of glass and coloured with the pigments used for plaster. Concrete forms a cold,

heat- and scratch-resistant floor. Mixed with additives, it is less susceptible to chipping and cracking than the cement that is mixed in trucks and poured on footpaths.
Laying Concrete floors are economical for new homes, additions, or when new screed is required. You can pour it on existing tile floors and reinforce apartment floors with steel rods to accommodate its solid-state style. It takes 28 days of curing to set.
Treatment Concrete can and should be sealed to be impervious to oil, food stains and water. Ask the supplier to recommend a stain best suited to the type of concrete mixture used. After the sealant dries, an application of several heavy coats of commercial paste wax followed by machine buffing will give a concrete floor a warm texture. Treating a grey concrete floor with an acid wash preserves its hard-edged character but adds a refined interior finish. Adding copper sulphate, a mineral with non-fading, saturated green colour, gives a verdigris finish.

VINYL

Practical, low-cost, non-allergic vinyl is comfortable under foot and well suited to family life. Vinyl comes in tiles and sheets (some wide enough to fit without seams) in a more limited colour range than linoleum or rubber. The thicker the vinyl, the more cushioning, more durable, more expensive and more stain resistant the floor.
Laying Sheet vinyl can be laid over existing floors. Vinyl tiles are a great DIY material, cheap and easy to

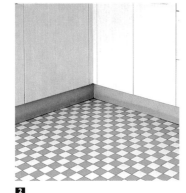

install, but they may shift and pry up if they are laid on wood or near constantly wet areas (like kitchen and bathroom sinks).
Treatment Manufacturer's polish can build up to an unpleasant yellow. Never-wax floors should be buffed, and no-wax ones vinyl polished.

RUBBER

Made from the rubber tree's milky sap mixed with chalk, powdered slate, asphalt, cement, cork, or marble chips, rubber is tough and waterproof. It can take a pounding and is flexible and durable. Rubber comes in more than 25 different textures from smooth to studded.

Textured surfaces are visually bewitching, but they show stains and hot items may burn. Rubber jigsaw tiles, originally made for sports halls and gym floors, don't require adhesive and can be loose laid, making them suitable for damp-proof basements, outdoor patios and children's playrooms.
Laying Since undulations and dust interfere with rubber's adhesion on

level floors, apply an acrylic adhesive to a latex screed on concrete, and then lay the tiles. Alternatively, you can overlay floorboards with plywood and then glue rubber tiles in place. The acrylic adhesive is easy and simple to work with, making rubber tiles a DIY project. Sheets require a metal or timber edging.
Treatment Sweep and mop clean with non-acidic detergents. Use a natural bristle brush to loosen dirt from crevices in pattern treads.

METALS

Though hardly conventional, aluminium, stainless and galvanized steel are nonetheless original and resilient flooring materials. Aluminium (specify the calibre of aluminium used for aeroplanes) and zinc can be polished, oxidized, sandblasted or brushed (a finish which hides scratches). Zinc is a coating on iron which does not corrode with water and oil. Aluminium and steel buffed with a sander or pressed with a diamond or chevron design reflect light in unusual patterns.
Laying Metal comes in sheets which should be welded and laminated to a level timber, fibreboard or plywood base so that it doesn't sound like a tin can when walked on. Solder metal sheet seams together.
Treatment Sealed with epoxy or polyurethane, sheet metal is a forgiving, non-slip flooring surface. An occasional rub down with a wire wool pad will keep zinc, aluminium and other metals from getting dull. Expect zinc and aluminium to wear to a natural patina.

1 White painted and glazed concrete.
2 Vinyl.
3 Machine-pressed stainless steel.
4 Studded rubber.

Natural flooring

LINOLEUM

Linseed oil, ground cork, wood, flour and resins are baked slowly at high temperatures and pressed on to a jute or hessian backing. Linoleum is static free, resists burns and is available in sheets or tiles, in a huge range of colours and patterns.
Laying Glue tiles and sheets to a level timber or fibreboard floor for best results. A straight edge, tape-measure and Stanley knife is all it takes to lay tile; borders and sheets require professional tools.

Treatment Simply sweep, wash and wipe linoleum down with an emulsion or wax polish.

CORK

Natural cork is compressed with binders and baked to form tiles. Thicker grades provide greater insulation and resilience.
Laying Cork tiles are easy to cut and quick to lay on smooth, dry floors (but not over radiant heating; they will lift). If laying on a concrete floor, install a damp-proof membrane beneath the cork or vapours will rise up from the concrete slab and the cork tiles will expand and lift. Cover floorboards with thin plywood or hardboard. Use the manufacturer's recommended adhesive and a serrated spreader to apply glue to the right depth.
Treatment Untreated cork tiles work in bathrooms, where their absorbent quality is appreciated. Otherwise, cork needs sealing. Four coats of high-gloss polymer sealant keep the surface from dulling and pitting. Wipe and polish occasionally.

SISAL

Sisal is anti-static, relatively easy to keep clean, hardwearing and versatile. Sisal comes latex-backed, in sun-bleached earth tones and it can be expressively dyed. Bright sunshine eventually fades deeper colours.

Sisal has been elevated to designer status – as a result, you pay more than seagrass or coir for its sophistication. Sisal can be close fitted like carpeting, or made into loose-laid mats or runners.
Laying As with all natural floorcoverings, the level of wear depends on how it is fitted. Sisal is moisture sensitive. To ensure a secure fit and prevent bubbling, overcut by 30mm (1¼in) on each edge and unroll in position for at least 48 hours before laying so it can adjust to the temperature and humidity. Underlay is recommended if the sub-floor is at all uneven, or if more than light household traffic is anticipated. It may be necessary to lay a solid rubber underlay on the floor and then an additional underlay for the natural flooring.

Firmly fix edges down. Gripper rods stop the edges from fraying and flipping up and can prevent any water from seeping underneath. To join sisal edge to edge, use a latex bonding glue or a hot melt tape to give a quick, strong bond.
Treatment Vacuum and protect as carpeting. Treat with a stain-inhibitor and mop spills with absorbent paper or a sponge. Trim small knots with scissors, taking care not to sever a complete weft or warp yarn.

COIR

Modern production techniques have turned coir into a stylish alternative to carpet. Tougher and less expensive than sisal, it is available in loose mats, tiles and wall-to-wall strips which are stitched together. Latex backing prevents dust penetration and increases durability. Coir works well in heavy-traffic areas.
Laying As easy to lay and shape as carpet. For wall-to-wall, stitch lengths together and bind edges with jute tape. Underlay may be required depending on the level and quality of the floor. Acclimatize coir as for sisal; coir reacts to moisture by expanding, buckling and wrinkling and shrinks when shedding moisture, which can result in open joints.
Treatment Vacuum clean and protect as carpet. Brush off any mould that may occur because of damp or humid conditions.

SEAGRASS

Seagrass is grown in paddy fields. The hard, almost impermeable fibre is spun into tough strands and woven into practical flooring the colour of sand with hints of russet and grass.

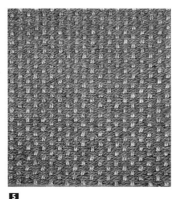

Seagrass is soft underfoot, relatively smooth, and is more resistant to food and wine stains (and unfortunately dyes) than its natural cousins. Price wise it is a good choice and is at home in every room.
Laying Even latex-backed seagrass needs 48 hours' breathing room to allow it to expand or shrink before it is fitted wall-to-wall. Stick down firmly with adhesives that will uplift without mess later, or with underlay. For stairs, lay seagrass with the warp (the heavy seagrass fibre) parallel to the stair tread for maximum traction and wearability. Stairs likely to be used frequently should have protective nosing on the tread. Organic, natural floorcoverings wither like the plant fibres they're made from when subjected to feet scuffing against the risers.
Treatment Choose a stain-inhibiting treatment, usually a soapless chemical applied at the factory, which will put an invisible shield around each fibre. Vacuum regularly. For severe mud or dirt, use a stiff brush along the grain once it has dried, then vacuum.

JUTE

Jute – which has the same innocent charm as other natural floorcoverings – is cheap but less hardy. It will last provided it's treated with respect. The combination of woven jute and cotton provides the natural colour of hemp mixed with cream, blue or red and is a way of bringing in colour without pattern.
Laying and Treatment As with other natural floorcoverings.

RUSH

Also called medieval matting, rush is made up of hand-plaited strips sewn together to the size of the room or hall. Be careful with castors (lift, don't push, the sofa), do not lay it on stairs and step lightly in heels. It is not backed. Sprinkle weekly with water to keep it lush and prevent tears, cracks and flaking.
Laying Normally loose laid even when used as a fitted floorcovering; underlay is optional.
Treatment Lift and dust underneath periodically. Use a watering can to douse rush matting at least once a week.

1 Rush.
2 Linoleum.
3 Cork tile.
4 Coir.
5 Sisal.
6 Jute.

Wood flooring

NEW WOOD

Wood is savoured for its warmth and ability to make life seem richer. It can be expensive, so it's important that you select a species that will provide a durable floor. Oak satisfies traditionalist expectations and is the most hard-wearing of European timbers. Red oak is the cheapest. White oak is fine grained, stable, more sedate and considerably denser. French oak, the same species as English, is slightly paler in colour and straighter grained.

Once common, elm is hard to procure, valued now for its strength and its dark, rich umber hue (though its grain is prone to shrinkage and movement). Chestnut is even stronger. Museums favour North American maple, renowned for its toughness. Ash, beech, sycamore and lime are good general-use floor timbers, but require more upkeep than oak, which is less perishable and more water-resistant.

Wood is relatively easy to maintain and repair and will mature gracefully, actually improving in appearance with age. While most objects will bounce if dropped on wood, tricycles and prams leave behind a strong mark, cigarettes burn and stiletto heels dent. These intrusions break the sealant and leave wood floors open to water damage, the more so if the veneer is not sufficiently thick or hard.

Dry air can cause a timber floor to contract, shrink or twist, so monitor humidity levels; water and other fluids can seep through, causing the floor to warp. If a pipe bursts, floorboards are likely to swell with water and the wood floor could rise, buckle, or warp. Butt-jointed boards are particularly susceptible. In a centrally heated home, it is important to stack timber inside for 10 days so that the moisture-content reduces and the wood shrinks and acclimatizes. Some species require up to two months to prepare.

Laying Timber is available in strips and planks of many widths, pre-sealed tiles and parquet (pieces set in a formal, repeating pattern). Tongue-

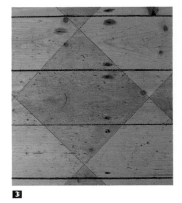

and-groove flooring should be no less than 20mm (¾in) thick and slotted or snapped together. Choose boards cut with a secret nail profile; the tongue is angled so that when a nail is inserted it is concealed when the next board is laid. Short and narrow planks are the most economical choice; in the saw-milling process narrow and short boards are often discarded, burnt or made into wood chips. They have the same 20mm (¾ in) thickness of tongue and groove and, at half the price, make an equally durable and beautiful floor.

Laying boards in random lengths and widths is quite a skill; for the best results random planks should be nailed to oak battens. Parquet and herring-bone floors are less uniform in appearance, fairly indestructible, non-slip, and take a good semi-matt finish, though laying is time-consuming.

Lay wood block and wood mosaic on screeded concrete, ply or chipboard (over a damp course on ground floors). Lay parquet on a concrete base fixed down with adhesive. Wood-strip floors should be suspended on battens or laid on level timber, plywood or hardboard above joists or concrete. Lay parquet panels on a complex series of joists with noggings to support the panels. DIY floors fitted with metal clips and glue are installed without nails.

Misjudging the location of joists and knocking nails through electric cables and water pipes is not an uncommon error, so map out services carefully. Another mistake made by amateurs is to start laying the floor in a recess or alcove on either side of a hearth or protruding wall. Since walls are rarely square, when boards come forward they will not be straight or aligned. Professionals recommend plumbing a line along the front of a fireplace or protruding wall, then working back into recesses, and taking skirting-boards off so the new floor tucks underneath; this also covers up any bad cuts along the edge.

Treatment Some species change colour when sealed; oak simply deepens with an oil finish, whereas elm darkens dramatically. All timber floors rely on a sealant applied with the grain to keep them immune from water. European alkyd-resin compounds and new water-based lacquers are the best; they resist moisture and household chemicals, mop clean with a damp cloth and won't yellow like polyurethane. Perfect for DIY, organic primers (with a base of linseed oil and citrus oil as solvent) and water-based lacquers won't make your eyes water, are less flammable and dry in about 30 minutes. Floors coated with these safer sealants need wax polishing every three to six months, depending on traffic. Urea formaldehyde sealants provide a colourless film suitable for blond woods. Finishes and sealants wear off and must be reapplied. If the floor is unsealed, polish or wax thoroughly and regularly. Vacuum or sweep clean and wash with mild detergent.

TROPICAL WOOD

Tropical timbers from properly managed forestry projects are durable, exotic woods that are ecologically acceptable. Lesser known species are generally less expensive. Buying exotic timbers from ethical plantations and forests is also a way to supply indigenous people with trade instead of aid, since projects are often run by communities, cooperatives or local groups whose aim is to minimize damage to the environment.

Chontaquiro from Peru has a ruddy red complexion and is extremely versatile. Vitex is a teak lookalike available at less than the price of ash and it won't oil spot or discolour like teak. However, no timber has teak's anti-slip characteristic, attributed to its inherent oiliness. Though pricey, kwila (a dense brown with black specks) from the Solomon Islands can be walked, chopped and splashed on. Straight-grained taun, planchonia and calophyllum from Papua New Guinea are bargains and good mahogany substitutes. Turupay, which matures from yellow to chestnut in sunlight, is so tough you need tungsten carbide-tipped blades to shape it. Kamarere is a fast-growing and strong tropical redwood from Papua New Guinea that dries and machines easily.

For elegant, dark floors, there are dense and stable newcomers in toasty shades of brown – ruddy merbau and dillenia, a striking timber that looks like rosewood. Celtis has the open, uncomplicated appearance of pine but the working properties of hardwood. It is comparable to oak in hardness, to beech in cost.

Avoid buying endangered woods and those from over-exploited rainforests. Contact the Forest Unit of the Worldwide Fund for Nature,

4

the United Kingdom Soil Association or the Rainforest Campaign at Friends of the Earth (see Useful Addresses, pages 258-65). These associations keep track of tropical, domestic and imported certified timber from managed forests and ecological plantations. Trust only those certificates with a logo or seal from the Forest Stewardship Council, an international and independent certifying body working in conjunction with these organizations. All new timbers should be kiln-dried to 12 per cent of moisture content; this is particularly important with tropical timber.

Laying and Treatment Lay and seal as native tongue-and-groove plank. Choose a species several weeks in advance of laying the floor. Timber is cut in whatever widths and thicknesses possible from felled trees and the vendor may need to accumulate the square metres required for a floor.

OLD WOOD

Before polishing, staining or painting inherited boards, they must be brought back to decent condition. To strip them down to naked wood before finishing requires a lot of hard work and often entails hiring expensive sanding equipment. Bare boards are noisy though durable, but can get dirty, damaged or splintery. Seal gaps between the boards with filler material to prevent draughts; test filler materials before applying since some may turn a different colour when sealed or stained. Don't be tempted to insulate below ground-level boards or block up sub-floor ventilation – this will lead to

5

damp. Stains and sealants can only darken the original colour of wood, not lighten it. If you want a light timber floor,you can try stripping the boards and then liming them or scrubbing with a bleach solution. The only other option is to begin afresh.

Buying salvaged old floors is a good economy; the expense is in re-laying. Most recycled wood floorboards have been sanded and revarnished repeatedly so they are different thicknesses which makes it tricky to

6

re-lay them. The best buy is recycled parquet wood blocks. Old strip flooring is slightly more expensive than parquet, but cheaper to lay. Old, wide boards are the costliest.

Laying When restoring bare boards, fill gaps with old wood where you've removed badly damaged boards. For a butt-jointed floor, ensure the fit is as tight as possible. Punch nail heads below the surface.

To preserve the lovely surface patina of old and recycled wood, lay the thickest board in the batch first. Then tack fillets to bring the remaining boards level, working from the thicker boards down to the thinnest. Alternatively, you can sand boards down to the same thickness, and at the same time remove old paint and finishes. Since even the grain of sixteenth-century oak will move when it is shifted from a warehouse to a centrally heated home, store old wood flooring in situ for at least a week before installing.

Treatment To refresh floorboards, first give them a thorough scrub with strong detergent and hot water. If the boards have been covered up by rugs or carpet, rubbing them down with sandpaper or paint remover may be all that is needed. If the boards are soiled or have a surface coating, remove damaged boards and then – working with the grain of the wood – use a natural bristle brush and stripper solution. Scrape up residue and sponge-rinse wood with water. Then hire a professional sander. Sand along the length of the boards with the grain; sanding across boards leaves ugly scratches. Empty the dust bag regularly and wear a mask. With a damp cloth, wipe down the floor, then clean with white spirit. Allow boards to dry thoroughly. Boards can be sealed, stained, limed, waxed, bleached or painted.

Stains look patchy unless applied evenly. Use a natural bristle brush, wiping the stain in with a cloth rag along the grain. Gloss or eggshell paints make attractive finishes, but are less durable than proper floor paints, which usually contain polyurethane, acrylic or epoxy resin and dry to a hard finish. Stain and paint can be applied in patterns, using stencils, cardboard squares or the floorboards as a guide for stripes.

7

Stained finishes are not enough to protect a wooden floor, however, so you need to apply a varnish or other sealant. Using a wide, natural-bristle brush, apply three coats of varnish or clear, matt, semi- or high-gloss polyurethane. For best results, let the floor dry overnight between coats and sand lightly with a very fine-grain sandpaper. Seal salvaged floors with polyurethane or water-based lacquer, or polish regularly. Spills will mark the traditional wax finish.

PLYWOOD

Not normally thought of as a final covering, timber-faced plywood at least 20mm (¾in) thick, can be cut into squares or bought tongued-and-grooved and fabricated into an inexpensive floor. Birch plywood from Scandinavia and maple plywood from America are tough and the likeliest candidates; most plywood comes in from the tropics and is not made to withstand walking on. Check with a sheet merchant specialist. With a good finish this flooring has presence or it can be transformed with paint or stain. Plywood's thin veneer is easily damaged and prone to de-laminate.

Laying Lay like any other wood, on boarding in older homes, directly on joists if sufficiently thick, or bed in bitumen or screeded concrete. Ensure the ply surface is laid in the same direction. Plywood is hard to cut into precise shapes and nail. Try serrated-head hardboard nails and ask the merchant to cut to size.

Treatment Seal thoroughly and immediately upon laying. Emulsion polish works well. Sweep and wipe with a damp cloth.

Carpet

Carpet is soft, the essence of luxury, an all-but-weightless flooring with plush, pile and flat weaves meant to skim the floor. Carpet conforms to the keep-it-simple philosophy of decor. It is a cushion to sprawl out on and can be safely crawled over by even the tenderest young knees.

The choice of carpeting, let alone texture and colour, is perplexing. To decide where you stand, you need to acquaint yourself with some of the broad categories and – when you've narrowed down the options – live with samples. Don't buy into brand names; big retail groups provide excellent lines of quality carpeting at low prices because they can guarantee volume sales.

To assess durability, look at the thickness, resilience, the material and weight of a carpet's pile. Press your thumb firmly into the pile; the quicker it recovers, the denser and more resilient the carpet (unless it is a long-hair shag). A carpet's density is determined by how closely knitted each individual fibre is to another, not how low or high the carpet measures. To evaluate the density of

woven carpets, look at the back of the material. Prise open the tufts. If there is too much space between tufts, the yarn will collapse into itself when it gets worn.

Weight should be printed on the label. Check the pile weight per square centimetre and compare like with like, Berber with Berber, nylon with nylon. Short, dense-fibre carpets, the kind that you're practically unaware of, are the most durable. Carpets of long strands and large loops have greater presence

2

and bulk, but weigh less. Velvet-cut pile camouflages dirt but is slightly harder to clean than loop pile.

Match the quality of the carpet with its use. Read the labels and use your common sense. The average life span of a carpet is between five and seven years. Put light-use carpets with a light, feathery pile in bedrooms rather than in the hall or living-room. If you intend to carpet stairs and high-traffic zones choose a dense, tight, low-pile tuft. Professionals recommend buying extra stair carpeting so that you can replace the odd few steps as they wear with material that came from the original roll. This will also enable you to stretch your budget. Consider buying a few more metres of a less hard-wearing, less expensive carpet if you are planning to run the same carpet throughout the whole house and stairs, rather than longer-lasting, costlier weaves which will ensure stair wear but whose durability will be wasted elsewhere.

For years the best choice for an all-purpose carpet was considered to be 80 per cent wool, 20 per cent nylon. A 40 per cent wool, 60 per cent acrylic can be just as durable. These standard blends are much less expensive than pure wool, although they are slightly more commercial and not quite as soft.

There's a natural inclination to shift into neutral for large-scale, long-lasting home furnishings like carpets. Darker colours win out over lighter colours when it comes to traffic and dirt. Consider indulging in a bolder, well-loved colour in more private rooms in your home.

Before you buy, make a rough estimate of how many square metres you need, then do some comparison shopping. Most reputable retailers provide a measuring and fitting service to avoid the most common mistake of over-ordering. Check estimates, which should be accurate to the centimetre, and sign off on a floor plan before the carpet is cut at the factory or shop. In the main, the supplier of the carpet should also be responsible for fitting it. If you split the two jobs, and a problem arises with the carpet, the fitter tends to blame the factory while the factory will blame the fitter.

Laying Fitting carpet yourself is manual labour with injury potential ranging from the discomfort of cuts and bruises to those necessitating a visit to the doctor. Hands and knees are most likely to be hurt. For lightweight and foam-backed carpet and for carpet tiles, wear gloves and knee pads. For all other carpets, hire a professional carpet fitter with the requisite specialist skills and tools. Proper installation will mean the difference between carpet wearing well or badly.

3

Treatment Carpets stain. Stain-inhibitors are an insurance policy, not magic potions. Treatments such as Scotchguard make it easier to wipe off spills as they happen and before they have a chance to settle down on the surface. Stain-resisting chemicals are usually applied at the factory or warehouse for a nominal extra charge per square metre. Some firms can provide in situ fibre sealing accompanied by a comprehensive, active maintenance service. Professionals essentially treat a newly laid carpet, monitor the bonding of the stain protector, supply a kit of chemicals for DIY stain removals and offer a call-out service including advice and cleaning. Such service is costly, but is a worthwhile investment for those partial to pale colours or who have a tendency to discover stains after they have dried and been absorbed.

New carpets tend to shed fluff. Comb them lightly with a hand brush, then vacuum regularly to prevent dirt from embedding itself at the base of the pile where it can rub

1 Wool-and-nylon twist.
2 Pure wool with relief pattern.
3 Wool-and-polypropylene twist.
4 Pure wool.
5 Wilton carpet with a combination of cut and loop piles.
6 Loop-pile Wilton.

1

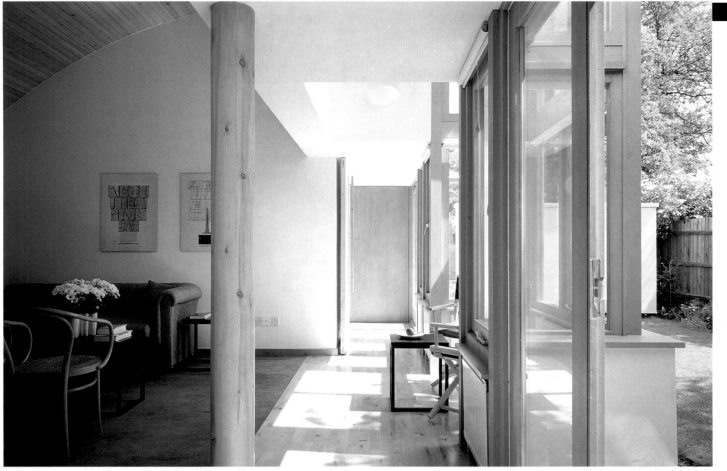

4

and cut fibres loose. To shampoo, follow manufacturer's instructions. Spray extraction cleaning is best left to the professionals.

UNDERLAY
Invest in a good underlay. A heavy-duty one can outlast the carpet. The best padding is a felt or rubber-top underlay made of hair and jute. This natural fibre doesn't flatten, crumble or dry out, is mildew proof and anti-microbial. Bouncier, thicker pads can eventually cause carpets to ripple.

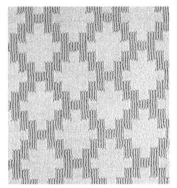

5

CARPET GLOSSARY
Acrylic Wool's synthetic twin in appearance, but slightly less resilient and stain resistant.

Axminster Like an oriental rug, fibres are woven in and out through the surface backing on an Axminster machine. This loom inserts pile tufts into the weave from above so that strands need not run along the back, enabling a multitude of colours to be used. Chosen by hotels and commercial lobbies for its durability

6

and cleanability, the surface is a cut pile, available in long and shaggy, short and smooth, stubbly or carved carpets. Metre for metre, it is comparatively more expensive than carpets made on high-speed modern tufting machines.

Berber A looped, nubbly pile carpet in natural, undyed wool. Now 'Berber' is the name coined for a flecked wool or a wool-blend looped carpet that is not shirred on top. Not advisable for stairs.

Bonded Yarns are bonded to an adhesive base rather than woven.

Broadloom Carpet wider than 1.8m (6ft).

Carpet tiles The selection includes loop pile, velours and tufted tiles. Tiles can be chequerboarded or used for random design patterns.

Tiles don't require underlay, are very flat, thin and hard-wearing, but lack the 'give' of carpeting. Stained and damaged tiles can be lifted up and cleaned or replaced. Bought by the box, carpet tile is a good DIY project. Spread bitumen on a level sub-floor and press tiles into place.

Cord Fibres are woven to give an effect similar to corduroy.

Cotton Cotton carpeting is exceptionally silky and very fine. It won't wear out but does matt down. Rugs with a soft back, in which cotton yarns are secured, can be tossed into a washing-machine or commercially laundered.

Cut pile Yarn filaments are cut rather than looped into the carpet.

Linen Textural, with loose-end pile, and expensive, linen carpet looks very rich and more unconventional than sisal, but still brings a natural feel to the floor. Bought for decoration rather than durability. Linen can be custom dyed to any colour. Best with at least a 5mm (¼in) rubber underlay pad.

Looped pile Uncut continuous loops on the surface. Pile can be short, like Berber, or shaggy.

Nylon Available in a more extensive range of hues than wool and with a clarity of lovely clear colours that can't be reproduced in wool.

Good-quality nylon carpets come with built-in stain-resistant treatments and score high marks for wearability (though not on a par with wool blends). Carpets incorporating metal or carbon-coated fibres have less static. Should static prove a problem try using a simple humidifier (a bowl of water, for example). Nylon is fire-retardant and self-extinguishing; however, burn holes permanently mar.

Polyester Often used for making into shag carpets and other piles that play with texture. Polyester carpets are remarkably soft, durable and stain resistant, but less resilient than acrylic and wool.

Polpropylene (olefin) Relatively cheap, this synthetic material is blended with other fibres to produce excellent quality carpets. Polypropylene cleans quite well. It is hard-wearing and dirt-concealing, but flammable and not self-extinguishing.

Shag pile A pile that's 25-50mm (1-2in) long. Dangerous for stairs; heels catch. It's often as appealing to dirt and bugs as it is to people. Susceptible to tangles and matting.

Silk Among the best weaving fibres, silk yarn is hand-loomed and machine made into fantastically expensive, exotic carpet. Non-colourfast silk carpet fades in strong sunlight.

Tufted Conventional carpeting that looks trimmed. Each individual fibre is punched into a base material, and usually sealed with a waterproof backing. The pile itself may be looped or cut (or both).

Twists Carpet with one-way pile direction. Ideal for places where tread always wears, such as in the hall and on stairs.

Wool As a natural resource wool is an environmentally friendly carpet material. It is also as insulating, durable and hard-wearing as the best wool coat. Wool is available in short runs and limited productions, whereas nylons and acrylics are strictly mass production.

Wilton Derives its name from the type of loom which weaves the yarn in a continuous strand. This method limits the number of colours that can be used. Wiltons have a smooth, velvety, woven surface.

Viscose A synthetic used in combination with other fibres in cheap carpets. Easily flammable and with low dirt resistance.

CARPET WEAVES

Axminster

Wilton

Tufted

Bonded

WINDOWS

Window dressing is the balance between the outside world and your home. It is, in effect, do-it-yourself light control. Curtains or drapery can obscure structural imperfections or eclipse an undesirable view. Window dressing shields us from neighbours in urban areas, shades us from the baking sun in hot climates and keeps out the chill of winter nights. But bear in mind that windows are important architectural features in a room, and that you may not wish to cover them up so much as make a feature of them. Window dressing is not only about framing the view outside or coordinating the scheme with the other furnishings in your room; if the windows themselves are unusual or noteworthy, the way in which they're dressed should not detract from their intrinsic merit.

To give your windows the treatments they deserve, give some kind of nod to the architecture of your home and complement the framework of the window. Furnish windows in accordance with the room's function and with the degree of natural light. Harmonize or consciously contrast its style with the walls, floors and furnishings, but make it an integral part of your overall decorative scheme rather than a casual afterthought. Base your choice on site and context, personal need and privacy. Simply redraping and refitting curtain rods, changing hardware, picking unusual fabrics or a more provocative valance may not be enough - you may decide to change the window.

As you become more comfortable selecting window treatments, you will be inspired to experiment with unusual pairings. Assembling different colours, patterns and textures works well. Opposites attract: drape lustrous brocade beside homely muslin, or sweeps of rich, thick velvet beside the crisp clean lines of tailored Roman blinds. Materials can be left plain or paired with a decorative border; curtains may be simple and sculptural or patterned and pleated; valances and pelmets can be used in an understated way to draw attention to the view or they can provide decorative flourish in a room with little architectural detail. Remember, though, that less is often more. Too much clutter at a window can make a room feel oppressive and hemmed in – simple blinds will often fulfil everything you need of a window dressing with a lot less fuss and for a lot less cost than fancy curtains.

1 A mullioned window frames the view outside.
2 Painting the frames of these mini-sash windows with a jolt of colour draws the eye away from the room and out into the countryside beyond.

1

3 Light marches across this bedroom through a large, mullioned window cut into the sloping roof. Roof windows and skylights are often used to make rooms brighter and to open up small spaces.

2

4 Interior windows elegantly borrow light from adjoining rooms. Most exterior windows can be fitted indoors.

3

5 Venetian blinds regulate heat, reduce noise and maximize privacy without relinquishing all access to daylight. Their spare, clean lines integrate them seamlessly with the window and blend well with modern interiors.

4

Shapes

Windows let in light and air, shut out the cold and stand out as an important architectural feature. The right window makes all the difference. For buildings of considerable architectural value as much as for houses of little distinction the size, shape and material of windows should be consistent or in balance with the original façade so that the building is pulled into visual order. Windows need to be sympathetic to the period of your home and the architectural

framework. One of the fastest ways to devalue a house is to replace the original windows with new metal, timber or plastic renditions.

It is important when adding windows or designing anew not to incorporate big picture windows and patio doors without any sense of composition or rhythm. Let big windows speak for themselves, to frame a fine view or make a bold focal point. But use with discretion and don't compromise the existing proportions of a room: fine examples of 1940s and 1950s architecture are being spoiled by home owners putting in wooden picture windows.

If you want to play down the size of a window, mullions can contain an expanse of glass, becoming part of the visual structure, so that large windows assume a more domestic scale. Mullions work particularly well on windows with a span of more than 1m (3ft) of uninterrupted glass.

When existing windows are beyond repair, it pays to find replacements as close to the originals as possible. If your home needs more

light, then increasing the size of existing windows is one option. If you do not want to disturb the façade, you could add windows at the side or back or cut skylights into the roof. For a room at the top, you can take away the roof itself, leaving the party walls of a terraced house and the front parapet to the street. Light floods in but the front of the house remains the same.

Unless you are building from scratch, new windows should look as though the original home owners installed them. Match the pane sizes and proportions. Align new window heads and sills with the old. If your house is historic or has some mullioned windows, you have an obligation to continue the tradition, the more so if it contributes to the overall look of the community or street front. Don't settle for ersatz substitutes. It's better to have plain glass and a window that is well made than one with snap-in mullions that will lend your home a cartoon quality.

Windows are a long-term investment so select the best you can afford. Powder-coated steel frames are more expensive than timber, but the thinness of their profile and their flat, fine surface make them ideal for double glazing. A good window will be as well suited to its task 30 years from now as it is today.

For an original approach, rather than filling an interior with solid planes – walls and doors – consider using exterior windows to fill in voids. Glass blocks allow light to pass through, but they aren't entirely transparent and so work well as a screen to more private areas. Their industrial aesthetic complements modern interiors.

GLAZING

About 15 per cent of the total heat lost in homes is through windows. Double glazing windows minimizes condensation and the cold zone that you get near windows. This conceivably reduces fuel bills by cutting the heat loss from each room by half, though this saving has to be offset against the high cost of installation. As a heat insulator, the narrower the gap between the exterior window and the secondary glazing, the more effective it is.

DIY double glazing is more cost effective than professional installation; both methods are sensible if you plan to stay put for many years. For windows of old and historic houses, be sure double glazing is not at the cost of architectural integrity and that frames are matched to those of the existing window.

WINDOW DRESSING

Like people and their clothes, what a window wears should accentuate its best attributes, provide some warmth and a degree of disguise. Windows and their wardrobe should be stylish, practical, flexible when possible, even unexpected.

Tall and narrow windows look good in just about every context. Flat Roman blinds accentuate the frame, curtains with plenty of material show off their grace; only top-heavy pelmets are to be avoided. Treatments that extend beyond the sill to the floor act as a visual extension for windows that stop at chair-rail height or are centred on a

wall. Making Roman blinds or curtains from a translucent fabric filters light but blurs it where the window sill ends.

When windows are awkwardly low or stunted in proportion to the room, mounting bamboo shades and relaxed Roman blinds on the ceiling will visually extend the apparent height of the window. Simple valances which focus the eye on the area above the window, or a cornice added to the top of the window

1 Traditional sash windows.
2 Circular window with skylight in ceiling.
3 Small sash window.
4 Mullioned casement window.
5 Casement windows with arch.
6 Sandblasted glass.
7 Glazed internal window.

4

frame also add an illusion of height. With low ceilings, windows seem to hit the roof. Elegant drapes or tails and pelmets that dip to a lower point on each side will draw the eye comfortably down.

If you have a radiator under a window, keep the area of coverage to a minimum to avoid losing heat – make sure there is another heat source in relative proximity. Floor-length curtains or fabric screens work well as a means of additional heat insulation. Both can be pulled

5

back when not required. Curtains that fall in front of a radiator should not be interlined or they will block heat from the radiator entering the room when drawn.

SMALL WINDOWS

Even tiny windows appear bigger if the frame is painted white. Louvred or panelled shutters broaden narrow windows. They look best when the shutters are about half the width of the window itself. Hanging dramatic

curtains on windows not large enough to accommodate them results in visual discomfort. Fabric on tiny windows minimizes them further. Shutters, tailored Roman blinds and flat treatments draw less attention to the window's diminutive proportions. Recessed windows allow only a limited amount of light to permeate so leave them bare, perhaps using the sill for interesting collections of objects.

LARGE WINDOWS

For large windows, subtle and unfussy decorative treatments work best. Avoid small prints and mini-blinds which create a blurred impression when spread over big expanses. If windows are broad, the flat, horizontal folds of a large Roman blind bordered with coloured tape offers a tailored, tasteful solution; pull-down shades made with a metal mesh so they are semi-transparent when down also work well.

Picture windows benefit from a straightforward plain set of shutters. Textural fabrics, such as muslin and lace, diffuse light and reduce unattractive views to a soothing blur. Walls of windows are less domineering when they are united under a valance or treated to panels of sheer curtains suspended from a steel tension wire. Sandblasting some panes to an opaque finish cuts down glare and softly filters light.

Large rear windows at the back of a house can be framed within a pergola. Remember, though, that if the pergola is then planted with climbers this will cut down the amount of light let in. At the front of the house, running trellising to the height of a picture window and planting climbing shrubs will similarly disguise and soften sheets of glass. If a window is too much of an open book for neighbours or allows in too much sunlight, louvred shutters can be inserted over one or more sections and painted to contrast with or match the window frames.

Arched and Palladian windows are a problem to dress well because of their shape and proportion. Custom-made curved blinds or curtains hung high above the arch and falling to the floor look good. For arched windows, suspend curtains from the ceiling.

MISMATCHED WINDOWS

Professional decorators generally discourage using more than one type of window treatment in a room. Mismatched windows present problems of asymmetry and proportion. Rooms with small windows and French doors or dado-height windows and oversized patio doors are not uncommon but are ill-suited to uniform window dressing. Use curtains or blinds made from the same fabric or colour as a means of relating different windows in a room.

6

On the exterior, painting windows of varying shapes and proportions white makes light of the differences. Since glass appears as black or dark grey from a distance, you can paint the windows' inner framework black or grey so that the glazing pattern virtually disappears.

NATURAL LIGHT

Light is a wonderful house guest; it is bright, illuminating, warm, cultivated and never stays too long in one place, casting shadows and changing in intensity through the course of the day. With sunny exposures, however, you can have such a thing as too much sun. Several treatments used in tandem – such as curtains lined with blackout over wooden venetian blinds – provide layers of control. Shade cloth comes in different colours and several degrees of opacity. Pull-down roller shades made from 50 per cent shade cloth mean nobody can see in but you can see out. Shade cloth is available from suppliers of awning fabric and makers of patio and boat covers.

Sandblasting window glass into opaque sheets or with patterns lessens the likelihood of faded fabrics. New production techniques have made available windows that moderate light – which look great when paired with bare sills and sashes – and others with electrical low-voltage charges that 'frost' at the touch of a button, diffusing light.

Another option is one developed for windshields by the automobile industry. It consists of a plastic filament centred between sheets of

7

glass. The milky white surface allows light to pass through but prevents passers-by from seeing in. Like sandblasting, this treatment obscures the view until the window is opened.

Fabrics with textural qualities, such as hessian and sheer metallics, and Venetian blinds fracture the morning sun. Window treatments in 'Indian punch' colours of fuchsia and saffron, as well as bruised colours like vermilion and indigo, warm the cool blue-grey tones of shady exposures.

ORDER OF PAINTING A WINDOW

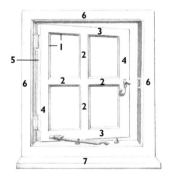

Following the grain of the wood, paint a casement window in the following order: (1) glazing putty; (2) glazing bars; (3) top and bottom rails; (4) outer uprights; (5) hinged edge; (6) frame (top, then bottom, then sides); (7) sill.

Curtains

Never skimp on fabric. Floor-length curtains benefit from a generous mass of fabric. Choose a less expensive fabric to save money, or add a valance on top or sheer underneath for another layer.

1 Café clips.
2 Half-height sheers.
3 Resist-dyed cotton.
4 Roman blinds behind pinch-pleated curtains.
5 Fabric tie-back.
6 Curtains on steel tension-wire track.
7 Cotton curtains bow-tied to track.
8 Cartridge-pleated cotton curtains.
9 Goblet-pleated curtains.

Any material can be fashioned into window treatments, even silk. The sun doesn't break down silk; it is the dirt that builds up on the fabric that is then broken down by the sun. If you vacuum your curtains regularly, they'll last a lot longer. Over time, sunlight, dust, and daily wear and tear lead to general fading and eventual disintegration of even the most colour-fast fabrics.

Think laterally: using café clips – which snap shut around fabric like clip-on earrings – a sari, an old piece of embroidery or a sheet of burlap can be attached to curtain rails with the greatest of ease and at minimal expense to give you instant curtains. Environmentally sound sackcloth (no bleach, no dye) offers a good finish and, at a low price, makes good sense. Other materials that are meant to be worn – like the striped fabric used to line men's waistcoats and Indian madras used for shirts – can be stitched up into a window dressing. The cloth used for sarongs falls softly when used as a window drape and turns a white room into something sensuous.

However, it often pays to invest in one good fabric rather than to dress your windows with a variety of contrasting and disparate styles. The architecture of the room should have an influence on your choice of fabric, as will the general decorative

scheme. Duck (untwilled linen used to make small sails), canvas and muslin are examples of fabrics that are able to hold a fold, and which give depth to shades and blinds. Dark fabrics on lighter window frames graphically delineate a window's sculptural silhouette.

Fabric should look wonderful all the time – both by day and night. A vibrantly dyed piece of muslin, lit from behind during the day, has all the luminescence of a stained-glass window. At night, when it is time to settle down and burrow in, curtains illuminated in front by artificial light sources become opaque and blanket the room. Solid colours can range from the bold to the subtle, and will create very different effects from patterns or printed designs.

MAKING CURTAINS

To calculate the amount of fabric you need, multiply the length of the finished curtain (allowing for hems and headings) by the number of curtain widths. To determine the degree of fullness for curtains, the rule of thumb is to allow two to two and a half times the finished width for pencil and pinch pleats and three times the track length for sheer fabrics. Loose drapes with a single swag need one and a half times the fullness. Add another 40mm (1½in) for each side seam and each join.

Use the window as a template for proportion. Accurate measuring is essential. Measure both vertical sides for curtain drops; subsidence often causes windows to become slightly distorted. If this is the case, fabric bunching on the ground will save you from having to make each curtain to a different measurement. If curtains are to be dressed back most of the time, you'll need less length than if they spend most of the time hanging out on a pole.

For lightweight materials and sheer fabrics, allow an extra 150–250mm (6–10in) overall for hems and heading and 250mm (10in) for heavy fabric. On patterned fabrics, order one extra pattern repeat for each curtain. If fabric isn't pre-shrunk, wash or dry clean it before the curtains are cut out and made.

LINING

A lining protects fabric from light, gives extra weight and body and conceals all the hems and raw edges. Linings also provide a professional finish to window dressing and prolong the life of your curtains. In colours, they offer an interesting view from the street, but you should first check the effect the coloured lining has on the appearance of the curtain material. Blackout linings (not necessarily black) totally or partially block light. They successfully make fabrics opaque, but detract from the overall beauty. Blackout linings suit bedrooms and nurseries.

INTERLINING

Usually a soft blanket layer of padding between the fabric and the lining, interlining improves heat

retention in a room, buffers window draughts and helps curtains hang better and look fuller by softening the folds as the curtain falls. It is sold in various weights.

8

CHOOSING A STYLE

Traditionalists tend to view windows as opportunities to swathe and swag, trim and tassel, tail and tie. Modernists address the fact that we live in the twentieth century; since

6

we don't wear nineteenth-century clothes, our windows should be dressed in curtains that share the same simplicity, tailoring and low maintenance of current fashion.

A window shouldn't be an excuse to go overboard with chintz. When selecting curtains, considerations such as climate control, a room's architecture, and the style and proportion of the windows and their surrounds are as important as the colour, design and texture of the curtain material itself. These are the caveats in a choice that would otherwise be limitless.

The maxim is to keep curtains floor- or sill-length, unless they are hung outside the window frame as a means to disguise badly proportioned windows. Keeping it simple lets the curtain fabric or architecture of the room speak for itself. If the room lacks architectural elements, you can create them in your choice of window dressing. Curtains can be rich in a tailored, deliberate and structural way, with pelmets and valances or a sheer petticoat. (But err on the discreet side – with each element you add, you take away some precious light.) The taller the ceiling, the more elegant curtains look. Masses of curtain tend to appear squat, over elaborate and ungainly, particularly in rooms with very low ceilings.

Coloured borders provide definition to plain curtains. Headings can be nautically knotted or bow-tied to poles. Plain curtains can be given a more sophisticated edge with contrasting bias binding.

Long curtains can be used in place of cupboard doors to hide hanging spaces, to cordon off a vestibule and behind closed front doors for heat retention. Bedhangings are again fashionable, though without the primary emphasis on creating a draught-proof box. Simple muslin draped over plain frames evokes exotic and romantic associations.

HEADINGS

Fabric conveys the desired effect, but the heading defines the curtain style. A heading is the gathering or pleating at the top of a curtain. The tape

7

sewn on to the curtain back determines both the shape and size of these gathers or pleats, or the heading can be hand-stitched.

Pinch, or French, pleats are small clusters of three pleats grouped at regular intervals; they suit heavy, floor-to-ceiling curtains. Pencil pleats are tighter and run continuously across the curtain and work well with lightweight and sheer fabrics.

Gathered headings are a cross between pencil and pinch pleats, best for short, light curtains paired with a pelmet or valance.

Goblet pleats are elaborate and rather formal, with stiff cuffs that are stuffed with interlining or filling fibre. Smocked headings look as if they have been embroidered and must be painstakingly sewn.

PELMETS AND VALANCES

These are three different pieces of window furniture, separate from curtains and positioned at the top of the window over curtain headings. Pelmets are generally made from wood, MDF (medium-density fibreboard) or buckram and are either painted or covered in fabric. Valances are made entirely from cloth. Soft, deep valances convey a mood of relaxed luxury. Lambrequins are essentially pelmets with arms that reach down each side of the window. They are usually made of wood, MDF or plaster to retain their shape. All three define the window treatment and connect it with the architectural framework of a window.

POLES AND FINIALS

Poles are another visual element, available in various diameters and materials including brass, wrought iron, steel, pine and bamboo, though driftwood can be used to great effect, while steel tension wires are modern and unobtrusive. Make sure curtain rings run freely across the pole for easy opening and closing.

Finials are the decorative denouement, traditionally capping off each end of the pole. They range from the discreet to the gaudy. Wood, plaster and metal finials are available in various shapes and designs.

TRACKS

Curtain tracks secure curtains and are normally hidden behind the curtain heading, a valance or pelmet or they are disguised by swags. Tracks range from plain plastic to sophisticated metal. Aluminium track can be carefully bent to fit awkwardly shaped bow and bay windows so that curtains follow the exact contour of the window. For window treatments starting at ceiling height and for those using a heavy fabric, it's a good idea to use stronger ceiling-mounted track. Before hanging curtains, ensure that the track is correctly and safely attached to the wall or ceiling and that it is able to take the weight of the curtains. Tracks can be corded so the fabric of the curtains is handled as little as possible.

TIE-BACKS

Tie-backs help a curtain to drape or fall gracefully when drawn back, and alleviate the stress that the weight of the curtains puts on the track or pole. They're decorative restraining elements holding back curtains to make way for light from the window. A tie-back can be fashioned from almost anything, but usually consists of a doubled straight piece of fabric that is attached by rings to a hook on the window frame or wall. Bows, tassels, cord, metal chains – each serves the tie-back function well and offers a range of looks.

9

MEASURING FOR CURTAINS

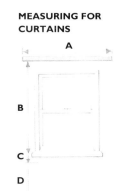

To calculate the amount of curtain fabric you will need, first measure the width of the track ('A') – not the window – and multiply this by the number of times a heading requires. Add on the appropriate amount for seams and hems. To calculate the length, measure from the bottom of the track or curtain rings to the required point: usually the sill ('B'), about 100mm (4in) below the sill ('C'), or to the floor ('D'); then add an allowance for the heading and hem.

CURTAIN HEADINGS

Gathered pleats

Pencil pleats

Pinch pleats

Cartridge pleats

Smocked

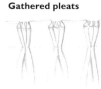

Drapery

There is relaxed, individualistic drapery and there are traditional forms. Swags and tails are a swanky decorative arrangement of fabric hung at the top of windows, used with sewn curtains and those draped over poles. Swags are draped horizontally, tails hang on either side of the curtain.

Draping fabric over poles can be achieved simply with one fabric or by using several that harmonize or contrast. The layered look can be assembled with an eye to luxury or

1 Cotton draped to form a pelmet.
2 Muslin.
3 Complementary sheers.
4 Cotton sari.

2

1

with ingenious economy, depending on your choice of fabric. Drapes can be swagged, folded and looped, formally cut and sewn, or turned artfully over a pole and allowed simply to hang. Egyptian cotton voile thrown across the pole so that both ends bunch a little at floor level is quietly, but unabashedly, extravagant.

Classic romance can be achieved without excessive frills or cost. Muslin, synthetic translucent materials and medium-weight fabrics drape well. Fabrics with a contrast lining can be wound around a pole to create an effect of bulk; the twisted section of fabric needs to be twice the pole length. Revealing part of the pole lends an air of informality. For classical beauty, drape a single length of fabric over a simple pole and allow it to hang symmetrically on either side of the window.

Resist the temptation to use drapery as a shorthand means to creating more elaborate curtaining. Excessive drapery looks both fussy and ill considered. Stick to simple, edited-down effects for best results.

SHEERS

Whether you want a dramatic sweep of colour to cut out cold winter light, or romantic drapery, sheers or semi-transparent hangings are among the easiest window dressings to rig up. The thinnest sheers dilute light, while patterned ones dapple it. Often used with curtains, sheers provide privacy and an element of light control.

Special attention to scale and line is in order since sheers are usually unaccompanied by frills, swags or elaborate headings. There are sheers that shine – silks, synthetic translucents, parachute silk, organdie – and those that are dull and textured – voiles, cheesecloth, gauze, muslin, batiste. When a breeze lifts the panels, or light filters through simply hung sheers, there is a gossamer effect. Sheers can also be remarkably economical. Saris of clashing colours can be clipped to tracks and poles and hung as simple, ethereal drapes. Stripy gauze takes the edge off even the most severe examples of modernism. Builders' cloth hung on tension wire and stretched in horizontal bands across a skylight creates a tent-like effect. Fine linen scrim used in theatres comes in widths of up to 4m (13ft). It is billowy and light, and can be thrown in the washing-machine.

LACE

Lace comes in hundreds of subtle off-whites, including chalk, eggshell, ivory, gardenia, alabaster and cream, as well as colours. Lace doesn't have to look overly feminine or florid. Without spending a lot of money, you have a window treatment that can go in any direction.

Much of the lace available today is based on nineteenth- and early twentieth-century designs, including French window panels (narrower than usual to cover the width of the window only) and half-sized horizontal panels which cover the lower half of a window. Roller blinds can be made out of the harder-wearing laces, such as Nottingham or Madras. Old lace can be found in antique shops and markets – at a price. Designs don't have to match. Windows look pretty with different patterns at each pane, particularly if they are panels.

SCREENING

Unlike curtains, screens don't crowd a window with solid material. Instead, they recreate nomadic life, giving a window constant potential for change and focusing on the contents of the room. Screens are especially good if you don't want to spend money on expensive, properly tailored curtains because you are living in rented accommodation or planning to move home.

3

Bracketed rods, mounted on either side of a window, can suspend layer upon layer of opalescent sheers in a pageantry of lengths and widths. Moveable rods make it simple to maximize light or to play it down.

Designers are taking industrial fixtures and giving them a new twist as neutral foils for windows. Framed in steel, a rolling door of translucent, corrugated fibreglass can leave a view wide open or close off a window when privacy is required. Steel

4

tubular frames on castors or commercial dress rails on wheels can shut out the world, allow slivers of light through, or be whisked away for an unobstructed view.

Sandblasted glass screens resting on the sill and reaching halfway up deflect strong sun, but still allow in light and outside views above eye-level. Simpler still is to bring lattice-work in from the garden to obscure the view partially and to filter light, generating privacy and shade simultaneously.

Blinds

1

2

Blinds, shades and shutters help regulate heat, reduce noise and ensure privacy. They have spare, clean lines which enable all types of window to remain uncluttered. These are the blue jeans of window treatments – immensely practical and always appropriate. Less overpowering and simpler than curtains, they are a relatively inexpensive form of window dressing. Blinds work particularly well on small windows and alleviate the comparative gloom of constricted spaces. At large windows, it usually looks better to hang two or three separate blinds rather than a single blind across the whole width. This also allows you greater flexibility in controlling light and shade in the room.

ROLLER BLINDS
The pull-down white roller blind is a classic. Containing just a single key piece of apparatus, roller blinds can be used independently or as 'blankets' for sleeping when paired with curtains or delicate sheers. The simplicity of their technique makes them available in DIY kit form, custom-made and ready-made in a stock range of sizes. Sill-mounted roller blinds that pull up rather than down are a great urban solution, simultaneously giving privacy while letting in natural light.

Unsuitable fabrics roll unevenly; tight, flat weaves are best suited to constant unravelling. Roller blinds have started moving away from the white and natural materials of most contemporary interiors, and take on very different looks when made from gold mesh or taffeta.

VENETIAN BLINDS
Venetian blinds are available in wood, metal, plastic and fabric, in horizontal and vertical louvres. With their simple structural function, they seem almost integral to the window, part of the serene passing of time. Venetian blinds give a faceless window graphic definition. The warm natural tones of wooden Venetian blinds are, surprisingly, all the stronger against vivid curtains or painted frames and actually mellow the incoming light.

3

Vertical Venetian blinds pivot open or closed, and are usually made of fabric-covered plastic or wooden slats attached to track or suspended from curtain rails. Slats can be linked to a continuous chain or weighted to hang free. Vertical louvre blinds are particularly useful on windows with difficult angles since the slats can be graduated in height or hung from a curved track in a bay or bow window. Slat widths typically range from 75-125mm (3–5in).

ROMAN BLINDS
Roman blinds have all the grace, strength and durability of a sail. Operating on a simple cording system, the Roman blind draws up into a series of broad, flat folds. Dowel rods, secured horizontally and concealed within pockets made from tucks in the fabric, keep the blind taut and supported. Unrolled fully they are somewhat of a let down, resembling ordinary blinds. They look good in isolation or in combination with curtains, and are economical on fabric. Lining Roman

blinds will improve the way pleats fall and keep out more light. Avoid large-scale patterns because the design will be interrupted by the horizontal pleats. Dowel rods can be made of timber (half dowels to rest flat against the fabric) or perspex with lightweight and sheer fabrics.

Roman blinds can give a twist to the simplest of fabrics. A thin, sheer organdie Roman blind edged with linen and stretched across a window filters an ethereal light.

AUSTRIAN AND FESTOON BLINDS
Austrian blinds fall like curtains to end in a series of deep, ruched scallops which need a surplus of about 0.5m (20in) of fabric. Festoon blinds are flamboyantly ruched from top to bottom and gathered from side to side, differing from Austrian blinds in that the fullness is distributed along their entire length. When calculating the amount of fabric, allow twice the length of the finished drop for festoon blinds.

These window treatments combine the drapery of curtains with the economy of a blind. Cords running through looped tape at the back draw up Austrian and festoon blinds into a ballooned effect. When gathered and pulled, both blinds, suffer from the reputation of being overdressed. It's usually the excessive bows, ruffles and florals that make them too over-the-top for most rooms. Plain fabrics display the form of these blinds best. They contain as much material as full-length curtains and – because of their weight – it's advisable to choose lightweight fabrics.

4

NON-FABRIC BLINDS
Non-fabric blinds made from split cane, burnt bamboo, metal, wood, plastic or stiff, pleated paper are both cheap and practical. Make sure the mechanisms run smoothly. Pinoleum blinds are made from ultra-thin slats of wood – either stained darker or left in their original colour – and woven together with cotton. Wood and bamboo blinds have a colonial quality about them. Bold, deliberate colourings are reminiscent of early Modernist and Bauhaus furnishings.

5

6

SHUTTERS
Shutters can give a room a comforting sense of enclosure. Mounted on each side of the frame, interior shutters give definition and presence to a window. Their clean appearance doesn't detract visually from the window's architecture or view. They keep out the light when you want them to while continuing to let in fresh air (if they are louvred). Shutters provide additional security and insulate against noise from outside.

Plantation shutters fold back with accordion hinges to each side of the window. Most shutters are louvred to let in fresh air and filter a little light, but some – typically in older town houses – have solid wooden panels. Old shutters can be bought cheaply, cut down and trimmed to fit your windows. While some people treat their shutters to an elaborate paint treatment – for example, painting *trompe-l'oeil* scenes on the exterior face – they are best left alone, simply painted with a few coats of white gloss paint.

1 Sill-mounted, upwards-rolling blind.
2 Roller blinds.
3 Venetian blinds.
4 Roman blinds.
5 Pinoleum blind.
6 Shutters.

FURNISHING

Furnishing a home involves translating the ideas that stir us into rooms that content us. Our homes should be as personal, eclectic and full of character as we are, reflecting our different lifestyles, preserving our memories and expressing our own brand of taste. At the same time, most people desire a sense of timelessness in design – materials that wear and weather well, furnishings that are comfortable, practical and easy on the eye.

How do you make a confident choice from the vast range of furnishings available? How do you combine different elements in a way that looks natural and instinctive rather than contrived? One of the best approaches is to allow yourself time to assimilate items into the pattern of daily living. Reconstructing a room set down to the last cushion cover stifles individuality and rules out the creative changes which keep homes alive.

It's equally important to respect what you already have. Take cues from an interesting floor, good ceiling height or fine architectural detail. Consider the quality of light and general spatial elements of each room: both of these elements can dictate or initiate colour and furnishing schemes. Trying to deny a room's innate character is self-defeating. Use space, volume and history as the starting points for your decorative ideas. If your home doesn't have much in the way of architectural detail, everything has to come from the contents. If there's a strong period flavour, expressed in mouldings, panelling, fireplaces and architraves, you can echo the basic framework with sympathetic furnishings, or play up the contrast in a bolder fashion.

There's always room for wit and reinterpretation. Crafting a table from builders' trestles, pulling up antique chairs to a modern, glass-topped table, juxtaposing an old rolled-arm sofa with folding metal park chairs marries old with new, the treasured with the ordinary. Interiors which lack surprise and conform to some proscribed notion of style lack any sense of vitality.

The bottom line is practicality. Visual pleasure is rapidly undermined by poor performance. Dining-chairs that are too uncomfortable to sit in, upholstery which swiftly deteriorates under the onslaught of children, or tables which are too rickety to bear the weight of a cup of coffee are ultimately sources of frustration whatever the superficial merits of their appearance.

1 The uncluttered lines of glass shelving are perfect for those who believe that less is more. Glass shelves add the illusion of space and light, but their pristine surface requires regular cleaning.

2 Quilts thrown over a pair of large, slouching sofas, big, generously filled cushions and deep, pillowy armchairs create an air of charm and comfort.

3 Modern chairs and tables are often categorized by designer or decade. Lloyd Loom chairs are less likely to bruise and scar the floor than more formal dining-chairs. The Philippe Starck table combines function with an original design.

4 Loose covers disguise worn upholstery and mismatched pieces of furniture, guard finishes from sunlight and dust, and instantly update and redefine a room by bringing in style at little expense.

5 Using the corridor as a space for a vast book collection creates a literary forest and a wonderful transition space between the hall and living-room.

Upholstery

3

The price of an upholstered piece varies according to the quality. Ideally, a well-upholstered piece of furniture will last a lifetime, just needing re-covering as the fabric wears out or your taste changes. Choose hardwood frames that are jointed with screws, dowels and glue (not just glue). Double-coil springs, hand tied and anchored so that the front edge is separated from the springs behind, indicate long-lasting, good-quality pieces. This attention to detail is costlier, but you'll have a more comfortable piece of furniture.

Medium-range, more affordable upholstery often consists of trapeze construction and steel frames. It is easier and less costly to construct furniture with fluid shapes, or made from a frame of tubular steel with internal straps of steel. Cheap sofas are built of sheet material or out of various densities of foam. A sofa bed is a poor compromise, neither a good sofa nor a good bed. They're expensive, and most people don't use them often enough to warrant the cost and loss of comfort.

MATERIALS

The quality of filling is a question of personal preference. It depends on how you want the upholstery to look and how you want it to sit. The comfort of a sofa and chair can be gauged by its appearance. If it's entirely foam, it is probably not going to be too interesting to look at or sit in, though cushions will bounce back into shape. A 50:50 mix of feather and down is a better choice than pure down. A mixture of down fibres and synthetic material offers a good balance between appearance, comfort and maintenance. A blend of horsehair and coir fibre bonded with latex is a good new filling. All-weather foam is best for outdoor furniture.

If upholstery feels soft, plump but firm, it is probably well made. Weight is a fairly accurate measure of quality; pieces that feel heavy probably have reasonable components and frames of hardwood rather than man-made boards. Steer clear if you can feel the back rail, or your legs bang against the timber edge at the front. Hard edges wear out the upholstery and are a sign of poor springs and bad crafting.

CHOOSING THE STYLE

Allow yourself to get used to the curves and dimensions of a chair or sofa. Typically, young adults want a deep-seated lounge and older adults prefer a frame chair where they feel more upright. If your family is likely to use the piece to watch television, you'll want a high enough back for relaxed viewing to rest heads and engulf occupants when seated. Smart, tailored pieces with a lot of ground clearance encourage correct posture. Upholstery with a tight back rather than loose cushions and those with a single-seat cushion tend to look neater. Sofas and chairs with a slight exaggeration of proportion – deeper, longer, more voluptuous and low to the ground – encourage sprawling. To create softness in square spaces, use large, moon-shaped or curved upholstered pieces.

REUPHOLSTERY

A piece of furniture is worth reupholstering if it's an antique, or if it simply sits comfortably and you like what you're looking at. As a

1

general rule, contemporary pieces merit reupholstering if restoration and renovation will cost no more than 50 per cent of the price for a replacement. For period pieces, reupholstering with traditional methods, hand-stitching and horsehair is generally a smart investment, even though it's expensive. Reupholstering a piece enables you to redesign it. You can tuft it or not, change the height of a skirt or cushion, box or bullnose arms and edges.

Treatment Stain-resisting treatments can be applied to upholstery fabric before tailoring. Removing stains from upholstery pieces is thereafter usually done on site by cleaning services.

LOOSE COVERS

Loose covers are a stylish and practical way of dressing furniture. They can be used to disguise worn upholstery and mismatched furniture, to guard wood finishes from light and dust and to update and redefine a room. With loose covers you can self-confidently and informally bring texture, pattern and colour into a room without going to the expense of changing the whole scheme.

Loose covers can be used to ring the changes on a seasonal basis or to extend the life span of the fabric underneath, thereby postponing major re-covering. Skirts carried to the floor and shallow kick-pleats improve the figure of ungainly sofas.

Used as a flexible wardrobe, loose covers act as extra protection for your furniture. You can keep covers on all day for pets and children, then take them off at night for guests.
Treatment Though loose covers offer the precision finish of upholstery for less money, it is the saving in laundering that makes them substantially less costly. Loose covers made of a single, colourfast fabric (no linings or trims) with a simple construction that won't collapse when wet can be safely machine-washed. Laundering or dry cleaning fabric before sewing will prevent shrinkage. Canvas, heavy calico and linen can be purchased pre-shrunk from professional suppliers.

2

MAKING COVERS

Loose covers should be tailored to fit tightly the way a suit hugs a dress form. If you are making the covers yourself, begin by cutting out a pattern of pre-shrunk calico to use as a guide. This saves costly cutting mistakes, ensures a good final fit, and can double as a lining or be reused when it is time to replace the loose cover. Unless you want a translucent look, it is advisable to line lightweight fabrics with muslin, calico or padding. Lined loose covers hang better, have more body and last longer than unlined covers. In many cases, lining the arms, backs and skirt is less expensive and time consuming than a full lining and can be equally effective.

Loose covers are best kept simple, with bound or piped seams. A fitted cover free of seams and details at the hem highlights the fabric pattern and shape of the furniture. Contrasting piping lends covers a crisp look.

CHOOSING FABRIC

Before deciding on a fabric, estimate how much you'll need. The cost of loose covers and upholstery will vary dramatically according to your choice of fabric. Fire and safety codes restrict the choice of material; flammability, cigarette and match tests vary from country to country.

For upholstery, you need hardy stock. 'Upholstery weight' refers to the durability of a fabric. Manufacturers are required to subject upholstery-weight materials to a rub test, in which a sample is mechanically rubbed hundreds of times. Any good fabric supplier should be able to supply you with this information. Though almost any

1 Tubular-steel and leather armchair.
2 Loose sofa cover.
3 Loose chair cover with ties.
4 Armchair upholstered in kelims.
5 Fitted sofa covers.
6 Dining-chairs with drop-in seats.
7 Fitted armchair covers.
8 Bolster.

4

fabric can be used, it is wise to start out with a heavy-duty neutral fabric that can easily be incorporated into different decorating schemes or adapted when you change homes. Stripes – such as grey and taupe or beige and cream – will blend with almost any decor. To avoid bland rooms, consider using bold stripes about 75mm (3in) wide. Stripes radically change the shape of upholstery. Vertical stripes lengthen squat furnishings, horizontal stripes add girth and elongate. Solid fabrics and those with an all-over pattern tend to look best kept simple. Piping and covered buttons add structure and emphasize curves.

If you intend moving the same piece of furniture from one room to another, steer towards colours such as straw, paper-bag brown, grey, beige, and neutrals with tone. White can look too fresh and harsh. Jacquards, damasks and small geometric prints are also flexible choices. They have visual interest and character, but lack the kind of strong personality that might clash with other furnishing schemes.

When choosing upholstery fabric, it is tempting to go for the darkest and busiest pattern in the hope that it won't show the dirt. It will, and this can prove a false economy since you need more fabric to ensure a good pattern match.

For longevity, choose a synthetic viscose blended with linen and cotton and weaves with a slub. Kelims make hard-wearing covers, but are thick and more labour-intensive to work – they are also flammable, a risk you should carefully consider. Chintz and silk aren't

durable upholstery materials. As the sheen comes off chintz, lending it its coveted appeal, it becomes, like silk, prone to rips.

Brushed denim, Indian cottons and vibrant cotton velvet are all comfortable, hard-wearing and possess an amazing softness and slight twill. Velvet is losing its old-fashioned connotations of stuffy clubs and airless rooms. The effect of using this simple and luxurious fabric on unusual shapes of upholstery is evocative and wickedly indulgent.

Medium-weight cotton or linen, a cotton-linen blend or a light wool that will behave well with everyday use are good for loose covers. Washable and more resistant to fading than synthetics, these natural fabrics are soft, comfortable and pliable, yet stiff and substantial enough to be a durable loose cover. The tighter the weave, the longer the cover lasts. Tartan plaids and some floral prints can look striking and contemporary when used on sofas with fairly clean, modern lines in a simply decorated room.

5

TRIMMINGS

When covering a chair or sofa with a solid colour, use a striped fabric for piping to provide a crisp, graphic note. Fringe can be pinned in place at the bottom of the upholstery or applied with hot glue to give a dressy, formal look and to cover the gap between the bottom of the frame and the floor. In a contemporary setting, this rich detail is a particularly nice juxtaposition. Trim can also be used to accentuate the lines of shapely legs.

CUSHIONS

Cushions are the easiest way to personalize and dress up a chair or sofa thanks to a multitude of shapes, sizes and patterns. Using bursts of colour and pattern in your choice of fabric for cushions can also add drama and variety to the whole room, without overwhelming it in the way that curtains or upholstery in the same fabric would. Collections of cushions have a habit of moving from one chair to another, even one room to another, changing the feeling of the home.

The size and shape of cushions should be a combination of personal preference and the proportions of the room and its furniture. Square and rectangular cushions are the most popular as well as the most versatile. Ottomans range in size from that of a foot-stool to something big enough to sprawl across. Scatter cushions – a luxury for some, a necessity for others – encourage nodding off. Bolsters make beds more comfortable and add a touch of luxury to sofas.

6

Cushion covers in matched pairs or that coordinate with the curtains are fine, but to generate contrast, you could try using one bright shade of a colour that has nothing in common with anything in the room. Don't overlook 'scraps' of inherited or vintage fabric which can be used as cushion panels; even very small pieces can be sewn into a patchwork. It doesn't take much in the way of braid, piping, tassels and fringe to be effective – when it comes to trimming, less is very often more.

7

FORMAL CHAIRS

Seat covers for dining-chairs are either nailed right over the chair frame, built up over coiled springs or built on to a drop-in seat which fits snugly within the seat rail. Drop-in seats make repairing and replacing upholstery relatively easy – if you are doing it yourself, you should experiment first with a pattern guide cut from calico to make sure you get the dimensions and fit right.

Since chairs are one decorating area in which people are prepared to be far more modern and eclectic in taste, there is a vast range of choice if you are looking to buy a new set of chairs for the kitchen or dining area. Mixing and matching different chairs around a table can lend a relaxed, informal mood to supper time. In addition to furniture retailers, chairs can be commissioned from artists, or bought from local auctions and in second-hand shops. Some furniture workshops specialize in copying antique chairs with such accuracy it's hard to spot the reproduction from the original.

8

Light fixtures

Select your light fixtures according to the quality of light that is suited to the task and function of the room. Although lamps offer an additional and versatile form of lighting – because they're portable – they will only deliver maximum benefit if they are used to supplement the fixed lighting, which must be planned with care from the outset, if at all possible (see pages 74-9).

Artificial lighting is used to create a number of effects, and you'll require some fixtures to provide soft, relaxing, general light, others to do a specific job – a combination of decorative and effective lighting. For instance, if the dining-table is primarily a place for homework and writing cheques, the bright light of a halogen fixture will provide a level of illumination that allows you to concentrate without straining your eyes. But if the table is primarily used for dining, there would be no escaping the paralysing spell of such a fixture: the ambient glow of candlelight or wall sconces would be more evocative and appropriate.

1 Track lighting for halogen spots.
2 Recessed halogen spots.
3 Halogen downlights.
4 Custom-made pendant light.
5 Wall-mounted uplight.

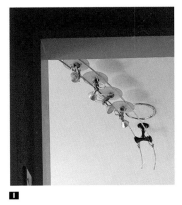

If you walk into a room and the first thing you notice is the lighting or if you find yourself squinting at the light fixtures, the room is overlit. Layer lighting for optimum effect and maximum flexibility. Overhead pendants provide good, general background light. Table and floor lamps are secondary light sources used to cast pools of light and illuminate reading material. Spotlights are good for task lighting in a kitchen or for highlighting a painting or architectural features.

In recent years there has been a rash of 'designer' lighting. But spotlighting a jumble of contrived objects or lighting a single bowl in the centre of a table will only ever be as interesting as what it is illuminating. This sort of lighting can appear melodramatic and tends to make furnishings look static; it often creates too severe a distraction from the overall feel of a room. Picture lights work in areas such as a hallway, where you want to highlight family photographs or to wash the walls to display a collection of art.

When choosing wall sconces and table lamps to flank the sofa, most people choose pairs, but mismatched light fixtures offer the charm of imperfection. Taking a more individualized approach to light fixtures assumes that they can be as varied as the people who meet their gaze. However, too much witty ingenuity can be uncomfortable.

QUALITY OF LIGHT

Different light-bulbs create varying qualities of light, and this will have a direct effect on how a room looks, particularly at night-time, changing the colours of curtain fabrics, upholstery and wall finishes.

Tungsten bulbs are still the most commonly used, generally with screw-in or bayonet attachments. The tungsten filament glows a warm, yellow colour, its intensity dependent on the wattage. The bulbs have a shorter life-span and are more expensive than fluorescent tubes, but they emit a far more flattering quality of light. They are most often used in table lamps and hanging fixtures. Some bulbs are silvered across their top to reflect light back to the fittings, reducing glare.

Halogen bulbs provide a clear, white light that has the least perceptible effect on colour. They are, in fact, a combination of halogen gas and a tungsten filament. Standard halogen fixtures provide focused, controllable light thanks to built-in reflectors. They generate a specific wash of light or a spot of light which, because of the strength of the bulb, is often used to good effect in uplights, since the light bounces off the wall or ceiling and reflects back into the room.

Low-voltage halogen fittings were originally developed for commercial use and can be recessed or mounted on tracks in a domestic context. The main attractions of low-voltage halogen are the pristine quality of light it creates combined with the tiny scale of the fixtures themselves. But the sparkling quality that attracts consumers in off the street and into a lively retail shop can be glaring and harsh in the home. Installing these low-voltage lights in a domestic situation should be planned with care. To reduce the glare of low-voltage fixtures, set bulbs back into the fitting or use a baffle or honeycomb grille to shield the light.

Fluorescent bulbs have a long life, low-energy use and a tubular shape. They are used in a boxed housing that diffuses light over a large area, but they cast an unpleasantly artificial green tinge. Fluorescent light fixtures evoke unpleasant memories of offices and schools. They are still viewed as unhealthy; a plant under fluorescent light is barely able to stay alive.

New compact fluorescent lamps (CFLs) are thin, energy-saving 10mm ($\frac{3}{8}$in) tubes folded into a cluster. They are used in place of traditional tungsten bulbs, and last considerably longer (though they cost more). CFLs distribute light slightly less evenly than tungsten or halogen and cannot be fitted to dimmers.

OVERHEAD LIGHTS

Overhead lights create an illusion of greater space and provide good general lighting. However, the problem with all overhead fixtures is how to control glare. Too much overhead lighting is distracting, and

banishes the potential for creating shadow and contrast. Fitting overhead lights to a dimmer switch greatly increases their potential, while the glare can be reduced according to the type of shade. Overhead lighting is good in halls, corridors and on staircases, where you need to be able to see where you're going; in rooms where you want to have more control over mood, pendant fixtures (see below) offer greater flexibility.

PENDANT LIGHTS

Pendant light fixtures hang down from the ceiling. Both the quality and quantity of the light produced depends on the type of bulbs and shades used. Choose fixtures wisely; it's not always flattering to have light coming down on the top of your head. Generally, light is more attractive when it is at average human height. Over a dining-table, suspend the fixture between 2.5–3m (8–10ft) off the ground so adults can stand in the room without being

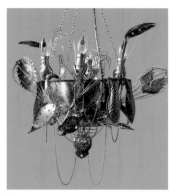

4

blinded by eye-level bulbs; at mealtimes, it helps if the pendant is adjustable so that the light can be brought closer to the table to give a more intimate focus to the room.

A central light source from the ceiling is often used to form an axis, or boundary, between two prevailing outside sources of light. An overhead fixture with a dangling centre bulb is often inherited. It is a mistake to try to organize all the illumination in a room from this central point. The down side of these fixtures is glare. Rather than trying to achieve illumination from one light source in a fixed position, vary the sources. Use centred pendant lights for atmosphere and general lighting.

If you have a ceiling rose, the lamp shade can provide a complementary focus. Translucent shades – a glass globe and brown paper, for instance – scatter light. A crumpled paper cylinder is a clean, modern choice. An opaque shade enclosing the bulb is more attention-seeking. A metal shade, open top and bottom, gives good, general light over a desk.

DOWNLIGHTS

Downlights do exactly as the name suggests. They are versatile and compact, surface mounted or recessed into the ceiling. Depending on the bulb and fitting, downlights create a range of effects from the narrow, focused beam of light from a low-voltage halogen bulb through to the broader, gentler wash of a tungsten bulb.

Downlight fixtures can provide general, mood and task lighting. As with most types of light, their versatility is increased if they are attached to a dimmer switch, though this is not appropriate for task lighting. Modern fittings are small and unobtrusive, great for rooms with low ceilings and those in which furniture is often moved around.

Recessed ceiling lights are completely anonymous. Recessed compact fluorescents are energy efficient and the quality of light is a more comfortable colour than that provided by fluorescents. Recessed light fixtures are installed by cutting a hole in the ceiling and connecting wiring as for a simple pendant fitting. Recessed lighting cannot be used if you live in a flat or in a maisonette with other dwellings above.

Low-voltage fixtures can only be used with a special transformer, which requires the services of a qualified electrician.

Track lighting allows you to position fittings anywhere along the track, and to move them as you require. However, this versatility has to be offset against the rather lumpen appearance of many track systems. Low-energy halogen tracking is sleek and modern.

UPLIGHTS

With an uplight, the ceiling acts as a reflector. Light bounces off it and scatters in such a way that shadow and glare are totally reduced. Other advantages are that uplights are inexpensive and don't require an electrician to install them. As fixtures, uplights are less casual than either downlights or lamps. The shape of the shade or fitting – from directional cones to half-round wall dishes – will have an effect on the area illuminated and the intensity of

5

the light, though this will also, of course, be affected by the type of bulb used. You can't work in uplighting, but it provides good general background illumination. Since uplights flood a ceiling with light, they make the most of plaster mouldings and ceiling cornices, but will magnify any unattractive faults. Used lower down a wall, uplights can be used to cast dramatic shadows behind plants or large free-standing decorative objects.

DIMMERS

Dimmer switches offer maximum flexibility and control of light. Turned low, they can create a romantic, soft glow; turned high, a cool bright light is achieved. As well as being wired to overhead and pendant lights, dimmers can also be wired to the electrical circuit for lamps. However, be wary of going overboard. If you are one of those people seldom likely to use a dimmer in anything except the high position and off, skip the added electrical expense.

LIGHT-BULBS

Tungsten

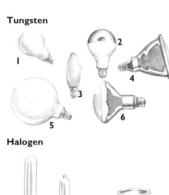

Halogen

Fluorescent

LIGHT-BULBS
(1) Standard tungsten filament.
(2) Crown-silvered tungsten reflector.
(3) Tungsten candle.
(4) Parabolic aluminized reflector.
(5) Tungsten globe.
(6) Spotlight reflector.
(7) & (8) Standard-voltage halogen.
(9) Low-voltage halogen reflector.
(10) Standard fluorescent tube.
(11), (12) & (13) Low-energy compact fluorescents.

LIGHT FIXTURES
(14) Ceiling-mounted globe.
(15) Garden spotlights.
(16) Wall uplight.
(17) & (18) Pendants.
(19) Spotlight with clamp-on fitting.
(20) Picture light.
(21) Wall light.
(22) Track-mounted spotlights.
(23) Recessed downlight.
(24) Eyeball downlight.
(25) Semi-recessed downlight.
(26) Low-voltage track fittings.
(27) Striplight.

LIGHT FIXTURES

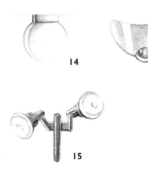

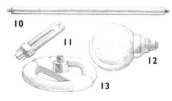

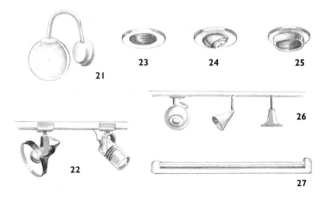

Lamps

1 Anglepoise.
2 Sconce with candle bulb.
3 Clamp-on desk lamp.
4 Paper-shaded table lamp.
5 Table lamp with halogen bulb.

LAMPS
(1) & (2) Table lamps.
(3) & (4) Desk lamps.
(5) Standard lamp.
(6) Pole-mounted spotlights.
(7) & (8) Floor uplights.

Table and floor lamps are used either for task lighting or for local illumination. Consider the function of the lamp and its shape, colour and impact on a room. Does the lamp have to be very powerful, pushing light up towards the ceiling, or do you want something soft and warm for low, ambient background light? Other criteria to consider include the quality of light (and so choice of bulb), maintenance, how long you want the lamp to last and how much energy it uses.

Floor lamps can be used for general light or to light up corners of rooms; table lamps shed localized light for reading, sewing and other close work – as long as they have an appropriate shade. Many modern floor lamps, particularly those using halogen bulbs, have adjustable heads, so that they can be used for general uplighting but, when necessary, the head can be swivelled around to point downwards and provide task lighting for reading by. The traditional standard lamp remains an invaluable piece in the lighting

equation, though their siting should be carefully considered to avoid trailing flexes and awkward paths through a room.

Table lamps often function as a decorative focus of the room, though this shouldn't necessarily equate with lamp shades coordinated with the soft furnishings. Over the century, the design of table lamps has changed dramatically, though the major styles all still have their advocates: from the Art Nouveau look of a Tiffany (or reproduction) lamp through plastic

lamps of the '50s and '60s to the sculptural pieces of Philippe Starck and numerous Italian designers. If the choice seems overwhelming, you can soon narrow it down by considering the context in which you'll place the lamp – what looks cool and modern in a study or home office may appear harsh and confrontational in the bedroom or living-room.

It generally makes practical sense to distinguish between table lamps and desk lamps. The former are primarily decorative 'tools' providing general ambient light, whereas the latter offer specific task lighting. The design history of the desk lamp is a lesson in the dictate that 'form follows function', epitomized by the classic cantilevered Anglepoise. Modern updates of the Anglepoise take advantage of the sharper light made available by halogen bulbs.

If you want lamps to add a subtle but rich warmth, those with bases of textural porcelain and terracotta make good choices. There is a vast choice in the shape, size and colour of bases for table lamps: colour will

largely be determined by the scheme of a room; shape and size should reflect the proportions of the room and the location of the lamp in it. Clear- and coloured-glass bases sparkle and refract the light from the bulb. Small lights, such as candle lamps on a mantel and lamps tucked into bookcases, instill mystery and charm. Commercial studio lamps and pharmacy-style floor lamps are practical and barely make their presence known.

LAMPSHADES
The shade acts as a form of control. It either allows light through, in which case it acts as a diffuser, or it is opaque and allows light out through the top and in a distinct pool below. Lampshades need to look good whether the light is on or off. A shade colours the quality of light. When lit from behind, a shade shouldn't appear too textured or take on a garish tone.

Hold a swatch of your chosen lampshade material a few centimetres in front of a bare, lit bulb to gain a fairly accurate idea of the effect it will have on the light. Look for fabrics or materials with 'give' in them so that they can be stretched around the frame. Anything that isn't too stiff, thick or bulky is suitable. Fine-textured linen, thin cotton and silk are good choices.

Lining a shade with gold warms up the light and gives it a rich glow. A pale-blue lining slightly cools the colour of the light; a pink or peach lining warms it. Lining the inside of a shade with flesh-coloured silk gives the room a flattering peachy glow, which works well in a bedroom.

Well-suited lamps and shades are comparable in style, shape, size and type of hardware fittings, all subject to personal taste. A rough principle is that the bottom diameter of the shade should be equal to the height of the lamp base. This varies according to the shape of the lamp. If a lamp base tapers or is tall and skinny with a bulbous bottom, alter the shade to suit. The look of the room as a whole is almost more important than the lamp base when choosing a shade.

Generally, the more formal the lamp, the richer the shade material should be. Brass can take card shades as well as silk. Silk and fine linen are good choices for ormolu and porcelain bases. Textural materials such as parchment, raffia, pierced metal and Indian cotton work well with simple and modern lamp bases.

Shades usually follow the geometry and shape of the lamp base. Rounded lamps are best suited to rounded shades, oval lamps to oval shades, square or rectangular lamps to panelled shades. A shade must also be wide enough to allow the bulb at least 25mm (1in) of space all around; 50–75mm (2–3in) for bulbs of 100 watts and above. In principle, a lampshade should be long enough to cover the electrical fittings and stop just above the lamp base when viewed at eye-level; lower for lamps made from Chinese vases whose long skinny necks demand greater coverage. Narrow, tapered shades work nicely as candle shades, since candles or flame-shaped bulbs fit easily inside.

Rugs

There is a lot of snobbery associated with buying rugs and it is not always justified. Antique kelims and specially commissioned designs can cost a fortune, but perfectly acceptable – and cheaper – alternatives can still deliver the desired effect. As a rule, rugs bought to coordinate with the decor work less well than rugs treated as a piece of art on the floor.

A rug can be as nonchalant as a white T-shirt, used simply for warmth underfoot, a place where sleepy cats curl up and friends sprawl. Rugs can be used in combination with other flooring materials, or as one large cloak for the floor. Runners take the chill off a stone-flagged floor and highlight the foot of a staircase or make a hallway more welcoming. A rug can assume a central role in your design motif without overwhelming the room. Conservatory and basement floors, liable to damp, benefit from rugs which can be taken up and aired from time to time. Another point in their favour is that you can take rugs with you when you move.

Natural floorcoverings – such as sisal and jute – and carpets sometimes look better if they are loose laid, made up into mats and runners. Linen and cotton pile are almost unaffordable fitted wall-to-wall but become more attainable scaled down.

Rugs represent amazingly good value for money. The cost of a hand-knitted, hand-sheared, hand-dyed carpet that will provide a lifetime of pleasure is equal to the price of a designer suit or a new set of car tyres. If you can't afford the perfect kelim or Oriental now, consider taking inexpensive coir and binding it yourself. Rather than settling for a reproduction with less integrity than an antique, choose from the wide range of modern possibilities, not the least of which are contemporary rugs that are an artisan's free expression.

If the rug is going to be laid over bare floorboards you should include a layer of underlay for protection. It's important that a rug should lie flat on the floor, not only so that it looks good, but to prevent people tripping. Lightweight rugs and any rugs placed on a slippery floor surface should be lightly secured in place.

TYPES OF RUGS

Bokhara or Turkoman These rugs have small, repeating geometric designs and are normally fine quality. The elephant foot and octagonal 'gul' motifs tend to look best in smaller sizes that make the most of the intricate pattern. Not the hardest wearing, they are recommended more for decorative use than high-traffic areas. Woven in areas of Turkmenistan, Uzbekistan, Kazakhstan, Afghanistan and Pakistan, the Russian examples tend to generate the most interest in investment circles.

Caucasian With their distinctive bright colours, stylized childlike figures and elaborately decorated borders, Caucasian carpets are appealing and simple. They work well in both traditional and contemporary settings and are flexible enough for new or old homes. The simplicity of their patterns makes them easy to work with, although they are only available as scatter rugs: it is rare to find an example over 2×3m (6×9ft). The opening up of eastern Europe has made available some exciting Caucasian kelims.

Dhurry This is the Indian word for flatweave (the Persian word is kelim). Inexpensive, reversible, casual and easy to live with, dhurries are available in a wide range of sizes and colours, as well as in a stonewashed finish. Made of hand-woven cotton, they are not advisable as heat-insulators in winter. Although made of cotton and therefore washable, strong colours are likely to run if put through a washing-machine; gentle hand-washing should minimize the risk of the rug shrinking.

Flokati Made in Greece, these are heavy, shaggy wool rugs in white or off-white with very long pile. The shag tends to matt down.

Kelim This is a tapestry rug woven from fairly harsh, thick wool. The artistry is high compared to the price and there is a fantastic variety of designs. The best pieces are often in long, narrow strips rather than room sizes. As a flatweave they are arguably not as practical as some other rugs and have a tendency to pucker up. They are made by

nomadic peoples in Turkey, Iran, Iraq, Russia, China, Pakistan, India and Morocco. Kelims were originally intended as a pliable warm carpet that could be placed on a sandy desert floor and easily packed on a camel or horse. Kelim designs represent different tribes and regions. Kurdish versions are brighter, sometimes mixed with embroidery, and generally cheaper. Turkish kelims feature Mediterranean colours of gold, orange and turquoise. Iranian kelims are grounded in burgundy, rust, heavy blues and heavy greens.

Oriental Thick and rich, high in art content, often in multi-coloured patterns or featuring representational designs. The typical colour range includes black, soft yellow, pastel pink, peach, apricot and blue. Originally hand-woven in China, Oriental carpets are now made in Romania, Iran and India as well. They represent good value as labour costs remain low. The most expensive rugs are woven from silk, cheaper ones from wool.

Persian The main advantage with Persian rugs is that the older they get the better they look. These are high-quality carpets of knotted wool, and are not deemed to be at their best for some 30 to 40 years. There is a wide variety available, some of fine wool and others coarser. Usually rectangular in shape or made up into long runners, they come in rich colours with stylized motifs. Deep red and blue are the most popular ground colours.

Rag With a lineage back to the seventeenth century, rag rugs are pieces of fabric looped or stitched together using odds and ends. They can also be custom-made from cloth that matches the curtains or upholstery. Rag rugs wear well. Their popularity recalls Scandinavian and German folk art.

Rya High-pile rugs from Denmark and Finland with a 1960s shag effect, these are now coming back into fashion. They are available in strong colours which matt together in contemporary, abstract designs and quite often in less conventional shapes such as circles and ovals.

Serape Coarsely woven Mexican and south-west American tribal blankets, these are coarsely woven flatweaves with fringed ends. Old serapes with Navaho Indian designs are expensive and highly collectible.

Turkish The Turks have turned back the clock on the Industrial Revolution and are going back to the old ways of hand-spinning wool and using vegetable dyes. These are incredibly good value for hand-made rugs. Each region has its own distinct look, although religious motifs can often be discerned in the design.

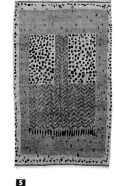

1 Cotton dhurry
2 Kelim.
3 Persian.
4 Kelim
5 Contemporary.

Shelving

Shelves fulfil two functions – they can provide a concentrated form of storage, either open to the room or hidden behind cupboard doors; and they offer a surface on which to display objects in a room. These are not, of course, mutually exclusive roles. If, for example, you enjoy your books and often refer to them, it is worth showing them on open shelves: they will be easily accessible, protected from accidental damage and will add visual interest and a personal note to the room.

Shelving doesn't have to be lined up against the wall or made from thin strips of wood. However, it is important to get the proportions right – if the shelf is too thin it will not only look weak; it will buckle, too, unable to take the weight of the objects it is supporting. Use shelving to add interest to the architecture of a bland room, by boxing in a window, for example, running low shelving around the perimeter, or continuing it from one room into another.

Shelves can be fashioned from almost anything. The traditional material is wood, but a wall of wooden shelves will be expensive and many people these days choose man-made boards – such as MDF – which are considerably cheaper, and are a sensible choice if you intend to paint the shelves (a waste of money if you're using wood). Melamine shelves are made from board covered with a wipe-clean, laminated surface. The joins along the edges can look rather ugly, but melamine is a good choice inside kitchen cabinets or in a child's room, where practical concerns outweigh aesthetic ones.

Shelves of wood seldom fail to tantalize even the least aesthetically inclined, but they must be sealed against dust and dirt. If you choose wood for new shelves, make a virtue of the material, and don't clutter them with an overwhelming display. Glass shelves add depth and the illusion of space, but their reflective surface is hard to keep clean. Industrial grid shelving allows air to circulate but is awkward to dust.

Whatever material you choose, it is important that the shelves are adequately supported and firmly fixed to the wall. As a general guide, shelves should have supports at each end and at 900mm (36in) intervals along their span. The traditional method of support is to screw a fixing batten along the wall for the shelf to sit on, with additional battens or brackets at each end. More sophisticated methods are available, though you'll probably need to call in a carpenter. Angle brackets which screw up in to the shelf and to the wall (or which slot in to special vertical shelving tracks) are cheap and efficient, but not very attractive.

You can give thin shelves the illusion of greater depth by adding a 'lip' to the front edge, which will also help to conceal the fixing battens. Attaching beading or decorative mouldings to the front of the shelf similarly adds to the visual appearance for minimal extra cost.

1 Plywood box shelves.
2 Glass.
3 Plastic-coated metal.
4 Built-in wooden ledge.
5 Free-standing shelf unit.
6 Shelves recessed into frame of blocked-off doorway.
7 Fitted alcove shelving.

Pictures

Paintings and drawings can fundamentally affect the way in which we perceive a room. A large painting on a wall will attract attention, a group of misaligned prints will irritate and distract. Like any other element in the decorative vocabulary, pictures can be used as foreground or background elements. Hanging pictures at eye-level encourages you to study them. Anchoring a room with a handsomely framed mirror or an outstanding painting will augment the room's classical proportions.

People tend to get complacent about their displays. Any picture that hangs in one place for too long will get taken for granted. Rotating artwork from one room to another revitalizes a room, celebrates the quality of a piece and invites you to see it with a fresh eye. As a contrast, lean favourite objects against the wall or on bookshelves. Side by side, artwork and books speak volumes about your range of interests. Propping art on a shelf or table also discourages objects from becoming too precious and is much less staid than permanent hanging. This also frees you to buy something without the worry of where it will go. If you are hesitant about drilling holes in the wall, you can run picture rails above a mantel or along a blank wall, add a ledge, or use traditional picture moulding and hang your paintings from picture hooks.

In a bland space it pays to be decisive and organize a graphic focal point. You can design your own by mixing different shapes, sizes and styles of artwork. The conventional approach arranges pictures with symmetry as a guide; the unconventional alternative foregoes linear logic and aims for whimsy. Settle on an arrangement that pleases your eye. Lay out your design on the floor first before committing yourself to drilling holes.

Things you love – the expressions of your taste – will probably complement one another and work well together. Often the friendliest of interiors is a magpie's collection of drawings and art from different centuries and cultures, muddled together by instinct. Themed groupings arrest the eye too, such as in a room hung with architectural prints. A collection of botanical prints of the same fruit or vegetable will transform an area into an eighteenth-century print room, which may have its attractions but will inhibit general activities. Pedigree isn't important; mood is.

Framed vintage fabrics, photographs, old postcards, or childhood drawings all qualify as 'art'. What is deadening is to choose artwork based on decor, such as

choosing a green painting for a green room. Whether you have one painting or a large collection, let the room grow around it. Though buying art can be an investment, it should be bought for pleasure. There's nothing wrong with living with a bare wall for a while at first. When in doubt, a mirror might provide the necessary magic. Mirrors liberate small rooms by opening up and lightening tight spaces. There is a wonderful range available, including frames in kit form.

FRAMES

If a picture is worth a thousand words, it is worth showing it off to its best advantage. This not only means choosing an appropriate place to hang it, but selecting an appropriate frame. Medium and large frames help expand spaces by lending a sense of proportion and depth. Small frames focus the eye on detail.

It is important to match the style of frame to what it displays. It's worth spending money to have any art you value well framed, and to invest in mounts made from cotton or linen paper. Make sure paper mounts are acid-free, otherwise you risk irreparable damage to your print or painting. Wood oxidizes images and causes stains unless there is a protective layer between it and the piece of art. Never apply glue or sticky tape to the back of a valuable print or drawing.

When it comes to boxing pictures in, options range from the spare to the elaborately ornate. The clip frame consists of two plates – one of glass the other a backing board – and a dog clip at the top and bottom. It is a frame with no defined edge, designed simply and elegantly to allow what is inside to be the focus.

Antique frames can artfully hang on a wall empty, savoured for their intrinsic merit, or made into mirrors. Shop at flea markets and auction houses for frames with character and replace missing border details with modelling clay and gesso. But make sure that what you then place within the frame is appropriate to it: a humble watercolour bought on holiday will look pretentious and lose its charm hung in an elaborate frame.

Carved and gilded Louis XIV and Louis XVI frames, fluted frames from nineteenth-century France and hollow 'trench' frames (oak with matt gilding) were designed to be seen in candlelight. These frames are well suited to take mirrors and in many instances can be bought for considerably less than a new mirror of similar size and scale.

Making your own frames is also a worthwhile venture. Mouldings are available from local timber yards, decorative plaster suppliers and print shops, which also sell mounts. You can gild the frames yourself by painting them with a good-quality gold paint, or brighten up dingy crackled frames with metallic waxes from arts and crafts shops.

1 Large painting as focal point.
2 Themed collection.
3 Pictures propped up on ledges.
4 Sketches hung from tension wire.
5 Empty frame hung in front of bookshelves.

Finishing touches

As life becomes more complex, we tend to demand greater simplicity at home. Finishing a room does not imply that you need to fill it with clutter, to weigh it down with frills and bows. Quietly comfortable, pared-down interiors soothe us and serve our needs far more than thematic set-decorating and pre-digested packages of style. Instead of agonizing over a room's contents, focus on finding a few well-chosen items that reflect your personal style and the way you live.

It helps to think of finishing touches in a broader context than just the living-room. The appurtenances of everyday life offer opportunities for simple self-expression. Lining up a row of bathroom towels in bright tones of saffron yellow, navy or fuchsia makes an artful statement. The undulating lines of a ribbed-glass bowl and the symmetry of milk pitchers ranged in ascending size on a kitchen shelf have a simplicity and subtle beauty that is easy to appreciate. Pots and pans hanging close to the oven, a glass-fronted dresser packed with plates and dishes or a gleaming *batterie de cuisine* combine aesthetic appeal with practical purpose.

In the living-room, displays are often most effective if they take their cue from an interest or hobby. A battered microscope from your childhood, a brass music stand or an old dress mannequin can form the basis for a display. Often, the more idiosyncratic the combination of items, the better. The kiss of death is to display items which you believe

will accord you a certain status in the eyes of your guests. Display doesn't mean showing off; it means sharing your true enthusiasms and passions.

Discretion is the necessary counterpart to display. This entails taking account of those ordinary but essential elements – such as wastepaper baskets, light switches and door furniture – to ensure that unlovely or poorly designed details don't strike a jarring note.

COLLECTING

Home is a natural haven for collections. There's something organic and faintly dotty about the true collection, which both defies logic and ignores market value. Most natural born collectors can't help themselves and go on acquiring the objects of their desire long after they have run out of house-room. Teapots, antique telephones, tin toys, salt and pepper shakers and many more ephemeral artefacts have all inspired grand collecting passions. For most of us, collecting never quite reaches such heights of obsession. But everyone has an acquisitive streak, and displays of favourite things give life and humour to everyday surroundings. Weathered wood, shells and beach stones trawled from the sea shore, fragments of broken patterned pottery unearthed in the garden, postcards, packaging and snapshots serve no earthly purpose at all, but may be treasured for the memory of a perfect holiday, the thrill of discovery or the simple attraction of colour, graphics or form. There are no rules for this instinctive impulse, only pure personal pleasure, but you can heighten what you display by contriving like groups based on common colours, shapes or provenance.

OCCASIONAL TABLES

In the 1920s the occasional table became part of domestic life. A low table was the hard surface next to the divan to park a cocktail glass and cigarette case. The 'coffee table' made its debut in a 1939 American furniture catalogue which pictured it as a knee-height table set out with an after-dinner coffee pot. Though sneered at by some, for most of us

the occasional table is an indispensable accessory in the living-room. You want to be able to shed light on its surface with reading and table lamps and be able to put a glass down without thinking. In this respect, the height and dimensions are important points to consider. You don't want occasional tables to block important traffic routes through a room, nor do you want them to involve you in awkward manoeuvres when you reach out for your cup of coffee.

One large coffee table can overly dominate a room. Scattering several small tables more or less in front of a sofa is as appealingly functional but less overbearing. Foot-stools, as long as they are not over-upholstered, can make useful substitute occasional tables. Wicker tables recall more exotic climes. A straw-coloured tabletop provides a neutral background on which to display lamps and objects to great effect. If you're looking for something a little

different from the central coffee table, antique trunks and blanket boxes can be put into service, and at the same time provide you with an additional source of storage.

SCREENS

A screen allows you to dispense with doors but still defines the boundaries of space. Screens can be covered in fabric, wallpaper, postcards, greeting cards, or sketches, padded with one luxurious piece of material or pieced together patchwork fashion from scraps of fabric, and trimmed with tapes, gingham or rope.

You can use a screen to close off a section, hide things behind, create a sleeping alcove or eating area. A screen can be pieces of MDF or chipboard hinged together, fabric stretched over padded panels, or wallpaper glued to plywood boards. Frames of glass and glass windows hinged together form a barrier that you can see beyond. Brass mesh and aluminium screens likewise divide off rooms. In lieu of cupboard doors, hemstitched linen curtains or sandblasted glass screen panels make sensible partitions.

HANDLES AND CATCHES

Novel door pulls, handles and hinges are easy upgrades. They are a fast and affordable way to bring change to even the humblest surface. Hardware can counteract the negative characteristics and age of a house, door or piece of furniture.

Traditionally a cupboard had a crystal knob, a door to a dining- or living-room had a bronze or brass knob, and front doors a lever or big pull. Hardware made from inexpensive resin and cast aluminium or from bits of nature furnish dull and tired doors and cupboards with spirit and renewed vigour.

An old chest of drawers can be spruced up with with a new set of pulls or handles that are simply attached with the turn of a screw. Choices include bronze stars and flowers, twigs gathered on a camping trip and seashells. You can match the door handle with the function of a room – open the bathroom door with a fish or scallop, a door to a child's room with plastic dinosaurs. Pulls need not match; designers often

1 Vase of flowers.
2 Bathroom accessories.
3 A themed display.
4 Occasional tables.
5 Folding screen.
6 Door catch and hinges.
7 Door knocker.

4

5

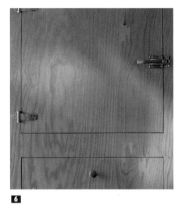

6

7

mount complementary but not identical hardware on bureau drawers and upper and lower cupboards, an attention to detail that lifts a room without making a dramatic statement.

As a rule, it is advisable to relate door hardware to the shell of the space rather than the furnishings. Silent unseen catches and bare doors that spring open at a touch are modern. Nothing jars or intrudes in the open space, not even handles.

Old door accessories don't cost more than new, you just need to have the determination to find them. Shop in salvage yards and flea markets for old hammered and hand-forged wrought-iron and brasswork hinges, eighteenth-century strap hinges and rat-tail hinges.

The way a door knob opens is important. Hinges should enable a door to swing nicely and operate soundlessly; door pulls and handles should be tactile and easy to turn. If a wooden door pull twists, it is inadequately fixed and will probably snap off. Wooden hardware should be both glued and screwed in place. Bolt-fix ceramic knobs from the back. Good porcelain knobs should have a plastic or rubber washer separating the porcelain collar from the pull; two pieces of porcelain rubbing against each other will set up high stress and the back plate will eventually crack.

If left matt, brass must be polished or moisture in the air and on your hands will tarnish it. Handles and pulls of solid brass are undentable.

Hollow brass hardware rings less true and if one handle bangs into another from doors opening back to back, they are liable to bruise.

Stainless steel and iron hardware is trouble-free. Black iron tends to be made in foundries and stainless steel in engineering factories. The most appropriate door handles from the perspective of multi-generational design have generous oversize grips that are easy for the arthritic and older children to grasp.

FLOWERS

Flowers are the quintessential finishing touch, at home in every location. They bring colour, life and the invigorating dimension of scent to a room, reflecting the changing seasons and providing a potent reminder of the natural world. If you have a garden, potted plants and cut flowers are a way of merging outdoors with in; if you live in a city, flowers offer a breath of country air.

You can pick up a dominant colour in a decorative scheme by choosing flowers in the same shade, or inject a note of bold contrast. In spare, minimal rooms, the sculptural forms of contorted twigs and branches have a Zen-like quality. Formal florist's arrangements always look stiff and contrived; a generous mass of simple garden flowers in a plain vase has a natural appeal which is hard to better.

Keeping your home supplied with fresh flowers need not involve horrendous expense. Flowers which are currently in season tend to be cheaper than more exotic specimens or those brought on early in hot-house conditions. If you have a

garden, you can grow flowers specifically for cutting and bringing indoors, and supplement the blooms with foliage, twigs, blossom or berries. In winter months, when there are few flowers, seasonal arrangements of evergreen, seedpods, dried leaves and bright berries more than compensate.

There are endless variations for the creative. Single blooms in test-tube containers, bright flowerheads floating in a low glass dish as a table centrepiece, cottage garden flowers

spilling out of an old watering-can make witty displays that owe as much to the choice of container as the selection of flowers. You can also arrange flowers in old jam jars filled with water and conceal the jars inside containers – such as baskets – which aren't strictly waterproof.

As with any decorative arrangement, size and massing create impact. A number of small vases of flowers dotted around the room have a fraction of the interest provided by one sumptuous display in a key location.

As the lure of the conservatory testifies, houseplants also look best grouped together, which tends to make practical sense, since there are generally only a number of places in the home which provide the right growing conditions. Pots of herbs ranged on a sunny window-sill make an indoor kitchen garden; ferns thrive in steamy bathroom atmospheres. Indulge in several specimens of your favourite variety for maximum impact; a scattering of different species lacks coherence.

AVOIDING TROUBLE

Over the last **30** years the incredible popularity of DIY as a disparate set of craft skills practised in millions of homes has also created a worrying trend to alter, remodel and 'improve' just for the sake of it, or to hone newly acquired talents. No matter how non-materialistic you believe yourself to be, a house or an apartment is a working machine. Like a car, it needs regular servicing and fuel, but if it is going well, leave it alone. If you don't, you can easily upset the fine balance which often exists between working order and breakdown. You'll also create problems which tend to have punitively expensive remedies, reflecting the professionals' dislike for sorting out an amateur's botched work.

A roof-top Jacuzzi, a loft extension, yes, of course you can do them yourself, and very well too. But not before fixing the leak in the roof or, more importantly, taking precautions against it leaking in the first place. Almost everything in this section is achievable, and achievable without breaking your neck, your budget or creating such domestic mayhem that even the cat leaves home.

However, nothing is for nothing. Time, even your own DIY time, is money which might be better spent. Usually, the only commodity you have to offer is time, but this is a judgement only you can honestly make. So don't fall into the easy trap of starting off with the enthusiasm to do everything yourself unless you're quite sure you have the necessary skills. Most importantly, ensure you really want to do the work. That way you'll become interested, involved and enjoy the experience. If you approach a project with fear and loathing, it's doomed before you even start.

Making your home both a place that reflects your own sense of style and one in which potentially hazardous situations are minimized is largely a matter of common sense. Here, the brake at the foot of the ladder secures it firmly to the floor.

1 Many accidents in the home involve children in kitchens. By keeping work surfaces as clear of clutter as possible, you will be able to prepare food more efficiently while minimizing the chances of accidents. **2** Stairways are a potential hazard, particularly for the young, old and infirm. Make sure halls and staircases are well lit, and that there is a banister or safety rail along the stairs to hold on to.

2

Planning and maintaining a schedule for a job is difficult; unexpected snags happen, and these cause depressing delays. Installing a new window frame, for example, can reveal dry rot which has to be totally eradicated before the original project can proceed. So you'll have to live with a large hole in the wall covered with a piece of polythene until that's done. But, more positively, you will have diagnosed, investigated and cured an extremely serious fault which might have been plastered over in the past. As a general rule, don't start anything on a Saturday that you cannot finish by early on Sunday night. For on Monday morning, another life awaits.

Be organized, make work lists, prioritize jobs and order materials in time. If you like to write things down, keep a daily diary of work, note peculiar lessons learnt, problems encountered, mistakes made or short-cuts discovered. All this information could be valuable in the future. In the rush of things, it's simple to forget which bare wood has been primed, and which has been undercoated. Both look similar, so you could waste time doing the job again to be sure. If you feel you're confronting the impossible, be convinced that there is almost always an easier way of doing things if you sit down with a cup of coffee and spend a pleasant half hour or so thinking about the problem in hand.

Take care of yourself and make time to be safe. Dress properly, in overalls or whatever is comfortable and practicable. Jeans, open-neck shirts and trainers may look fetching in advertisements but they're scant protection in a dusty and potentially dangerous situation.

Wear work gloves and goggles whenever you can; use masks and earmuffs in dusty and noisy situations even if they seem inconvenient, or even irrelevant.

You may feel too embarrassed to wear a hard hat in your own home until a piece of wood, a length of pipe, or clump of masonry falls on your head. If you see a rusty nail poking out of a wall,

stop and take it out at once. Read up on basic first aid and know where the first-aid box is kept.

Safety precautions are mainly a matter of common sense, but there are a few which apply to most DIY jobs. Don't work with tools or climb ladders when you're tired. Make sure anything you're working on is absolutely secure. Never overreach when you're up a ladder – climb down and move it along.

Carefully read all instructions for tools, chemicals and so on well before you use them, and file for future reference. Lock up all tools and chemicals well out of the reach of children.

You can't do anything well without good tools. Doing it yourself should save you enough money to be able to afford to buy the best tool dedicated for a particular task, whether it's cutting, smoothing, or drilling. Hiring tools is expensive and time-consuming unless you're certain you'll never need one like it again, or the purchase price is more than you can afford.

Avoid becoming a collector of gadgets. Outside the mail-order catalogues there is no such thing as the all-purpose tool. The accuracy of a power tool that is dedicated to a specific job can help compensate for lack of skill. But remember that all tools, even the innocent screwdriver, are potentially dangerous if they are abused or misused. Read and understand the instructions and practise using the tool in a relaxed but alert manner.

Few aphorisms are more profound than 'Measure twice times, cut once'. Accurate measuring and marking out is vital otherwise things simply will not fit. The retractable pocket measuring tape can take measurements up to about 5m (16ft) and it can be locked at any dimension. Buy one with a tape as wide as 16mm (⅝in) which makes it rigid over long lengths. (Consider the advantages of this when there is no one around to hold the other end taut against a wall for you.)

4

3

3 A purpose-built shed or tool cupboard offers ideal storage space for woodworking equipment, garden furniture, lawn-mowers and the like.
4 If you are an enthusiastic handyman it makes sense to take good care of your tools. A tool cupboard provides dedicated space for each item, encouraging you to put equipment back after use, and ensuring that pieces do not become damaged or pre-maturely worn because of carelessness. Make sure the tool cupboard has a lock on it, and that it is out of the reach of children.
5 The attractions of an open fire have to be offset against the potential hazards. A fire guard prevents burning fuel falling from the fire on to the floor, while the adjacent cubby hole here allows coals or logs to be stored discreetly nearby.

A good 60cm (24in) spirit-level is also a vital purchase; it will ensure that things are properly horizontal or verti-cal. So too is the versatile, all-steel com-bination square. This provides a 90° angle, a 45° angle (for mitres) and a lockable sliding blade of up to 30cm (12in) which is invaluable as a depth gauge for marking out and accurately repeating or transferring measurements. Get one with the measurement mark-ings clearly etched into the blade. On cheap squares they're lightly printed and quickly rub off.

There always seems to be a mass of things to buy, even before you begin a project. You can't have everything in stock, but you will always need a good supply of one of the most basic compo-nents – screws. These are most economi-cally bought in boxes of 100 or 200 from mail-order distributors who generally give a discount for large orders. Going out and buying screws as you need them is both expensive and tedious.

Much DIY work involves lifting heavy things; a bag of cement will seem rooted to the ground. Keep your back straight and use your knees to power the lifting. If you are unfit and over-weight, don't even attempt to do it!

Take extreme care with demolition work; do not tamper with structural things such as chimney breasts or load-bearing walls – call in professionals.

5

Home safety

FIRE SAFETY

Fires don't just happen to other people. Carelessness with matches, deep-fat fryers, open fires and discarded cigarettes all regularly contribute to fatal infernos.

- Many fires happen at night. If you smell smoke, you may have only a few seconds to escape.
- Forget about valuables, wake everyone, and if you quickly establish where the fire is, close the door to that area. All doors, in fact, should be kept shut as they inhibit the spread of fire through the rest of the building.
- Get out fast and get neighbours to call the fire service.
- If the stairs are blocked, go to a bedroom, close the door and seal around it with bedding or clothes. Only then open the window and call for help.
- Jump out of an upper-floor window only as a last resort, and reduce the drop by lowering yourself feet first from the sill.
- Security keys for window locks should be stored close to a window, but not on the frame itself.
- Practise an emergency fire-drill but, above all, try not to panic.
- Remember how to deal with particular fires. Fat fires in chip pans and frying pans erupt without warning. Never throw water on them or use a fire extinguisher. Don't attempt to move the pan. If you can reach the cooker controls, turn them off. Cover the pan with its lid, a damp tea towel or chopping board. Better still, always have a fire blanket ready in the kitchen. Leave it over the pan for at least 30 minutes, or the fire could reignite.
- Smoke and fumes from blazing polyurethane foam-filled furniture kill, and although the manufacture and sale of untreated foam filling was prohibited in 1989, any older furniture should be sprayed with a DIY flame retardant, which offers some protection. If the furniture does catch fire, get out of the room, close the door and call the fire brigade.

- Only use an extinguisher on electrical fittings or appliances after unplugging them, or switching off power at the fuse-box. Never use water on televisions or computers.
- Cut off power and cover electrical appliances with a fire blanket or damp coat or blanket.
- Remember that, even in a smoke-filled room, the 50-75mm (2-3in) of space above the floor will be clear.

PREVENTION

- Install smoke alarms in rooms where there is a fire hazard – except for bathrooms and kitchens where steam from hot water or smoke from cooking may trigger them off accidentally. Even a small house should have a minimum of two alarms – one at the foot of the stairs, the other on the landing. Test alarms regularly and replace the batteries annually.
- If you have double-glazing, or security grills, ensure that all windows will open in an emergency.
- A fire blanket for the kitchen is a necessity; most other domestic extinguishers, because of their size, can only deal with small fires. As there are different types for different fires, it would be unsound to invest in them all unless you live some way from a fire station; make sure you know how to use them and have them checked and serviced regularly.
- Water extinguishers are only effective on common materials such as wood or cloth, and must not be used on flaming liquids or on electrical fires. Foam and dry-powder extinguishers are for liquids like fats, oils and spirits and are very messy.
- Carbon dioxide, BCF or Halon extinguishers deal with electrical fires. They need to be used with great care as they smother fires with gases which are toxic or an asphyxiant.
- Don't store combustible materials such as paints in the house, never leave deep-fat fryers unattended or

dry clothes in front of an open fire or electric heater. You'll also be safer, healthier and richer if you stop smoking.

GAS SAFETY

- Even a small gas leak can produce a large amount of highly inflammable vapour which could cause a fire or explosion. If you smell gas in the home, turn off the mains gas tap near the meter, open all doors and windows, turn off all naked lights and electric fires. Do not operate any other switches and do not smoke.
- If you cannot detect an obvious cause, such as extinguished pilot-lights on the central-heating boiler or cooker controls left on but unlit, call the gas board.
- LPG – liquefied petroleum gas – is in popular use. Accidents happen when it leaks from cylinders or cartridges when they are being changed or connected to appliances. This must be done in the open air. Never smoke or have a naked flame near an LPG cylinder that is being changed. Check all hoses and connections regularly; leaks can be detected by applying a soapy water solution around the suspect area. It will bubble around any gas leak. Store spare cylinders upright, outside the house but locked away securely.
- Only buy appliances that are approved by the gas regulating body.
- All installations and, vitally, regular annual servicing should be carried out by the local gas board or a registered member of CORGI (Confederation of Registered Gas Installers).
- The servicing should also include safety checks on ventilation, which means having efficient trickle ventilators above windows and an air-brick in an outside wall. Only appliances such as gas boilers with balanced flues, which take their air supply from the outside, are exempt from this strict safety rule.

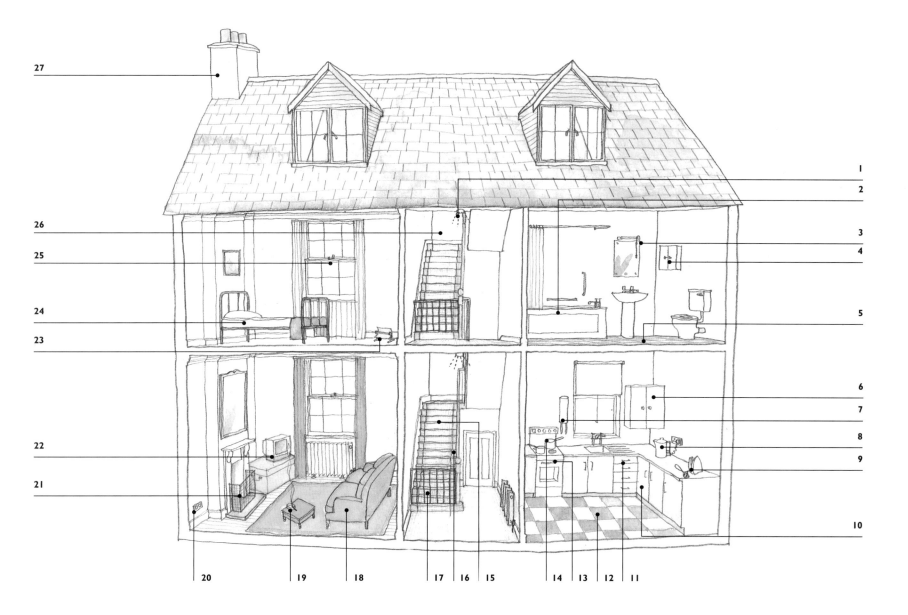

1 Fit at least one smoke alarm on each floor: they will give you vital minutes to escape, are cheap, and are easy to install. Check the batteries routinely, and change them annually.
2 The bath should have a non-slip base. Additional hand grips are a good idea.
3 Pull-cord light switches are essential in the bathroom. Electrical equipment in the bathroom is potentially very dangerous.

4 Keep medicines out of children's reach. Make sure the bathroom cabinet is fitted with a lock.
5 Fit a non-slip flooring material.
6 Store household cleaners out of the reach of children.
7 Keep a fire blanket near the oven and hob.
8 Kettles should have a coiled flex or be cordless.
9 Turn off the iron immediately after use, and put it somewhere safe to cool down.

10 Fit safety catches on low-level cabinets that contain potentially dangerous equipment.
11 Keep sharp knives in a drawer or knife rack, out of the reach of children
12 Wipe up any spills straight away.
13 Ideally, keep small children away from the cooking area.
14 Always keep saucepan handles pointing inwards; and never leave chip pans or deep-fat fryers unattended.

15 Keep the stairs clear of clutter and in good condition.
16 Make sure there is a firmly fixed banister or safety rail.
17 If you have young children, fit safety gates at both the top and bottom of the staircase.
18 Fabrics and furnishings should be fire-resistant; make sure they are retreated after washing.
19 Extinguish cigarettes properly; better still, stop smoking.

20 Fit safety covers over low-level sockets if you have small children, and never overload individual sockets.
21 All fires and heaters should have a safety guard ; check open fires are safe before leaving the house or going to bed.
22 Switch off electrical appliances after use; safer still, unplug them from the mains supply, particularly at night or before going away on holiday.

23 Portable fires and heaters should be kept away from furniture, bedding and curtains; never dry clothes near or over them, and switch them off and unplug from the mains before going out or going to bed.
24 If you have an electric blanket, follow the manufacturer's instructions precisely.
25 Fit safety catches or locks on windows, but make sure they can be opened quickly in an emergency.

26 Stairs should be well lit; artificial lighting on staircases should be operable from both upstairs and downstairs with two-way switches.
27 If you have an open fire, keep the chimney regularly swept.

ELECTRICAL SAFETY

Many people are put off electrical work because they imagine it to be a complicated and potentially dangerous business. It is relatively straightforward; much of the work involves lifting floorboards and carefully routing wiring. It's perfectly safe, interesting and productive as long as you are careful and thoroughly understand what to do. However, in some countries – such as Australia – it is illegal for anyone other than a qualified electrician to undertake electrical work.

- Always switch off at the mains before starting work and never, under any circumstances, assume that any wire or electrical part which you are about to work on is dead.
- If you feel you are getting out of your depth, stop straight away and call in a qualified electrician.
- Never make temporary repairs. Always have the installation tested before connecting it if you haven't got proper test equipment yourself.
- Provided you test and re-test every bit of wiring and every component before working on it, you'll be safe.
- Simple tests on fixed house wiring are easy with an electrical tester. You can, for example, check that a new circuit or circuit extension is wired up correctly. But testers are no substitute for a proper inspection and test carried out by an electrical contractor. For instance, you would not be able to prove that an installation has an adequate earth, nor that the modern residual current safety devices are operating correctly.
- There are several good mains testers available. They all come with clear instructions and have two properly insulated probes, a needle indicator and/or lights, as well as an AC setting; they are capable of handling voltage up to 240V. The best are called multimeters which can be used for continuity and mains voltage testing. Don't confuse these with a test

screwdriver which has a neon light inside the handle. Even so, test the tester before starting work. Touch it on a fitting you know to be live.

- Every electrical appliance which you propose to wire up to a plug will have at least two leads – one brown and one blue. Many will have a third coloured in green and yellow stripes. If you have any other colours – red and black for example – the appliance is old and may be potentially dangerous, or it could be imported and not comply with local specifications.
- Appliances that are all plastic or marked with a double-insulated symbol – a square within a square – are modern and safe. They don't need an earth. Sloppily wired plugs are very dangerous.
- The amount of insulation you'll need to pare away from the raw wire will vary from plug to plug. Some appliance manufacturers thoughtfully bare the wires for you, but they're never the right length.
- Few householders have any idea how healthy their electrical installation is and consequently are unaware of trouble until it happens. Fuses blow for a reason. It's conceivable that this could be old age, but more likely that there is a fault in the circuit which the fuse protects. So don't, as many people do, just mend the fuse, or switch the miniature circuit-breaker back on and hope for the best.

CHECKING THE SYSTEM

You can run a simple check of your electrical system. Start at the consumer unit or, in older installations, the fuse-box. Turn off the power at the main switch, and with a torch make sure the unit is securely mounted on its fire-resistant board and that the casing is undamaged. Look at the cables running in and out of it. The sheathing should go right into the unit. If you find rubber, or even older lead-sheathed cables, they should be replaced as soon as possible.

With the power still off, open up the unit and look for any cracks or signs of overheating. Remove any of the older, re-wirable fuses, one by one, and look out for signs of damage or charring. Check re-wirable fuses for wire of the right rating – simply compare this with new fuse wire – and ensure that the wire is securely held by the terminal screws but is slightly slack in the holder; taut wire burns out earlier.

A dangerously out-of-date wiring system will include separate fuse-boxes for individual circuits, re-wirable circuit fuses, rubber-sheathed cable, socket outlets with round holes, light switches mounted on wooden blocks, no earth continuity tester on lighting circuits and no protection against current leaking to earth. If your system has any or all of these features, it is time your house was completely rewired, and you should call in an electrician.

DEALING WITH ELECTRIC SHOCK

As long as you treat it with due sense and respect, electricity is relatively safe. Modern appliances are stringently monitored and are properly earthed, but shocks do occur, particularly when the hazardous combination of electricity and water is present.

- If someone gets an electric shock, turn off the current by removing the plug or switching it off at the consumer unit. If you can't do this, don't touch the person – the current may pass through to you. Instead pull the victim free with a dry towel, rope or something similar. If you can, knock them free of the electrical source with a piece of wood; as a last resort use their loose clothing to pull them free.
- People who have fallen badly may have sustained other injuries; wrap them in a blanket or coat to keep them warm and seek medical advice.
- Electrical burns should be treated similarly to other burns. Reduce the heat of the injury under cold running water and seek medical advice.

FLOODS

The most serious flooding occurs when a water main bursts or a river bursts its banks. On a domestic level, however, flooding is far more commonly the result of human oversight or mechanical error – an overflowing bath, defective overflow pipe or a leaking washing-machine or dishwasher. You can take precautions if you live somewhere where natural flooding is a known hazard. Common sense and regular maintenance will help guard your home from small-scale flooding.

- If you live in an area at risk from flooding, be prepared with strong, plastic shopping bags filled with sand or soil. These can be placed outside doors and against air-bricks at the bottom of the house walls. If you do have a sudden flood, the doors may quickly become too swollen to open and you may have to smash open a window to gain access.
- Flood water is often contaminated with sewage, so – once water levels have subsided – floors and walls will need scrubbing with a strong antiseptic solution.
- Turn gas and electricity supplies off and, when the flood has subsided, remove as much furniture as you can, lift carpets and other floor coverings and mop up. If the flooding has been severe, remove some of the floorboards so that the under-floor area can be pumped out using an electric submersible pump when it is safe to use power supplies.
- In less drastic flood situations, bail out and mop up as much water as possible. 'Wet and Dry' vacuum cleaners will help to dry out soaking carpets, and a dehumidifier can be hired to dry out a room. These are also invaluable for removing heavy condensation and speeding up the curing of plaster before decorating. Be careful not to use dehumidifiers too enthusiastically, however, as they could also cause severe cracking.

SAFETY FOR CHILDREN

Most parents have horror stories of near-tragedies involving children in the home. But how do you childproof a house or flat? It's not easy second-guessing a two-year-old who, given a moment, can crawl or clamber into the most dangerous places and with devilish dexterity open an upstairs window and climb out on to the ledge. It sometimes happens, so it's best to be prepared.

Some of the danger zones are pretty obvious; stairs and bedroom windows seem to share a fatal attraction to young children, as do medicine cabinets and the kitchen cupboard where you store the bleach.

- If you have a baby or toddler, buy safety gates for the stairs – shop around for the type that can be opened, by adults, with one hand.
- Think about how many pieces of glass you have at child-height, not just French windows, but pieces of furniture such as glass-fronted bookcases. Shattered glass can, and does, kill and glass window- and door-panes should either be replaced with safe laminated glass or covered with special film (conforming to BS6206).
- There's some confusion about types of 'safety' glass: laminated glass crazes on impact, but is held together by the strong transparent interlayer; whereas toughened glass shatters into tiny pieces in the same way in which a car windscreen smashes.
- Never put anything a child can climb on to near a window and decorate large and low panes with stickers to re-emphasize their existence.
- If you're going to use painted second-hand furniture in a nursery or child's bedroom, it is safest to strip it completely and repaint it, just in case the original paint finish contains lead. The lead content of paint and varnish is now limited by law, though paint for use on metal furniture still has a relatively high lead content. Look for lead-free paints (labelled 'non-toxic').

- If you do buy second-hand items like cots, make sure they conform to current safety standards, particularly with regard to details such as the spacing of the bars.
- When your child moves into a 'grown-up' bed, fit a safety rail on the side; the better versions form a tubular framework and have a soft mesh infill. You'll certainly need one of these if you intend putting children in bunk-beds.
- Before decorating a child's room consider whether there are enough suitably placed electrical sockets. Make sure that every socket has a safety cover and that there is absolutely no need for trailing flexes.
- Fit guards that totally enclose radiators in a child's room, or that have a thermostatically controlled valve fitted so that you can modify the radiator's temperature to a safe level.
- A three-year-old has enough strength to pull a packed bookcase over, so secure any free-standing furniture firmly to the wall.
- Fit proper safety catches to all the windows – buy locks which allow the window to open slightly for ventilation. Make sure that windows can be quickly unlocked in an emergency.
- The kitchen is potentially the most dangerous room in the house – even half a cupful of hot water in a kettle can cause scalds, so fit a kettle guard which is secured to the wall at the back of the work surface. You can lessen the risk of pans being overturned by habitually cooking on the back rings or burners, out of the reach of children.
- Kitchen cupboards and drawers and fridge/freezers can be locked with a number of simple and inexpensive devices, but it's worth buying a door-slam protector to prevent tiny fingers being crushed.
- Keep sharp knives out of reach in a knife-rack out of sight or in a drawer fitted with a safety catch.

Emergency plumbing

Pipes burst when the water inside them drops below 0ºC (32ºF) and expands, splitting the casing. You may not know about it until the pipe thaws and the flow is re-established. However, if, during a cold spell, water fails to flow from a tap or won't drain away then a freeze-up is the most likely culprit.

An occupied and heated house stands little chance of suffering a burst, as long as the pipes in vulnerable places, such as under the ground-floor floorboards and in the loft, are well insulated. This is most easily done by encasing them in foamed plastic tubes. So if you go away for a weekend, or even a night in mid-winter, it will prove an absurdly false economy to turn off the central heating for the whole of the time you are out of the house. Some recently installed heating systems can be left in charge of a 'frost-thermostat' but as these have been known to stick, it's safer to rely on heating the water by a timer.

There are pipe-heating systems to prevent freezing – these are usually in the form of low-wattage electrical cable wrapped around the pipes and connected to a 13-amp electrical outlet. Some are linked to a thermostat which will switch them on as the temperature drops to freezing, others have a control which progressively increases heat output as the ambient air gets colder.

If you leave a house empty for a long time in winter, the only safe measure is to drain both the hot and cold systems, but not the central-heating system if this contains antifreeze, as it should.

After first switching off the boiler or immersion heater or raking out a solid-fuel boiler, turn off the main stopcock on the rising main and run off the water from all hot and cold taps. If there is a draincock on the rising main, drain what water is left in the pipe from that point. Drain the hot-water cylinder and flush all lavatories.

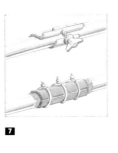

7 If a leak occurs in a pipe, you can make a temporary repair using a clamp-type repair kit (above); or improvise using a piece of hose-pipe reinforced with wire and insulating tape (below).
8 Where a leak occurs at a joint, you can use two-part repair tape (above): wind the first tape around the pipe; cover this with the second tape; make a third covering with the first. Alternatively, pack putty around the leak (below).

Don't forget to refill the system before lighting the boiler or switching on the immersion heater.

The minimum you will need to undertake an emergency repair to the plumbing is a slip coupling and leak sealant, a pair of plumber's grips or a Mole wrench, a large adjustable spanner, a sink plunger, penetrating oil, a radiator key, a junior hacksaw, a length of hose-pipe with a jubilee-clip fastener (for draining), a shallow container such as an old ice-cream carton to catch leaks in inaccessible places and a torch with leak-proof alkaline batteries.

9 If the lavatory is blocked, try plunging the pan using an old mop with a plastic bag tied around the head. Move the mop up and down to try and dislodge the blockage. This can be messy but is surprisingly effective.
10 If the lavatory remains blocked, use drain-clearing rods to clear the pipes, working from the nearest inspection chamber. You may have to call in a specialist drain cleaner for this.

ACTION IN AN EMERGENCY

Despite the best precautions, bursts and leaks happen. Once you've mopped up the flood as best you can, set about repairing the damage (or containing the leak until a plumber arrives). A semi-permanent repair can be made quite easily by using sealants for small leaks and clamps and couplings for bursts.

Some sealants are two-part; you mix the contents of two tubes and apply to a clean and dry pipe. They set very hard in a day, but you can shorten this time by playing hot air on it. Some kits recommend you reinforce the repair with special glass-fibre or self-adhesive PVC tapes, just to be sure.

1 A gate valve controls the water flow in some low-pressure pipes. When the metal gate (wheel) is open, the water flow is unrestricted; turn the gate to cut off water.
2 The mains stop cock is connected to the rising main and controls the flow of water. Turn the handle clockwise to cut off the water supply.
3 Replace the washer on a dripping tap: turn off the water supply, then turn the tap on; remove the cover (it may pull off or be fixed with a screw) and unscrew the head gear (the large nut above the jumper unit, 'A'); remove the jumper unit and replace the washer ('B'); grease the joints and threads and reassemble.

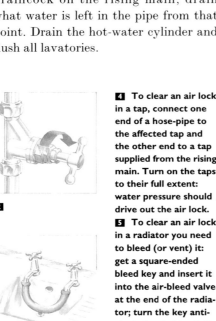

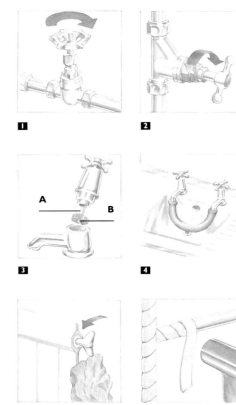

4 To clear an air lock in a tap, connect one end of a hose-pipe to the affected tap and the other end to a tap supplied from the rising main. Turn on the taps to their full extent: water pressure should drive out the air lock.
5 To clear an air lock in a radiator you need to bleed (or vent) it: get a square-ended bleed key and insert it into the air-bleed valve at the end of the radiator; turn the key anticlockwise; hold a cloth under the valve to catch any water, then retighten the valve once the air is cleared.
6 Frozen pipes can be thawed using a hair dryer: undo the lagging and blow warm air over the whole pipe to disperse the ice plug as soon as it starts to melt.

11 A rubber plunger may be all you need to unblock a sink. Hold a damp cloth tightly over the overflow, and plunge up and down over the plug hole.

12 If the above fails, you can try probing the waste trap in the pipe below the sink with a piece of wire hooked down through the plug hole (not shown). Should this fail, you will need to access the waste trap more directly. If the waste trap is old and made of lead, place a bucket underneath it and undo the drain plug using a spanner. Lead piping is very easily damaged, so you should hold it steady while you work with a piece of scrap wood.

13 With newer piping made of plastic, you can simply unscrew the nuts to disconnect the trap. This can be messy, so wear rubber gloves and overalls.

14 If the blockage is within the waste pipe, flexible drain-clearing wire may be enough to dislodge the block. Place a bucket or other container beneath the pipe to catch the debris.

15 If the outside gully is blocked, use a small trowel or a stick to break up sediment in the trap, and then remove it (wear a pair of strong rubber gloves). Finally, flush the gully clean with water from a hose-pipe.

Clamps wrap around the pipe to encase a leaking section. They are generally made of rubber-cushioned gaskets enclosed in a stainless steel casing. They are tightened on to the burst section with a wing nut or hexagon nut. The coupling repair is by far the most permanent, although it is a bit more complicated. Cut out the burst section and replace it with a 'slip' coupling which can be slid on to one pipe and back up on to the other.

Refilling water pipes often creates air locks. These will be indicated by an erratic flow from the tap, often accompanied by hissing and spluttering. Air locks can be unblocked by running a length of hose-pipe from a tap that is supplied from the rising main to the affected tap and securing each end. Turn on the tap from the rising main. The pressure of the water should force the air bubble out. If airlocks regularly occur, the cold- water cistern could be too small, or the ball valve supplying it may be blocked.

Leaking lavatories are yet another problem. Water may come out of the outlet joint, leading to the drains, when the pan is flushed. This often happens in an upstairs lavatory because the warmer atmosphere there has dried out the putty joint between the pan and the branch to the soil pipe. Clean out the remainder of the dried-out putty with a screwdriver or filling knife and bind a couple of turns of waterproofing builder's tape around the pan outlet, prodding it firmly into and around the soil-pipe socket. Pack some non-setting mastic into the rest of the space, and bind another few turns of the tape over the joint to secure it. This should stop the leak on a semi-permanent basis, but you should budget for having to fit a new pan connector in the near future.

The only other place a lavatory is likely to leak is at the inlet joint to the pan. This is normally made of rag-and-putty and can be easily replaced by a rubber cone connector.

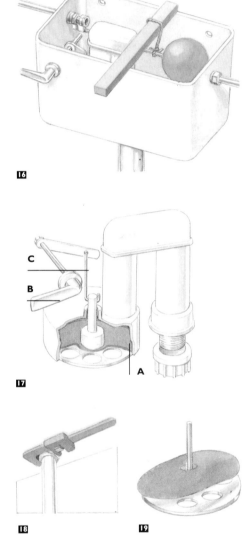

16 To make repairs to the lavatory cistern, you first need to empty it of water. Remove the cover of the cistern and tie the arm of the float to a scrap of wood resting across the top. This will stop the water flow. Now flush the lavatory and mop up any remaining water in the cistern.

17 If the lavatory needs repeated attempts before the cistern flushes, you need to replace the flap valve ('A') in the siphon assembly. First, empty the cistern (see step 16). Then follow the procedure below.

18 Use an adjustable spanner to undo the pipe nut immediately underneath the cistern, and also the nut holding the siphon assembly in place inside the cistern (not shown).

19 Disconnect the flushing handle ('B') from the metal link ('C') attached to the flap valve ('A', see step 17). Lift the siphon assembly up, replace the flap valve with a new one, then reassemble the siphon and refill the cistern.

Simple roof repairs

Leaking roofs and gutters are a constant source of trouble. There is nothing very difficult about repairing them, though it is potentially dangerous work. Safe access is of paramount importance, even for the smallest repairs. Consider it an imperative to have professionally erected tower scaffolding installed for anything more complicated than the routine cleaning of gutters. Tower scaffolding will give you confidence to complete most repairs. If you cannot arrange a safe way of getting on and off the roof, don't even think about trying.

You'll certainly need to hire a roof ladder with a ridge hook. This is slid up the roof on its wheels, and flipped over so that the hook secures on the apex of the roof. You only need a few basic tools, a soft pair of shoes and a still, preferably overcast, day.

You probably won't have much idea about the size and type of slate, clay or concrete covering, or how many tiles

■

2

1 A roof ladder runs up the tiles on wheels.
2 When the wheels reach the ridge, turn the ladder over so that the hook engages over the ridge.

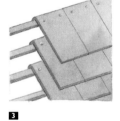

3   **4**   **5**

3 Plain tiles overlap one another to give a double thickness. Nibs at the top of each tile hook over horizontal tiling battens which are nailed to the rafters.
4 Slate tiles are fixed using two nails in each slate to attach it to the tiling battens. To keep the covering waterproof, slates should be staggered to overlap the previous row.
5 Interlocking roof tiles are laid in a single layer. Like plain tiles, they have nibs and are nailed to tiling battens.

you need to repair the roof until you get up there. Make sure you know where to get replacements and that they definitely have what you want in stock.

Most roofs suffer from cracked tiles or slates at some time. If you think you have a leaking roof, the site of the damage probably won't be obvious from inside the house unless you climb into the loft when it's raining. You can then trace the drip back to its point of entry, which may be some distance from where it drops on to the loft floor. Use a pair of binoculars to make an external inspection of the roof. Ask a neighbour if you can look out of an upstairs window.

Leaks can happen at abutments, typically the head of a lean-to extension, or around a chimney stack where weak fillets of mortar crack or break away. These can be inexpensively cured, in the short term at least, by bitumen-backed self-adhesive flashing strip. Professionally installed lead flashings last longer, but are much more costly and difficult to fix. Don't try to repair cracked slates or tiles – replace them. However, a mastic sealant can be used as an emergency stop gap.

Replacing a plain tile is easy, as they're usually piggy-backed on top of each other, secured by two nibs which hook over roof battens or laths. Use wooden wedges to lift the tiles in the row above the damaged one and slide a brick layer's trowel underneath the broken tile. You'll see how simply it is fixed when you remove the broken one, and replacement is similarly straightforward. Support the new tile on the trowel and slide it into place until the nibs hook in place.

Concrete tiles are more difficult to replace because they have interlocking grooves on the side. You may discover wire clips holding some types of tile, or they may be individually nailed, but a bit of wiggling about will free any tile that needs replacing.

6

7

6 Replacing a broken roof tile is relatively straightforward. Fit wedges to lift the tiles in the row above clear, then remove the broken tile: you may be able to do this by hand, but it will probably be easier to use a trowel.
7 Slide the replacement tile in place, and hook the nib over the tiling batten. However, you will not be able to nail the tile in place. Remove the wedges from the row above, taking care not to damage adjacent tiles.

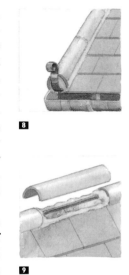

8

9

8 Hip tiles are fixed to the eaves of a sloping roof. A hip hook (metal bracket) at the end should be screwed to the hip rafter before the hip tiles are fitted: this will help prevent dislodged tiles sliding off the roof.
9 Damaged ridge tiles (which seal the apex of the roof) and hip tiles are easily replaced by bedding a replacement tile on new mortar. Leave a gap below the tile as shown to allow air to circulate freely.

Ridge tiles are used to waterproof the apex of the roof, while hip tiles seal the external corners where two roofs join. These can often work loose in high winds because the mortar they're fixed with is merely a fill-in material and has no real strength.

Ridge tiles should be carefully pried up and away (they are not difficult to crack), given a thorough soaking in a bucket of water and then bedded down again on a cement mortar (one part cement to four of sharp sand). You will need to clean off the old mortar first, and seal all the ends and edges of the replacement tile, but endeavour to keep the underside of it clean and open to enable air to circulate and prevent the roof timber below from rotting.

Alternatively, builders' merchants sell clips which will give ridge and hip tiles a much stronger hold on the roof. End hips are kept in place with curly ended irons which are screwed directly into the rafter. If the mortar between hip or ridge tiles is only slightly cracked, use a caulking gun to inject a non-setting mastic.

A slate has to be replaced differently. Elderly slate roofs suffer from 'nail sickness' – the copper nails fixing them rot, allowing the slate to slide down and away. If the slate is damaged and loose,

10

11

12

10 To replace a damaged slate you will need a specialist slaters' ripper. Slide this underneath the broken slate and move it to one side until you feel one of the fixing nails. Pull the rip down so the barb on the end pulls out or cuts through the nail. Repeat for the nail on the other side. With both nails removed, pull out the damaged slate.
11 Next, nail a strip of lead about 200mm (8in) long and 25mm (1in) wide to the roof timbers in the position shown, using galvanized nails.
12 Slide the replacement slate in place, and fold the bottom of the lead strip so that it holds the lower edge of the slate, doubling it back to keep it firm.

it will simply pull out. If it's firmly fixed, you'll need to hire a sword-like weapon called a ripper which is slid underneath the damaged slate, moved sideways over the nail and then pulled down to sever the nail. If you do have occasion to re-nail tiles, copper or aluminium nails should be used. Never use galvanized, or anything else.

Roof slates are replaced using 'tingles'. These are lead strips about 20cm (8in) long and 25mm (1in) wide, the top part of which is nailed to a fixing batten. The new slate is then pushed into place and the bottom of the tingle is folded up to hold it. It is a simple repair, but can come undone if, for example, a heavy load of melting snow slips down the roof, unfolding the tingle.

Heatwaves play havoc with a roof, continually expanding and contracting its timbers and tiles, cracking cement flashings around the chimney and, on flat roofs, shifting the felt coverings and blistering them. The first sign of trouble is likely to be a damp patch appearing on the ceiling. Most flat roofs are built up from a three-layer felt construction laid on a sub-base and bonded to each other using a bitumen-based adhesive. Unlike tile and slate roofs, which are built of several separate parts that are designed to move independently of each other, roofing felt relies on its elasticity to expand and contract in response to changes in the atmosphere.

Flat roofs should be inspected at least once a year. Their maintenance involves very little time or trouble: just the common sense removal of debris; the careful inspection of the points where the felt covering reaches the side of a chimney stack, surrounds on central-heating flues or soil pipes or the edge of a dormer window; and clearing the gutters of chippings and debris before they block downpipes.

Look for patches where chippings are missing; it is in these areas that you are likely to find cracks, blisters and bubbles. Deal with a crack by first

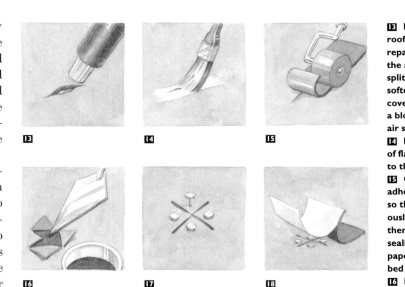

13   **14**   **15**

16   **17**   **18**

19

20

19 Lead flashing seals the join where a roof meets a wall. Fine cracks can be repaired using a generous layer of bituminous mastic to fill the crack and make it waterproof.
20 You can replace flashing with a self-adhesive strip. Clean and prepare the surface, then press a strip of flashing to the roof and wall. Fit a second strip to overlap the first.

scraping away any embedded chippings around it. Use a hot-air stripper gun to dry out the area and soften the felt; don't use a gas blowtorch.

When the area is dry, brush it clean, reapply the hot-air gun to melt the felt further and press the felt down with a wooden wallpaper-seam roller. Finally, coat it with flashing-strip primer, and then roll down a strip of self-adhesive flashing tape along the crack. Should you find a wide crack, fill it first with bituminous mastic before covering it with flashing tape. If you find a crack in flashing tape where it is covering a join in a building (for example, where an extension roof meets a wall) then it can be sealed using bituminous mastic.

Blisters and bubbles are caused by rainwater finding a way between the layers of felt, and then being 'boiled' by the sun. Repair them in the same way as you would a crack, except that an X-shape cut should first be made in the blister, enabling the edges to be folded back while you dry the felt underneath. The flaps are then sealed with a cold bitumen compound before being pressed and rolled back into place. The repair is completed by sticking a patch of self-adhesive flashing over it. Cover all repairs with a good layer of chippings for further protection.

13 Minor splits to flat roofs are easily repaired. First, clean the area around the split, then dry out and soften the asphalt roof covering using either a blow torch or a hot-air stripper.
14 Next, apply a coat of flashing-tape primer to the damaged area.
15 Cut a piece of self-adhesive flashing tape so that it will generously cover the split, then press this in place, sealing it using a wallpaper-seam roller to bed the patch firmly.
16 Blisters are repaired in a similar way to splits. Dry out and soften the area around the blister, then, using a sharp knife, make two cuts in a cross shape across the blister. Apply a generous coat of bituminous mastic.
17 Press the flaps back down on to the layer of mastic, and fix them in place using galvanized clout nails. Brush flashing-tape primer over the repair to seal and waterproof it.
18 Peel the backing paper off a piece of self-adhesive flashing tape and press it over the repair. Ensure the flashing tape is firmly sealed using a wallpaper-seam roller.

Damp and rot

RISING DAMP

If it is left unchecked, rising damp can, in a couple of months, lead to wet rot, which is bad enough, or dry rot, which is catastrophic. It will transform your desirable house into something even the estate agents couldn't describe as being 'in need of some decoration', their euphemism for demolition. Even if you find *merulius lacrymans*, dry rot fungi, sprouting in the cellar, there's a sporting chance you can cure it. Otherwise, call in a specialist company.

If your house was built before 1875, its unlikely to have a damp-proof course (dpc). Rising damp will introduce itself in a number of ways, most likely by blistering paintwork, peeling wallpaper and crumbling plaster.

There are several remedies, all rather tedious and time consuming, so first check that the damp isn't caused by broken downpipes or gutters, damaged rendering, porous or damaged flashing, plumbing leaks, faults in the drainage, or broken window-sills. All these can have the same effect as rising damp, as can garden soil banking up against an outside wall, effectively bridging the damp-proof course.

Some damp is caused by poor ventilation underneath the floorboards. This can be cured by fitting a bigger air-brick. It is worth hiring a battery-powered damp meter which has two prongs for prodding gently into plaster and lights that indicate damp; these meters have to be carefully calibrated.

The most effective remedy is also the most difficult – installing a new dpc. Cut out a row of bricks – 1m (3ft) at a time – and insert impervious engineering bricks in mortar mixed with a water-proofing compound. The dpc should be about 15cm (6in) off the ground.

It is tempting just to cure the spot where damp occurs, but far better to do the whole wall. Alternatively, hire an angle grinder and cut out a horizontal mortar course between the bricks, again 1m (3ft) at a time.

You then insert a new purpose-made membrane strip into the gap and seal it with mortar. The easiest DIY solution is to inject a silicone water repellent – a chemical dpc – which acts as a barrier throughout the thickness of the wall. You can hire the complete unit: an electric pump with half a dozen nozzles.

The efficiency of this method depends on how well the fluid permeates the wall. It involves drilling 2cm (¾in) diameter holes 10–15cm (4–6in) apart, preferably from the inside of the house, although it's easier and less disruptive to work outside.

The floors and walls of basements and cellars are below the normal line of a dpc and are therefore particularly prone to damp if the damp-proof membrane protecting them has failed – but there may be an obvious, easily fixed fault such as a broken drainpipe.

The traditional method of 'tanking' the walls with a four-coat sand and cement render containing a damp-proof compound is still the most reliable, but difficult work for an amateur. Floors are more easily treated by a damp-proof compound covered with a sand and cement screed. But if they are really wet, the only solution is to dig up the floor and re-lay it over a thick, damp-proof plastic sheet membrane – this is only for the brave and very fit! Seek professional assistance.

ROT

Houses are incredibly resilient things. They can withstand a considerable amount of assault and battery from the most unskilled hands, yet will capitulate quite quickly in the face of a rot attack, especially if this gets into the structural timbers of the floor or roof. Don't think that you're safe because you've bought a brand new home. Bad practices in the building trade, when wood is left around sites getting soaked for months before being used, means that some houses actually have dry rot built into them.

If you do discover dry or wet rot in your house, you can be assured of one thing; the damage is likely to be far worse than it looks. It is vital to take some immediate, elementary measures towards a cure, but first identify what sort of decay it is. Rot happens when the wood soaks up more than 20 per cent of its mass and remains wet for a considerable time – months rather than weeks.

The misleadingly named dry rot, far worse because it spreads very quickly, relies on damp to breed in places like roof voids, bathrooms and kitchens. Its effect on timber is to produce a rusty red spore dust on the surface, while the body of the wood will shrink, splitting into cubical patterns, and cracks will appear along the grain of the timber. Brittle grey strands by which the rot spreads can often be the first sign of attack, or there could be cottonwool-like patches on the timber. In the worst possible form of attack, a soft pancake-like growth develops.

Wet rot is found in damp places like cellars and roofs and exterior doors and window frames. The wood is darkened, with severe cracking along the grain.

The treatment for dry rot amounts to quite drastic surgery; rotted wood must be cut out allowing a safety margin of at least 1m (3ft) each side of the damaged portion and replaced with sound wood which has been soaked in a dry rot killing liquid. This liquid should also be liberally sprayed on to surrounding timber. The best method of fixing the replacement timber is by bolting pairs of steel connector plates on to it and the existing sound timber. Remove and burn the infected timber as soon as possible.

Infected plaster must also be removed and, allowing a similar 1m (3ft) safety margin, the walls scrubbed with a wire brush, and sterilized with a masonry dry-rot killer. The treatment of wet rot is similarly messy and tedious. In both cases it is vital to discover the original source of the dampness which led to the rot and cure that.

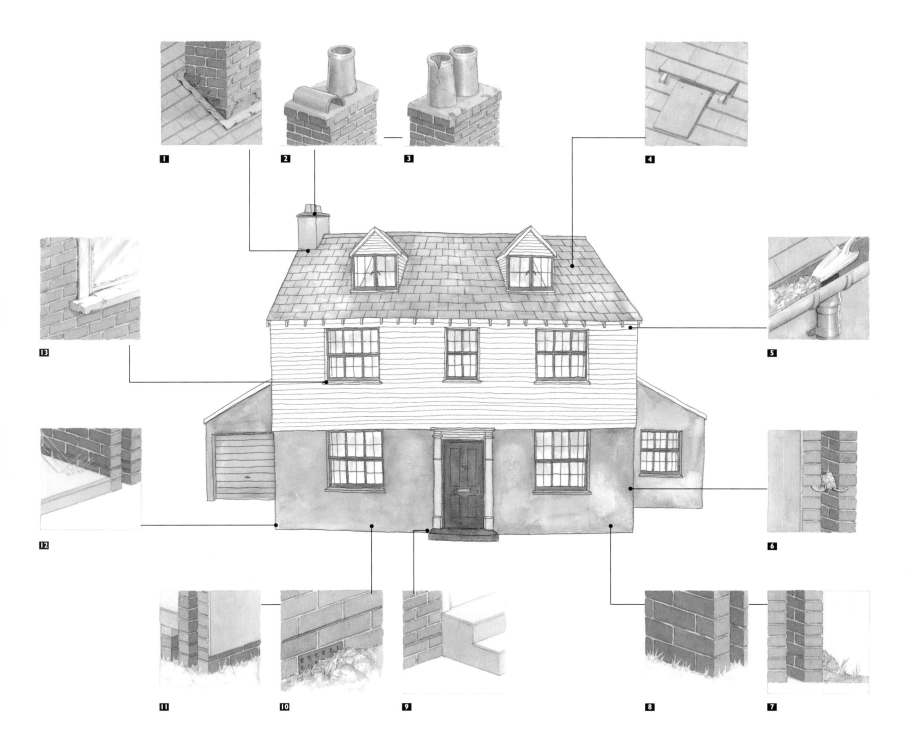

1 Make sure that lead flashing around the chimney is not loose or damaged. You can undertake simple repairs yourself (see page 247).
2 Rain falling down the chimney can cause damp if a fireplace has been blocked up without ventilation. Vent the chimney with an air-brick and fit a capping pot or a half-round ridge tile in mortar at the top.
3 Replace loose, cracked or broken chimney pots.

4 Replace missing, loose or damaged roof tiles (see pages 246-7).
5 Clear gutters of waste and debris, working away from the downpipe outlet. If the downpipe becomes blocked, use drain-clearing rods to remove the debris, working from the top.
6 Ensure debris does not become stuck in cavity walls.
7 One common cause of rising damp is soil piled up above the dpc. Ensure the dpc is not blocked.

8 House settlement can fracture your dpc. Have a new dpc professionally installed.
9 Concrete steps built above and across the dpc will allow damp to rise into the walls, and will also rot the door and its frame.
10 Air-bricks provide essential ventilation: keep them clear and make sure they do not become clogged.
11 Make sure that rendering to the exterior of the house is not extended below the level of the dpc.

12 A path built alongside the wall of the house should fall clear of the dpc; further, it should be low enough to ensure that, during spells of heavy rain, water does not splash up on to the wall above the dpc, as this can lead to damp.
13 Keep window frames and door frames in good order. Fill any cracks and gaps you find. Keep drip grooves clear under the windowsills and replace crumbling putty.

Insulation and subsidence

INSULATION

Insulating the loft is not difficult work, just messy and dusty – wear some eye protection, a dust mask and rubber gloves. Remember that once insulated, your roof space will probably be one of the coldest places in your entire house. Consequently, wrap an insulation blanket around the cold-water tank. Make a cover for it out of a piece of plywood and insulate that too. It doesn't have to look pretty, just warm. Do not, however, insulate under the tank – rising heat will help prevent the water from freezing in the coldest weather.

All pipes in the loft can be easily lagged using lengths of foam-moulded tubes designed to fit around them. An economical black-light heater can also be installed in the loft. The heater, which can be run from a junction box into a socket, can be safely left on throughout the winter months. It simply takes the chill out of the air; its heat is otherwise imperceptible.

If you use your loft for storage, you should lay the insulation between the joists and board over them. If you can see the underside of your roof tiles, staple heavy-duty polythene sheet to the underside of the rafters, keeping the ventilation of the eaves clear. But if you don't do another thing, ensure that the domestic hot-water cylinder has a smart new jacket (to conform with British Standard Kite Mark BS 5615). Measure the height and circumference to ascertain the right size. This alone could pay for itself in a couple of weeks.

SUBSIDENCE

Cracks that suddenly appear in ceilings and walls can strike terror in the bravest home-owner. Don't panic, but don't ignore them either. Although it is very rare for a property to become so badly damaged by subsidence or settlement that it is on the point of collapse, cracks give due warning that something has to be done. This might not be anything more drastic than redecoration.

Subsidence happens when the earth supporting a building's foundation dries out and starts collapsing. Clay soils are particularly prone to this. Subsidence shows up after an especially long, hot summer, but trees planted too close to a house are more often blamed as a serious contributory factor to drought because they have sucked moisture out of the ground. Willow, poplar and oak are particularly thirsty.

If you have a mature tree near your house, don't fell it just to prevent cracks. Doing so could cause 'ground heave', created by the swelling of clay as the water returns and the water-table rises. It can affect even very deep foundations, lifting them and cracking walls below ground level, and those below floor and sill levels. Tree roots can extend a considerable distance and, as a rough guide, if the distance between the tree and the house is less than the height of the tree, then the tree is likely to be the root of the cracking problem.

There are no hard and fast rules with trees, but remember that they play an important part in stabilizing the water-level, so if the tree was there before the house, particularly if it is fully mature, leave it alone beyond pruning it back. In the early spring fill in any cracks in the walls you suspect it has caused. They shouldn't reopen.

If the tree has been planted more recently, it is probably best to remove it altogether. You may see cracks appear in the walls afterwards, and these should be filled in the following spring.

Ground shrinks vertically and horizontally, but as the house itself shelters the ground beneath it, that part remains fairly stable. Beyond the house the ground tends to shrink down and away from the house, resulting in diagonal cracks at doors and windows.

If, after heavy winter rain, the ground is getting waterlogged and the cracks in your house show signs of closing up again, this indicates that they are typically caused by clay shrinkage.

Some degrees of subsidence can be caused by overloading the foundations, which could occur after alterations to the property. Although houses usually impose a fairly even load all around their strip foundations, sometimes – typically when a large hole is made in a wall to install a patio door or bay window – the lintel carrying the load of the building exerts too much pressure on the piers at each end of the gap and the foundations settle further down into the ground. Clay ground, in particular, exaggerates this effect.

Inadequate foundations to porches or conservatory extensions can lead to cracks occurring at the point where the extension joins with the main wall of the house; these cracks will also tend to close up during spells of wet weather.

Problems often occur where houses are built on ground such as old ditches, ponds, or even bomb craters. On these 'soft' sites special attention should have been given to the types of foundation used at the time of construction, but if large cracks appear in steady progression you should ask your local surveyor's department whether there are any maps of the plot on which your house is built; if there are, look to see if they show reclaimed ground.

Subsidence caused by soft ground will almost always call for some form of underpinning. The foundations may need to be widened rather than deepened in order to spread the load, or some form of piling may have to be undertaken. If it is necessary to deepen the foundations, this is carried out close to the wall, so it may have to be done by hand – and at some expense.

Inside the house, it is common for cracks to appear at the junction of the ceiling and wall. This is the weakest point of the structure and the cracks open due to normal seasonal movement. Filling the cracks with plaster filler is only a short-term cure: the permanent solution is to fit coving, which will permanently conceal the problem.

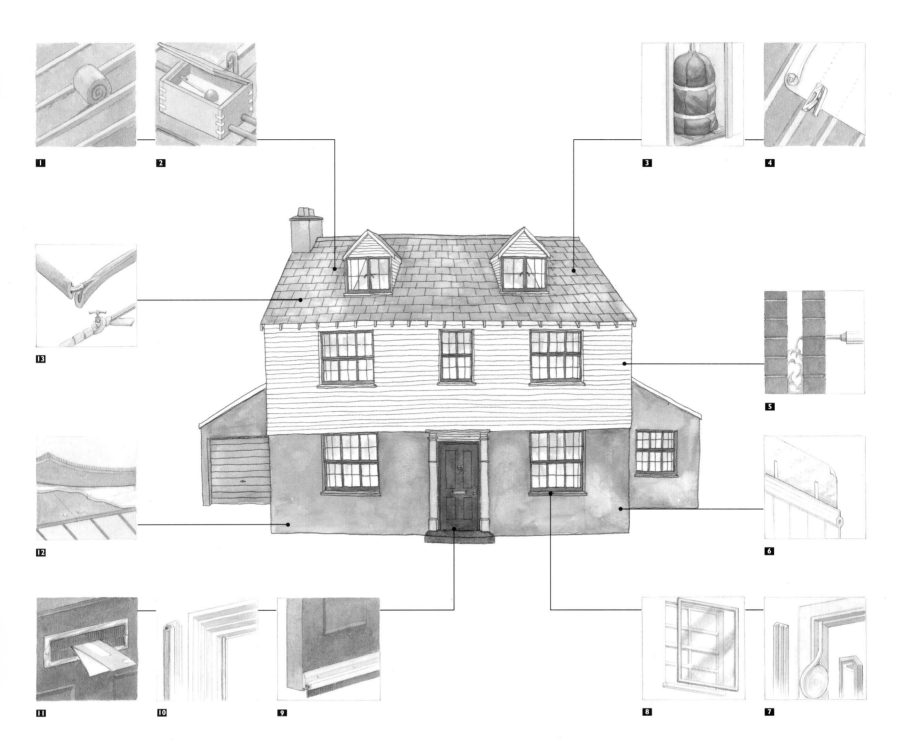

1 Fit insulation blanket between the joists in the loft. If the loft is already insulated, check that it is adequate: the blanket should be at least 150mm (6in) thick.

2 Your storage tank should be insulated with insulation blanket, polystyrene sheets or a purpose-made jacket. Leave cut-outs for the pipes, and fit a lid. However, the tank should not be insulated underneath.

3 The hot-water cylinder should be lagged with a jacket at least 75mm (3in) thick.

4 Line the roof with building paper or polythene sheeting stapled below the rafters.

5 Cavity-wall insulation can reduce heat loss. It is injected through exterior walls and should be carried out by professionals.

6 Specially coated foil paper can be stuck behind radiators to reflect heat back into the room.

7 Insulate windows using brush seals for sash windows, and V-shaped plastic strips or self-adhesive PVC foam strips on casement windows.

8 Secondary glazing is expensive but may be worthwhile as a form of insulation, particularly at windows you seldom open. It also makes windows more difficult to use as a point of entry for intruders.

9 Fit a threshold draught excluder to the inside of the front door at the bottom.

10 Fit rigid brush or tubular strips around the door frame.

11 Fit a brush-type draught excluder to the letterbox, or fit a secondary flap on the inside of the door.

12 Fill any gaps between floorboards with wood strips or filler. Cover the floorboards with chipboard and foil-faced reflective foam underlay beneath carpets. You can incorporate additional insulation beneath the floorboards using loft-insulation blanket or polystyrene boards.

13 Lag hot-water pipes with special pre-formed moulded foam insulation, which is split along its length. For more complicated pipework use pipe lagging which is taped or tied in place.

Home security

Domestic break-ins these days are an all-too-common occurrence, and it's easy to become paranoid about home security as result, turning your home into a high-security fortress. Different homes require different security arrangements. If you live in the country and your home is some distance from the neighbours', your priorities in terms of how to protect your property will be different from those of someone who lives in a busy city. But while no amount of precautions will protect you against the truly determined burglar, there are a number of simple, common-sense measures you can adopt.

Never leave money or valuables lying around, and don't carry keys in a pocket or handbag that also contains your address or a means of identification. Similarly, it may seem to make life easier if you hide a spare key under the door-mat, hidden in a flowerpot or hanging inside the letter-box, but thieves will look in all the usual places; it's far better to leave a spare set of keys with a trustworthy friend or neighbour.

Your household goods insurance policy can never recover the sentimental value that may be attached to a stolen piece of jewellery, for example, but you should make sure that it allows you to replace goods at their real cost. Keep an inventory, and note the serial numbers of electrical goods, etc. The policy may also stipulate certain security requirements: make sure you conform to these, or your claim may not be paid.

SECURING YOUR HOME

• For very little expense you can make each window difficult – though not impossible – to use as the means of entry favoured by two out of three burglars. Ground-floor and basement rear windows are the most vulnerable. Window locks do work, but don't hang the keys from the window frame.

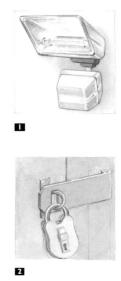

1 Make sure that the exterior of your house is adequately lit. Fit a detector light, which automatically switches on when someone approaches. Models are also available that automatically switch on when dusk falls and switch off at dawn.
2 Doors to any outside buildings such as a garden shed should be securely padlocked. If you have been using a ladder and need to leave it out, keep it locked to something secure, away from the house.

• Whether you live in a house or a flat, the softwood-framed front door found in most homes is the first and fairly poor line of defence. Panelled doors with inset glass panels should be protected with simple wrought-iron

3 If you have patio doors at the back of the house, fit purpose-made locks at the top and bottom. Keep the key out of sight, but close at hand so that you can get out easily in an emergency.
4 If you have French windows, fit bolts to the top and bottom of both leaves, as well as a five-lever mortise lock half way down.

5 A viewer enables you to identify the caller before opening the door.
6 Hinge bolts help to reinforce the frame on the hinged side of the door, reducing the chance of the door 'giving' under force.
7 A mail holder across the letterbox makes it more difficult for someone to tamper with the locks by sticking a hand in through the letterbox.
8 Rim-mounted cylinder deadlocks lock automatically from the outside, but can be opened without a key from inside.
9 A door chain allows you to check a caller's identification.
10 Five-lever mortise deadlocks can only be opened with a key, making entry difficult.

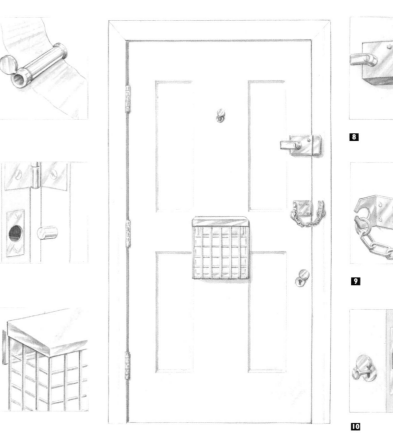

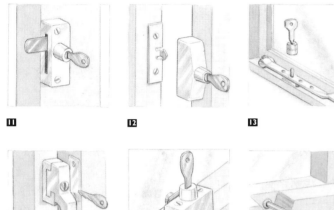

11   **12**   **13**

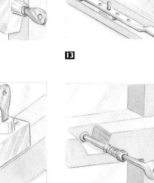

14   **15**   **16**

You should fit locks on all windows that can be opened, but especially on all downstairs windows and those on upper levels that are easily accessible. A wide range of locks is now available.
For casement windows:
11 A pivot lock prevents inward-opening windows being forced.
12 A snap lock is fitted to the surface of the window surround and the frame.
13 A stay lock bolts the stay to the frame when the window is closed.
14 A surface-mounted lockable handle.
For sash windows:
15 A sash bolt fits most wooden frames. The bolt in the top unit locks into a plate fitted to the bottom frame.
16 A dual screw is recessed into the frames, locking them together when closed.

grills, and thin plywood panels must be reinforced with stronger outer panels. It is best to replace a door like this. The most effective door is made of hardwood or has a solid hardwood core not less than 45mm (1¾in) thick.
• Replace a two-lever lock with a five-lever mortise deadlock (ensure it meets BS3621 which satisfies most insurance requirements). Mortise locks do have an in-built weak point though, because cutting the hole for them weakens the door at the point where it should be strongest. This can be overcome by reinforcing the wood in the lock area with a metal plate.
• With the exception of the front door, all doors need to be reinforced with strong, preferably key-operated bolts fitted at the top and bottom. Hinge bolts on all doors, which would prevent them being jemmied out of the frame, are a sensible extra. There is little point in fixing strong locks if the door frame isn't in good condition. If it is weak, the frame and door can be levered out in a matter of seconds.
• If you still feel your home is vulnerable, then consider installing a burglar alarm. If you cannot fit it yourself, consult your Crime Prevention Officer who will be able to provide you with a list of approved installers.

You'll save money and rental charges by fitting an alarm system yourself, but buy kits with care. They should comply with British Standards – look for the kite mark – as well as meeting the requirements of the National Supervisory Council for Intruder Alarms. Some DIY systems fail because they use cheap, unreliable components. Don't buy a dummy box – thieves can spot a fake.

Surface-mounted door contacts may be easy to fit but do not have the same security rating as the type that are hidden in the edge of the door. Pick a system with four-core, double-pole cable rather than the twin-wire frequently offered. Some kits have the facility for adding on devices like movement detectors, but the significant factor is that a system should be tamper-proof, so that any criminal interference with the circuit sounds the alarm.

Door contacts can be effectively backed up by passive infrared (PIR) sensors which react to rapid changes in temperature caused by an intruder's body heat. They can be very effective in switching on outside security lights, but they have to be positioned with some care to avoid dazzling innocent visitors.

The best sensors for inside a house are dual units which incorporate PIR and ultrasonic or microwaves. Both ele-

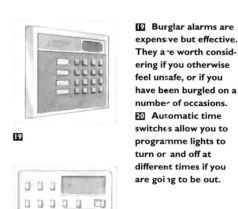

19 Burglar alarms are expensive but effective. They are worth considering if you otherwise feel unsafe, or if you have been burgled on a number of occasions.
20 Automatic time switches allow you to programme lights to turn on and off at different times if you are going to be out.

17

17 Exterior side doors and rear doors should be fitted with lockable bolts at both the top and bottom.
18 A five-lever mortise deadlock offers an near-impregnable line of security.

18

ments have to be activated to trigger an alarm system. Some systems are linked to a monitoring company or to a designated friend's phone, who will then alert the police of a break-in. A fee is often levied in the case of a false alarm.

The control panel, which supplies the power, monitors the system and triggers the alarm, is connected to the mains supply via a fused spur. It contains a standby battery in case of power failure. It is always fitted on the main exit/entry route, but should be out of sight of anyone peering through the letter-box.
• Plug-in time switches that can be programmed to go on and off at random within a pre-chosen timescale are far preferable to the ones that light up at precisely the same time each evening. Always leave curtains half drawn in rooms fitted with these switches.
• Before going on holiday – having cancelled the paper and milk, and arranged some reliable neighbourhood watch – deposit valuables at the bank. Hide items such as portable televisions and video recorders in the attic; burglars seldom look there. They usually won't bother looking under carpets either, so remove a section of floorboard, place a box containing precious things there and screw the whole thing down again.

Multi-generational design

Multi-generational, or universal, design approaches the design and layout of a home with the idea of finding solutions that work regardless of age or disability. Over the years, we have learnt to fight shy of labelling somebody a 'disabled person': impairments such as loss of sight or lack of mobility are often compensated for by an increase in other faculties. Design that caters for the special needs of the elderly or the physically impaired often used to underline the disparity between them and the rest of the population; current thinking, however, recognizes that design which seeks to increase ability rather than handicap the less able works well for everyone.

Designing homes for people with physical disabilities is a complex matter which is difficult, if not impossible, to resolve simply by means of a universal checklist: the needs of a young, fit adult paraplegic in a wheelchair will be quite different from those a frail, elderly person. Each disability is different, and the needs of individuals – and the solutions – are necessarily a matter of detailed consultation at the planning stage. It is important that the demands, requirements and suggestions of the individual are addressed towards the aim of improving their independence; the fact that homes so redesigned will perform more efficiently for all users is not only fortuitous, but a positive aim.

Bathrooms and kitchens are important areas in any house, and should be designed with particular care. Specialist doctors, occupational therapists and registered charities may have valuable advice on general requirements.

Converting a kitchen to meet the criteria of universal design is probably the greatest challenge, not least because, in a family context, children no more fit into a kitchen designed for mobile adults than do wheelchair users. However, many of the fashionable design elements in modern kitchens allow for some flexibility of appliances and their layout. The separation and

Designing a kitchen for use by people with varying degrees of mobility requires careful planning. The layout shown here incorporates a number of features that can aid the less mobile, incorporating plenty of under-counter leg room so that people can comfortably sit and work. In a small kitchen such as this, storage is a problem, and the wall-mounted units would not be accessible to a wheelchair user: you need to check the limits of a person's reach upwards, downwards and across.

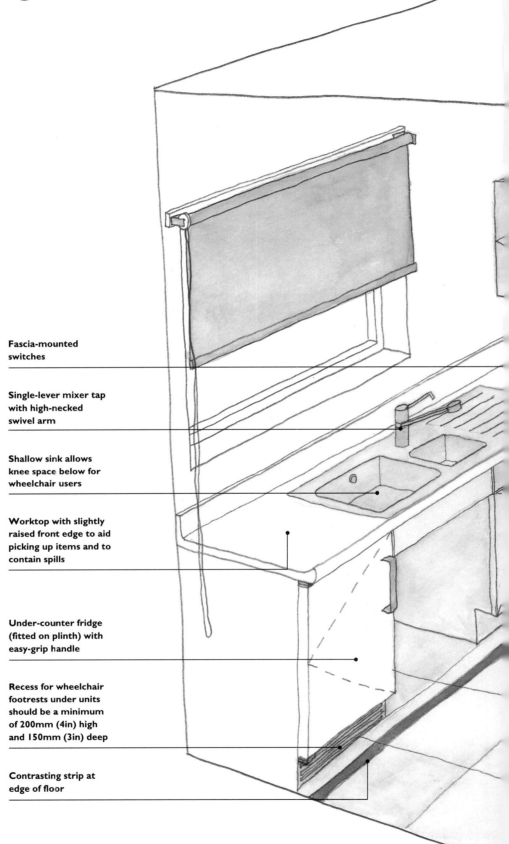

Fascia-mounted switches

Single-lever mixer tap with high-necked swivel arm

Shallow sink allows knee space below for wheelchair users

Worktop with slightly raised front edge to aid picking up items and to contain spills

Under-counter fridge (fitted on plinth) with easy-grip handle

Recess for wheelchair footrests under units should be a minimum of 200mm (4in) high and 150mm (3in) deep

Contrasting strip at edge of floor

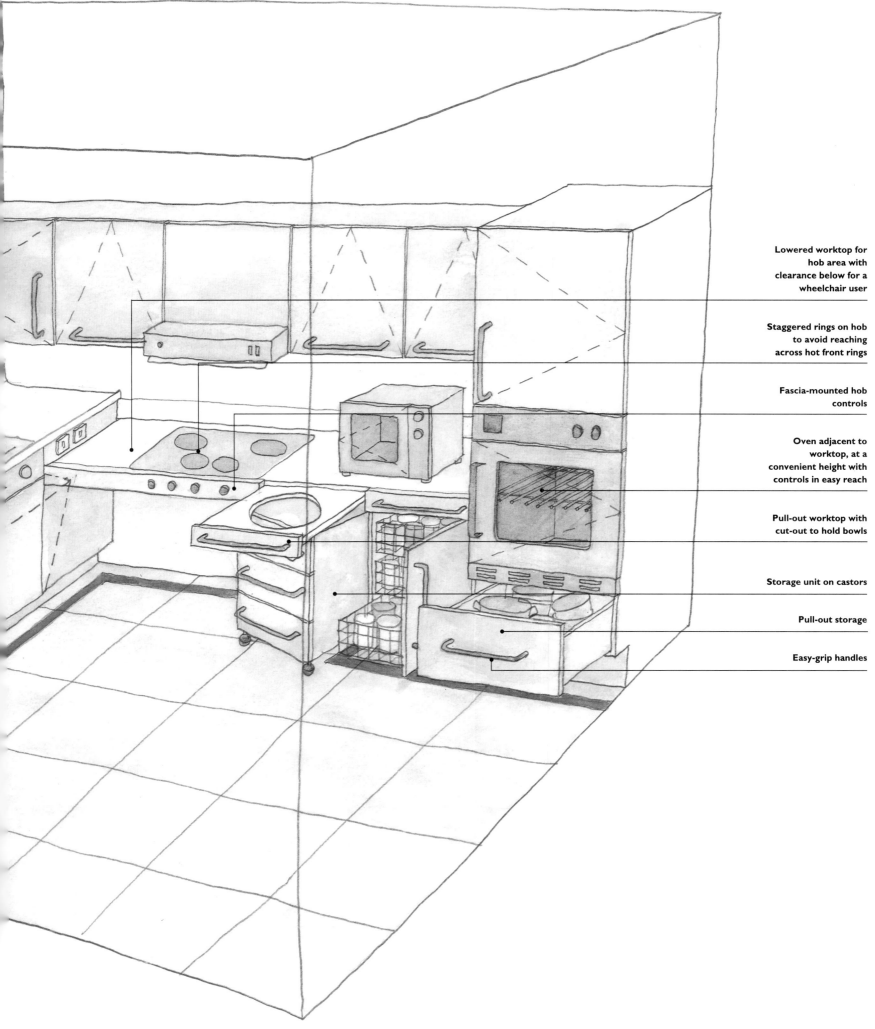

Lowered worktop for hob area with clearance below for a wheelchair user

Staggered rings on hob to avoid reaching across hot front rings

Fascia-mounted hob controls

Oven adjacent to worktop, at a convenient height with controls in easy reach

Pull-out worktop with cut-out to hold bowls

Storage unit on castors

Pull-out storage

Easy-grip handles

1 A bath seat should be adjustable to fit most baths. It locks in position close to the hand grips to make getting into and out of the bath a much easier process for the elderly and infirm.
2 A hinged, fold-down shower seat and grab rail allow people with a range of disabilities to take a shower on their own. Both the seat and grab rail should be positioned with care, preferably in consultation with the person for whom its use is intended.

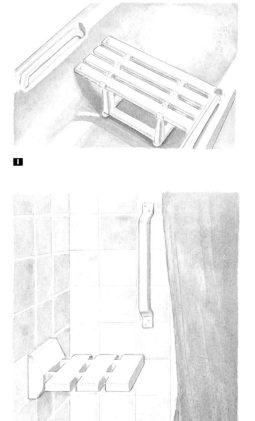

juxtaposition of the hob and oven is essential: splitting these appliances should enable them to be placed at heights which make cooking easier and safer, although the presence of young children would obviously have to be taken into consideration.

Hobs can be installed side by side in pairs so there is no need to reach over a front burner to a pot cooking behind. Controls mounted on the edge of the worktop, in front of the hob, are easier to reach and operate safely. Ovens with drop-down or side-hung doors can be installed at any height, according to requirements. Both appliances should be close to a generous area of worktop.

The U- or L-shaped kitchen layout is the most convenient for disabled users, particularly those confined to wheel-chairs which don't readily move side-ways. Such a configuration enables a number of tasks to be carried out from approximately the same spot provided there is enough space to position a wheelchair beneath lower work surfaces. Accessories such as pull-out boards, some with holes cut out for bowls, and cupboards with slide-out shelves that hold heavy appliances ready for use are available from commercial kitchen companies as part of their range. Slightly raised nosings on the leading edge of worktops make it easier to pick up things and contain spills.

It is essential that all kitchen fittings should be robustly installed, as a person with reduced mobility may grab them for support. Drawers should obviously open smoothly, and their design should include stays to prevent them being inadvertently pulled out completely.

Power sockets could be extended to double switches on the front of, or directly underneath, the worktop nosing for easy access. The front edge of the worktop should be rounded over to min-imize potential injury.

Suitable ceramic or quarry tiles pro-vide a firm, level and slip-resistant floor surface which is easy to clean. However, unless the tiles are exactly flush, they may cause people to trip and limit the mobility of wheelchair users; and any-thing breakable will shatter if dropped. Sealed cork tiles, or even washable car-pet tiles are viable alternatives.

BATHROOMS
Bathrooms require careful planning and, for wheelchair users in particular, need to be a generous size. If your home is on more than one level, there should be provision for a lavatory, at least, on every floor. A shower may seem like a good alternative to a bath, allowing many disabled people to bathe independ-ently. A seat and grab rails are safer,

3 You can buy special taps that can be easily operated by the elderly and arthritic. You can also convert existing taps with lever covers. Both solutions enable users to turn the water on and off with much greater ease
4 A grab rail can be fitted at the foot of the stairs for support. Well-designed versions are available in left- and right-handed models; these are not interchangeable and should be bought according to which side of the stairs the banister is positioned.
5 Plugs with large, easy-grip handles allow elderly and arthritic people to operate electrical appliances much more easily.

less intrusive and cheaper modifications to make to a shower cubicle or bath-tub compared to hoists over a bath.

Shower areas can also be designed to incorporate a toilet and wash-basin, with carefully sited drop-down rails and pull switches. Such an integrated unit would also solve problems by containing water supplies and other plumbing services within it, while at the same time keeping the rest of the bathroom dry.

Access to showers should provide few difficulties for the ambulatory disabled, but there could be problems for wheelchair users. Careful siting could provide a shower over the bath.

If a progressive disability makes the provision of overhead hoist tracks imperative in the future, careful in-line planning of the layout of the fittings, together with the strengthening of the ceiling joists, could save disruption and expense. Although baths can be lowered into the floor, this is a complicated, and therefore expensive, option.

Non-slip tiles are a necessary and obvious floor covering, providing their surface does not make cleaning difficult.

Whether bathroom doors open in or out depends on the available space, but sliding or concertina doors could be an alternative. Whatever the type of door, provision should be made for opening it – both from inside and outside the bathroom – in an emergency.

AIDING MOBILITY

Although most public places now provide dedicated and designed parking facilities for the disabled, it is just as important that a person should be able to park as conveniently outside their own home. Private parking bays should be clearly identified for disabled drivers or passengers only, as close to the home as possible and wide enough to allow car doors to be fully opened to enable someone to transfer to a wheelchair. The car-parking area should be smooth and kerbs between it and the house should be dropped for wheelchairs.

Wheelchair users need ramps outside their home; a gradient of 1:15 would be considered normal, and 1:12 the maximum. Portable or semi-permanent ramps made of timber are a possible alternative, as long as they have a slip-resistant finish.

Some ambulant disabled prefer steps to ramps. The going, or tread, should be no less than 28cm (11in) and the riser a maximum of 15cm (6in). Handrails made of a 'warm', non-slip material such as hardwood or plastic-coated steel are essential and should be coloured to be more easily distinguishable.

Sheltered entrance areas, in the form of porches or canopies, provide protection for people who may take a long time to open a door and enter a house.

Doors for wheelchair users should have a minimum opening of 80cm (31in). Doors should be of solid construction for security and to provide fixing for pulls and fittings, although some glazing in laminated glass extending low enough for a wheelchair user to be seen and to see in and out may be preferred.

Door locks are important, both in terms of easy operation by disabled people and in an emergency when helpers may need to gain access.

While the selection of surface materials and finishes is important to all disabled people, they are vital to people with sight and hearing impairments. Hard surfaces reverberate more than soft, and this can confuse people with impaired hearing. Glossy walls and floors reflect light which can hamper people with poor sight.

Wheelchairs move more easily on firmly fixed floors, which should be of a shallow, dense pile if carpeted. The joins between different flooring materials should be carefully executed so as not to hamper the wheels, or trip ambulant disabled, or those with poor sight.

Lightly textured walls and floors provide important information of their whereabouts to people with little or no sight, but boldly patterned flooring can confuse people with impaired sight. Floor surfaces should be slip resistant, particularly in an area where they may become wet, such as just inside a front door, in the kitchen or bathroom.

Although good lighting is essential for everyone, the partially sighted require greater levels (up to three times as much) to achieve a satisfactory level of illumination. Perhaps the main criterion is that lighting should be controllable and adjustable to meet individual needs. Passive infrared sensors could activate booster lighting, but keeping windows, blinds and lamps clean will also maximize the amount of available light, both natural and artificial.

Lights should be positioned so as not to cause glare, reflection or confusing patches of light and dark. Uplights fixed above 2m (6ft) deliver a good level of comfortable, glare-free illumination.

Components in fluorescent lighting can cause a loud hum in hearing aids, and the background noise from heating and air-conditioning units can similarly be distracting and tiring. Radiators and other heating units should be recessed wherever possible to avoid sharp angles.

If windows aren't carefully considered, they will introduce problems of glare and loss of privacy as well as difficulty with controls and cleaning. Their sheer size is not necessarily an asset and should be secondary to that of their position. Smaller windows are easier to open and clean, and a combination of, say, a large window to give overall light to a room, and a small window to provide a view for a bed-bound person may be the formula arrived at. Tolerances of heat and cold and other discomforts are often very fine with disabled people.

Bad positioning of windows can create glare from too much sunshine for a person confined to bed, or too much reflected light from light-coloured paving for the wheelchair occupant. Adequate, variable and easy-to-operate ventilation without opening the main window should be incorporated in the plan.

Useful addresses

ADVICE

Advertising Standards Authority
Brook House
2-16 Torrington Place
London WC1E 7HN
Complaints should be in writing, with a copy of the advertisement

Association of British Insurers
51 Gresham Street
London EC2V 7HQ
Publishes a list of members

Association of Consultant Architects (ACA)
Buchanan's Wharf
Redcliff Backs
Bristol BS1 6HT
Publishes a list of members for £25

Association of Manufacturers of Domestic Electrical Appliances
Leicester House
8 Leicester Street
London WC2H 7NB
Publishes a list of members for £10

British Bathroom Council and British Ceramic Tile Council
Registered Office
Federation House
Stoke-on-Trent ST4 2RT
Publishes a list of members

British Carpet Manufacturers Association Ltd
Royalty House
72 Dean Street
London W1V 5HB
Publishes a list of members

British Coatings Federation
Alembic House
93 Albert Embankment
London SE1 7TY
Represents the wallpaper and paint industries. Publishes a list of members

British Electrotechnical Approvals Board
Marks House
The Green
Walton-on-Thames
Surrey KT12 5NA

British Gas Corporation
Headquarters
326 High Holborn
London WC1V 7PT

British Woodworking Federation
82 New Cavendish Street
London W1M 8AD
Part of the Building Employers Confederation. Publishes a list of architects and contacts for general joinery

The Building Centre Group
26 Store Street
London WC1E 7BT
Information on everything to do with building and building materials. Offers advice to members of the public on general building enquiries

Building Societies Association
3 Savile Row
London W1X 1AF

Chartered Society of Interior Designers
29 Bedford Square
London WC1 3EG
Contact the Information Section

The Consumers' Association
2 Marylebone Road
London NW1 4DF
Set up to improve consumer goods and services; publish Which? magazine and offers a legal advisory service at a set fee

Council for Registered Gas Installers (CORGI)
4 Elmwood
Chineham Business Park
Crockford Lane
Basingstoke
Hants RG24 8WG
All gas installation businesses must register with CORGI

Crafts Council, Information Unit
44a Pentonville Road
London N1 9BY
National organization for promoting contemporary crafts. Apply for the Index of Selected Makers which lists

craftsmen and women with considerable experience and reputation

Design Council
28 Haymarket
London W1Y 4SU
Houses a permanent display of well-designed British products, and an index of modern consumer products

Dyno-Locks
Zockoll House
143 Maple Road
Surbiton
Surrey KT6 4BJ
Operates a nationwide emergency locksmith service

Dyno-Rod plc
Address as Dyno-Locks (above)
Operates a nationwide emergency drain-cleaning service

Electricity Association
30 Millbank
London SW1P 4RD

Electricity Board
Templar House
81-82 High Holborn
London WC1V 6NU
Contact for local boards

Electrical Contractors Association Ltd.
Esca House
34 Palace Court
London W2 4JG
Publishes a list of members

Federation of Master Builders
Gordon Fisher House
14-15 Great James Street
London WC1N 3DP
Contact regional office for list of members: admits only experienced builders

Gas Consumers' Council
Abford House
15 Wilton Road
London SW1V 1LT
Offers independent help and advice to customers of British Gas and third-

party suppliers

The Heating and Ventilation Contractor's Association
Esca House
34 Palace Court
London W2 4JG

Incorporated Society of Architects and Surveyors
41 Queensgate
London SW7 5HR

Incorporated Society of Valuers and Auctioneers
3 Cadogan Gate
London SW1X OAP
Publishes a list of members

Institute of Plumbing
64 Station Lane
Hornchurch
Essex RM12 6NB
Publishes a list of members

Institution of Environmental Health Officers
15 Hatfields
London SE1 8DJ
Professional body with a regulatory role, members must subscribe to a code of conduct

Law Society
113 Chancery Lane
London WC2A 1PL

Master Locksmiths Association
Unit 4/5
The Business Park
Woodford Halse
Daventry
Northants NN11 6PZ

National Association of Citizens' Advice Bureaux
(Registered Charity)
Middleton House
1 5-123 Pentonville Road
London N1 9LZ
Contact for local branches

National Association of Plumbing, Heating and Mechanical Services
Ensign House

Ensign Business Centre
Westwood Way
Coventry CV4 8JA
Publishes a list of members

National Association of Tile Distributors
39 Upper Elmers End Road
Beckenham
Kent BR3 3QY
Publishes a list of members

National Consumer Council
20 Grosvenor Gardens
London SW1W ODH

National Federation of Painting and Decorating Contractors
82 New Cavendish Street
London W1M 9FG
Publishes a list of members

National Federation of Roofing Contractors
24 Weymouth Street
London W1N 3FA
Publishes a list of members

National House Building Council
Registered Office
Buildmark House
Chiltern Avenue
Amersham
Bucks HP6 5AP
Publishes a list of members and registers newly-built houses

National Inspection Council for Electrical Installation Contracting
Vintage House
36 Albert Embankment
London SE1 7TL

Public Health Inspectors
Local councils will put you in touch with public health inspectors: contact them before undertaking any alteration to drainage

Rainforest Campaign
Friends of the Earth
26-28 Underwood Street
London W1N 4AD
Can recommend suppliers of ecologically farmed timber

Registry of Friendly Societies
15-17 Great Marlborough Street
London W1V 2AX
Regulatory body of Building Societies and Friendly Societies

Rentokil Group plc
Felcourt
East Grinstead
Sussex RH19 2JY
Operate guaranteed service for the eradication of dry rot and woodworm. Pest Control Division will also deal with pests

Royal Institute of British Architects
66 Portland Place
London W1N 4AD
Publishes a list of members

Royal Institute of Chartered Surveyors
12-24 Great George Street
London SW1P 3AD

Royal Society for the Prevention of Accidents
Canon House
The Priory Queensway
Birmingham B4 6BS

Society of Designer Craftsmen
24 Rivington Street
London EC2A 3DU
Will put the public in touch with craftspeople

Soil Association
86 Colston Street
Bristol BS1 5BP
A registered charity. Looks into all aspects of organic farming

Timber Research and Development Association
Stocking Lane
Hughenden Valley
High Wycombe
Bucks HP14 4ND

Trading Standards Departments
Give civil advice on consumer goods. Contact your local authority for the nearest department

Water Boards
Should be contacted about alterations to plumbing

Worldwide Fund for Nature
Forest Unit, Panda House
Weyside Park
Godalming
Surrey GU7 1XR
Can recommend suppliers of ecologically farmed timber

WALLPAPERS

Laura Ashley
256-258 Regent Street
London W1R 5DA

Cole & Son
18 Mortimer Street
London W1A 4BU

Colefax and Fowler
110 Fulham Road
London SW3 6RL

Designers Guild
271 and 277 King's Road
London SW3 5EN

Donghia
Chelsea Garden Market
Chelsea Harbour
London SW10 OXE

Hamilton Weston Wallpapers Ltd
18 St Mary's Grove
Richmond
Surrey TW1 9UY
18th and 19th century reproduction of designs and wallpaper borders

Harlequin Wallcoverings Ltd
Cossington Road
Loughborough
Leicestershire LE12 7RU

Nairn Kingfisher Ltd
Lancaster
Lune Mills
Leicester LE1 5QN

The Nursery Window
83 Walton Street
London SW3 2HP

Osborne & Little plc
49 Temperley Road
London SW12 8QE
Coordinated wallpapers and fabrics

Sandersons, Arthur and Sons Ltd
100 Acres
Oxford Road
Uxbridge UB8 1HY

PAINT

Auro Organic Paints
Ashdon
Saffron Walden
Essex CB10 2ET

Blackfriar
E. Parsons & Sons
Blackfriars Road
Nailsea
Bristol BS19 2DJ

Papers and Paints Ltd
4 Park Walk
London SW10 0AD
Specialize in 18th and early 19th century paint colour, plus a full range of modern paints

Courtaulds Coatings
50 George Street
London W1A 2BB

Croda Paints Ltd
Bankside
Hull HU5 1SQ

Crown Berger Europe Ltd
PO Box 37
Crown House
Darwen
Lancs BB3 0BG
Advisory service available, matt/silk emulsion, acrylic eggshell

Dulux
ICI Paints plc
Wexham Road
Slough
Berks SL2 5DS

Harlequin Paints
Harlequin Wallcoverings Ltd
See Wallpapers

International Paint Ltd
24-30 Canute Road
Southampton SO14 3PB

Johnstones Paints plc
Stonebridge House
Edge Lane
Droyosden
Manchester M43 6BX

Manders Paints plc
PO Box 9
Old Heath Road
Wolverhampton WV1 2XG

Sandersons
See Wallpapers

The National Trust
36 Queen Anne's Gate
London SW1H 9AS

John Oliver Wallpapers and Paints
33 Pembridge Road
London W11 3HG
Bespoke paint mixing

TILE AND STONE

Art Marbles Ltd
Dawson Road
Kingston-upon-Thames
Surrey KT1 3AX

British Ceramic Tile Council
Federation House
Station Road
Stoke-on-Trent ST4 2RT

Corres Mexican Tiles
15 Ewer Street
London SE1 ONR

Domus Tiles Ltd
33 Parkgate Road
London SW11 4NP

Fired Earth Tiles plc
Twyford Mill
Oxford Road
Adderbury
Oxon OX17 3HP

Focus Ceramics Ltd
Unit 4 Hamm Moor Lane

Weybridge Trading Estate
Weybridge
Surrey KT15 2SF

Elaine and Arthur Goodwin
4 Devonshire Place
Exeter EX4 6JA
Mosaic artists

Interface Flooring Systems Ltd
Shelf Mills
Halifax
West Yorkshire HX3 7PA
*Tiles: tufted, fusion bonded, fibre
bonded*

Kirkstone Green Slate Quarries
Lower Farm
Ampfield
Nr Romsey
Hampshire SO51 9BP
*Lakeland green slate and patented
sealant*

Langley London Ltd
161-167 Borough High Street
London SE1 1HU
Tiles and glass blocks

The Life-enhancing Tile Company
Unit 4A, Alliance House
14-28 Saint Mary's Road
Portsmouth
Hampshire PO1 5PH

Marley Tiles and Waterproofing
Dickley Lane
Lenham
Maidstone
Kent NE17 2DE

Naturally Terracotta
116 Bewdley Road
Kidderminster
West Midlands DY11 6RX

Paris Ceramics
583 Kings Road
London SW6 2EH
and
31 East Elm Street
Greenwich
Connecticut 06830
*Mosaic tiled floors in a range of
patterns*

Pilkington's Tiles Limited
PO Box 4
Clifton Junction
Manchester M27 2LP
*Glazed and unglazed ceramic, wall
and floor tiles, bathroom accessories*

Pittsburg Corning
South Court
29 South Street
Reading RG1 4QU

Rye Tiles
Rye
Kent TN31 7DH

Terra Firma Tiles
70 Chalk Farm Road
London NW1 8NA

TileStyle Ltd
89-90 North Wall Quay
Dublin 1
Eire

Vitruvius
20 Ransome's Dock
35 Parkgate Road
London SW11 4NP

VW Aldershaw Bricks and Tiles
Kent Street
Sedlescombe
Nr Battle
East Sussex TN33 0SD

World's End Tiles
Silverthorne Road
Battersea
London SW8 3HE

FLOORING

Altro Floors
Works Road
Letchworth
Herts SG6 1NW
Rubber flooring

Amtico
The Amtico Co Ltd
Kingfield Road
Coventry CV6 5PL
*Linoleum and vinyl flooring available
as sheets or tile*

Campbell Marson
Unit 34
Wimbledon Business Centre
Riverside Road
London SW17 0BA
*Bespoke floor designs in all types of
wood*

Carpet Tile Centres
227 Woodhouse Road
Finchley
London N12 9BD
and
150 Pinner Road
Harrow
*Specialists in carpet tile, with a
comprehensive range including Heuga*

Crucial Trading Ltd
The Market Hall
Craven Arms
Shropshire SY7 8ZZ
*Natural floorcoverings (sisal, seagrass,
coir, jute)*

Dalsuple
P.O. Box 140
Bridgwater
Somerset TA5 1HT

Ecological Trading Company
1 Lesbury Road
Newcastle-upon-Tyne NE6 5LB
Environmentally managed timber

English Woodlands Timber
Keepers Lodge
Bury Road
Market Weston
Diss
Norfolk IP22 2PB

Fine Wood Floors
Unit 5
Gibson Business Centre
rear of 800 Tottenham High Road
London N17 0DH

First Floor
174 Wandsworth Bridge Road
London SW6 2UQ

The First Flooring Company
2 Jowett Street
London SE15 6JN

Forbo-Nairn Ltd
PO Box 1
Kirkcaldy
Fife KY1 2SB
Linoleum

4 Wood Floors
Unit B
Wellington Industrial Estate
Wellington
Somerset TA21 8ST
Natural floorcoverings

Grass Roots
102 Portland Road
London W11 4LX

The Hardwood Flooring Company
146/152 West End Lane
London NW6 1SD
*New and reclaimed hardwood floors
and worktops*

Heritage Woodcraft
Heritage House
Wheatfield Way
Hinckley Fields Industrial Estate
Hinckley
Leicestershire LE10 1YG
*Wide range of traditional wood
flooring and treatments, including a
liming service*

Interface Flooring Systems Ltd
Shelf Mills
Halifax
West Yorkshire HX3 7PA
*Tiles: tufted, fusion bonded, fibre
bonded*

Junckers Ltd
Wheaton Court Commercial
Centre
Wheaton Road
Witham
Essex CM8 3UJ
Timber flooring

Kährs UK
Timberlaine Estate
Quarry Lane
Chichester
West Sussex PO19 2FJ
*Specialists in pre-finished laminated
flooring*

Milland Fine Timbers Ltd
The Working Tree
Milland
near Liphook
Hampshire GU30 7JS
*Suppliers of environmentally managed
hardwoods*

Sinclair Till
793 Wandsworth Road
London SW8 3JQ
Linoleum floors

Stonell
Unit 1
Bockingford
Ladham Road
Goudhurst
Kent TN17 1LY
Natural slate flooring

Tarkett
PO Box 173
Poyle House
Blackthorne Road
Colnbrook
Slough
Berkshire SL3 0AZ
*Pre-finished cross-laminated
hardwood flooring.*

Treework Services Ltd
Cheston Combe
Backwell
Nr Bristol BS19 3JQ
Timber flooring

Victorian Wood Works
118 Carpenters Road
Stratford
London E15 2DY

Wallis Wood Floors
Bush House
294 Ongar Road
Writtle
Chelmsford
Essex CM1 3NZ
*All forms of timber flooring including
refurbishment*

**The West Sussex Antique Timber
Company**
Reliance Works
Newpound

Wisborough Green
West Sussex RH14 0AZ
*Salvage specialists also offering new
floors with an 'antiqued' finish*

Wicanders
Amorium House
Star Road
Partridge Green
Horsham
West Sussex RH13 8RA
Natural wood and cork floors

CARPETS

Axminster Carpets Ltd
Gamberlake
Axminster
Devon EX1 5PQ

BMK Ltd
Head Office
Burnside Street
Kilmarnock
Ayrshire
Scotland KA1 1SX
London Office and Showroom:
9-10 Savile Row
London W1X 1AF

Brintons Ltd
PO Box 16
Exchange Street
Kidderminster
Worcestershire DY10 1AG
Showrooms in London, Glasgow,
Bristol, Manchester, Newcastle-
upon-Tyne and Telford

Brockway Carpets Ltd
Hoobrook Works
Kidderminster
Worcestershire DY10 1XW

Bronte Carpets Ltd
Bankfield Mill
Greenfield Road
Colne
Lancashire BB8 9PD

Cavalier Carpets Ltd
Thompson Street
Industrial Estate
Blackburn
Lancashire BB2 1TX

Coats Viyella Carpet Group
Head Office
PO Box 18
Lees Street
Swinton
Manchester M27 2LX

Hugh Mackay Carpets
PO Box 1
Durham City
County Durham DH1 2RX

Northern Ireland Carpets Ltd
Comber Road
Newtownwards
Co. Down
Northern Ireland BT23 4QR

Resista Carpets
255 New King's Road
London SW6 4RB

Sanderson Carpets
(A division of Arthur Sanderson &
Sons Ltd)
Union Road
Bolton
Lancashire BL2 2HH

Stoddard Carpets Ltd
Glenpatrick Road
Elderslie
Johnstone
Renfrewshire PA5 9UJ

Tomkinsons Carpets Ltd
PO Box 11
Duke Place
Kidderminster
Worcestershire DY10 2JR

Victoria Carpets Ltd
Green Street
Kidderminster
Worcestershire DY10 1HL

Wilton Royal Carpets Ltd
(A division of Coats Viyella)
Romsey Industrial Estate
Greatbridge Road
Romsey
Hampshire SO51 0HR

WINDOWS

Anglian Windows
(Commercial Division)
114-118 Oak Street
Norwich NR3 3BP

Caradon Everest Ltd
Everest House
Sopers Road
Cuffley
Potters Bar
Herts EN6 4SG
Hermetically sealed glazing units

Computerglaze plc
11-15 Chase Road
Park Royal
London NW10 6PT
Double glazed windows and doors

**The Original Box Sash
Window Co.**
Unit 10
Bridgwater Way
Windsor
Berkshire SL4 1RD
Vertical sliding sash timber windows

CURTAINS AND BLINDS

Manuel Canovas Ltd
2 North Terrace
Brompton Road
London SW3 2BA

The Curtain Shop
54 Abbey Gardens
London NW8
*Take top-quality second-hand curtains
and sell on 50% commission.
Branches outside London*

Designers Guild
See Wallpapers

Faber
Kilvery Road
Brackmills
Northampton NN4 0PB

John Lewis Partnership
278-306 Oxford Street
London W1A 1EX
And stores nationwide

Liberty
210-220 Regent Street
London W1R 6AH

The Louvre Blind Co.
7 Forward Drive
Harrow
Middlesex HA3 8NT

Ian Mankin
109 Regent's Park Road
Primrose Hill
London NW1 8UR

Monkwell Ltd
10-12 Wharfdale Road
Bournemouth
Dorset BH4 9BT

**Osborne and Little Fabrics and
Wallpapers**
304-308 King's Road
London SW3 5UH

The Shutter Shop
Queensbury House
Dilly Lane
Hartney
Witney
Hampshire RG27 8EQ
Custom-made interior shutters

Timney Fowler
388 King's Road
London SW3 5UZ

Tidmarsh & Sons
1 Laycock Street
London N1 1SW
Blinds and shutters

LIGHTING

Artemide
17-19 Neal Street
Covent Garden
London WC2H 9PU

Chelsea Lighting Design
Unit 1
23A Smith Street
London SW3 4EJ

Christopher Wray's Lighting
600 King's Road

London SW6 2DX
*Vast emporium with traditional and
repro designs*

Fergus Cochrane
570 King's Road
London SW6 2DY
Chandeliers

Concord Lighting
174 High Holborn
London WC1V 7AA
*Lighting system manufacturers. State-
of-the-art showroom*

Mrs M. E. Crick Chandeliers
166 Kensington Church Street
London W8 4BN
*Comprehensive stock of old
chandeliers, mainly 19th century*

John Cullen Lighting
216 Fulham Palace Road
London W6 9NT
*Specialist in low-voltage, with a
demonstration studio*

Davey Lighting
1 Chelmsford Road
Industrial Estate
Great Dunmow
Essex CM6 1HD

The Egyptian Touch
76 Goldhawk Road
London W12 8HA
Brass lanterns perforated with stars

Elementer Lighting Ltd
Progress House
Whittle Parkway
Slough
Berkshire SL1 6DG

Erco Lighting
38 Dover Street
London W1X 3RB
Hi-tech lighting systems manufacturer

Inhouse
24-26 Wilson Street
Glasgow G1 1SS
and
28 Howe Street
Edinburgh EH3 6TG

Isometrix Lighting & Design
Exmouth House
3 Pine Street
London EC1R 0JH
*Mostly commercial work, but some
large-scale domestic installations*

London Lighting Company
135 Fulham Road
London SW3 6RT

Mr Light
275 Fulham Road
London SW10 9PZ
*Ceramics, also plaster wall lights,
downlights, uplights*

Ragdon Art
Ragdon Manor
Ragdon
Church Stretton
Shropshire SY67 EZ
Glass star lanterns

SKK
34 Lexington Street
London W1R 3HR
*Ranging from minimal low-voltage to
more frivolous lighting designs*

Space
12 Dolland Street
London SE11 5LN
Futuristic paper lanterns

Stiffkey Lamp Shop
Townshend Arms
Stiffkey
Wells-next-the-Sea
Norfolk NR23 1AJ
*Restored antique lights from about
1860 to 1920*

W. Sitch and Company Ltd
48 Berwick Street
London W1V 4JD
Period lighting

Wilchester County Lighting
Stable Cottage
Vicarage Lane
Steeple Ashton, Nr Trowbridge
Wiltshire BA14 6HH
*American-style chandeliers and wall
sconces hand-made in tin*

Woolpit Interiors
The Street
Woolpit
Bury St Edmonds
Suffolk IP30 9SA
*Hand-painted wooden lamp bases
and large selection of shades*

Switches:

Forbes and Lomax Ltd
205b St John's Hill
London SW11 1TH
'Invisible' transparent switches

R Hamilton & Company Ltd
Unit J, Quarry Industrial Estate
Mere
Wiltshire
*Wooden light switches; contact for
retail outlets*

FURNITURE AND HARDWARE

Aero Wholesale
96 Westbourne Grove
London W2 5RT

David Armstrong Furniture
Pitway Lane
Farrington Guerney
Bristol BS18 5TX

John Barnard and Craftsmen
The Granary
Trowsebridge
Bracondale
Norwich
Norfolk NR1 2EG

A Bell & Company Ltd
Kingsthorpe Road
Northampton NN2 6LT

Rebecca Bell
Islington Workshop
39a Islington Road
Southville
Bristol BS3 1BQ

Andrew Beswetherick
Venn Launcells
Bude
Cornwall EX23 9LJ

Chalon UK Ltd
Old Hambridge Mill
Hambridge
Nr Langport
Somerset TA10 0BP

Harvey Clark Design
61 Broucker Road
London W3 8AF

The Classic Brass Company
1 West Road
Westcliff-on-Sea
Essex SS0 9AU

The Conran Shop
81 Fulham Road
London SW3 6RD

Cowrie and Roberts
15 Ddole Road Industrial Estate
Llandrindod Wells LD1 6DF

Designcare
124-128 Barbly Road
London W10 6BL
Upholstery

Divertimenti
45-47 Fulham Road
London SW3 6SD

En Attendant les Barbares
50 Rue Etienne Marcel
Paris 75002

Forgeries
Old Butchery
High Street
Twyford
Hampshire SO21 1RF

Thomas Goode
19 South Audley Street
London W1Y 6BN

Henry Gordon-Jones Furniture
Chapel Road
Rendham
Saxmundham
Suffolk IP17 2AT

Johnny Grey
Fyning Copse
Rogate

Petersfield
Hampshire GU13 5DH

Habitat UK Ltd
The Heal's Building
196 Tottenham Court Road
London W1P 9LD
And branches nationwide

CP Hart & Sons
Newnham Terrace
Hercules Road
London SE1 7DR

Heals
The Heal's Building
196 Tottenham Court Road
London W1P 9LD

IF (Interior Furniture)
359 Portobello Road
London W10 5SA

Ikea
255 North Circular Road
London NW13 0QJ
And branches nationwide

John Lewis Partnership
278-306 Oxford Street
London W1A 1EX
And branches nationwide

Liberty
210-220 Regent Street
London W1R 6AH
And branches nationwide

Marcatré
179-199 Shaftesbury Avenue
London WC2H 8AR

Merchants
Olmar Wharf
Olmar Street
London SE1 5AY

Muji
39 Shelton Street
London WC2H 9HJ
And branches

Neal Street East
5 Neal Street
London WC2H 8AR

Newcastle Furniture Company
Unit 4
Green Lane Buildings
Pelaw
Tyne and Wear NE10 0UW
and
128 Walham Green Court
Moore Park Road
London SW6 4DG

Plain English
The Long House
Tonnery Road
Combs
Stowmarket
Suffolk IP4 2EQ

Sainsbury's Homebase
Beddington House
Railway Approach
Wallington
Surrey SM6 0HB

Solent Furniture Ltd
Pymore Mills
Bridport
Dorset DT6 5PJ

Study Products Ltd
41 Shad Thames
London SE1 2NJ

Top Knobs
4 Brunel Buildings
Brunel Road
Newton Abbot
Devon TQ12 4BP

David Wainwright
249-251 Portobello Road
London W11 1LT

Whitton Wood Designs
37 Crown Road
St Margaret's
Twickenham
Middlesex TW1 3EJ

Tim Wood Furniture Ltd
128 Grandison Road
London SW11 6LN

Woodstock Furniture
23 Pakenham Street
London WC1X 0LB

RUGS

Ambiencé
273 Brighton Road
Belmont
Sutton
Surrey SM2 5SU

Simon Boosey
The Tun House
Hitchin
Herts SG4 8AG
Persian and Oriental Rugs

Christopher Farr Handmade Rugs
115 Regents Park Road
London NW1 8UR
*Specifiers and design commissioners
of high quality handmade rugs*

First Floor
See Flooring

Signature Carpets
Linden Mill
Linden Road
West Yorkshire HX7 7DN
Designs to order

SAFETY

Crime Concern
David Murray John Building
Brunel Centre
Swindon
Wiltshire SN1 1LY
*National Organisation to support and
develop the Crime Prevention Act*

Crime Prevention Officers
*Will give expert advice on making
your home safe. Contact your local
police station*

Fire Protection Association
140 Aldersgate Street
London EC1A 4HX
*Publish useful leaflets on fire
prevention and extinguishing, electric
blankets and DIY fire safety*

**Royal Society for the Prevention of
Accidents**
Canon House
The Priory Queensway

Birmingham B4 6BS
*Provides up-to-date information on
safety requirements and legislation*

SECURITY

Age Concern
Astral House
1268 London Road
London SW16 4ER
*A welfare group for pensioners with
offices all over the country. Age
Concern runs projects to fit security
devices in elderly people's homes*

Help the Aged
St James's Walk
London EC1R OBE
*Call the Senior Line for free
information service:*
0800 289 404 Monday to Friday,
10am-4pm
advice line:
071 250 3399
031 556 4666

Banham Alarms
10 Pascal Street
London SW8 4SH

Banham Locks
Address as Banham Alarms

Bell Intruder Alarms
125 Cambridge Street
Aylesbury
Bucks HP20 1BT

Brace Ltd
Imperial House
64 Willoughby Lane
London N17 0SP

Chubb Alarms Ltd
42-50 Hersham Road
Walton-on-Thames
Surrey KT12 1RY

Chubb Locks
Address as Chubb Alarms

Honeywell Control Systems Ltd
Charles Square
Bracknell
Berks RG12 1EB

Ingersoll Security Products
Wood Street
Willenhall
West Midlands WV13 1LA

Home Security System *from*
Sainsbury's Homebase
Beddington House
Railway Approach
Wallington
Surrey SM6 0HB

Thorn Security Ltd
Security House
The Summit
Hanworth
Sunbury-on-Thames TW16 5DB

Yale Security Products Ltd
Wood Street
Willenhall
West Midlands WV13 1LA

UNIVERSAL DESIGN

Atkinson Engineering
Unit 7, Premier Mill
Begonia Street
Darwen
Lancs BB3 2DP
Height-adjustable worktops

The Boots Company plc
1 Thane Road West
Beeston
Nottingham NG2 3AA
*Contact for catalogue of easier-living
aids and equipment*

Care Design
Moorgate
Ormskirk
Lancs L39 4RX
*Kitchen and bathroom specialists for
the elderly and disabled*

Castlewood Kitchens
Unit 5
Enterprise Park
Beckview Road
Beverley
East Yorkshire HU17 0JT
*Bedrooms, bathrooms and kitchens
designed and custom made to suit the
needs of a disabled person*

**Centre for Accessible
Environments**
60 Gainsford Street
London SE1 2NY
*Literature and reference on universal
design*

Contact (Helping the Elderly)
15 Henrietta Street
London WC2E 8QH

Disability Information Trust
Mary Marlborough Lodge
Nuffield Orthopaedic Centre
Headington
Oxford OX3 7LD
*Publishes a series of books on
equipment (books are used by
therapists)*

Disabled Living Centres
*An up-to-date list of centres
throughout the country is available
from:*
Disabled Living Centres Council
286 Camden Road
London N7 0BJ

Disabled Living Foundation
380-384 Harrow Road
London W9 2HU

Jonathan Fisk
Airedale General Hospital
Skipton Road
Steeton
Keighley
West Yorkshire BD20 6TD
*Consultant Psychiatrist/Designer for
the elderly*

Grays Fitted Furniture
Unit 1
Drayton Industrial Estate
Taverham Road
Drayton
Norwich
Norfolk NR8 6RU

HTH Kitchens
28-30 Castle Street
Kingston-upon-Thames
Surrey KT1 1SS
*Kitchen furniture designed for disabled
or elderly people*

Mr M. McLachlan
39 Westerton Avenue
Busby
Glasgow G76 8JS
*Manufactures alarm for blind or
visually disabled people which buzzes
when cupboard doors are left open*

Nicholls & Clarke Ltd
Phlexicare Division
3-10 Shoreditch High Street
London E1 6PE
*Kitchen cupboards electrically
adjustable by height*

Royal Association for Disability
and Rehabilitation (RADAR)
25 Mortimer Street
London W1N 8AB
*The Publications Department issues a
comprehensive range of books and
pamphlets*

RICA
2 Marylebone Road
London NW1 4DF
*A charity which tests goods and
services that help disabled or elderly
people to live more independently*

Scanflex Ltd
2 Thursby Road
Croft Business Park
Bromborough
Wirral
Merseyside L62 3PW
*Mobile and adjustable units designed
to give easy access to the elderly or
disabled*

The Silverdale Catalogue
15 Aquinas Street
London SE1 8AE
*The catalogue features implements
designed to help the elderly or
disabled in the home, the garden and
whilst travelling*

ECOLOGICAL DESIGN

Association for Environment
Conscious Building
Windlake House
The Pump Field
Coaley
Gloucs GL11 5DX

British Earth Sheltering
Association
The Caer Llan Berm House
Lydart
nr Monmouth
Gwent NP5 3JJ

Centre for Urban Ecology
c/o The Birmingham Settlement
318 Summer Lane
Birmingham B19 3RL

Earthwrite Co-operative
Unit 1b
Carlisle House
Carlisle Street East
Sheffield S4 7QN

Ecological Design Association
20 High Street
Stroud
Gloucestershire GL5 1AS

Ecology Building Society
18 Station Road
Cross Hills
Keighley
W Yorks BD20 7EH

Gaia International
66 Charlotte Street
London W1P 1LR

Institute for Baubiology
PO Box 82
Grinstead
Sussex RH19 3YB

London Ecology Centre
45 Shelton Street
London WC2H 9HJ

Scottish Ecological Design
Association
15 Rutland Square
Edinburgh EH1 2BE

DESIGNERS
AND ARCHITECTS

Alford Hall Monaghan Morris
9 Alfred Place
London WC1E 7EB

Allies and Morrison
42 Newman Street
London W1P 3PA

Architype Design Co-operative
4-6 The Hop Exchange
24 Southwark Street
London SE1 1TY

Pierre d'Avoine
Tapestry Court
Mortlake High Street
London SW14

Sergison Bates
94 The Drive Mansions
Fulham Road
London SW6 5JH

Tony Fretton
21 Hanson Street
London W1P 7LP

Gaia Environments Ltd.
Umberella Studios
12 Trundle Street
London SE1 1QT

Michael Gold Architects
4 Campden House Terrace
Kensington Church Street
London W8 4BQ

Cowper Griffiths Associates
The Barn College Farm
Whittlesford
Cambridge CB2 4ZX

Mark Guard Associates
16 Whitfield Street
London W1P 5RY

Louisa Hutton
Sauerbruch Hutton
74 Ledbury Road
London W11 2AH

James Lambert Architects
Top Floor
42/43 Gloucester Crescent
London NW1 7PE

Kiss and Zwigard (Architects)
3rd Floor
60 Warren Street
New York
New York 10007

Richard Lavenstein
Bond Street Design
33 Bond Street
New York
New York 10012

Rick Mather Architects
123 Camden High Street
London NW1 7JR

Munkenbeck and Marshall
3-11 Pine Street
London EC1 0JH

Powell Tuck Associates
12 Barley Mow Passage
London W4 4PH

Domenico Rensch
2 Sydney Cottages
Aldenham Road
Elstree
Herts WD6 3AQ

Tugman Design Partnership
The Old Station Works
119 Sandycombe Road
Kew
Richmond
Surrey TW9 2EP

Deborah Weintraub
1540 North Sierra Bonita
Los Angeles
CA 90046

David Wild
44 Rochester Place
London NW1 9JX

Jonathan Woolf Architects
49-51 Rathbone Street
London W1P 1AN

Index

Acknowledgments

The publisher thanks the following photographers and organizations for their kind permission to reproduce the photographs in this book:

1 Geoffrey Frosh;
2-3 Paul Ryan/Conran Octopus; Architects: Deborah Weintraub & Scott Lane; Designer: Richard Lavenstein (Ronald K. Smith);
6-7 **above left:** Arcaid/Richard Bryant; Architects: Chapus/Domaine de Sperone; **below left:** Studio Brackrock; Architect: Richard J. Neutra; Stylist: Luis Ortega; **above centre:** Arcaid/Richard Bryant; Architect: Gabriel Poole; **below centre:** Paul Ryan/Conran Octopus; Architects: Deborah Weintraub & Scott Lane; Designer: Richard Lavenstein (Ronald K. Smith); **above right:** Eric Morin; Designer: Christian Liaigre; **below right:** Esto/Scott Frances;
10 Stylograph/Côté Sud/Bernard Touillon;
12-13 **1** World of Interiors/Simon Upton; **2** Ianthe Ruthven; **3** Ianthe Ruthven (Gene Garthwaite); **4** Jean-Pierre Godeaut;
14-15 **1** Geoffrey Frosh; **2** Michael Freeman; **3** Henry Bourne; Designer: Sue Skeen; tongue and groove supplied by Charles Hurst; **3** JB Visual Press/Paul Ryan;
16-17 **1** Francis Hammond; Designers: Giuseppe & Ada Tolla; **2** Cookie Kinkead; Designer/Owner: Melanie Martin; **3** Arcaid/Richard Bryant; Architects: GEA/Domaine de Sperone; **4** Gross and Daley; **5** Paul Warchol; Architects: Agrest & Gandelsonas; Struct.Eng: Robert Sillman (Villa Armore);
18-19 **1** Arcaid/Richard Bryant; Designer: Gian Franco Brignone; **2** Hotze Eisma; Stylist: Hugo Kostevo; **3** Henry Bourne; Architect: Jonathan Woolf (Patricia Ijaz-Ul-Haque);
20-21 **1** Peter Cook/Conran Octopus; Architect: Jonathan Woolf (Brian Mindel); **2** Dominque Vorillon courtesy of Elle Decor; Architect: Tom Bosworth; **3** Studio Brackrock; Designer: Gustav Lange; **4** Elizabeth Whiting & Associates/Rodney Hyett; Architect: McGuaran Soon;
22-23 **1** Marie Claire Maison/Gilles de Chabaneix; Stylist: Catherine Ardouin; **2-3** Marie Claire Maison/Christophe Dugied; Stylist: J. Postic; **4** Dominque Vorillon courtesy of Elle Decor; Architect: Robert Hull; **5** Deidi von Schaewen; Architect: Claudio Silvestrin; Designer: Monica Donati (Chantal Scaler);
24-25 **1** Elizabeth Whiting & Associates/Rodney Hyett; **2** Jonathan Pilkington; **3** Elizabeth Whiting & Associates/Di Lewis; **4-5** Esto/Scott Francis; **6** Elizabeth Whiting & Associates/Neil Lorimer; **7** Jerome Darblay; **8** Marijke Heuff (Maria de Haan); **9** Eric Morin;
26-27 **1** Paul Warchol; Architects: John Randolph & Bruce Tomb; **2** Christian Sarramon/Conran Octopus; Designers: Olivier Gagnières and Yyoyyo Maeght; Designer: Vincent Strebell; **4** Robert Harding Picture Library/Joanne Cowie; **5** Stylograph/John Hall; **6** Dominque Vorillon courtesy of Home Magazine; Architect: Bruce Davis;
28-29 **1** Stylograph/Christian Sarramon; **2** Archipress/Luc Boegly; Architect: Godivier; **3** Elle Decoration/Christophe Kischerer; Designer: Ted Muehling;
30 International Interiors/Paul Ryan;
32-33 **1** Arcaid/Julie Phipps; **2** Arcaid/Richard Bryant; Architect: David Chipperfield (Nick Knight); **3** Paul Warchol; Architect: François DeMenil; **4** Arcaid/Richard Bryant; Architects: Grose Bradley; **5** Arcaid/Richard Bryant; Designer: Brian Murphy;
34-35 **1** Peter Cook; **2** Eric Morin; Designer: Christian Liaigre; **3** Hotze Eisma; Stylist: Hugo Kostevo (David Seeler and Ngare Macray); **4** Peter Cook/Conran Octopus; Architects: Paxton Locher; **5** Todd Eberle; Architects: John Randolph & Bruce Tomb (Larry Sultan);
36-37 **1** Esto/Mark Darley; Architects: Chase Architects; **2** Archipress/S.Couturier; Architect: M.Bokura;

3 Todd Eberle; Architects: John Randolph & BruceTomb (Lewis Baltz);
38-39 **1** Antoine Bootz/Conran Octopus; Architects: Anderson & Schwartz Associates (John Newman); **2** Antonio Garbasso (Giorgio Vigna); **3** Esto/Scott Frances; **4** Archipress/Alain Goustard; Architect: Y. Tsiomis;
40-41 **1** Vogue Living/Ken Israel; **2** Aki Furudate; Architect: Massimiliano Fuksas (Yvan & Marzia); **3-4** Michael Moran; Architects: Anderson & Schwartz Associates;
42-43 **2** Paul Ryan/Conran Octopus; Architects: Deborah Weintraub & Scott Lane; Designer: Richard Lavenstein (Ronald K. Smith); **4-5** Paul Ryan/Conran Octopus; Architects: Deborah Weintraub & Scott Lane; Designer: Richard Lavenstein (Ronald K. Smith);
44-45 **1-7** Paul Ryan/Conran Octopus; Architects: Deborah Weintraub & Scott Lane; Designer: Richard Lavenstein (Ronald K. Smith);
46-47 **1-2** Jerome Darblay; **3** Arcaid/Alberto Piovano; Designer: Lustig; **4** Peter Cook; Designers: Surgeson and Bates; **5** Paul Warchol; Designer: Jay Smith (Dente Apartment);
48-49 **1** Christian Sarramon/Conran Octopus; Architect: Philippe Gazeau; **2** Kari Haavisto;
50-51 **1** Todd Eberle; Architects: John Randolph & Bruce Tomb; Artist: Lewis Baltz; **2** Marie Claire Maison/Jean Pierre Godeaut; Stylist: Valentine de Ganay; **3** Peter Cook/Conran Octopus; Architect: Paxton Locher;
52-53 **1** JB Visual Press/Paul Ryan; Architects: Stamberg & Aferiat; **2** Arcaid/Alberto Piovano; Designer: Jeff del Salle; **3** Fritz von der Schulenburg (Sophie Hicks); **4** Marie Claire Maison/Alexander Bailhache; Stylist: Catherine Ardouin;
54-55 **1** Marie Claire Maison/Nicolas Tosi; Stylist: Catherine Ardouin; **2** Tim Street-Porter; Designer: Russ Leland; **3** Reiner Blunck; Architect: Alberto Ponis;
56-57 **1** Elizabeth Whiting & Associates/June Buck; **2** Peter Cook; **3** Paul Warchol; Architect: Richard Rice;
58-59 **1-2** Peter Cook;
60-61 **1** Arcaid/Richard Bryant; Designer: Steve Lyman; **2** Eigenhuis & Interieur/John Van Groenedaal; Architect: Kris van Zeebroeck;
62-63 **1** Bridgeman Art Library/National Gallery, London; **2** Dennis Gilbert; Architects: Allford, Hall, Monaghan, Morris;
64-65 **1** Paul Ryan/Conran Octopus; Architects: Deborah Weintraub & Scott Lane; Designer: Richard Lavenstein (Ronald K. Smith); **2** Reiner Blunck; Architect: Manfred Koratsch; **3** Reiner Blunck; Designer: William Stout; **4** Elizabeth Whiting & Associates/Tom Leighton; **5** Antoine Bootz/Conran Octopus; Architects: Anderson & Schwartz Associates (John Newman);
66-67 **1** Peter Cook/Conran Octopus; Architect: Domenico D. Rensch;
68-69 **1** Michael Garland; Designer: Lena Raymond; **2** Esto/Scott Frances; Architect: Turner Brooks; **3** Elizabeth Whiting & Associates/Ed Ironside; Designer: Trevor Horne;
70-71 **2** François Roche; **3** Todd Eberle; Architects: John Randolph & Bruce Tomb (Tom Bonauro); **4** Arcaid/Richard Bryant; Designer: Bulter Redice;
72-73 **1** Tim Street-Porter; Architect: Brian Murphy; **2** Christian Sarramon; Architect: Christine Menjaud; **3** Antoine Bootz courtesy of Metropolitan Home (A.Freime);
74-75 **1** Todd Eberle; Architects: John Randolph & Bruce Tomb (Tom Bonauro); **2** Geoffrey Frosh; Architect: David Chipperfield; **3** Peter Cook/Conran Octopus; Architect: Domenico D. Rensch; **4** Residence/Sigurd Kranendock; **5** International Interiors/Paul Ryan; Architects: Deborah Weintraub & Scott Lane; Designer: Richard Lavenstein (Ronald K. Smith); **6** Mick Hales; Architect: Turner Brooks;
76-77 **4** Christian Sarramon (Terence Conran);

5 Christian Sarramon; Architect: Erik Vene (Brigitte Forgeur); **6** Christian Sarramon/Conran Octopus; Architect: Philippe Gazeau; **7** Peter Cook/Conran Octopus; Architects: Munkenbeck & Marshall;
78-79 **2** Esto/Scott Frances; **3** Peter Cook;
80-81 **1-2** Andy Glass; Architects: Gaia Architects (Peter & Majorie Bourne); **3** David Spiro;
82-83 **1-2** Arcaid/Richard Bryant; Architect: Gabriel Poole; **3-5** Lars Hallen; Architect: Sverre Fehn (The Eco-House); **6** Arcaid/Richard Bryant; Architect: Gabriel Poole; **7** Lars Hallen; Architect: Sverre Fehn; Furniture Designer: Alvar Aalto, supplied by Artek (The Eco-House);
84-85 **1** Deidi Von Schaewen; **2** Arcaid/Richard Bryant; Architect: Rick Mather; **3** Arcaid/Alberto Piovano; Designer: Jef del Salle; **4** International Interiors/Paul Ryan; **5** Claudio Silvestrin;
86-87 **1** Arcaid/Richard Bryant; Architect: Ron Brinks; **2** Peter Cook; **3** Camera Press/Thurman; **4** Antonio Garbasso; Designer: Oscar Turco;
88-89 **1** Aldo Ballo; Architects: Tomaso Gagliardi & Stefano Turi; **2** Archipress/S. Couturier; Architect: M.Bokura; **3** Dawson-Brown and Ackert; **4** Todd Eberle; Architects: John Randolph & Bruce Tomb (Larry Sultan);
90-91 **1** Arcaid/Richard Bryant; Architects: GEA/Domaine de Sperone; **2** Jean-François Jaussaud; Architect/Designer: Antti Lovag; **3** Arcaid/Richard Bryant; Architects: Pawson and Silvestrin; **4** Vogue Living/Gerald Jenkins (Greg & Patrica Anderson);
92-93 **1-2** Peter Cook/Conran Octopus; Architects: Munkenbeck & Marshall;
94-95 **1-4** Peter Cook/Conran Octopus; Architects: Munkenbeck & Marshall; **5** Dennis Gilbert; Architects: Munkenbeck & Marshall;
96-97 **1** Nadia Mackenzie/Conran Octopus; Designer: Kate Fontana; **2** Camera Press/Peo Eriksson; **3** C. David Livingston;
98-99 **1** Peter Cook/Conran Octopus; Architect: Domenico D. Rensch; **2** Tim Street-Porter; Architect: Mark Mack; **3** Jerome Darblay; **4** Paul Ryan/Conran Octopus; Architect: Yanni Petsopculos;
100-101 **1** Camera Press; **2** Elliot Kaufman; Architect: Anderson & Schwartz Associates (Ross Anderson); **3** Eric Morin; **4** JB Visual Press/Paul Ryan;
102-103 **1** Marie Claire Maison/Roland Beauffre; Stylist: Billaud; **2** Todd Eberle (Joe U'Urso); **3** Deidi Von Schaewen (Chantal Scaler); **4** Antoine Bootz courtesy of Metropolitan Home; **5** Peter Cook/Conran Octopus; Architect: Domenico D. Rensch;
104-105 **1** Christian Sarramon/Conran Octopus; Designers: Olivier Gagnières and Yyoyyo Maeght; **2** David Phelps courtesy of U.S. Homestyle Magazine; Architect: Paul Dierkes; **3** International Interiors/Paul Ryan; Designer: Lee Mindel; **4** Reiner Blunck; Architect: Mark Mack Summers; **5** Nadia Mackenzie/Conran Octopus; Designer: David Benson-Bunch;
106-107 **1** Esto/Mark Darley; Designer: Christopher Alexander; **2** Esto/Scott Frances; Designer: Jeff Cole; **3** Paul Warchol; Architects: Claire Weisz & Ursula Warchol (Bismuth Residence); **4** Richard Davies; Architect: John Pawson; **5** Peter Cook; **6** Elizabeth Whiting & Associates/Graham Henderson; Architect: John Pawson;
108-109 **1** Antoine Bootz/Conran Octopus; Architects: Anderson & Schwartz Associates (John Newman); **2** Elizabeth Whiting & Associates/SIP/W.Waldron (Smith); **11** Michael Moran; Architects: Anderson & Schwartz Associates;
110-111 **5** Antoine Bootz courtesy of Neotu Gallery; **8** Marie Claire Maison/Christophe Dugied; Stylist: Catherine Ardouin; **9** Paul Ryan/Conran Octopus; (Meryl Lloyd & John Lakin); **10-11** Ianthe Ruthven; Architect: Kevin Waltz (Jade Albert);
112-113 **1** Peter Cook/Conran Octopus; Architects: Munkenbeck & Marshall; **2** Nadia MacKenzie/Conran Octopus; Designer: Kate Fontana;

3 Reiner Blunck; **4** Paul Ryan/Conran Octopus; Architect: Yanni Petsopoulos; **5** Tim Goffe/Conran Octopus; Designer: Justin Meath-Baker for Study Products Ltd; **6** Richard Davies; Architect: Peter Wilson; **7** Nadia MacKenzie/Conran Octopus; Designer: Kate Fontana;

114 Peter Cook; Architect: Tony Fretton;

116-117 **1-2** Peter Cook/Conran Octopus; Architect: Domenico D. Rensch; **3** Arcaid/Julie Phipps; **4** Eric Morin; Designer: Christian Liaigre; **5** David Phelps; Designer: Barbara Levin Interiors Inc.;

118-119 **1** Peter Cook; Architects: Levin Berstein Associates; **2** Elizabeth Whiting & Associates/Tim Street-Porter; **3** Elizabeth Whiting & Associates/David Giles; **4** Robert O'Dea; **5** Geoffrey Frosh; Architect: John Knepler of Survey & Design Partnership; **6** Robert O'Dea; **7** Dominque Vorillon courtsey of Elle Decor; Architect: Tom Bosworth; **8** Peter Cook/ Conran Octopus; Architect: Jonathan Woolf (Brian Mindel); **9** Robert O'Dea **10** Peter Cook/ Conran Octopus; Architect: Jonathan Woolf (Brian Mindel);

120-121 **1** Archipress/Peter Cook; Architects: Tugman Design Partnership; **2** Arcaid/Richard Bryant; Architect: David Wild; **3** Dominque Vorillon courtsey of Elle Decor; Architect: Tom Bosworth; **4** Antoine Bootz; Architects: Dennis Wedlick; **5** Arcaid/Julie Phipps; Architect: Charles Rutherfoord;

122 Peter Cook; Designers: Surgeson and Bates;

124-125 **1** Elizabeth Whiting & Associates/Rodney Hyett; Designer: John Morgan; **2** Christian Sarramon; **3** Residence/Sigurd Kranendock; **4** Hotze Eisma; Stylist: Hugo Kosters (Jeremy Switzer and Mario Montes); **5** Christian Sarramon (Terence Conran); **6** Jean-François Jaussaud (Jane Birkin); **7** Mick Hales; Architect: Lee Skolnick (Suzanne Slesin & Michael Steinberg);

126-127 **1** Nadia Mackenzie/Conran Octopus; Designer: David Benson-Bunch; **2** Gross and Daley (Paul and Rebecca Rotherdam); **3** Archipress/S. Couturier; Architect: D.Colomb; **4** Elizaberth Whiting & Associates/Rodney Hyett; Architect: Robert Troup; **5** Elizabeth Whiting & Associates/Rodney Hyett; **6** Gabriele Basilico courtesy of Domus; Architect: Colin Glennie; **7** Camera Press; **8** Geoffrey Frosh; Architects: Munkenbeck & Marshall; **9** Kari Haavisto; Designer: Valerie Boom (Mimi & Mal MacDougall)

128-129 **1** Peter Cook/Conran Octopus; Architects: Paxton Locher; **2** Tim Street-Porter; Designer: Laurie Franks; **3** Reiner Blunck; Architect: Helmut Raff; **4** Ianthe Ruthen/Conran Octopus; Architect: Kevin Waltz (Chris Calles & Lisa Jenck); **5** Eigenhuis & Interieur/Verne Fotografie bvba;

130-131 **1** Simon Brown; **2** Ornella Sancassani courtesy of Elle Decor; Architect: Piero Castellini; **3** Esto/Scott Frances; Designer: Gwathmey Siegel; **4** Jonathan Pilkington; **5** C. David Livingston; **6** Esto/Mark Darley; **7** Elizabeth Whiting & Associates/Rodney Hyett; Architect: Craig Jones; **8** Kari Haavisto; Designer: Susan Ratcliff; **9-10** Nadia Mackenzie/Conran Octopus; Designer: Kate Fontana; **11** Kari Haavisto; **12** Ianthe Ruthen/ Conran Octopus; Architect: Kevin Waltz (Jade Albert); **13** Kari Haavisto;

132 Christian Sarramon (Anne Delhougne);

134-135 **1** Derry Moore (Jasper Conran); **2** Arcaid/Richard Bryant; Architects: GEA/Domaine de Spirone (Pochy); **3** Michael Mundy; Architects: Bentley, La Rosa, Salaski (Nisselson); **4** Ianthe Ruthven; Architect: Kevin Waltz (Jade Albert); **5** JB Visual Press/Paul Ryan; Designer: Raymond Waites; **6** International Interiors/Paul Ryan; **7** Simon Brown (Polly Dickens & Mark Gilbey);

136-137 **1** Jean-Paul Bonhommet; **2** Dominque Vorillon courtsey of Elle Decor; Architect: Robert Hull; **3** Deidi Von Schaewen (Nicole de Vesian); **4** Dominque Vorillon; Architect: Koenig-Heigenberg; **5** Camera Press; **6** Paul Ryan/Conran

Octopus; Architects: Munkenbeck & Marshall (Ben Richardson); **7** Antonio Garbasso; **8** Esto/Scott Frances; Designer: Weiss Manfredi;

138-139 **1** Jerome Darblay; **2** Gross and Daley (Michael Smith); **3** Reiner Blunck; Designer: Geoffrey Pie; **4** Guy Bouchet; **5** Elizabeth Whiting & Associates/Tom Leighton; **6** Residence/Sigurd Kranendock; **7** Elizabeth Whiting & Associates/Tom Leighton; **8** Kari Haavisto; Designer: Kerstin Enbom (Kerstin & Sten Enbom); **9** Yves Duronsoy;

140-141 **1** C. David Livingston; **2** Tom Leighton; Designer: Charles Rutherfoord; **3** International Interiors/Paul Ryan; **4** Hotze Eisma; **5** Belle/Earl Carter; Architect: Nicholas Gioia; Furniture Designer: Mark Douglass; **6** Arcaid/Richard Bryant; Architects: Grose Bradley; **7** Bill Stites;

142 **1** Camera Press;

144-145 **1** Jean-François Jaussaud (Michel Klein);**2** Arcaid/ Richard Bryant; Architects: GEA/Domaine de Sperone; **3** Jean Pierre Godeaut; **4** Elizabeth Whiting & Associates/Simon Upton; Designer: Lucianna Martine; **5** Jean-François Jaussaud (Harry Sigle); **6** Dominque Vorillon courtsey of Elle Decor; Architect: Tom Bosworth; **7** JB Visual Press/Paul Ryan; **8** Arcaid/Richard Bryant; Architects: GEA/Domaine de Sperone (Roux);

146-147 **1** Mick Hales; Architect: Ted Smith; **2** Peter Cook; Architect: Tony Fretton; Designer: Axel Vervoort; **3** Christian Sarramon; Designer: Axel Vervoort; **4** Arcaid/Richard Bryant; Designers: Ada Dewes and Sergio Puente; **5** Marie Claire Maison/Gilles de Chabaneix; Stylist: Catherine Ardouin; **6** Guy Bouchet; **7** Eric Morin; Architect: Bougon;

148-149 **1** Antoine Bootz; Architects: Morsa; **2** Christian Sarramon; **3** Cookie Kinkead; Designer/Owner: Melanie Martin; **4** Hotze Eisma; Stylist: Hugo Kosters (Jeremy Switzer & Mario Montes); **5** U.S. Conran's Habitat/James Merrell; **6** Trevor Richards; **7** Arcaid/Richard Bryant; Architects: GEA/Domaine de Sperone (Voisin);

150-151 **1** Elizabeth Whiting & Associates/Tom Leighton; Designers: Wilson & Gough; **2** Arcaid/Richard Bryant; Architect: David Chipperfield; **3** Esto/Scott Frances; Architect: Steve Harris; **4** Maison et Jardin/Françoise Lemarchand; **5** C. David Livingston (Brown Residence); **6** Peter Cook; Designers: Sergeson and Bates; **7** Michael Moran; Architects: 1100 Architects;

152-153 **1** Eigenhuis & Interieur/Verne Fotografie bvba; **2** Peter Cook/Conran Octopus; Architects: Paxton Locher; **3** Esto/Mark Darley; Designer: Richardson Bulter Associates; **4** Peter Cook/Conran Octopus; Architect: Domenico D.Rensch; **5** Eduard Hueber; Architect: Zaroni Architeketen; **6** Peter Cook/ Conran Octopus; Architect: Jonathan Woolf (Brian Mindel);

154-155 **1** Mick Hales; Architect: Bobby McAlpine; **2** John Hall; Architect: Mark Kaminski (Robert Wilson); **3** JB Visual Press/Paul Ryan; **4** Jean-Paul Bonhommet; **5** V.T. Wonen/Hotze Eisma; **6** Paul Ryan/Conran Octopus Architects: Munkenbeck & Marshall (Ben Richardson); **7** John Hall; Architect: Mark Kaminski; **8** Marie Claire Maison/Jean Pierre Godeaut; Stylist: Marie-France Boyé;

156-157 **1** JB Visual Press/Paul Ryan; **2** Tim Street-Porter; Architect: Brian Murphy; **3** Jacques Dirand; Designer: Christian Liaigre; **4** Elizabeth Whiting & Associates/Tom Leighton; **5** Simon Brown (Polly Dickens & Mark Gilbey); **6** Tim Street-Porter; Architect: Mark Mack; **7** Eigenhuis & Interieur/ John Van Groenedaal; **8** Christian Sarramon/ Conran Octopus; Designers: Olivier Gagnières and Yyoyyo Maeght;

158-159 **1** Tim Street-Porter; Architect: Richard Meier; **2** Christian Sarramon; **3** Fritz von der Schulenburg; Designer: Chicita Astor; **4** Dominque Vorillon courtsey of Elle Decor; Architect: Tom Bosworth; **5** Arcaid/Richard Bryant; Architects: GEA/ Domaine de Sperone; **6** International Interiors/ Paul Ryan; **7** Elizabeth Whiting & Associates/

Tim Street-Porter; Architect: John Chase; **8** Jean-Pierre Godeaut;

160 **1** Arcaid/Richard Bryant; Architect: David Wild;

162- 63 **1** Arcaid/Richard Bryant courtsey Ser or Brignone (Architect: Gian Franco Brignone); **2** Arcaid/ Richard Bryant; Architects: GEA/Domaine de Sperone; **3** Jerome Darblay; **4** Simon Mc Bride; **5** Elle Decoration/Christophe Kischerer; Designer: Ted Muehling (African stool and bench from Craft Caravan, 63 Greene St., New York); **6** International Interiors/Paul Ryan;

164- 65 **1** Guy Bouchet; **2** Paul Warchol; Architects: Henry Smith-Miller & Laurie Hawkinson (Moss Apartment); **3** Elizabeth Whiting & Associates/ Peter Woloszynski; **4** Stylograph/Côté Sud/Bernard Touillon; **5** Jean Pierre Godeaut courtsey of Elle Decor; Designer: Patrick Naggar; **6** Michel Fernin; **7** International Interiors/Paul Ryan; **8** Paul Warchol; Architects: Henry Smith-Miller & Laurie Hawkinson; **9** Reiner Blunck; Designer: Reiner Blunck;

166-167 **1** Deidi von Schaewen; Architects: Ecart/Andrée Putman (Bartos); **2** JB Visual Press/Paul Ryan; **3** Arcaid/Richard Bryant; Designers: Ada Dewes and Sergio Puente; **4** Jonathan Pilkington; Designer: Hazel Gomez; **5** Elizabeth Whiting & Associates/ SIP/W. Waldron; **6** Arcaid/Richard Bryant; Architects: GEA/Domaine de Sperone; **7** Jean Pierre Godeaut; **8** Jean Pierre Godeaut; Stylist: J.P. Billaud; **9** Hotze Eisma; Stylist: Hugo Kosters (Jeremy Switzer and Mario Montes);

168-169 **1** Richard Davies; Architect: John Pawson; **2** Abitare/Fregoso (Basalto); **3** JB Visual Press/Paul Ryan; **4** Tim Street-Porter; Designer: Mick Haggerty; **5** Arcaid/Alberto Piovano; Architect: Annig C. Sarian; **6** Vogue Living/Ashley Earber (Luigi Rosselli); **7** Nadia Mackenzie/Conran Octopus; Designer: Kate Fontana; **8** Fritz von der Schulenburg; Designer: Sophie Hicks; **9** Simon Brown; **10** JB Visual Press/Paul Ryan;

170-171 **1** Jerome Darblay; **2** Richard Waite; Designers: Robert Sakvla & Lany Ash; **3** Jean Pierre Godeaut; **4** Elizabeth Whiting & Associates/SIP/W.Waldron; **5** Elizabeth Whiting & Associates/Shona Wood; **6** Christian Sarramon; Designer: Jean de Meulder; **7** Peter Cook/Conran Octopus; Architects: Paxton Locher; **8** Camera Press; **9** Paul Ryan/Conran Octopus (Meryl Lloyd & John Lakin);

172 Richard Davies; Architect: John Pawson;

174-175 **2** Camera Press; **3** Jean-Paul Bonhommet; **5** Aldo Ballo; Architect: Antonia Astori; **8** Reiner Blunck; Designer: Mike Dolinski; **9** Elizabeth Whiting & Associates/Graham Henderson; **10** Guy Bouchet;

176-177 **1** Jean-Pierre Godeaut; Designer: Patrick Naggar; **2** Nadia Mackenzie/Conran Octopus; Designer: Kate Fontana; **3** Residence/Sigurd Kranendonk (Wolterinck Bloemen); **4** Simon Browr (Polly Dickens and Mark Gilbey); **5** Elizabeth Whiting & Associates/Neil Lorimer; **6** Jean-Paul Bonhommet; **7** Geoffrey Frosh; Architect: John Pawson; **8** Arcaid/Richard Bryant; Architect: John Pawson; **9** Richard Davies; **10** Elizabeth Whiting & Associates/Rodney Hyett; Architect: Bruce Kirkman; **11** Paul Warchol; Architects: John Randolph & Bruce Tomb; **12** Peter Cook/ Architect: Tony Fretton;

178-179 **1** Marie Claire Maison/Gilles de Chabaneix; **2** Deidi Von Schaewen (Nicole de Vesian); **3** Paul Warchol; Architects: John Randolph & Bruce Tomb; **4** Archipress/Peter Cook; Architect: M C. Ajlan; **5** Fritz von der Schulenburg; Designer: Richard Mudditt; **6** François Roche (Odile Filior); **7** Claudio Silvestrin;

180-181 **1** Camera Press; **2** Archipress/Luc Boegly; Architect: Godivier; **3** Elizabeth Whiting & Associates/Marie O'Hara; **4** Ianthe Ruthen/Conran Octopus; Architect: Kevin Waltz (Jade Albert); **5** Marie Claire Maison/Alexandre Bailhache; Stylist: Jean Pascal Billaud; **6** Fritz von der Schulenburg; Designer: A. Wadsworth; **7** Cookie Kinkead; Architect: Don Chappel (Chuck Winslow);

8 Arcaid/Richard Bryant; Architects: Pawson and Silvestrin; **9** Christian Sarramon (Terence Conran); **10** Ianthe Ruthven;

182-183 1 Peter Cook; Designer: Tugman Design Partnership; **2** Eduard Hueber; Architect: Ming Wu; **3** Gross and Daley (Ryan Gainey); **4** Elizabeth Whiting & Associates/Tim Street-Porter; **5** Antoine Bootz courtesy of *Metropolitan Home*; **6** Peter Cook; Architect: Stanton Williams; **7** Tim Street-Porter; Designer: Russ Leland; **8** Stylograph/*Côté Sud*/Christophe Dugied; Designer: Alberto Pinto; **9** Elizabeth Whiting & Associates/Neil Lorimer; **10** Deidi Von Schaewen; Architects: Ecart/Andrée Putman;

184 Henry Bourne; Architect: Jonathan Woolf (Patricia Ijaz-Ul-Haque);

186-187 1 Elizabeth Whiting & Associates/Dennis Stone; Designer: Robert Budwig; **2** Studio Brackrock; Designer: Gustav Lange; **3** *Eigenhuis & Interieur*/Paul Wiering; **4** Camera Press; **5** Gabriele Basilico courtesy of *Domus*; Architect: Colin Glennie; **6** Aldo Ballo; Architect: Flavio Albanese; **7** Todd Eberle; Architect: John Randolph & Bruce Tomb (Tom Bonauro); **8** Antoine Bootz; Architects: Dennis Wedlick;

188-189 2 Elizabeth Whiting & Associates/Tim Street-Porter; Designer: Dan Benjamin; **3** Antonio Garbasso; **4** Eduard Hueber; Architects: Resolution 4 Architecture; **5** Christian Sarramon/Conran Octopus; Designers: Olivier Gagnière and Yyoyyo Maeght; **6** Elizabeth Whiting & Associates/Dennis Stone; **7** Esto/Mark Darley; Designer: Christopher Alexander;

190-191 1 Jean-François Jaussaud (J.C Nicolas); **2** Jean-François Jaussaud (Christian Audigier); **3** Michel Fernin; Designer: Pascal Maingourd/Stylist: Catherine Cornille; **4** Aldo Ballo; Architect: Glenn Murcutt; **5** Camera Press;

192 Antonio Garbasso; Architect: Carlo Nepi;

194-195 1 Christian Sarramon; **2** Arcaid/Alberto Piovano; Architect: David Chipperfield; **3** Tim Street-Porter; Architect: Barton Phelps; **4** Tim Street-Porter; Architect: Mark Mack; **5** Arcaid/Richard Bryant; Designer: Michael Carapetian;

196-197 1 Elizabeth Whiting & Associates/Rodney Hyett; **2** *Eigenhuis & Interieur*/Verne Fotografie bvba; **3** Todd Eberle; Designer: J.Michele Oka Doner; **4** Amparo Garrido; Architect: Joseph Lembo;

198-199 1 Tim Street-Porter (Kelly-Low); **2** Arcaid/Richard Bryant; Designer: Bulter Redice; **3** Fritz von der Schulenburg; Designer: Richard Hudson; **4** Fritz von der Schulenburg; Designer: Richard Mudditt; **5** Eric Morin; **6** Eric Morin; Designer: Christian Liaigre; **7** Elizabeth Whiting & Associates/Rodney Hyett;

200-201 1 Donghia; Designer: John Hutton; **2-3** The Nursery Window/Kim Sayer; **4** International Interiors/Paul Ryan/Designer:Sasha Waddell; **5** Christian Sarramon/Conran Octopus; Designers: Olivier Gagnière & Yyoyyo Maeght; **6** Peter Cook/Conran Octopus; Architect: Jonathan Woolf (Brian Mindel); **7** Fired Earth; **8** Deidi Von Schaewen;

202 1 *Eigenhuis & Interieur*/Verne Fotografie bvba; **2** John Miller; **3** Arcaid/Richard Bryant; Architects: Grose Bradley; **4** Jean-Pierre Godeaut;

203 1 Paul Ryan/Conran Octopus; Architects: Munkenbeck & Marshall (Ben Richardson); **2** Abitare; **3** Deidi von Schaewen (Silvie Blanchet); **4** Edifice/Philippa Lewis;

204-205 1 Studio Brackrock; Designers: Peter Ibens and Claire Bataille; **2** Peter Cook; Architect: Tony Fretton; **3** Antoine Bootz courtesy of *Metropolitan Home*; **4** Paul Ryan/Conran Octopus; Architects: Deborah Weintraub and Scott Lane; Designer: Richard Lavenstein (Ronald K. Smith) **5** Deidi von Schaewen; Architects: Ecart/Andrée Putman;

206-207 1 Reiner Blunck; Designer: Alberto Ponis; **2** Arcaid/Richard Bryant (Ron Brinkers); **3** Michael Garland; Designer: Alice Copeland; **4** Deidi Von Schaewen; Architect: Franco Bombelli;

208-209 1 Nadia Mackenzie/Conran Octopus; Designer:

Kate Fontana; **2** Fired Earth; **3** Reiner Blunck; **4** Elizabeth Whiting & Associates/Michael Dunne; **5** Paul Ryan/Conran Octopus; Architect: Yanni Petsopoulos; **6** Simon McBride; **7** David Phelps; **8** Peter Cook/Conran Octopus; Architects: Paxton Locher; **9** Elizabeth Whiting & Associates/Tim Street-Porter; **10** Paris Ceramics/David George;

210 1 David Massey; **2** *Eigenhuis & Interieur*/John Van Groenedaal; **3** *Eigenhuis & Interieur*/Henk Schuurmans; **4** JB Visual Press/Horst Newmann;

211 1 Crucial Trading/Richard Holt; **2** David Parmiter; Stylist: Martin Bass/Supplier: Sinclair Till; **3** Antoine Bootz/Conran Octopus; Architects: Anderson & Schwartz; **4-6** Fired Earth;

212-213 1 Elizabeth Whiting & Associates/Rodney Hyett; Architect: Angela Carlton; **2** Arcaid/Richard Bryant; Designer: Colin Gold; **3** John Miller; **4** Belle Magazine/Earl Carter; Architect: Steve Whitford; **5** Houses and Interiors; **6** Tim Goffe; Furniture designer: Christopher Nevile for Study Products Ltd.; **7** Peter Cook/Conran Octopus; Architect: Domenico D. Rensch;

214-215 1 Arcaid/Richard Bryant; Architect: Rick Mather; **2** Michael Mundy; Design: Dialogica; **3** Mr.Tomkinson; **4** Archipress/Peter Cook; Architects: Greenberg & Hawkes; **5-6** Steeles Carpets Ltd.;

216-217 1 Elizabeth Whiting & Associates/Jerry Harpur; **2** Bill Stites; **3** *Marie Claire Maison*/Gilles de Chabaneix; Stylist: Catherine Ardouin; **4** Stylograph/Le Toureur; **5** Richard Davies; Architect: John Pawson;

218-219 1 Elizabeth Whiting & Associates/SIP/W.Waldron; **2** Tim Street-Porter; Architect: Brian Murphy; **3** Studio Brackrock; **4** Elizabeth Whiting & Associates/Neil Lorimer; **5** Camera Press; **6** Arcaid/Richard Bryant; Architects: Munkenbeck & Marshall; **7** Paul Warchol; Architect: François DeMenil;

220 1 Peter Cook/Conran Octopus; Architect: Domenico D. Rensch; **2** Antoine Bootz; **3** Manuel Canovas; **4** Jean-Paul Bonhommet; **5** John Miller;

221 1 Deidi Von Schaewen; **2** Stylograph/*Maison Française*/Nicolas Millet; **3** Christian Sarramon/Conran Octopus; Designers: Olivier Gagnières and Yyoyyo Maeght; **4** David Parmiter; Stylist: Martin Bass;

222 1 Ianthe Ruthven (Mandy Baird); **2** Christian Sarramon; Designer: Yvonne Hulst; **3** John Miller; **4** International Interiors/Paul Ryan (Charles Rutherfoord);

223 1 Peter Cook/Conran Octopus; Architect: Domenico D. Rensch; **2** Peter Cook/Conran Octopus; Architects: Munkenbeck & Marshall; **3** JB Visual Press/Paul Ryan; **4** Deidi von Schaewen; Architects: Ecart/Andrée Putman (Dr. W. Felten); **5** Elizabeth Whiting & Associates/Spike Powell; Designer: Dagny Duckett; **6** Nadia MacKenzie/Conran Octopus; Designer: David Benson-Bunch;

224-225 1 Arcaid/Richard Bryant; Architects: Munkenbeck & Marshall; **2** Christian Sarramon (Terence Conran); **3** Esto/Mark Darley; Designer: Bauer Design; **4** Habitat UK; **5** JB Visual Press/Paul Ryan (Bernardo Urquieta);

226-227 1 Martin Trelanney/Conran Octopus; Supplier: Authentics shop; **2** Eric Morin; **3** Christian Liaigre; **4** International Interiors/Paul Ryan; **5** Donghia; Designer: John Hutton; **6** *Marie Claire Maison*/Gilles de Chabaneix; Stylist: Catherine Ardouin **7** U.S.Conran's Habitat/James Merrell; **8** Stylograph/*Maison Française*/Nicolas Millet;

228-229 1 Arcaid/Richard Bryant; Designers: Butler Redice; **2** Peter Cook/Conran Octopus; Architects: Paxton Locher; **3** Paul Ryan/Conran Octopus; Architects: Munkenbeck & Marshall (Ben Richardson); **4** Elle Decoration/Rory Carnegie; Designer: Michael Rainsford; **5** Elizabeth Whiting & Associates/Peter Woloszynski;

230 1 Christian Sarramon (Terence Conran); **2** Antoine Bootz courtesy of Neotu Gallery; **3** U.S.Conran's Habitat/James Merrell; **4** Antoine

Bootz/Conran Octopus; Architects: Anderson & Schwartz (John Newman); **5** U.S.Conran's Habitat/James Merrell;

231 1 Christian Sarramon (Terence Conran); **2** International Interiors/Paul Ryan; **3** Elizabeth Whiting & Associates/Anaya; **4** Jerome Darblay; **5** Christopher Farr Handmade Rugs; Designer: Michael Rainsford;

232 1 Antoine Bootz/Conran Octopus; Architects: Anderson & Schwartz (John Newman); **2** Antoine Bootz courtesy of *Metropolitan Home* (A.Freime); **3** Reiner Blunck; Architect: Helmut Raff; **4** Deidi Von Schaewen (Silvie Blanchet); **5** Gross and Daley (Paul Smart); **6** Paul Ryan/Conran Octopus; Architect: Yanni Petsopoulos; **7** Elizabeth Whiting & Associates/Rodney Hyett;

233 1 Jean-François Jaussaud (André Dubreuil); **2** David Phelps courtesy of *Food & Wine Magazine*, U.S.; **3** Deidi Von Schaewen; **4** Abitare/Gabriele Basilico; Architect: Paolo Nova; **5** Cookie Kinkead; Designer/Owners: Scott Waterman & Brett Landenberger;

234-235 1 Tim Soar (Mr. & Mrs. J. Myers); **2** Peter Cook/Conran Octopus; Architects: Paxton Locher; **3** Todd Eberle (Jack Lenor Larsen); **4** Antoine Bootz; Designer: Bob Patino; **5** Christian Sarramon/Conran Octopus; Designers: Olivier Gagnières and Yyoyyo Maeght; **6** François Roche; **7** John Miller;

236 Antoine Bootz; Architects: Dennis Wedlick;

238-239 1 Camera Press; **2** Michael Freeman; Architects: Carroll, Dempsey & Thirkell; **3** Paul Ryan/Conran Octopus; Architects: Deborah Weintraub & Scott Lane; Designer: Richard Lavenstein (Ronald K. Smith); **4** Hugh Johnson/Conran Octopus; **5** Stylograph/John Hall:

Every effort has been made to trace the copyright holders, architects and designers and we apologize in advance for any unintentional ommission and would be pleased to insert the appropriate acknowledgement in any subsequent edition.

ILLUSTRATIONS
The publisher thanks the following illustrators whose work appears throughout the book as follows:
Brian Ma Siy: 8-9; 42-5 (Architects: Deborah Weintraub & Scott Frances; provisional site plan by Kiss & Zwigard); 122-3; 125 (sculpture table, Benchmark); 132-3; 135 (Jake dining-chair, Ryan & Co); 137; 141 (Barcino chair, Indecasa); 142-3; 145 (sofa, Jasper Morrison); 147 (Papu coffee-table, Punt Mobles); 150 (Adorno tub chair, Conran Shop); 153 (Revista magazine rack, Piersons Wireworks); 154 (Wave shelving, Aero); 156 (Kronso vases); 160-1; 165 (Bandera bedside table, Conran Shop); 171 (Cabina wardrobe, Evoluzione); 172-3; 184-5; 186 (Bernice lamp, Luceplan); 189 (desk, Ricardo Boffill); 191 (crockery, Despaul-Halez).

Angus Shepherd: 48-9; 78-9 (room sets); 95; 97; 129;1 74-5; 188; 241; 249 (house); 251 (house); 254-5.
Paul Bryant: 51; 66; 70-2; 76-7; 78-9 (excluding room sets); 81; 91; 109-11; 199; 219; 229-30; 243-4; 245; 146-7; 249 (details); 251 (details); 252-3; 256.

PLANS
The plans in this book are copyright © the architects listed below and are illustrated by kind permission:
42 **(above)** Deborah Weintraub, A.I.A. & Scott Lane
42 **(below)** Kiss & Zwigard Architects
45 Deborah Weintraub, A.I.A. & Scott Lane
95 Munkenbeck & Marshall Architects

See 'Useful Addresses' for details.

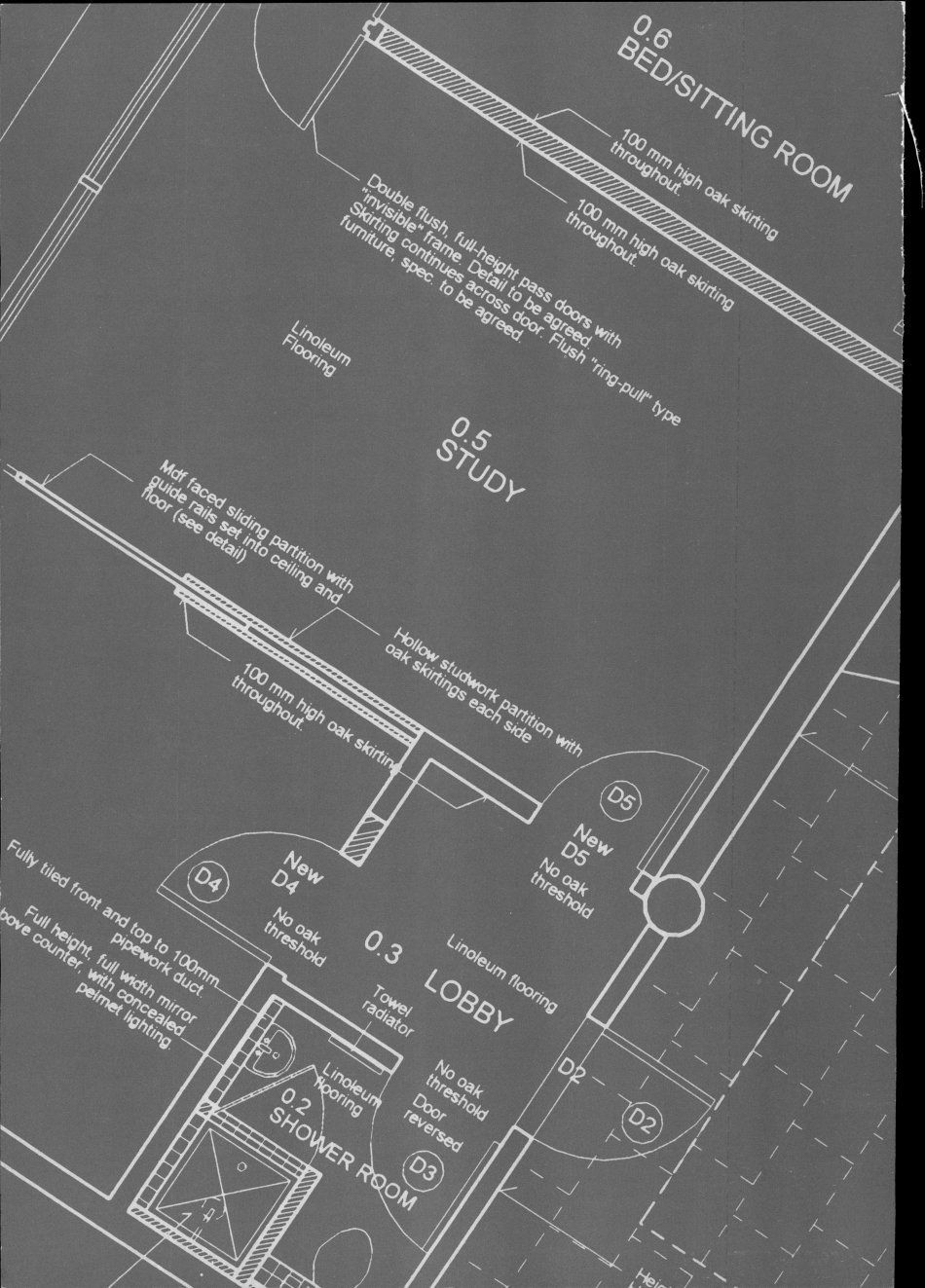

0.6
BED/SITTING ROOM

100 mm high oak skirting
throughout.

100 mm high oak skirting
throughout.

Double flush, full-height pass doors with
"invisible" frame. Detail to be agreed.
Skirting continues across door. Flush "ring-pull" type
furniture, spec. to be agreed.

Linoleum
Flooring

0.5
STUDY

Mdf faced sliding partition with
guide rails set into ceiling and
floor (see detail)

Hollow studwork partition with
oak skirtings each side

100 mm high oak skirting
throughout.

D5

New
D5
No oak
threshold

Fully tiled front and top to 100mm
pipework duct.

Full height, full width mirror
above counter, with concealed
pelmet lighting.

D4

New
D4
No oak
threshold

0.3   LOBBY

Linoleum flooring

Towel
radiator

No oak
threshold

Door
reversed

Linoleum
flooring

D2

D2

0.2
SHOWER ROOM

D3